PLYMOUTH
As Time Draws On
Volume 2

written and illustrated by

Chris Robinson

with a foreword by
the Rt. Hon. Michael Foot MP

Pen&inK
PUBLISHING

British Library Cataloguing in Publication Data

Robinson, Chris, 1954—
    Plymouth, as time draws on, vol. 2.
    1. Devon. Plymouth, history
    I. Title
    942.3′58

    ISBN 0–9510747–1–7

Designed by Chris Robinson and Rob Warren
© Chris Robinson 1988

First published September 1988

Typeset, printed & bound in Great Britain
by Latimer Trend & Company Ltd
Crescent Avenue
Plymouth PL1 3AW, Devon

Published by
Pen & Ink Publishing
34 New Street,
Barbican
Plymouth PL1 2NA

for James & Ben

Rt. Hon.
Michael Foot MP

 House of Commons

Plymouth, my father told me – and he was the one who truly knew – had played a bigger part in the modern story of freedom than any other place on earth.

As a child, he had stood on Plymouth Hoe when the statue of Francis Drake was erected, and, like Drake, he had looked out across Plymouth Sound a thousand times. No other stretch of water (with the dockyard round the corner thrown in) had seen such scenes in the establishment of the English freedom-loving state.

Then Plymouth too had played the foremost part in the protection of Parliament in its just war against the Stuart Kings. Just across the road from the birth place of most of his children in Lipson Terrace, stood Freedom Fields where the victory, against the Royal odds, was properly celebrated. We passed it every day when we went to school and learnt more from the inscription maybe than from our instructors at Plymouth College.

Then, in the years between 1939 and 1945, Plymouth led the rest of the nation in its endurance and its triumph. Without Plymouth, the whole resistance of our people could have been crushed beneath the Nazi tyranny. In 1945, when my father became Lord Mayor – no prouder title was ever bestowed on him – he went to every school within the city and told the children how Francis Drake and the citizens of Plymouth had helped save England and freedom again, as in 1588.

When I read Chris Robinson's first volume, my thoughts naturally turned to what my father had taught us. So many of these were his favourite, sacred places too. No better modern picture of our city had been contrived, and I pictured how fascinated he would have been to turn those pages. But now, believe me, the miracle has been repeated. My father's boast about Plymouth in all its infinite variety looks truer than ever.

Armada Day 1988

Introduction

The idea for the first volume of these drawings and articles grew about a year and a half into the newspaper series. This volume, however, is altogether more premeditated. Designed to cover most of the more major omissions from the first book, I hope that together they give a reasonably comprehensive view of this beautiful city. To cover every school, church, inn, historic house or landmark would be an almost never ending task. So for the time being at least this is where the line has been drawn.

It often takes longer to research and write one page than it does to complete the drawing it accompanies. And, certainly, the drawing is always the easier part. Information for the text is often sparse and difficult to come by while the subject is always there, just waiting to be drawn.

Plymouth
July 1988

Acknowledgements

First and foremost thanks must go to the two women in my life, my mother Brenda and my wife Clare; the former for helping me to meet the regular deadline at the last minute each week by patiently typing my jumbled manuscript, full of crossings out and insertions; the latter for putting up with the 'working all hours' routine and all the hours of reading. Thanks too to my in-laws – Laurence and Patricia Greathead – for all the proof reading and encouragement. And to my father Des, ever patient, for the many, many hours of assistance in all the directions this work takes.

To Rob Warren whose services with the pen, brush and typewriter help make 34 New Street a successful hive of industry and a happy place to work. To his wife Nita who left New Street to concentrate on their latest product Davy. To Julie Dent who joined us in 1986 for a two-year training scheme and who, in that time, has coped admirably with all the diverse tasks we've thrown at her, including the compilation of the index for this book.

Thanks to Jim Mitchell from the *Evening Herald* who launched the 'Time Draws On' series in February 1982 and to his successors behind the Editor's desk, Alan Goode and Alan Cooper who have carried it on. To Ken Fenn, Chris Collins and Mike Longhurst who make sure it arrives each week on time. And for all the promotion, to Lesley Martin and John Dudley.

To Devon County Council for the Local History Library; to John Elliott the librarian, Jenny Ward (and before her Anique Skinner) the local history librarian; to my Godfather John Smith and Polly Lamb who have helped with the many inquiries. At the same time thanks to Tony Clement the Barbican bookseller from whose shelves I have equipped my own local history library.

As to the actual production of the two volumes of *Plymouth – As Time Draws On*, enormous thanks to John Turner, Bill Bugler, Roger Bossom and John Coates of Latimer Trend.

And once again, three years on, thanks to Angela Lanyon at the Theatre Royal for organizing my second exhibition of work and giving us a focal point around which to launch this second volume.

I am also extremely grateful to Britain's best known Argyle fan, Michael Foot, for his foreword to this book.

Finally a few others, 'without which not' – Jim Woodrow and the Barbican Association, Clive Hooper and Dennis Gibbs of Planographic, Ron, Joe and Co., from PDS, Mike Newton Perks from Reprocraft, Vic Brimacombe, Dinah Livingston, Mary Browning, Tony Evans, Mike Billinghay, Bill Hodges and Audrey Hosier – from little acorns . . .

CJR

Latimer Trend

Later this decade it will be exactly 100 years since the Plymouth printing firm of Trend & Co., established themselves in the former home of Bradbury's sewing machine depot at 163 Union Street. Harold Trend was one head of the business, the other was Alfred Latimer.

Alfred Latimer's father, Isaac, had moved to Plymouth in 1844. A Londoner, friend of Charles Dickens and a former reporter on the *West Briton* in Truro, Isaac went on to become owner/Editor of the *Plymouth Journal*. However, when the *Western Morning News* appeared in June 1860, he quickly followed its lead and 5 months later started the *Western Daily Mercury*, the paper that in 1895 gave birth to the *Western Evening Herald*. Isaac Latimer, later with his son Alfred, continued to publish the *Mercury* well into the 1880s. Late in the decade, however, Isaac Latimer & Son Publishers passed over the proprietorship of the paper to W. J. Pearce and it would appear that Alfred then channelled his energies into Trend & Co.

A little more than thirty years later the firm moved to its present site in Crescent Avenue. Here its front entrance is overshadowed by a single large and impressive *Populus Nigra*, Black Poplar. A protected tree, common in the South East and Wales but not indigenous to this country, the Black Poplar is a straggly tree with furrowed bark, resinous buds and fruiting catkins. Because its timber is soft, light and evenly textured, difficult to splinter and fire resistant, the poplar 'enjoys' widespread use on factory floors, in packing cases, plywood, matches and pulp. However, it will be a long time before any paper manufacturers get their machinery into this tree to put it the way of a printer, as not only is it protected, but it stands, not in the grounds of Latimer Trend but St. Andrew's Primary School. Established the year after the *Morning News* and *Daily Mercury* in 1861, St. Andrew's was demolished exactly 100 years later to make way for the new law courts adjacent to the Guildhall. One present member of staff, Miss Cooper, was there in 1961 and remembers the grand old Victorian edifice with affection. The present school was opened on 26th April 1961 and still stands on church property. This time though it is the site of the blitzed St. James-the-Less.

Latimer Trend also felt the effects of enemy bombing as their roof was blown clean off which, temporarily at least, devastated production schedules. Before the war a great deal of Latimer Trend's work was the production of timetables and various items of printed matter for the Great Western Railways. Immediately prior to the war the company increased their book production, a development that took a further step forward when first Faber & Faber and later David & Charles purchased the firm. In 1981 against the flow of mergers into ever expanding conglomerates, John Turner and his directors bought the company, thereby returning its independent status.

Currently a wide range of technical and scientific books are produced here for major publishers including the Oxford University Press and the National Trust. The past five years as well have seen the firm assisting in the production of the supplement to the *Oxford English Dictionary*.

With some of the latest Monotype Lasercomp typesetting equipment and computer control in the whole of the West country, Latimer Trend is well geared up for the twenty first century, a situation that would doubtless please and impress the pioneering Victorian Isaac Latimer. As indeed, might one of their latest productions, my own books, beautifully printed and based on the articles and drawings produced over the last three and a half years for the newspaper he himself established.

Contents

PLYMOUTH
As Time Draws On
Volume 2

The Plymouth Coat of Arms

'Plymouth is, unquestionably, entitled to two Coats of Arms'. Such was the opinion of Victorian historian R. N. Worth in 1890, who based his statement on the evidence concerning two distinctly different crests, the earliest records of which go back to 1368 and 1439 respectively.

In 1368, sometime before the 1439 Act of Incorporation of the three Suttons (the town of Sutton Prior, the tithing of Sutton Raf and the Hamlet of Sutton Valletort), we find record in a contemporary deed, of a seal bearing the legend 'SI-COMMVNITATIS-VILLE-DE-SVTTVN-SVPER-PLYMOVTH ...' of the fellowship of the town of Sutton on Plymouth. The wording runs in a circle around the image of a simple, single-masted ship with furled sail upon the waves.

No other record of this seal appears to have survived and it may well antedate 1368 by many years, perhaps even from the notable charter of Henry III in 1253, granting Sutton a 'Thursday market with a fair of three days at the festival of John the Baptist'. Whatever its earlier history, we find a similar image being recorded in 1575 after the Heraldic Visitation to the town.

This time however, the arms of Plymouth were shown as a three-masted ship upon the sea, again with furled sails, with each mast surmounted by a blazing fire beacon. A map of 1584 shows prominent fire beacons at Roborough, Pennycross (Beacon Park) and on the Hoe. The colours recorded show a gold ship set in a red shield. (Barbican signwriter George Rowe incorporated a version of this in his imaginative inn sign for the Barbican Arms). Worth also noted that 'a manuscript Armorial in the Exeter Cathedral Library of about the same date gives a three-masted ship on the waves with the motto, 'Si vela tendas nimium navis mergitur ...' If the sails strain too much the ship will sink.

Less than fifty years later however, the Heralds made another Visitation, at various times during the sixteenth and seventeenth centuries, officers of the College of Arms made visits to places all over the country recording, noting, local coats of arms and seals, and any they recorded were then accepted as being lawful. In 1620, when the two heralds 'St. George Richmond and Blewemantle' came to Plymouth with their 'Clarkes', they recorded a common seal bearing a saltire and castles on an escutcheon surmounted by a crown of fleur-de-lys. This of course is the basis for our modern coat of arms and is first recorded as the mayoral seal, back in 1439. A more elaborate seal, also believed to date from the time of the Act of Incorporation, shows St. Andrew, patron saint of the town, flanked by two smaller figures of angels; one bearing the cross of St. George, the other a shield of the Royal Arms with the earliest version of the four castles and the cross of St. Andrew's on a shield, supported by the national lions below. The castles depict the old castle quadrate on the Barbican of which only part now survives. This element of our Civic Crest would, therefore, appear to be almost 550 years old.

The motto 'Turris Fortissima est Nomen Jehova' however, is of a later date and it has been suggested that we may owe it to George Hughes the Puritan Vicar of St. Andrew's from 1643–1662. In July 1646, Hughes resigned all his property in the vicarage to the Mayor and Commonalty as it was 'much decayed by reason of the seige'. Who better therefore to suggest that Proverbs Ch. 18 V. 10 '... The name of

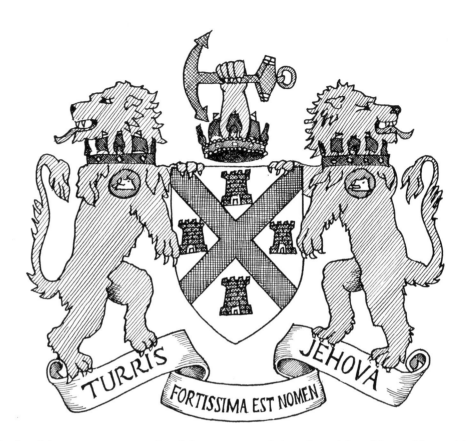

the Lord is a strong tower: the righteous runneth into it and is safe' would provide the city with a fine motto when the Puritan Plymouth had just successfully held off the Royalist cause, both factions fighting with God on their side.

It was around this time too that we find an entry in the municipal records — 'Town Colours altered' (1645–6). Chris Smith, in a recent article on the Arms of Plymouth, believes that before this, the saltire (cross) was probably black not the now familiar green.

For the next two hundred years or so, except for an adventurous attempt to combine the ship with it, (best seen on the 1837 Reform Act Tablet on the Hoe), this is how Plymouth's Coat of Arms remained. Then in 1931 the three towns of Devonport, Stonehouse and Plymouth, (amalgamated in 1914 with City status following in 1928) were granted as the 'City of Plymouth' by Letters Patent a new Coat of Arms. Essentially, this was the longstanding Plymouth Crest with the two naval crowns and anchor of the 1876 Devonport crest added, plus two boar's head medallions from the old Edgcumbe Arms which represent Stonehouse.

The colours today are gold (lions), blue (crowns), red (anchor and medallions) and the now traditional green cross and black castles set on silver. Perhaps it is these basic civic colours, as much as any other element, that accounts for Plymouth Argyle's unique strip in the English league.

27th September 1986.

1

Plymouth

'O dear Plymouth town, and O blue Plymouth Sound!
O where is your equal on earth to be found?'

Mother to, or inspiration for, some fifty Plymouths across the globe, it's interesting to reflect that there might not have been a single one were it not for a tenuous chain of name changes many centuries ago.

Although the various authorities are not in complete agreement, consensus appears to be that it all began in Plympton which, nominally at least, antedates Plymouth by several hundred years. A well used rhyme applied to places all over the country, has it locally that 'When Plymouth was a fuzzy down, Plympton was a borough town.' Certainly Plympton developed earlier and was recorded in 904 as Plymentun. However, as the Victorian historian R. N. Worth observed, Plympton is not and never was on the river now called the Plym, 'rather' he noted 'it was upon the estuary afterwards called the Lary'. He then puts forward the theory that Plympton, or Plintona as it was recorded in Domesday, derives from the possible Keltic name for the estuary 'lyn' — that is simply 'lake or pool'; penlyn then becomes the 'head of the lake' so that penlinton 'exactly expresses the site of the original Plympton'. By way of a similar verbal contraction, he cites Pelynt in Cornwall which, he says, is often called Plynt. The next stage then becomes, according to Worth, Plympton—giving its name to the Plym '. . . Penlin being first blunderingly applied by the Saxons to the estuary, and thence to the river'. Finally 'Plin passed into Plym through Plinmouth, whence Plymouth, just as at the present day, the local pronunciation of Lynmouth is Lymouth'.

Not everyone agreed with him, however. One contemporary J. Brooking Rowe, author of 'A History of Plympton Erle' thought that Plym or Plin could be a personal or class name, while Ekwall, author of the scholarly work 'River Names', opted for the old English plyme, meaning plum (tree) for his derivation of plymetun. The sequence of names Plympton then Plym then Plymouth however is not challenged.

So it is then that we find in 1238 a reference to the 'Bridge of the Plyme' and in 1254 the first mention of the 'port of Plymme' (one of very nearly 300 different spellings Worth found in various records through the years 'Plimu being the shortest and Pilimmouthe the longest'). Whether or not Plymbridge was new then is not known. The town at the mouth of the Plym however certainly was not new, having long since been known as Sutton, Sudtone, South town or 'ton'-the Saxon word meaning farm. Sudtone, or Sutona, manor was comparatively small at the time of Domesday; 'one serf . . . four villeins and two bordars with five ploughs. There are two acres of meadow and twenty acres of pasture . . .' there were also fifteen sheep which Crispin Gill suggests would have 'probably grazed on the short turf on the Hoe, where Lambhay means sheep enclosure.'

However, as the sea and the navy came to play an ever larger part in our nation's history and as Sutton was so well situated, the town rapidly grew and by the close of the fourteenth century, with a population approaching 7,000, was fourth largest in the kingdom behind only London, York and Bristol. In 1439 Plymouth, comprising the town of Sutton Prior, essentially the Barbican area as far as St. Andrew's, the tithing of Sutton Raf and the hamlet of Sutton Valletort, was incorporated by Act of Parliament, thereby consolidating the change in name and ensuring for posterity that the name that pioneers around the world would come to spread would be Plymouth, not Sutton. The now famous Plymouth Hoe, looked upon in medieval days as 'distinctly exterior to the town', was referred to in the 1439 Act as 'the hyll callyd the Wynderygge'—the hill called the Windy ridge!

30th August 1986.

2

The Royal Plymouth Corinthian Yacht Club

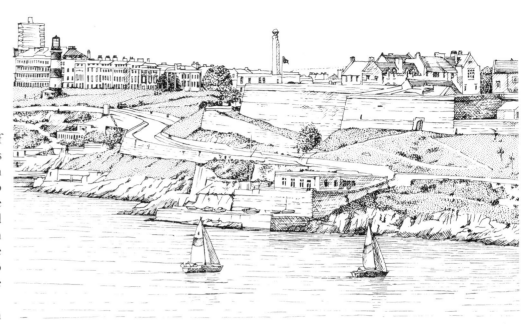

Rather like horse racing, yacht racing could easily have been dubbed the sport of kings. It was in 1660, the year he was restored to the throne, that Charles II was presented with the 100 ton yacht *Mary* by the Dutch East India Company and soon after he became the first to introduce the idea of sailing purely for pleasure into Britain. Indeed in 1661 his *Katherine* was launched at Deptford—the first yacht to be commissioned in the country—and it was in this 94 ton, 49 foot vessel that he raced against his brother the Duke of York in the *Anne*, from Greenwich to Gravesend, in what is regarded as being the first competition of its kind ever held. A definite enthusiast, Charles at one time had amassed 18 yachts and when he came down to Plymouth in 1671 with his brothers, to inspect the first five years work on the Citadel, he sailed down.

However, these yachts were a far cry from those we know today, not only much bigger but also, in the early days, they tended to be modelled on warships, often carrying a full complement of guns. Not surprisingly, the scale and cost of this pastime put the new sport well out of reach to all but the fantastically wealthy and although two yacht clubs were formed in the eighteenth century (1720 and 1775), it was not until the early part of the nineteenth century that any great advances were made. In the Regency days of George IV the Yacht Club (now the Royal Yacht Squadron) was formed (1815) and other clubs soon followed.

Plymouth witnessed its first regatta in 1823 and, four years later, the Port of Plymouth Royal Clarence Regatta Club was formed under the patronage of the Duke of Clarence, who attended the event himself that year attracting leading yachts from around the country in his wake.

In 1833 the Royal Clarence became the Royal Western Yacht Club, by which name it is still known today. Plymouth's second oldest yacht club meanwhile, takes its name from a word used to describe 'a gentleman sportsman who rides his own horses on the turf or sails his own yacht' (Brewer 1894). That word is Corinthian and it too was popularised in the Regency when it was also applied to those sportsmen 'devoted to pugilism'—boxing. In Shakespeare's time a Corinthian was a 'fast man' but an older association still is with Corinth itself, a veritable den of iniquity, proverbial throughout Greece and Rome such that a Corinthian became a fitting way to describe a licentious libertine.

The nineteenth-century sporting association however, survives through several organizations, including the Corinthian Casuals Amateur Football Club and various yachting clubs, the Corinthian Otters, the Royal Corinthian based at Burnham-on-Crouch and the Royal Plymouth Corinthian based since 1898 here in purpose-built premises, appropriately enough, under Charles II's Citadel.

Formed in 1876 by 'prominent local gentry', Royal since 1886 and with a recently restored warrant to wear the Blue Ensign, the Corinthian's move in 1898 to this little harbour, constructed fifty years or so after the Citadel itself, coincided with a major event in the City's yachting history—the staging of its first dinghy race.

Although this new class of yacht was not particularly quick to catch on, Jollyboats were popular by 1902 and by the mid 1920s Mayflowers and Sunbeams were becoming common. But it was still the 'big' yachts which dominated regattas and drew the crowds and the photographers, and the impressive 70-ton Bermudan-rigged 'J' class were still being raced here in the 30s.

Up until the advent of small dinghy racing, yachting was still a sport for the very rich. Even today you would need to be a multi-millionaire to challenge for the ultimate prize in the sport—the America's Cup. Despite the early inroads made by the dinghy class, it wasn't really until the social and technological changes that followed the Second World War, that sailing became more of a sport for all '...marine plywood and resin glues made boat building possible for amateur carpenters who before had tackled little more than kitchen shelves'.

In the early 1950s the Corinthian helped organise the first major dinghy championship to be held in Plymouth. This was for the Prince of Wales Cup, donated back in 1927 for the International 14 class—one of the first notable classes of dinghy.

Today there are hundreds of classes of yachts registered in this country alone and the spread of the sport is borne out by the fact that by the 1970s over 2 million Britons were participating in it, many of whom acknowledge Plymouth as one of the finest yachting centres in the country.

16th August 1986.

Gog and Magog

Plymouth Hoe has been the scene of a good many spectacles down the centuries but one, perhaps the most fantastic of them all, took place long before proper records began.

When Charles II had the Citadel built upon the Hoe (1666–71), to ensure the town would never again resist the royalist cause, his massive structure superseded the fortifications begun by Drake in the previous century, and the earlier Castle Quadrate on Lambhay Hill. It also swallowed up the land which, for centuries at least, had borne the figures carved out of the turf of 'Gog Magog'. Subjects of many stories through the years, their origin is somewhat uncertain; their existence as carvings at least however is well documented. Before the King stole this land from the people of Plymouth, 'the townsmen' would 'pass their time of leisure in walking, bowling and other pleasant pastimes, in the side whereof is cut the portraiture of two men of the largest volume, yet one surpassing the other in every way; these they name to be Corinaeus and Gogmagog; imitating the wrestling to be here between these two champions; and the steep rocky cliff affording aptitude for such a cast' (Westcote 1630).

Earlier in his Survey of Cornwall, Carew noted 'upon the Hawe at Plymmouth the pourtrayture of two men . . . with clubbes in their hands (whom they terme Gog Magog)'. From 1493 through to 1566 there are more than half a dozen references to the 'renewyng', 'clensyng' and 'cuttyng of Gogmagog the pycture of the Gyaunt at hawe' in the City's surviving municipal records. From these records it would appear that the general cost of such upkeep was 8d (about 3½p)—at least that was what was paid to Cotewyll in 1494, to John Lucas in 1514, and William Hawkyns, baker, 1540–41; although if left too long, the cost appeared to rise as in 1566-7, 20d was paid. Throughout these official records there is only mention made of a single figure, a little like the Cerne giant near Dorchester and the Long Man of Wilmington (Sussex), and T. C. Lethbridge, an archaeologist, believes that like these other figures,

the Hoe picture was of Helith or Hercules the sun god. A smaller figure, the other wrestler Lethbridge suggests may originally have been female and thus the earth goddess; the two together carved in the high slope were pagan symbols of worship in a natural temple, carved out two or three centuries before the Romans came. Then he suggests, as time eroded the memories of their original purpose but not the figures themselves, so now associated with the struggle of good and evil, they perhaps acquired their new names from the Bible where in Ezekiel 38, the 'son of man' is encouraged to 'set they face against Gog, the land of Magog'.

All this however, is to dismiss the colourful legends that begin with the thirty three infamous daughters of the Emperor Diocletian, who all murdered their husbands and were set adrift. They later landed in Albion (England), where they fell in love with a number of demons. 'The offspring of this unnatural alliance was a race of giants, afterwards extirpated by Brute and his companions, refugees from Troy' (Brewer).

Now according to one story Gog and Magog survived this conflict and were taken in chains to London. However, another version suggests that the two figures in London's Guildhall, lost in the Great Fire and replaced in 1708 and then reconstructed again after the Blitz, weren't Gog and Magog at all but Corinaeus and Goemagot. Now Goemagot or Goemot is supposed to be the last surviving giant and Corinaeus was one of Brute's or Brutus's Trojan chiefs, who held it 'a diversion to encounter giants'.

Brutus, according to the twelfth-century historian Geoffrey of Monmouth, 'least trustworthy of the old chroniclers', came to our shores around 1200 BC, landing somewhere near Totnes (hence the town's Brutus Stone), then moved west and settled around here. Then one day when the Trojans were holding a festival to the Gods on the Hoe, the local giants attacked them in force. In the fighting that followed all were slain except Goemot who was saved to do battle with Corinaeus. Goemot, 'twelve cubits high and of such strength that with one stroke he pulled up an oak as it had been a hazel wand', broke three of his opponent's ribs. Corinaeus then became so incensed that he hoisted the giant onto his shoulders, ran to the edge of the Hoe and hurled the monster down onto the rocks where he was torn apart, crashing into the sea, colouring the waves with his blood. Brutus, who gave his name to Britain according to our chronicler, was so pleased with Corinaeus's achievement that he gave him the Western Horn of this Isle, which was thereafter known as Corinea or Cornwall.

Meanwhile the high rock became known as Lam-Goemot or 'Goemot's Leap' and is today identified as Lambhay Hill.

2nd August 1986.

Commercial Wharf

Looking across to the eastern side of the Citadel with uneven grassy slopes running down from it to Commercial Road, separated from the water's edge by boat and car parking spaces, it is easy to imagine that this part of the Barbican has as yet done well to avoid any major concentrated development. However such is not quite the case. Older inhabitants will recall the great storehouses or warehouses that lined the seaward side of Commercial Road and which, between 1750 and 1940, witnessed a great deal of activity (much of which fascinatingly chronicled in Crispin Gill's book on Sutton Harbour).

Long before the building of the Royal William Victualling Yard at Stonehouse, which was completed around 1835, the Navy had been victualled from Sutton Harbour. As early as 1654 Cromwell had instituted Commissioners of Victualling who soon after began operating at Lambhay and, although there was a temporary move to Coxside for a decade or two, a proper Victualling Office was set up at Lambhay at the beginning of the eighteenth century and in 1750 a new bakehouse was built. Provisions baked here would have supplied the pioneering adventurers and colonists Byron, Wallis, Carteret and Cook, who embarked on his epic voyages of 1768 (in the Endeavour), 1772 and 1776 (in the Resolution) from Plymouth each time. Appropriately enough too, for when the gateways to Australia and New Zealand were well established, and the new Royal William Yard had rendered these Victualling buildings superfluous, they became the basis of probably the most sophisticated Emigration Depot in the country.

Between 1839 and the end of the century estimates suggest almost half a million people emigrated to Australia, New Zealand, the Cape or Canada from here. Most of the emigrants bound for America, excluding those notable voyagers the Pilgrim Fathers, left Britain from Liverpool. The emigrants themselves included a lot of Devon and Cornish people and, prompted by the potato famine of 1847, a lot of Irish folk. For half a guinea they could get from Cork to Plymouth and for another 14 guineas they could go all the way to Australia. This figure was later reduced as the various Australian states began to offer assisted places and grants of land which, when added to the fact that gold had been discovered 'down under' in 1849, made the trip very attractive to the nation's poor. Compared to other emigration ports, notably Liverpool, the poor were relatively well looked after at Elphinstone Wharf where the depot was situated. But standards were difficult to maintain and at times the death rate here was higher among inmates than in the rest of the town. In 1860 for example, 102 children died in Plymouth from measles and almost a third of them came from the depot. However the figure is put in some sort of context when it is remembered that, on average, around 10,000 souls emigrated from Plymouth each year between 1840 and 1890—then equivalent to about a quarter of the population of Plymouth on its own.

Today all that is left of the depot complex is the building that now houses the Mayflower Sailing Club, founded not long after the first world war. The rest were all, for the most part, pulled down when Commercial Road was widened and extended through the Citadel's south eastern limb which runs down to Fisher's Nose, so that it linked up with Madeira Road. Elphinstone Wharf (originally perhaps linked with Captain Thomas Elphinstone RN) now cleared, is a boat and car park. In 1815 Captain Elphinstone accommodated Lord Keith at his Peverell home Belair House, when the visiting dignitary received word of the fate of the French 'prisoner' Napoleon Bonaparte, who was being held on board the 'Ballerophon' in Plymouth Sound. Strangely enough, Napoleon's brother Lucien had come here five years earlier seeking asylum having fallen out with his brother. Lucien arrived at the old victualling office at a time when the Bakehouse still belonged to the Navy. Twenty years later, this building which stood on the northern side of Phoenix Wharf, was bought by a council alderman George Frean. Frean then started producing biscuits here, with subsequent assistance from millers Daw and Serpell.

Famous as a biscuit factory for many years thereafter, Frean himself left in 1857 and joined the Peek brothers in Bermondsey—it is only recently that amalgamations and name changes have seen the disappearance of the Peek-Frean label. Likewise with Serpell's, as Robert Serpell's son Henry moved the business to Reading, biscuit making centre of Britain in 1899.

Meanwhile in 1895, Phoenix wharf Pier was opened as a free public landing-place, thereby paving the way for a whole new chapter in this part of Plymouth.

12th July 1986.

The Commercial Inn

The advent of the railways gave a new lease of life to a man for whom transport had long been a problem—the 'Commercial Traveller'. Indeed the term 'Commercial Traveller' did not pass into common usage until 1855. Up to that time such a character tended to be known as a travelling chapman, a word derived from the medieval 'cheap' to buy, buy and sell truck. Before the railways he would generally have relied upon the public coaching routes, unless of course he had his own horse and saddle bag, which he would have undoubtedly needed if he wanted to call into any town or village not on a main road.

It's hardly surprising therefore, that as travelling became easier the number of travelling salesmen in this country expanded rapidly. An obvious consequence of this great increase in itinerant salespersons, was an upsurge in demand for overnight bed and breakfast and, so as to readily make it known to such travellers that they were happy and able to accommodate them, hundreds of innkeepers and hoteliers across the country changed the name of their establishment to the Commercial Inn, Hotel or whatever. Yet others were purpose-built. By the middle of last century Devonport had a couple of 'Commercials', Stonehouse had one and Plymouth had three or four; and there were literally dozens of them dotted around Devon. The whole phenomenon marked quite a change in the attitude of innkeepers and the status of the commercial traveller. In the very early days back in the seventeenth century, they were regarded for the most part as being persons of inferior status and their accommodation was often very basic, which presumably from the traveller's point of view had the advantage of being cheap. Before the wave of building, or renaming inns and hotels, it was not unknown for such establishments to have a

commercial room for the benefit of these people, indeed Dickens makes reference to just such a place in the Pickwick Papers (1837).

Locally, Hannaford's 'Commercial Inn' appears as an important coaching stop as early as 1830 and commonly, hotels and inns were marked as 'commercial' in directories if they offered accommodation. Some called themselves 'Commercial and Family' Hotels—this is what 'Chubbs Hotel' in Old Town Street became, while Fanny Farley in 1857, was calling her large establishment at the Plymouth end of Union Street, the 'Commercial Hotel and Family Boarding House'. One by one however, these places were either pulled down or changed their names again and Plymouth's only 'Commercial' today is here on Lambhay Hill, just up from Commercial Road and Wharf.

No longer the centre of commerce it was last century and well into this, the Commercial Inn now has a clear view of the Cattewater, which once would have been obscured by warehouses, factories and immigration buildings. Even the commercial nature of the Inn itself has changed in recent years. Until 1953, this was just a beerhouse but on 21 September that year, the full licence of the old 'Newport Inn' from Edinburgh Road, Devonport was transferred here; the 'Newport' being one of many casualties to fall by the wayside in the wake of the 1950s Dockyard extension of the South Yard.

'The Commercial' on the other hand, has survived when all around has seen change. Modern flats on either side have replaced the Inn's old neighbours and plans to build the new car park, so desperately needed by the Barbican, are still being considered for the site opposite. The Department of the Environment however, apparently feels that Lambhay Hill is not the best site for such a car park. Certainly, when so much of the City's coastline has been built upon or rendered otherwise inaccessible to the public already, it would be a shame to blot the landscape now, particularly if there is an opportunity perhaps to have that part of Lambhay Hill below the Citadel's eastern walls grassy and clear as it is around the corner. Lambhay, after all, is said to mean sheep enclosure and, at the time of Domesday, the original manor of Sutton was recorded as being 20 acres 4 pastures and sporting fifteen sheep. Then again, other writers have suggested that while the 'hay' probably does mean field, the 'lam' may come from the old Cornish meaning leap and, thus, we get leap field, this being the field from which the giant Goemot leapt, or was thrown, a legend which, while undoubtedly bizarre, many earlier Plymothians chose to believe.

This week, however, the Barbican has witnessed more concrete examples of the bizarre and the legendary as the Barbican Regatta has been in full swing. Established over 100 years ago around the time Jane Joy was licensee at the 'Commercial', the Regatta is the Barbican's annual week of mayhem and entertainment. Tug-of-war, greasy-pole climbing, dancing, fishing, leaping from boat to boat in fancy dress and today a cider race organized by the present licensee of the 'Commercial', Ian Wood, who came to the pub in 1980.

1st August 1987.

United Services Inn

An early reference to the 'United Services Inn' shows William Owen here at Garrison Green in 1857; however, prior to that there are no apparent references to Garrison Green at all. Although in 1852 we find presumably the same William Owen recorded as a shopkeeper in Citadel Green. Given that there are no subsequent references to Citadel Green, it would seem that William Owen began selling beer from his shop and that, around the same time, Citadel Green became Garrison Green. The Green in question being the open space that then existed in front of the Citadel's North entrance, which also gave rise to the old title of Lambhay Green for part of Lambhay Hill. This land was later taken over and developed by the Territorial Army and, at present, is being redeveloped for a training wing for 29 Commando.

Like much of the land south of the pub, this area belongs to the Crown and makes up part of the 28-acre site appropriated from the City by Charles II and mostly, now, leased by the Corporation from the War Office for a modest sum (less than £200 per year). The extent of the War Department land was staked out in 1867 by a series of over 20 boundary stones. The whereabouts of these stones have just recently been published, in the 'Transactions of the Devonshire Association' (December 1985) in a list compiled by Roger Serpell of the Old Plymouth Society. Two of these stones (numbers 17 and 18) can be seen on the two southern corners of the 'United Services' although a third, at the back of the Inn, seems to have mysteriously disappeared in the new developments around the Inn.

Among these new developments has been the rebuilding of accommodation in Castle Dyke Lane (formerly Little Hoe Lane), which runs down the Eastern side of the Inn. Bombed during the war, reputedly causing the back wall of the pub to buckle and bow, much of Castle Dyke Lane had been laid waste for many years. Now largely reconstructed, it is probably the narrowest public thoroughfare with adjacent living quarters in the city and it's not hard to imagine that this was among the 'more especially filthy' streets of Plymouth, in the middle of last century when, in a second major outbreak of cholera, some 10 per cent of the population of Plymouth died. At that time 146 people lived in the six houses that made up Castle Dyke Lane—four of which had no privy or w.c.

Accompanying this squalor the neighbouring beerhouses, of which the Barbican had the largest concentration, were host to scenes of 'everything degrading to human nature'. In his fascinating book on Sutton Harbour, Crispin Gill quotes one contemporary witness who talked of 'trawler "apprentices"', boys between 10 and 16, who made up to five shillings a week supplying fishermen with bait and spent this "squid money" in beer houses, each with his prostitute aged between 8 and 12 . . . In many cases boys and girls were not turned out of the beer houses until six or eight in the morning, drunk.' Castle Street alone, which runs east from here, in 1850 boasted 7 licensed houses and 5 beer houses—today it has none.

The 'United Services Inn' itself was formerly a beerhouse and it was only in 1957, when it acquired a spirit license from the defunct Spread Eagle, in erstwhile Kinterbury Street, that it became a full public house. Here then, to institute the changes were Reg and Maud Brenton, celebrated cat lovers, who left the pub with an air of its own and an inheritance of many stray cats, a legacy which Basil Bowden was not keen to assume, and he caused a minor outrage when he effectively banned the offending felines from the premises.

One man who remembers that era well is Tony Moy, who first drank in here in 1961. Then a young sailor, Tony, after 22 years in the Service, is the present landlord here and the 'United Services' is his first pub; as it was for his predecessor Roger Lillicrap. Roger, today at the 'White Thorn', Shaugh Prior, was born in Castle Street and just as the street and the Barbican have greatly changed in recent years, so Roger was responsible for beginning to ring the changes inside the Inn. Now, after yet more redesigning and refurbishment, the 'United Services Inn' is a far, far cry from its original nineteenth-century state inside, although from the outside it has probably changed very little in all this time.

8th February 1986.

The Admiral MacBride

'MacBride's a man and Sir Frederick's a mouse—MacBride shall sit in Parliament House.' So ran the 'campaign slogan' of the supporters of Captain John MacBride a little over 200 years ago in the Parliamentary election of 1784. MacBride, variously described as 'the faithful Irishman', 'an exceedingly troublesome, busy, violent man' and a 'gentleman whose gallantry has often been the theme of praise' was successfully elected. He was undoubtedly a popular hero. In those days elections were a far cry from what we recognize as democratic today and on the previous occasion, in 1780, Sir Frederick Rogers, the Government's man, and Admiral Darby, the Admiralty's nominee, had both been returned against the candidates supported by the local freeholders. However with MacBride they were more successful and both Rogers and the Admiralty's own man were beaten by the Irish Captain although the other victorious candidate, Captain R. Fanshawe, was another Government man.

As a Plymouth MP, MacBride 'distinguished himself very much, particularly by the opposition made by him to the expensive plan then in agitation for fortifying the dock yards'. This he did 'not merely as a member of parliament, but as a member of the board of officers, convened for the purpose of investigating the propriety of the measure.' Furthermore, we are told, he gave 'firm support' to every measure that could advance the good of the service or the welfare of his brother officers' and lastly he strove 'to remedy some abuses which had made their way into the civil departments of the service'. To these ends he brought two bills into the Commons, one for 'the relief of the widows of Warrant Officers' and another—'restricting Captains in the Royal Navy with respect to their holding Civil Appointments'.

Clearly John MacBride was not a pocket borough Parliamentarian. However, perhaps his most important achievement, for the bulk of his constituents, was the securing of the Government's grants which enabled the piers to be built across the entrance to Sutton Harbour. Storms presented a great danger in those days before any Breakwater at Mount Batten or even in the Sound, and the building of the East and West Piers transformed Sutton Harbour. It also, in the short term, caused the Pool to silt up somewhat thanks, in part, to the ever increasing amount of sewerage that the growing town was pumping into it. But MacBride didn't live to see that although he was still alive in 1798 when the account above of his Parliamentary activities was written and when Patrick Shea, who we also assume to be Irish, was licensee here at the 'Admiral MacBride'.

The land on which the pub stands was probably built up at the same time as the piers were constructed, between 1791–99 and in all likelihood the pub was built for the benefit of those working on the project. MacBride himself had moved on to Torbay in 1790 with the *Cumberland*. After becoming an MP it appears that he had spent a few years out of commission but in 1788 he was appointed to the *Cumberland*, a guard ship, which was at that time stationed in Plymouth. The year he left Plymouth he also left Parliament.

Although described as an Irishman, John MacBride was born in Scotland, 'the descendant of an ancient Scotch family'. His father, a Presbyterian minister, soon afterwards moved and settled in Ireland and so John grew up around Ballymoney, in County Antrim. It is not known when he was born and it is thought that he joined the Navy around 1754, after some years in the Merchant Service. His naval career was a long and distinguished one and he was first made a Rear Admiral in 1793. His full promotion to Admiral came six years later, on the 14th February, 1799. It was an honour he enjoyed but briefly, as he died of a paralytic seizure, at the Spring Garden Coffee House a year later on Monday 17th February. Twice married, he lived for a while in Plymouth with his second wife, at Leigham House, on the site of the modern Leigham Estate. However, one other of his activities was to have a much wider, long-term effect on Plymouth. Back in 1765 Captain John Byron returned from a voyage of discovery around the world. Byron's report on the Falkland Islands was so favourable that the Government determined to take effective possession of Port Egmont in West Falkland and the man they despatched, 'to carry out this purpose', was Captain John MacBride. That year, 1766, a small British garrison was established and another chapter in Britain's naval history was opened. MacBride even opened a few chapters of his own—he wrote a 'Journal of the Winds and Weather . . . at Falkland Islands from 1 February to 19 January 1767'.

Today 'his' piers are walked by thousands of visitors each year from all over the world and, as befitting to the pub, which is not only nearest to the Mayflower Memorial but, virtually, on the site of the original Mayflower Steps, it sports the flags of Britain and America.

31st January 1987.

Sir Francis Chichester

'Flying is the most fascinating sport in the world; it enters ineradicably into your blood ... That feeling of cutting out big distances in an apparatus controlled and directed by yourself alone; the attempt by you, a solitary soul from among two thousand millions, to do something that no other of the 1,999,999,999 has done tickles your vanity, your sense of power, your sense of romance, your love of excitement, as nothing else in the world can do!'

So wrote the 28-year-old Francis Chichester some 37 years before he completed his epic solo around the world voyage, on 28th of May 1967.

Born at Shirwell near Barnstaple on September 17th 1901, Francis Chichester was one of the greatest adventurers of the twentieth century. In 1919 he emigrated to New Zealand with £10 and, within as many years, he was earning £10,000 from his various enterprises, one of which was the formation of an Aviation Company. Having described himself as having few friends at school or at home, Chichester— twice married (his first wife died in 1929)—was perhaps always a bit of a loner and in late 1929 he became the second ever person to fly solo from England to Australia. At that time, Chichester had only been flying for about five months and, although he had planned his flight carefully, a contemporary newspaper reported that he had only made his intentions known at the last minute when a mechanic helping him to prepare, 'jocularly remarked', 'Going to Australia, aren't you?' and received from Mr. Chichester the unexpected answer 'Yes'. Chichester made that flight in a De Havilland Gipsy Moth aeroplane and it was that name he later gave to all four of his boats. The first he bought in 1953 and had rechristened from the Florence Edith. The others he had built himself. As an aviator, Chichester made many pioneering flights—the first solo flight from New Zealand to Australia in 1931 the first solo seaplane flight, in his converted Gipsy Moth, from New Zealand to Japan, also in 1931. He documented his exploits in a series of books—'Solo to Sydney' (1930), 'Ride on the Wind' (1936), the first chapter of which was entitled 'The Loneliest Man', whilst his autobiography, published in 1964, was called 'The Lonely Sea and the Sky'.

In between flying and sailing, Chichester established a fine reputation as a navigator, map maker and publisher. Indeed during the Second World War, the Air Ministry found his unique abilities extremely useful and he served as Chief Navigational Officer at the Empire Central Flying School.

At the age of 58 he helped organize, and won, the first solo transatlantic race and by the time he arrived in Plymouth after his round the world voyage, he had achieved several other sailing records. 250,000 people assembled around Plymouth Hoe and Sound to welcome him back in 1967 just four months after he had been appointed a Knight Commander of the British Empire. Fighting ill health, Chichester sailed to Greenwich in July to kneel before Elizabeth II, who knighted him with the sword which Sir Francis Drake, Devon's first circumnavigator, had presented to Elizabeth I. Drake himself would have walked the cobbles of the Barbican and so it was somehow fitting that when Starkey, Knight and Ford came to refurbish their Barbican inn, the Crown and Anchor, they should successfully seek permission to rename the pub the 'Sir Francis Chichester'—a ceremony that was ultimately

performed in the presence of the Lord Mayor, by the great adventurer himself, who sadly died in 1972.

Just as Drake has pubs in the area recording his name, so too is there one honouring his boat—the Golden Hind. So it was for a number of years with Chichester; however, the 'Hoe Park Hotel' in Citadel Road that became the 'Gipsy Moth IV', recently changed its name again and is now the 'Yard Arm'. Hopefully, however, the 'Sir Francis Chichester' will stay as it is as long as the building stands. Having enjoyed the best part of 200 years as the 'Crown and Anchor' already, it certainly looks in no danger of falling down. So far since 1967 the 'Sir Francis Chichester' inn has survived a dozen licensee changes, although strangely enough, before the name alteration, the pub had been in the hands of one family—the Glanvilles—for over 45 years.

There are many public houses recording great men of the past in the City but to date, there are only three remembering heroes of this century, the 'Lord Louis' (Mountbatten) at Plympton, the only 20th century pub in the trio, the 'General Moore' and the 'Sir Francis Chichester'. A fine time-honoured way of remembering great people, doubtless there will be many more to come.

21st June 1986.

New Street

The narrowness of the quaintly-cobbled New Street is an indication of its antiquity, the street was 'New' 400 years ago. In 1504 it was referred to as 'Mr. Sparke's new streate' and John Sparke, a major local landowner and developer, had just begun building behind the Island House. What we know today as the Elizabethan House was one of the first properties he completed here and it is unlikely that there were any earlier dwellings here, although the course of this thoroughfare ran up beyond the fourteenth century buildings of the Greyfriars monastery, which had only comparatively recently (1538) been taken from the Friars as part of Henry VIII's dissolution campaign. Sparke had already acquired the earlier monastic site of the Whitefriars at 'Friary' and building was also underway on part of that land. At that time, those two Friaries virtually marked the south western and north eastern extremities of the town.

While New Street (or Rag Street or Greyfriars Street as it has variously been known), has never extended much beyond the site of the old Friary, approximately where 43–45 New Street now stands, the path that ran beyond it, centuries ago, now marks the line of the present Citadel Road and, even as it did then, it runs down to the north eastern corner of Millbay.

Today New Street is probably the oldest and the narrowest of the well used thoroughfares in the old part of Plymouth. Indeed just after the war it was precisely these circumstances that almost led to many of the old, surviving buildings being pulled down. Fortunately, largely thanks to the Barbican Association which grew out of the Old Plymouth Society, most of these were reprieved and restored. However, because this was the era of the rambling housing-estate and the high-rise flat, and it was considered essential for every home to have an adequate amount of air

and natural light, New Street was judged to be too dark and too narrow to house the large number of people who had happily been living here and so everyone was rehoused. The buildings were now only considered to be fit for commercial purposes. Strict regulations ensured that any subsequent schemes should find a way around the light and air situation, something that the architects of Hanover Court achieved by building units at an angle obliquely to the street line. Today another major housing scheme is in progress directly opposite the buildings shown here and the street line once again is being preserved. This time, however, the ground floor residences will be slightly set back from the road, behind pillars which drop down onto the street line from the floor above. With modern artificial lighting, natural light is no longer as necessary as it became after the Window Tax was repealed in the middle of last century. Indeed in some respects, the history of New Street illustrates many aspects of the history of natural light and its place in the home. Long before the terraced house, the row house or the semi detached, the common men and women of this country, for the most part, lived in primitive dwellings that were both lit and ventilated by their main entrances. There was no readily available or affordable glass and, consequently, there tended to be no windows. Typically the door would be in two halves, the bottom half generally being kept shut to keep all the animals out. When unglazed windows did start to appear they were usually very small, this being as much a matter of security as practicality. In the absence of wooden shutters, of course, these 'windows' were obviously very draughty and that, indeed, is how they got their name—it comes from the old Norse 'vindauga'—'wind-eye'. Often placed well above eye level then, these windows were there simply to admit light and it wasn't until the craze for landscape gardening that windows were properly valued simply as something to look out of.

Nowadays, though, as artificial lighting improves this is tending to become the major function of the window. But back in the early days, only the wealthy could afford to think about such things—glass was very expensive and, working on the basis that you had to be very well off to afford any substantial number of windows, the Government in 1696 introduced a fairly heavy window tax. Only houses worth less than £5 per annum and dairies were exempt. This tax was raised six times between 1747 and 1808 until in 1823 it actually dropped a little. In 1851 the year appropriately enough of the opening of the Crystal Palace, the tax was abolished. In the meantime, however, many windows up and down the country had been blocked. Here in New Street of course, it is an indication of how wealthy the original inhabitants were that there was no shortage of windows. Built to house wealthy sea captains and successful merchants, it is ironic now, that after all this time the house opposite the Elizabethan House is currently being converted into luxury flats above ground floor level. The ground floor will become a shop and another trader will move into this bustling Barbican backstreet, where already you can find printers, potters, painters, designers and dressmakers and dieticians, artists and antique dealers and, in the original Elizabethan spirit, imported crafts from all over the world.

19th December 1987.

Southside Street

' ... This yere the kaye on southesyde, whereof the southe ende adjoneth to the Barbygan vnderneth the Castell, was Builded by the towne vnder full sea marcke, and Contayneth in lengethe one hundred and Thurtie Foot and in Bredethe fourtie and fower foot.' So reads the 1572 entry in the ancient 'Town Ligger'—a bulky volume in oak boards and tattered pigskin, long known by the name of the 'Black Book' (R. N. Worth 1893). This Black Book has contemporary record entries from 1540–1709 and is probably the most valuable source of information on early Plymouth history. Many earlier documents are known to have existed, but most have been destroyed.

It is not only this century that the ravages of war have seen important buildings and papers destroyed, as the Black Book itself tells us, Plymouth was burnt three times by the French and Bretons (1377, 1400 and 1403) and an entry of 1548–9 reveals that the town was assailed by the Western Rebels for the restoration of Catholicism '... then was our stepell burnt with all the townes evydence in the same by Rebelles ...' with the result that little was saved but a few scattered documents.

And so it is that we look to the Black Book to piece together the city's history from snippets of information about bye-laws, proclamations, acts of parliament, guild orders, lists of mayors and freemen, deed and the occasional note about events of national or local importance; which brings us back to the building of Southside Quay in 1572. Often assumed, as Crispin Gill notes, to be the oldest part of town, South Side is 'an Elizabethan suburb ... a good two centuries younger than the area north of Notte Street'. The original line of Southside street itself was, doubtless, a well trodden path from the old town to the medieval castle, which antedated the Citadel and stood between Lambhay Street and Castle Street, the fortification by the water that gives us the name Barbican.

Initially, however, this area was generally known as South Side and, although there were undoubtedly houses here earlier and the street was apparently paved in 1584, the first direct reference to the Southside Street is from 1591 and well into last century we find that buildings, whose address is now simply 'The Barbican', were given as Southside Quay—right around to the Admiral McBride, by the Mayflower Steps.

Clearly, virtually all the properties in Southside Street have been substantially redeveloped since the late 16th century; one, however, on the corner of Pin (formerly Pin's) Lane, has been rebuilt much as it would have originally appeared. Here it is believed that Captain Lucas Cocke, who was killed in the Armada fighting, once lived. Today it is the only building in the street to boast ground floor living accommodation, the rest of the street at this level being entirely used for a great variety of commercial purposes. A situation that makes it the most popular thoroughfare with tourists and locals on the Barbican.

Among the variety of businesses in this eastern end of the street is Parade Printing Works, the oldest such works in the city and one-time premises of the Royal Marines (the Guardhouse) before their move to Durnford Street. Their Parade was the quay on the northern side of this block. Roy Smith, who runs the print-works, has deeds for the site dating back to 1770 when two cottages stood here. These deeds provided for access, on alternate weeks, through each other's premises to their cesspits—a fact recorded in the recently lapsed Barbican Voice, a very local newspaper that for several years chronicled the changing face of the Barbican. Chief instigator of this noble organ, along with John Theobald, was Archie Roberts whose mother Mabel, now in her eighty-fifth year, must undoubtedly be the oldest pub landlady in the area. Mabel, who arrived at the Maritime in 1949, is probably also the longest serving licensee in Plymouth today, a feat which the cheery octogenarian makes little of.

Number 22 Southside Street, on the other side of the print works, is substantially an early eighteenth-century building and once housed an inn itself—the 'Custom House Tavern'. Beer was also sold in number 27, 44 (the Clarence), 46 and number 50, now 'Southside Wines' and one time 'Albion'. This end of the street, of course, also houses the long-established Yarmouth Stores and Jacka's, Britain's oldest working bakery. »Postscript

15th March 1986.

Jacka's Bakery

Were the Guinness Book of Records to list the 'oldest commercially working bakery in Great Britain', this humble building in Southside Street would almost certainly take the honours. A Nationwide appeal set up by the magazines 'British Baker' and 'Baking Today' found nothing to compare with it in England. (The famous Sally Lunns in Bath is now a tea room.) Records unearthed so far appear to date the bakery back to 1597 at least and in those days it would seem to have been a free-standing building rather like its Tudor counterpart the Island House nearby. Doorways and window frames, on both sides of this long narrow building, which

stretches two-thirds of the way back to New Street, suggest that it probably enjoyed unimpeded views of Sutton Pool long before the quay was extended and centuries before the fish market was built.

Describing the premises in a Devon Life article earlier this year, Mark Brayshay spoke of the medieval 'burgage plots'—'long strips with a narrow frontage facing the thoroughfare' on which townsmen or 'burgesses' would have built their streetline workshops. However, back in the sixteenth century, the stables at the rear of the building would have been approached via one of the side entrances, rather than through the shop itself as they were well into this century.

Strangely enough, the earliest record of the bakery coincides with the second mayoralty of Humphry Fownes—strangely, because not only did the Fownes family at that time own this business, but in 1684 when James Yonge came to catalogue all the Mayors of Plymouth—'togather with ye memorable occurrences, in their respective yeares', almost all he had to say about the year 1596–97 was that 'wheat was 30s. a bushell plym° measure' and 'barley twelve'.

During Humphrey Fownes's first Mayoralty, incidentally, Yonge records a somewhat more memorable occurrence—'the Spanish Armada Invade England and are destroyed'. That was obviously 1588 although another source suggests that 'Humfrie Fownes was mayor in 1585–86' when Yonge tells us that 'Tobacco was first brought into this country'.

With the dawning of the seventeenth century, another Fownes, Thomas, enjoyed two mayoralties, 1610–11 and 1619–20, a fact which is linked with the claim that this bakery actually supplied ships biscuits to the *Mayflower*. Certainly 'Fone's Captain's Ships Biscuits' enjoyed worldwide fame well into this century and Hugh Jacka, current owner/baker here, well remembers working long hours with his uncle in the 1930s, to supply the Russian fleet anchored off the Sound with the said biscuits. Hugh Jacka's uncle, John Jacka bought the bakery around that time from the Warren family who in turn around the middle of the last century had acquired it by the marriage of John Warren to a Fone's daughter. The bakery then is not only unique, on account of its age, but also because to date it has only really changed families twice in some 400 years. John Warren's son, Frank Fone Warren, took over the bakery from old man Fone towards the end of the last century. However, none of Frank's four sons went into the business. Two brothers Les and George, born in the bakery, later set up a garage business in Plymstock and, although long since retired, the Warren name is still preserved there. Meanwhile George still visits his native Southside Street to see two of his sons at work, as John Warren is current managing director of Topes long-established Barbican business and David Warren has his clock and watch making and repair shop there.

Meanwhile, it looks as though the bakery may soon change families again as Hugh Jacka's two daughters have not followed him in the business. However, Mr. Jacka is keen to see that whilst the ownership may change, the long-established style and traditions of the bakery do not and the indications are that this will, indeed, be the case. »Postscript

30th November 1985.

Barbican

'If it were anywhere on the Riviera or Provence, or in Spain, or Italy, English and American tourists would be found going into raptures over it, but here it is drab old England and we have not known how to make the most of it'. Sir Philip Pilditch, the historian, wrote that in his 1929 pamphlet, 'Elizabethan Plymouth' and was duly quoted, 14 years later, in the 1943 Plan for Plymouth. However, the authors of this much referred-to document believed that the war had brought this situation well and truly to a head and that now was the time to act '. . . We consider that in this small district (the Barbican) is an area worthy of preservation from every point of view, and we recommend an intensification of effort towards the reconditioning and reconstruction of the buildings so that, whilst retaining its historic features of narrow roads, winding step-crossed lanes, enclosed courts and tiered houses it shall possess those additional communal and personal facilities demanded by modern standards of living'. Central to their subsequent proposals was the drawing of 'a sharp distinction between the new Centre and historic Plymouth, by the construction of a real and physical wall, built in local stone'.

This wall was intended, approximately, to follow the 'original' walls or at least the perimeter of the Tudor town of Plymouth. The idea was that 'once a visitor had passed within the wall he would find himself, as it were, in another century'.

To date, however, although the new city centre has been developed largely in accordance with this visionary and optimistic plan, the Barbican has not altogether been ignored, but has certainly been overlooked. An area with the buildings, the history and the charm to sell the city far and wide, given a little more care and attention, it has so far failed to achieve its precinct status. Such is not to say that money has not been spent on it; Southside Street has been greatly tidied up and the Barbican Association have, over the years, done much to restore large areas of Looe Street and New Street and they have also part-filled another of the Watson/

Abercrombie plans by creating the attractive Elizabethan Gardens behind New Street. 'In the past' they wrote 'there was much more of gardens, courts and pleasaunces than can be seen today, since many of them have been built over to the exclusion of light and healthful conditions'.

A few trees have also been planted along from the Three Crowns and outside some of the new flats but for the most part, the flats that have been newly built rather than converted from warehouses, have tended to look somewhat ill-fitting in this historic part of town.

An area which, in 1967, was designated only the second Conservation Area in the country.

Three years later another report 'The Development of Plymouth' (1970) noted that the original sixteenth century street plan had largely survived here, thanks to the commercial centre of the town moving westwards. The report also quoted a 1966 policy plan that spoke of creating a new car park for the Barbican and an alternative route for the traffic passing through the area to the Hoe.

Twenty years later this road, first mooted in the original 1943 Plan, now looks under way, as does the construction of a large car park. The 1986 Plan states 'much of the environment of the area is spoilt by moving and parked vehicles . . .' so perhaps now Plymouth can look forward to the establishment of a truly historic area, a little more in harmony with its sixteenth century layout and a little less cluttered by the twentieth-century vehicles it was never designed to accommodate.

Plymouth grew out of the medieval town of Sutton and its roots are still there. Properly cared for, these roots will help keep the city healthy and confirm its status as a major attraction.

10th May 1986.

Unitarian Church Notte Street

On Saturday 31st of May 1958, the Rt. Hon. James Chuter Ede MP, a former Cabinet Minister, opened Plymouth's new Unitarian Church in his capacity as President of the General Assembly of Unitarian and Free Christian Churches.

Plymouth's earlier Unitarian Church was one of 20 destroyed or damaged during the heavy air raids of 20th and 21st March, 1941. Opened in May 1832, it had stood in Treville Street on a site, now partly buried by the viaduct above Bretonside bus station, between Charles Church and St. Andrew's Cross roundabout. However, the site had been used by Unitarians for over 250 years, the first purpose-built building being erected on that site around 1690. The present New England-style edifice, based on the Unitarians' traditional square chapel layout and designed by Mr. R. Fraser of a London firm of architects, Louis de Soissons, was built with the compensation from the Treville Street building. It cost £14,000 and is single storey with a tall copper-covered spire that tops 80 feet.

Between 1941 and 1958 local Unitarians gathered in a variety of places. For a couple of years they met in the house of Miss A. D. Drew at 10 Thorn Park. Before the war had finished, however, new premises were rented in Houndiscombe Road and it was from here that the Unitarians ran their services, committees and youth club until May 1958 when Notte Street was opened. Strangely enough, this opening came just six months after the re-opening and re-dedication of the blitzed St. Andrew's Church. It was the clergy of St. Andrew's who laid the local nonconformist foundations of the Unitarian movement in 1662. Following the countrywide ejection of 2,000 members of the clergy because they refused to use the Prayer book imposed upon them by Parliament that year, George Hughes, the Puritan vicar of St. Andrew's (1643–1662), together with his lecturer Thomas Martyn, was turned out of

the church. They were both arrested and subsequently imprisoned on Drake's Island. Hughes was sixty at this time and in the fearful cold and damp conditions, he was soon a victim of 'dropsy and scurvy'. He was released, on a bond of £2,000 (paid by his friends without his knowledge) nine months later, on condition that he did not come again within twenty miles of Plymouth. He retired to Kingsbridge, where he died five years later. It has been suggested, though, that he had paid clandestine visits to Plymouth and held unauthorised services.

But it was Nicholas Sherwill who, despite fines and periods of imprisonment, became the principal local nonconformist preacher and it was he who began the first register of the Unitarian congregation with a wedding in September 1662.

At first meetings were held in the 'Old Marshalls', the 'Marshalsea' in Southside Street and now the 'Distillery'. Thomas Martyn returned to preach, after the 1672 Act of Indulgence, and he recorded a series of baptisms in Greene Street—entered in the Unitarian registers through to 1675. Martyn's return appears to have led to a second dissenting congregation being established and almost 100 years later when Unitarianism properly asserted itself in the town, Treville Street both lost members to, and gained them from, Batter Street (where Sherwill's congregation had moved in 1705) as people either espoused the free-thinking Unitarian views or rejected them.

Unitarianism has been legally tolerated in England since 1813 but its rejection of the doctrine of the Trinity—the Father, Son and Holy Ghost—and its choosing to recognize only God the Father still causes some denominations to regard Unitarianism as non-christian. Certainly the Jews and Muslims are not amongst them as they share a monotheistic approach. Indeed, immediately after Treville Street was bombed the local Hebrew congregation, whose synagogue escaped damage (its roof and south facing wall are visible in this picture), allowed the Unitarians to use their hall on Sunday afternoons until alternative premises were found.

However, the Unitarians are not non-christian. They believe in Jesus and follow His teachings and see Him as an example of 'what human life can become when lived in obedience to God's will'. Furthermore they see the bible as a supremely valuable book from which much knowledge of God can be obtained. But their Church is essentially a creedless one as it allows its congregation complete freedom to think for themselves, to search for truth about God in their own minds and 'to take one world at a time'.

It is this open-ended faith that has led to the first church established by the Pilgrim Fathers in Plymouth Massachusetts back in 1620, being a Unitarian one today. Several American Presidents have been Unitarians. In this country John Milton, John Locke, Isaac Newton, Charles Dickens, Charles Darwin and Florence Nightingale are among those notables who, down the years, have been of Unitarian opinion.

It is perhaps significant too that the role of women in Unitarian Churches has been greater than in most other denominations. There have been women Unitarian ministers since the beginning of the century and the present minister, here in Notte Street, is a lady, the Rev. Patricia Womersley, M.A.

24th January 1987.

The Barbican Revival

'The finest house in Plymouth of the Queen Anne period is one in Notte Street ... set back from the street. The front is entirely of Portland stone, and the details are exceedingly good. Here lived for many years (and died) Cookworthy, of china-clay and Plymouth pottery fame. Can you picture him, the quiet Quaker in his drab suit, seated in his wainscoted parlour before the fire-place with its blue and white Dutch tiles? The house is unique in its way, and nothing half so good will replace it'.

That is what W. Hine stated in the local press on 17th November 1882. What he didn't say, however, was that the building was at that time multi–tenanted and very dilapidated and, in the last year or so, had had its fine doorway blocked up and the windows on either side of the original door opened up as separate entrances, each approached by a flight of eight steps. However, the reason for Mr. Hine's impassioned outburst was that he knew that the old Cookworthy house was about to be demolished. Earlier in the year (March 1882) Isaac Foot had bought the building for the princely sum of £640. It is to Isaac Foot's credit, though, that he did not remove all trace of the old building when he built his Christian Mission Hall immediately in front of it. Referred to in the deeds as the 'Old Mayoralty House', Cookworthy had lived in the grand building for a number of years, but it was by no means the first Plymouth residence of this young chemist from Kingsbridge.

William Cookworthy, always destined for a brilliant career, had lost his father when he was 12 and soon after his family lost a lot of money when the 'South Sea Bubble' burst. At 15 when an apprenticeship as a pharmacist was offered to him in London he accepted and being poor had little choice but to walk from Kingsbridge to London to take it up. Five years later in 1725, he opened a pharmacy in Nut Street (as Notte Street was then known). This later became very much a family business and remained as such until 1812. The exact location of the pharmacy is not clear, but it must have been very near 'Cookworthy House', the corner facade of which can be seen sticking out just a little at the rear of the present edifice. Isaac Foot also preserved the impressive sculpturing that had been above the entrance to the old house and this work can now be seen over the top two side windows.

Like William Cookworthy, Isaac Foot was temperate. However, whilst there would have been wine at the former's table, when he entertained his many and distinguished guests (Captain Cook, John Smeaton and others), Isaac Foot established the Mission Hall as a temple of temperance in an area which has always been famous for its high concentration of licensed premises. There was once a handful of pubs in Notte Street alone; Lourdes Bistro, next door, was for many years known as the 'Yarmouth Inn' although around 1920 it became home to the Plymouth Varnish and Colour Company Limited, Varnish Manufacturers.

Today there are far more restaurants in the Barbican area than there are pubs, the neighbouring Famagusta restaurant appearing in, what was for well over 100 years the base for the Gloyn family grocery business, dating back at least to Francis Gloyn in 1850. While since May of last year the opening of the Barbican Revival eating house has completed a hat-trick of licensed restaurants in this part of Notte Street. It is, undoubtedly, ironic that this hall of temperance should now be licensed, but Isaac

Foot cannot blame his descendants entirely for this. Sadly, his Mission Hall was gutted during the Blitz and David Nash, a grandson of Isaac Foot's, sold the shell for a nominal sum to the Elim Church, whose congregation had been worshipping in Stonehouse. They completely restructured the inside whilst preserving the exterior of the building and moved in around 1955. They worshipped here for 28 years before moving on again just recently, in 1983, to Embankment Road.

The Notte Street premises then changed hands once more. Now it is the Barbican Revival, with bare floors and attractive wood and stone furniture and fittings. Indeed some of the stonework has an interesting history of its own; the arches and pillars having been part of a grand Italian style house, the 'Gates of St. John', built near Henley. Just before the last war the house was dismantled, transported and rebuilt on the Isle of Wight, then sometime after the war it was dismantled again and shipped to Cornwall. It was never rebuilt. Over the years it was sold off bit by bit. Proprietors Michael and Jill Robinson bought some of the stonework for their Revival restaurant so now this curious building in Notte Street is even more of a hotchpotch but strangely enough, it works!

7th March 1987.

The Synagogue, Catherine Street

There appear to have been trading links between the Jews and Phoenicians and the people of Devon and Cornwall over 2000 years ago and there is evidence of an established Jewish community in Exeter as long ago as 1181. However, in 1290, after a number of anti-Jewish measures had been adopted by certain western European countries, the Jews were expelled from England.

Despite this policy though, records suggest that a few Jews continued to live in Plymouth, generally in work related to shipping. Indeed Drake noted in the log of the *Golden Hind* in 1527 that his quartermaster was 'Moses, the Jew, from the Barbican, Plymouth'.

Such references are rare, however, and it wasn't until 1656, under the Protectorate of Oliver Cromwell, that toleration was again granted in this country. At first, immigration was primarily from refugees of the Spanish and Portuguese communities—the Sephardim as they are known. These people had been expelled from Spain, in 1492 and Portugal in 1497 and some of them had already found their way into Britain in the guise of Protestants. Some became high-ranking servants of Elizabeth I and one of them, Hector Nunez, was the man who informed Walsingham of the sailing of the Armada.

In 1663, in order to safeguard their new-found liberty in this country, they renounced all interference in politics; a rule that was adhered to for some 200 years. In 1863 Benjamin D'Israeli (Disraeli), a Sephardim descendant, became Britain's 29th Prime Minister; however, it was a Plymouth Jew, Phineas Levi, who earlier became the first Jew in England to be elected to a public office. Until about 1700 almost all of England's Jewish community was Sephardic. However, just before the turn of the century a number of Jews arrived in this country; these were the Ashkenazim and in 1690 they established the first Ashkenazy Synagogue in London. Today the vast majority, about 85%, of the world's Jewry are Ashkenazim.

Towards the end of the seventeenth century an Ashkenazi group were beginning to come together in Plymouth and in the early part of the next century, they began to hold regular services in their own houses at first and then in rented rooms. In 1742 they set the wheels in motion for building and owning a synagogue which they could use as a permanent place of worship.

This was no easy matter at that time for Jews were not then allowed to own land or estates in this country, and so on 30th August 1742, a site for the synagogue was leased from the 'Mayor and Commonalty' by George Marshall, a sympathetic Protestant. That site in St. Catherine's Lane, was bounded on the north by the Hospital of the Poors Portion, and to the west and south by open land. In 1762 the Synagogue was built on this site and, from that day to this, here it has stood, little altered. One of only two major public buildings in the area to escape any damage in the Blitz, it is the oldest Ashkenazi Synagogue in the English-speaking world in continuous use.

Unassuming and uninspiring from the outside, almost all of its internal fittings and decorative work date from its opening. In fact the eight great brass candlesticks had to be pawned by the Founders to help pay for the completion of the building. Eventually they were returned of course and now they adorn the Bimah, the centre platform, from which the Pentateuch is read in an annual cycle. The pentateuch is in the form of a scroll and in Hebrew it is called a 'Sefer Torah' which is usually translated as the 'Scroll of the Law', but which should, more properly, be known as the 'Scroll of Teaching'.

Essentially the Synagogue, although a place of worship, is a place of teaching. Shool, rather like our school, is the dialect word for Synagogue and Jewish rabbis are religious teachers, not priests. The text of the pentateuch itself as evidenced by the Dead Sea Scrolls, has not changed in 2000 years.

Like all Synagogues, this building faces Jerusalem, east, and on its eastern wall is a cabinet in which the Scrolls of the Tarah are kept. This cabinet is known as the Ark and above it there are representations of the 2 stone tablets containing the Ten Commandments, with just the first word of each commandment appearing. The windows either side of the Ark are the only non-original windows in the building; they were cut after 1874, just ten years after the Ladies Gallery had been extended along either side of the building by Mr. Leon Solomon. Women do not take a formal part in the orthodox Ashkenazi services and here, on the Sabbath (sundown on Friday to sundown on Saturday), only male Jews who have celebrated their Bar Mitzvah—thirteenth birthday—can make up the Minyan (the necessary formal quorum of ten without which there would only be informal prayers in the synagogue).

Since the departure of Rabbi Dr. Bernard Susser in 1981 the congregation has been without an incumbent minister and now operates on a do-it-yourself basis from their own lay resources. President of the Hebrew congregation and Lay head of the local community today is Mr. Percy Aloof.

The Synagogue is a public place of worship and open to any person who wishes to be present at a service and from earliest times the Jewish Community of Plymouth has enjoyed a harmonious inter-faith relationship with all of the other religious communities of the City.

13th February 1988.

Catherine Street Police Station

Since its formal establishment in 1836 Plymouth's Police Force has had four principal headquarters. The old Guildhall—long since demolished—at the top of Whimple Street; the rear of the present Guildhall here in Catherine Street; the old prison, on Greenbank Hill, and the new multi-storey building, opened in 1976, at Crownhill. Of the four to date, it is the Catherine Street premises which have housed the force the longest; over 60 years between 1873–1935.

Built partly on the site of two early seventeenth-century establishments, the Hospital of the Poors Portion and Workhouse (1630) and the Orphans' Aid building (1615), later associated with Plymouth Grammar School, the Guildhall was part of the massive complex undertaken between 1870–73, which included its 'twin' municipal building which was destroyed during the Blitz. Included in the Guildhall building was the 'new Police Court, measuring 46 feet by 38 feet, and the Police Station-house muster room with drilling yard adjoining'. Police Superintendent at the time was Frederick Wreford, while William Thomas was Detective Superintendent. There were four inspectors, six sergeants and some sixty constables; the total force was 83.

In its form and structure, Plymouth's Police force was largely modelled, as were most Borough forces, on the Metropolitan Police. Created by Sir Robert Peel (hence the nicknames that soon spread far and wide—'Bobbies' and 'Peelers'), the Metropolitan police first took duty on 29th September 1829. This new force immediately took over from local parish constables and night watchmen in well over a hundred parishes. They also took over the duties of the 'Bow Street Runners' or 'thief takers' formed back in 1748 by Bow Street magistrate Henry Fielding, well known also as a novelist and playwright. Fielding's men started out as a small band of householders who joined together to provide some form of collective security. Life in those days was not always easy; mob rioting was not uncommon and crime was rife in densely populated areas. Cheap beer and spirits, particularly gin, added to the problems. The government's only answer was to offer rewards for thieftakers and increase the number of crimes for which the penalty was hanging. A figure, incidentally, which ran to over 200 at one time with young children by no means exempt from this ultimate penalty. The problem is, of course, an age-old one. Any society which attempts to establish a code of conduct must also have some means of securing effective observation of the same. Our modern police constable can be traced back at least 1500 years to the Anglo Saxon tithingman. A tithing (tything) was a group of ten 'free' men who were not only responsible for each other's conduct, but were also supposed to turn in any wrongdoer in the group. Ten tithings made up a local hundred and each county had, at the head of its hundreds, a local shire-reeve (later the County Sheriff). With the arrival of the Normans, the local tithingman became virtually a parish 'constable' and for centuries this unpaid local officer worked in the community. In the middle ages householders were expected to take turns in helping out with night-watch duties but, even when Charles II introduced a small payment for night watchmen (bellmen), the system proved unpopular, particularly as it became common for organized gangs to beat up these 'Charlies'. Small wonder that 'all over the country the householder slept with a loaded blunderbuss by his side'. Indeed in Elizabethan Plymouth there was not only an order for every person to 'aid constables as required' but also for 'every inhabitant to be provided with a good black bill, or a clubbe, for time of strife on penalty of 3s 4d.'

Today of course, citizens are still expected to assist their local police force and under common law all citizens have many of the same powers of arrest as the constable. Indeed the policeman has been described as 'a person paid to perform what is the right and duty of every citizen'. To this end the current promotion of neighbourhood watch schemes has been particularly helpful.

The technology at the disposal of the police, however, has clearly altered the role of the local bobby. Gone are the days when a shift would fall in here and march through the streets to their beat. Ernest Dickaty, in his book 'Rattles to Radio', catalogues many of the changes. Rattles were used as a quick communication medium until the introduction of whistles in the 1880s. The local call sign was one long blast followed by a short one, and it wasn't until 1967 that whistles were finally superseded altogether by radios. In 1926 the year after these Catherine Street premises were extended, a new automatic telephone exchange was installed here; however, the familiar emergency number 999 was not introduced until 1937. By that time all kinds of innovations had taken place. In 1929 the appearance of the city's first traffic signals started to relieve constables of point duty and around the same time motor cycle patrols were introduced as two Sunbeam machines were purchased.

A proper police traffic department opened in 1937, two years after the local HQ had moved out of these by now cramped quarters up to Greenbank. Last August, Plymouth City Treasury, who came here after the police left, vacated these premises and, although some of the building is still to be let, next year BBC Radio Devon will be moving into the building in behind the old police light—rattles to radio indeed!

12th September 1987.

The Coroner's Court

In the middle of the last century, opposite the 'Royal Exchange Inn' (now Heritage Preservation) in Tin Street, there was an empty site. Running down the side of that site was Tin Lane, which led in turn to Tin Quay; 'from this corner no doubt the tin from Dartmoor was shipped.' (Crispin Gill—Sutton Harbour.) Just as, from the next quay down—Dung Quay—all the street sweepings, products of the horse age, were shipped.

Dung Quay ran on from the bottom of Looe Street, beyond where it crossed Vauxhall Street and Tin Quay and Tin Lane ran on from How Street. In the latter part of last century Tin Street became an extension of Vauxhall Street and just a year or so before the close of the century, the empty site was filled by the building we see here today. Unassuming, grey and little-altered on the outside (the mullions on the main windows have been replaced by two old pillars), this building housed, for 80 years, the Corporation Mortuary and, for most of that time, the Coroner's Court, A reminder of its past is contained in the inscription that still runs across its frontage—'De Mortuis Nil Nisi Bonum'—'Say nothing but good of the dead'.

Today there is no longer an independent set of premises recognised as being the Coroner's Court. Local inquests are held either in Scott Lodge, at Milehouse, where the current Plymouth and South-West Devon coroner—local solicitor David Bishop—is based or if a jury is required, the Coroner generally conducts these larger inquests at Plympton Magistrates Court. The Vauxhall Street premises were not transferred to the Devon authorities when local government was re-organised in the 1970s and, as county policy was for coroners to hire halls for inquests where necessary, they decided against buying this block. Consequently in 1980 Plymouth City Council decided to sell the property and in January 1981 it was bought by Eddie Barron.

While some may lament the passing of this particular Coroner's Court, such purpose-built buildings are few and far between outside the Metropolitan areas, and Plymouth was undoubtedly unusual in the West country, for having such an establishment. Furthermore, prior to the construction of this building, around 1898, there appears to be no clear record of a previous purpose-built institution, although there are records of Plymouth coroners dating back to 1440 (the names of Devon coroners stretch back further still to Baldwin de Es). 1233 is given as the date that Baldwin died and, as coroners have traditionally been appointed for life, this would in all probability make him one of the first generation of recognised British coroners. 1194 is generally accepted as the date the office was first described, as an ordinance of Richard I set up 'the election in every shire of officers to keep the pleas of the Crown'—hence the title coroner. (In Latin corona or coronator means a crown). King Athelstan (924–939) had an officer known as 'coronator' and, although his functions are not clearly defined, it is quite possible that the origin of the office of coroner can be traced back to Saxon times.

The main task of a coroner has changed little over the years; it is to inquire into the cause of a death when it is thought to have occurred from other than natural causes. On average, David Bishop currently deals with about 150–160 such cases a year. Another principal duty of the coroner is to hold inquests into treasure trove. This

duty, however, could hardly be described as an onerous one. In his 46 years as City Coroner, Bill Major, who died two years after his retirement from the post in 1979, said he was never once called upon to decide whether or not valuables, which had been found, were treasure trove.

Well-known throughout local legal circles, Bill Major, both of whose sons Neil and John followed him successfully into the legal profession, retired at the age of 77. At the age of 31 he was the youngest coroner to be appointed in England, in his day, and he was by no means the oldest when he left the post. Indeed the oldest practising coroner in England today is believed to be 93.

As it is an appointment for life, Bill Major's retirement, while still in good health, contrasts starkly with some of his medieval predecessors for whom 'sick and broken by age' was a common grounds for a new appointment. A good number, however, clearly died in office although, in 1251 when a new coroner was chosen, it was recorded only that the previous officer—Roger Giffard—was 'said to be dead'; presumably his body was not available for examination. In recent years, prior even to the demise of the city mortuary, all bodies requiring post mortems, in coroners inquests, were dealt with in the city hospitals.

Since 1980, then, it is true to say that new life has, indeed, been pumped into what was once described as the city's 'mirror of tragedy'. Eddie Barron's EFB clothing stores, specialising in industrial and Army & Navy items, are now well established in this building, which is only marginally more unusual than his previous base; for many years he was a partner with Gould's clothing store, in Ebrington Street, and that, amongst other things, used to house the front of the old Cinedrome picture house.

Plymouth Arts Centre

It is undoubtedly appropriate that part of Plymouth's ever-expanding Arts Centre stands on the site of, probably, the first Inn to be mentioned by name in the pages of Plymouth's history—the Pope's Head, referred to in the White book of 1573. Appropriate, not on account of the drinking that takes place here today but because both institutions established fine reputations for their interest in things literary and cultural.

Looe Street, which itself dates from the end of the fifteenth century, was once one of the main streets of old Plymouth; Sir Francis Drake had a town house here as did the Trelawnys, who produced more than one generation of Plymouth mayors, and a few yards west of the 'Pope's Head' stood the original site of the town's first Guildhalls. The focal point then of the growing harbour town, the Guildhall, in 1500 stood alone at the junction of four streets which radiated, approximately, to the North (Buckwell Street), South (High Street), East (Looe Street) and West (Whimple Street). The 'Pope's Head', a large and impressive building, was the principal Inn of the Town until the building of 'Foulston's Royal Hotel' in 1811, part of the Theatre Royal complex and, significantly, the first lessee of the Royal left the Pope's Head to take up the new appointment.

The Inn was managed later last century by the Scott family, ancestors of Robert Falcon Scott. However, by this time the 'Pope's Head' had somewhat contracted and become just another Inn fronting Peacock Lane (running from here to the right). Gone were the days when the Otter Club, which had grown 'out of the companionship of men who were accustomed to meet at bathing parties off the Hoe' (Walling), would meet here regularly for literary talk. A one-time leading light of the Otter Club was Zachariah Mudge, Vicar of St. Andrew's from 1732–1769, and it is likely that in 1762 when Dr. Johnson spent some weeks in Plymouth with Joshua Reynolds as guests of Dr. Thomas Mudge, Zacharia's elder son, the group would have visited the Inn. It would be many more years, however, before such cultural activities would again be associated with this block. Used earlier this century as a butcher's shop and a flour factory, it later became a social settlement, and afterwards a Forces' Club and educational centre—part of the Virginia House development donated by the Astors.

Then, on 22nd October 1947, it was opened by Sir Kenneth Clark as an Arts Centre, since when it has gone from strength to strength as a venue for hosting the perhaps less commercial side of popular culture and entertainment. Over a period spanning almost 40 years now the emphasis has slowly shifted according to the demands of its membership. Early programmes tended to be dominated by talks, lectures and readings. Exhibitions and films (mainly foreign) had their place but were not as dominant as they are today. Music and drama also initially played a much greater part; Mike Westbrook and John Surman began their jazz careers here, and the writer Colin Wilson produced some of his own plays here in the early fifties. However, sadly, the live stage was a casualty of the internal redesigning a couple of years ago (ironically perhaps again because of the success of a Theatre Royal, this time its twentieth Century reincarnation). In place of the stage, the cinema triumphed and it is this, along with the highly successful and reasonably priced vegetarian restaurant, that makes the Arts Centre the busy place it is today. One should not, however, overlook the role of its newly restructured exhibition areas. It was, after all, here at Plymouth Arts Centre that the internationally-enjoyed work of Plymouth based artist Beryl Cook first saw the light of day. A fact duly noted and celebrated by the delightful pub-style signs that the artist painted to hang outside the building.

With the recent acquisition of premises in Batter Street conveniently connected to the main body of the Arts Centre, there is great potential for further development. Currently envisaged as the educational wing of the Centre which will include a special video workshop, the extra space promises to give Arts Centre Director Bernard Samuels even more scope to broaden the cultural horizons of his patrons.

1st March 1986.

Looe Street

The name Looe Street first appears around 1500, at which time all that probably existed of Plymouth lay to the south of a line now drawn between Friary Station and Old Town Street, east of Catherine Street and north of Notte Street, Plymouth's pre-Citadel Castle and the two friaries all standing a little outside this main development.

Within a hundred years this small area had become much more densely populated and Plymouth had spilled south towards the Castle and the entrance to Sutton Pools, where McBride later constructed his piers.

In those distant days of Elizabeth I and Sir Francis Drake (who at one time lived at the top of Looe Street where 'Drake's Stamps' shop now stands), Plymouth had several inns, many of which survived into the nineteenth century—the Mitre in Woolster Street, the Turk's Head in St. Andrew's Street (where the Abbey Hotel now stands), the Rose and Crown and Old Four Castles in Old Town Street and the Pope's Head which stood at the top of Looe Street, partly where the Arts Centre stands today. Now there is only one building left in the area of that vintage which houses an inn and that is number 31 Looe Street where we find the 'Minerva'. However, there is no record that it has always been an inn so it is possible that the neighbouring King's Head in Bretonside, whose existing deeds date back to the mid seventeenth century, is the oldest inn in town, whilst the 'Abbey' stands on the oldest Inn site.

Like its surviving Elizabethan contemporaries in Plymouth, the Minerva was essentially constructed around the mast of an old ship around which its spiral staircase connects each floor (save for the ground floor where the staircase has since been relocated). Known throughout several decades last century as the 'Looe Street Wine and Spirit Vaults', in 1804 (when the street itself was nearing the end of a long period of time when it had been called Pike Street), a lady called Agnes Johns was listed as licensee of the 'Minerva'. Strangely enough 170 years later in the television dramatisation of the story of another Agnes—Agnes (Aggie) Weston, the name of the Inn was very briefly changed again and on the little screen the 'Minerva' appeared as the 'French Maid'. However, perhaps more strangely still, the 'Minerva', this oldest local building to house an Inn, has also been for almost 20 years now, one of the best places to catch up on the latest off-beat trend in hairstyles as successive generations of hippies, punks and whatever have made this a favourite haunt. Over the last few decades it has also been well liked by its licensees—of the last three, Dave Bunker and Tommy Mutton each spent ten years here, whilst John Weston has been at the 'Minerva' now, with 'Mac', since 1970.

Named after the Roman Goddess of Wisdom and patroness of the Arts and Trades, it is somehow very fitting that the Arts Centre was established in this Street in 1947 and that in 1969 the Plymouth Incorporated Chamber of Commerce moved from Alton Terrace almost next door in the newly restored No. 29 Looe Street. Opened by Lord Mayor Ivor Lowe, the then Chairman of the Chamber was Peter Stedman, also a member of the Barbican Association, the body responsible for the excellent restoration of No. 29 and several other major buildings of historical note in the street and elsewhere in the area.

Renamed the Plymouth Chamber of Commerce and Industry in 1980, the origins of this august institution go back to 1813, making it the fourth oldest such chamber in the Country. First president of the chamber in 1813 was Lord Boringdon, later the 1st Earl of Morley and today's president is the sixth Earl of Morley. Meanwhile, one of the other main driving forces behind the establishment of the Chamber who became its first chairman was Henry Woollcombe, a descendant of whom, Humphrey Woollcombe, was in the chair 145 years later when the Port of Plymouth Chamber of Commerce combined with the Plymouth and the Devonport Mercantile Associations. And as if that were not enough to establish the continuity of this organization, it's interesting to note that in the Chamber's very first report in 1814 the authors were expressing the hope that the link with London might be speeded up and in the present annual report published this week the same hope is still being echoed. Only then measures were being sought 'for the (horsedrawn) arrival of letters two hours earlier', whilst today the talk is that, with Brymon's air-link, the whole journey, city centre to city centre, will be reduced to under two hours! »Postscript

16th May 1986.

23

Salvation Army Citadel

Plymouth has more than one citadel, there is Charles II's seventeenth-century military fortress on the Hoe and, here in Exeter Street, there is the somewhat more recent Salvation Army Citadel.

The term 'citadel', as applied to churches of the Salvation Army, was a logical extension of their self-styled adoption of military titles in 1878 and uniforms the following year. Initially, the title 'general' had been applied to the movement's leader, William Booth, as a convenient abbreviation of 'general superintendent'. Booth, a son of Nottingham, was born into an impoverished family and had been apprenticed to a pawnbroker before his contact with poverty and sin led him into preaching. By 1858 he had become an ordained minister of the Methodist 'New Connexion'. Three years later, however, he resigned from this body and in 1865 at the age of 36 he moved to London with his wife and children, and began working with like minded people in East London. Here, he helped set up the Christian Revival Association which later became the East London Christian Mission which, in turn, simply became the Christian Mission as its work spread to other areas. In 1878 it became the Salvation Army.

Earlier, in 1878, James Dowdle—a tall, well-built man with a strong, somewhat husky, voice—was sent from London to Plymouth by the Mission with just his wife, a bible and an 'Hallelujah Fiddle' to set up an outpost here. Before long, however, Captain Dowdle, as he became, was filling St. James's Hall with 1,500 people three times every Sunday and attracting large crowds to the old Central Hall in Manor Street on week nights.

Not that everything was plain sailing in the early days. Resistance was encountered from local 'rough-necks' and certain factions within the established church. Halls were often closed to them and, inside or outside, it was not uncommon for speakers to be pelted with rotten fruit or other missiles. However, the 'soldiers' persevered and soon afterwards General Booth came down to inspect the troops. Whilst here he met with Isaac Foot senior, a staunch methodist and local builder (responsible for Wesley Avenue, Cottages and Place and other streets with methodist linked names). Booth and Foot spoke at length on spiritual matters and Booth mentioned the problem of the Plymouth Salvation Army not having a hall of their own and their lack of funds to provide one. Isaac Foot's solution to these problems was a simple one; he would build such a hall and Booth could pay for it as and when he had the resources to do so. The two men shook hands and no legal document of any sort was drawn up. In February 1886 William Booth came back to Plymouth to open Congress Hall in Martin Street, built then at a cost of £4,724 7s.

Today 100 years on the Salvation Army in Plymouth is as strong as ever. There are three main halls, Exeter Street, Congress Hall (in Armada Way, opened by General Kitching on 23rd April 1960 as a replacement for the Martin Street Hall which was destroyed by enemy action in May 1941), another in Morice Town Devonport and a fourth, more modest affair, in Plympton. Every soldier still signs the 'articles of war' containing the beliefs and summarising the ethical conduct expected of him or her. Salvationists are teetotal and tobacco is also taboo in any form. Local officers, furthermore, are generally volunteers who are not only unpaid but who are expected to donate a tithe (one-tenth of their personal income) to the Army.

The role of women within the Salvation Army has always been on an equal footing with that of their male counterparts. Mrs. Catherine Booth was a zealous evangelist and competent theologian and a fearless upholder of her sex. Evangeline, their fourth daughter, was herself General of the Army from 1934–39.

Throughout the history of the Salvation Army, which now works in more than 70 countries and preaches in over 150 languages, a great deal of emphasis has also been placed on the role of music. William Booth, who believed that you should 'do all the good you can, to all the souls you can', also believed that there was no reason why the devil should have all the best tunes and consequently songs were often composed and put to popular airs. Today Salvation Army bands, first formed in 1878, present throughout the world the most visible face of the Salvation Army. Exeter Hall band itself has broadcast on many occasions in the past, and in recent years their songsters have toured Sweden and last year they represented England in a British Festival at Fairfield Hall, Croydon.

But the bulk of the Army's work goes on more quietly. During the summer open air services are held on Dingles' corner followed by a march up Royal Parade to Exeter Hall, where there are two services every Sunday. Regular summer services are also held on the Barbican and each year there is a Harvest of the Sea service for the Fishermen.

The Salvation Army has long since overcome its early difficulties and it has gained respect worldwide. Adapting to changing circumstances, these soldiers (who have to buy their own uniforms) have continued William Booth's traditions of mixing social work with evangelism, music and salvation and have, along the way, helped to make a better life for a lot of people.

14th June 1986.

The Black Horse

As long as black is black you might think that we know where we are and what is what but consider for a moment the following '. . . On past Moon-street on the left, past the old fashioned inns—the "Black Bull" and the "Red Cow" until we make a stand at the foot of Whitecross-street, opposite which is an ope leading to North Quay. We have here our choice of ways, all of them more or less squalid . . .' Obviously, as time goes by, we must expect areas to both develop and be redeveloped, but the all too frequent changing of names for an area or an establishment can often cause confusion and problems for the historian. Moon Street, formerly Moons Lane, still runs north from this part of Bretonside and the 'Red Cow' is no more, but the old-fashioned 'Black Bull' as described in 1879, is now the 'Black Horse'. Why the change from a bull to a horse you might well wonder? That is until you discover that for most of the time between 1879 and 1986 the inn has been known as the 'Friary Hotel'. Furthermore, for most of that time its address wasn't Bretonside at all but number 11 Exeter Street.

First of all then let us pick up the history of the 'Black Bull' in the middle of the last century. Here it then was—number 11 Briton side. Elsewhere in the area at that time was the 'Black Horse' in Bath Street, now gone, and the 'Black Horse' in Devonport—renamed the 'Lord Beresford' in 1890; there was also a 'Black Lion' in Exeter Street. A few years later Friary Station, built by the L&SWR, and already used for some time as a goods depot, was opened as a passenger terminus. Presumably, in an attempt to capitalize on this development begun in the summer of 1891, when Charles Allwright took over the 'Black Bull' around 1894, the name was duly changed to the 'Friary Hotel' and the unprecedented step of taking an advertisement in the local annual directory was taken. Sadly, it tells us little about the place other than it sold, in addition to wines and spirits, 'Bass's and Allsopp's Ale and Guinness' Stout'. It also, however, boasted a 'full size Billiard Table, by Thurston, magnificently fitted'. John Thurston of course was the man who, earlier last century, had revolutionized Billiards, particularly with his introduction in 1835 of rubber cushions and the introduction of the slate as opposed to a wooden bed. Thurston's firm had been founded in 1799, at which time W. Rider was here at the 'Black Bull'—a fact which is included only because, some hundred years later, another W. Ryder was licensee here—an unusual coincidence, despite the slight spelling discrepancy.

However, another spelling 'discrepancy' brings us forward to 1958 when Bretonside Bus Station opened and this part of Exeter Street was 'renamed' Bretonside (the inn, once number 11 Britonside, now became 51/53 Bretonside) and on 15th September 1958 Friary Station closed to passenger services. The station, incidentally, was called Friary after the Carmelite Friary established on that site at the end of the thirteenth century. But it was not the termination of Friary's most recent public guise that prompted the new name here at the 'Black Horse'. Rather this name change was, evidently, occasioned by an unfortunate incident that took place here over five years ago, when a local cowboy club met here and someone was shot. To avoid this association it became the 'Black Horse' because of the impressive old windows bearing the silhouette logo that harks back to when this was a Starkey

Knight and Ford pub and leading the visitor to perhaps assume it has been called the 'Black Horse' for a good number of years.

Landlord here when the last change took place was Reg Tregaskis, forty years ago a member of Argyle's playing list. Almost a foot shorter than his tallest Argyle contemporary and a good stone lighter than any other player, it's not hard to see how he earned his nickname 'Nipper'—the club handbook described him as 'diminutive but remarkably speedy'.

Today Ron Carkett, London born but from an old Exeter street family, is mine host here. An ex-naval contemporary of Garth Tuxford in the neighbouring King's Head, Ron has recently been responsible for reintroducing B & B Accommodation to the 'Black Horse', thereby re-establishing its traditional inn status. However, in the course of the conversion work he discovered a mattress and a few effects hidden under the eaves at the top of the building, suggesting that, at one time, accommodation was provided for someone who was, obviously, anxious to keep a low profile.

29th March 1986.

Friary

'With the closure of Friary after the last train had unloaded its passengers last night, Plymouth has lost its only remaining terminus station'. So read a local newspaper account from the 15th September 1958. It also said '. . . The last train, the 4 p.m., from Waterloo was late owing to an engine failure at Honiton, and arrived at 11.12 p.m., instead of 10.34'.

There were only 22 passengers on the last lap from North Road to Friary, 16 of them railway enthusiasts although, as the 'special correspondent' observed, 'a few more enthusiasts had assembled at the somewhat grim, badly-lit station, with water dripping through the roof, to see the train arrive'. A description that paints a subtly different picture to Ian Lane in his book 'Plymouth Steam 1954–63', 'Friary had', he wrote, 'style and a quiet gaslit charm which were lacking at the much busier, ex-GWR/LSWR joint station, Plymouth North Road'.

This station became just 'Plymouth', following the closure of Friary to passengers, and today, while part of this area continues to be used as a freight depot, the old passenger station has long since been demolished. The old stationmaster's house has recently been converted into a doctor's surgery. The area, however, is still known as Friary, a name that has a long pedigree.

It was in 1313 that the Carmelites or White Friars first arrived here and established themselves on this site and over the years they erected extensive buildings and a large and impressive church with a tall steeple. This was the only house established by this religious order in the whole of Devon and Cornwall. Their buildings and church apparently survived the Breton raid of 1403, when the invading Frenchmen entered Sutton, or Plymouth, via the 'bak haf' of the town just below their walled convent. The prominent steeple even survived the report from government engineer Robert Adams who, after consultations with Sir Francis Drake and Sir Arthur Champerowne on the town's defence requirements, recommended that the steeple be demolished, as it was feared that it might be an advantage to an attacker. The report was sent off in 1592 by the then Mayor of Plymouth John Sparke together with a map which deliberately left off the steeple; however, it was to stand for at least another 100 years.

Whitefriars, as it was known, had been appropriated by Henry VIII as part of the dissolution of the monasteries and Sparke acquired it, through marriage, some time before the turn of the century. While the Sparkes owned Whitefriars the romantic associations that led to its being referred to as the Palace of John of Gaunt were still conceivable. John of Gaunt (son of Edward III and father of Henry IV) had lodged here in 1386.

After three hundred years though the grandeur began to be eroded. In 1794 the buildings were converted into a hospital for sick soldiers, 'when great mortality prevailed among the troops detained at the port for the West India expedition' (Worth). Then during the Napoleonic Wars, at the time of the retreat from Corunna a large barn on the site became 'Friary Hospital'; here within three months more than 1,000 men died. 'The corpses were carried in cart loads to the burial ground in St. Andrew's parish, and interred there in large trenches dug for the purpose. Over 300 inhabitants perished of the same contagion' (Whitfeld).

At this time portions of the original Friary were still standing; part of the tower, the refectory and the kitchen. However, after its use as a hospital ceased the remaining buildings were used as dwellings and now re-styled 'Friary Court'. '. . . not being one of the most aristocratic purlieus of Plymouth' (Worth). Indeed, it became 'the resort of professional beggars, itinerant matchsellers, tape vendors, knife grinders, purveyors of full true and particular accounts of all bloody murders, pickpockets, and other conveyancers, blacking manufacturers, and every other variety of rogues and vagabonds might have been found among its habitués.' The beds in this establishment lined both sides of the floor with maybe a six inch gap between them. 'Bed clothes there were none, each traveller sleeping in the habiliments worn by day' (Nooks and Corners of Old Plymouth 1886).

With the construction of Friary Goods Yard in the 1870s and Friary Gardens passenger station in 1891 all this disappeared. Today the Roman Catholic Church of Holy Cross occupies part of the old Whitefriars site while, currently, another part is being used by the City as a car park. Meanwhile, the bustle surrounding this once-busy bridge is now mainly confined to road and not rail traffic.

12th December 1987.

Coxside Gasworks

'.. a Company for the purpose of supplying with Gas the districts included within the limits of this Act ... under the name of the "Devonport Gas and Coke Company" ... shall be a body corporate ... Twenty thousand pounds shall be the capital of the Company ... The number of shares into which the said capital shall be divided shall be four thousand, and the amount of each share shall be five pounds'. Don't bother to tell Sid, these shares were all sold a long time ago, back in 1845. The 'Plymouth and Stonehouse Gas-light and Coke Company' was incorporated, by a similar Act of Parliament, at the same time and in January 1846 this company set up its base here at Coxside. Prior to this there had been a plant at Meeting House Slip and in 1823 a company for 'manufacturing and supplying the town with Oil Gas' was incorporated; discussions had been taking place since 1817. In 1825, the 'United General Gas Company' was formed and the two companies merged in 1832. The main Gas Works were then at Millbay but these closed soon after the Coxside Works started up.

For many years the main use of gas was for lighting and the first house to be lit with gas was in Cornwall, in Redruth. It belonged, at the time, to William Murdock, a Scot, who is generally hailed as the father of the gas industry. However, although he had had his house and offices lit as early as 1792, it wasn't until 1801 that he took his experiments, researches and inventions in this field much further. Plymouth, incidentally, had first been lit with oil lamps. 250 had been ordered in 1770, '200 of which were to be mounted and the other 50 to be kept as reserve'.

In 1808 Frederick Winsor formed a company 'for providing streets, squares and houses with gaseous lights by means of conducting tubes underground from distant furnaces, on the principle as houses are now supplied with water'—not that many were at that time. Locally, up until the 'Plymouth Electric Lighting Order' of 1894 all the town's main artificial lighting was by oil or coal gas. In 1868 a new national standard decreed that the amount of light from a gas burner should be increased from the equivalent of 12 to 16 candles. Fortunately for the gas industry, however, the development of the gas mantle by Karl Auer, a pupil of Robert Bunsen (of bunsen burner fame), meant that for some time gas lighting held its own against the arrival of electricity. The chimneys, now defunct, of Plymouth's Power Station, can be seen to the left, here.

Gradually though, the role of gas moved from lighting to cooking and heating, and by the 1890s gas cookers were becoming relatively common domestic appliances and 20 years ago it was estimated that 12 million British homes used gas for cooking. Around the same time experts were saying that the gas industry's traditional reliance upon coal as its main raw material was unlikely to be superseded in the forseeable future. This coming after experiments with bringing gas into the country from the Sahara in liquid form at a temperature of about minus 258°F, occupying around one six-hundreth its bulk in a gaseous state; and after explorations in the North Sea had, thus far, proved fruitless.

Then in 1967 an 'ultra modern', 'gas from oil' plant was set up, at the Breakwater Works at Oreston, 'symbolising the dynamic growth of the gas industry in the 1960s'. The Coxside coal-based works were closed two years later. The discovery of North Sea Gas, however, soon changed everything again. The 'new' Oreston plant was closed down some time ago and is now being demolished.

Throughout all these changes over 140 years, including Nationalisation (1949) and Privatisation (1987), the grand Mona House, the corner of which is visible on the far left, here, has stood firm at the entrance to the site. Today, the Gas Social Club backs into it. The Victorian gas compressor house, the low, long building now used as a store, also survives as do the impressive and massive gasholders. The oldest and lowest of the three, dating from 1884, the second 1895 (both erected by Willey & Co. Exeter), the most recent and largest (far right) gasholder, 'C', dates from the mid 1930s.

These three gasholders (there used to be more), now hold up to 8 million cubic feet of gas. A further two holders at Ford have a capacity for another four million and, although gas can be stored much more effectively in pipes under pressure or in liquid form today, these gasholders look set to see a few more years yet.

Certainly the outlook for gas seems very healthy—people are even starting to revive the outdoor gaslight for their gardens or driveways, so who knows what the future holds?—maybe Sid does now!

21st February 1987.

North Quay

Up until the early part of the eighteenth century there was very little development around the east side of this harbour. The young town of Sutton, or Plymouth as it became, grew up around the northern and western side of Sutton Pool and ended at Friary Gate, which stood near the present junction of Sutton Road and Exeter Street. Even as the activity around this part of the harbour increased, large sections of the coastline ran into the sea in an almost natural state. A graphic description of the storms which ravaged England in 1703 and which destroyed Winstanley's Eddystone Lighthouse, gives us some idea of this area as it was then '. . . In Plymouth, the devastation was widespread, The Friary Green, Old Tree Slip, and other points were strewn with wreckage, and two sons of Mr. Collier met a tragic fate as they watched the mountainous waves rolling into the harbour. They had stationed themselves behind the Old Fish House, the whilom military store on the Barbican, which had so long served to break the rush of the waters into Sutton Pool. A huge bore suddenly swept towards the ruins, carried them away with the two victims, and the lads were last seen on the crest of the surf beyond the possibility of rescue.' (Whitfield 1899).

At the end of the eighteenth century the two great stone piers were constructed across the mouth of Sutton Harbour and in the Sound the Breakwater was begun in 1812. The character of this area began to change. In 1811 Sutton Pool Company had been formed and within three years Sutton Wharf (Vauxhall Quay) had been laid down on the seaward side of the warehouses that fronted on to Vauxhall Street. Prior to this, apart from the small 'Dung' and 'Tin' Quays, ships had pulled up right alongside the warehouses. In the 1830s Sutton Wharf was extended and at the end of the following decade North Quay was constructed. All this development still left two substantial inlets in the north eastern corner. However, these too went in 1878 when the Harbour Company spent £25,000 building North East Quay '. . . which cut through the clutter of old shipyards, quays and storehouses there, and cleared the path for both railways to reach North Quay in 1879' (Crispin Gill Sutton Harbour).

A railway had first appeared in the area with the extension of Thomas Tyrwhitt's horsedrawn Princetown to Plymouth line to the head of Coxside Creek in December 1825. The line was paid for by the quarry-owning Johnson's, who had a major contract to supply granite to the surface of the Breakwater. This was almost 30 years before the Great Western Railway opened their first Plymouth station at Sutton Harbour and even they employed horse power, until finally going over to steam locomotives in 1869. Ten years later both the GW and LSW (London & South Western) extended lines over the newly constructed North East Quay.

Because the two railway companies were using different gauges, it meant that three tracks had to be laid for the line that ran round to Vauxhall Quay. Three years later, however, GW went over to standard gauge and the third rail was taken up. Its line is still marked by a line of cobbles, although one piece remains; 'at a set of points under the gantry is the last piece of broad gauge line in the country in its original position' (Gill).

There is another historical curiosity under North Quay itself; a tunnel which runs down to the tide line and was used as a horsewash by the carters, who had formerly washed their animals on the beaches there. And while the railway stopped using horsepower in the 1860s here, the Co-op, who rebuilt their grocery warehouse on North Quay in 1951, used a certain amount of horse power right down to that time. The Co-op had moved here in March 1905, when they opened their imposing new warehouse; one official boasting that it 'would provide a monument to co-operative progress for future generations'. And, doubtless, it would have done were it not for the Blitz. In the mid seventies the new warehouse changed from groceries to dry goods, then in July of this year the building closed and now, having been sold by the Co-op, is about to be redeveloped as office and flat accommodation.

Increasingly, flats have appeared on the Barbican where warehouses once stood, like the recently completed Harbourside Court—a massive undertaking; there are now luxury flats behind an impressive facade, styled on the classic warehouse design standing on the corner of Hawkers Lane (formerly Old Tree Slip) and North Quay itself. This sympathetic development does much to preserve the old look of this area of Sutton Pool—an area which has changed greatly since the arrival of the Marina in 1972. Originally only 70 pontoon moorings were laid down. Within a year that number had more than doubled. Within two years it was almost trebled and today there are some 350 berths here.

And so, it is not just the character of the surrounding buildings but also the character of the sea-going vessels themselves which has changed radically in recent years; changes which, clearly, herald further developments in the near future. However, as long as there are little areas like Marrowbone Slip from which this view is taken then the memories of the trawlers, the commerce and the shipbuilding will be preserved. The name Marrowbone Slip itself conjuring up images of Shepherd's Manufactory, where bones from the nearby victualling yard were processed to produce—'foot oil'.

24th October 1987.

Queen Anne's Battery

'The name of Queen Anne has been perpetuated locally, by a small fortification, which stood at Teat's Hill on the eastern side of the approach to Sutton Pool. It was condemned, as useless, by Colonel Lilly in his report on our fortifications, in 1717, and its 14 guns removed'. So wrote C. W. Bracken at the beginning of this century in his History of Plymouth. He later went on to add, 'though known as Queen Anne Battery, it seems unlikely to have been built after the Citadel—it may therefore have been contemporary with the so-called Henry VIIIth towers at Stonehouse'.

While it is quite possible that there had indeed been some simple form of defensive outpost below Teat's Hill in Tudor times, there appears to be no record of any workings until 1667 when, as part of the measures undertaken in response to the threat from the Dutch, five guns and carriages were taken from the captured foreign ship 'Katherine' and 'landed at Peake's Point for the new battery' (F. W. Woodward The Citadel 1987). We are also told that Peter Buller carried warlike stores—'powder Match, Bullett, Springs and other necessaries' to, and from, St. Nicholas Island (Drake's Island), Mount Batten and Peake's Point.

Peake's Point is an earlier name for Queen Anne's Battery. It is also recorded as Pike's Point and also as Pigg's Point. In 1680 ten iron 8-pounder guns from Pike's Point were removed to the Citadel. Whether or not this then left the site without defences is not clear but just ten years later, when the French fleet were hovering menacingly off the coast, we find the following entered in the memoirs of James Yonge, 'We apphended the french might attaque this harbour made new forts, & kept. In Arms, with good watching'.

Meanwhile, in the Town Receiver's Book for that same period, we find '£88. 18s. 1d. spent on raising fortifications on Pigg's Point and Batten when French fleet on the coast, with ammunition and utensils of war'. And so a new, albeit hurried, battery was constructed here and this, we must assume, is what Colonel Christian Lilly, 'One of his Majesties Ingeniers', would have referred to when he recommended that the 14 guns here would be better employed in the Citadel.

Interestingly enough, Lilly's report still referred to the battery as being at Pigg's Point and yet at the time he wrote his report, Queen Anne had been dead for two years. It rather looks, therefore, as if Queen Anne's Battery was not only never known by that name during her lifetime or reign (1702–1714), but that whenever it did later acquire that name it was no longer being used as a Battery. Whatever the reasoning behind the name change, by 1835 we find Queen Anne's Battery being described as an irregular curve shape with 14 port holes for guns and as having 'long been allowed to go to decay . . . and although the smell and sound of gun powder are still frequently perceived there, it is only in blasting the rock behind'. However, it is suggested by our guide of 1835, 'The Perambulator', that these would be very familiar smells and sounds for the veterans, who resort to this place, 'smoke their pipes, and talk over the wars and politics of other days'.

Today over one hundred and fifty years later, any veterans here are more likely to be recounting past racing successes or failures for, in a little more than two years, Queen Anne's Battery has been rapidly transformed into one of the top sea-sport centres in the country. However, it might so easily never have been possible, not because of the politics and arguments of the present day but because of the proposals that were approved for this site back in 1894. Approved, that was, by everybody except the Lords of the Admiralty. It was the Chamber of Commerce who first floated the idea of establishing the Cattewater and Queen Anne's Battery as a dock suitable for the development of commerce and ocean liners. The Council thought it a wonderful idea but public opinion was divided and so the town was polled and the proposed bill was accepted, by 8,778 votes to 5,933. However, in the end the Admiralty blocked the scheme on the grounds that ocean liners in numbers, would draw too largely upon the two deep water channels leading into the Sound.

Of course, the irony of the Admiralty scuppering such commercial plans here is that this area, below Teat's Hill, was one of the first sites ever mooted for the establishment of the Royal Naval Dockyard.

Now in the 1980s, Queen Anne's Battery has at last been developed as a centre for commerce and ocean going sailing vessels. There are already 30 different businesses based here and there are berths on the Marina for 300 craft. At present, Plymouth's most successful ever boat show is being staged here and later this year the Carlsberg Single-handed Transatlantic Race will be one of the more major events to be organized. In 1986 the Royal Western Yacht Club, who expect to move to new premises at Queen Anne's Battery this autumn, organized the first major event, the Carlsberg Two-handed Transatlantic Race at QAB just months after the massive dredger, 'Hamburg', had first started clearing the seabed.

With every marine sport from diving to windsurfing available here, the future for this erstwhile grey area now promises to be very colourful indeed.

9th April 1988.

Ebrington Street Nissen Huts

Two hundred and twenty years ago you could have stood here and looked up to the right and seen the open fields which lay beyond Gasking Gate. Part of a network of gates which, together with various buildings, houses and walls, were designed to seal off the old City of Plymouth, Gasking Gate or North Gate as it was known adjacent to Resolution Fort, stood at the north eastern extremity of the town as it was at the time of the Civil War siege. So it appears on a contemporary map dated 1643. By 1768, however, such civil defence measures were not considered to be as important as the need to make the roads in and out of the city more functional in respect of the increased traffic, commercial and otherwise. The road here was then widened and Gasking Gate pulled down. In 1813 a plaque, by order of the Mayor and Commonalty, was erected on a wall nearby the site and today it stands on the Northern wall of the Woodside public house.

Gasking Street, formerly North Gate Street, takes its name according to H. Whitfield in his 1899 book *Plymouth and Devonport in Times of War and Peace* from a Dr. Gasking 'to whose memory a mural tablet exists in Charles Churchyard'. Quite why this happened he does not say, however, Gasking Street it has been for centuries now, despite various attempts at respelling it. Over the years it has appeared as Gascoyne, Gascoigne and Giascione Street, although Whitfield suggests that there were once two gates, Gasking's and Gascoyne's. The neighbouring Gascoyne Place, incidentally, is now part of Lipson Road. Whatever the story behind Dr. Gasking and this street, however, a more obvious name change has seen Ham Street disappear and the Victorian Ebrington Street stretch out and take it over.

All this happened towards the end of last century when the block between North Street and Gasking Street was restructured becoming 76–84 Ebrington Street instead of the former 16–17 Ham Street. One survivor of the change was William Vigus who was operating a cab business here in the last days of commercial, horse-drawn cabbying. His building was later destroyed in the Second World War enemy bombing raids and for over 30 years now two Nissen huts have occupied this site.

Thought to be the longest standing of such buildings in Plymouth today, Nissen huts were originally designed for use in the First World War by Captain Peter Nissen to provide accommodation for the great influx of Army personnel generated by the introduction of conscription in 1916. Although not alone in the field of easily erected 'temporary' accommodation, Nissen's bow-shaped hut proved most enduring and the design won him the DSO.

Used during and after both World Wars, Plymouth at one time had a great number of businesses operating from such premises. Many stood in the erstwhile Westwell Gardens and Westwell Street; others in Glanville Street, Tavistock Road opposite the Library and in North Hill Terrace (examples of which appear on the cover of Brian Moseley's newly published *Plymouth through the Lens*, Vol 2). Plymouth Police Station, Register Office, Dingles, British Home Stores, Freeman Hardy and Willis all had cause to thank Nissen. As did one Goodbody's Café, Stuart's Snack Bar and here in Ebrington Street, Weeks and Cundy's Café, later the Fountain Snack Bar and today the Bomb Shelter Café. Like its curved counterpart, several businesses have occupied this ageing curiosity whereas next door but one, George Symons newspaper shop has been consistently a stationers since the first decade of this century. While on the North Street corner of this block, another long established business changed only recently as the Albert Oak public house finally closed its doors after over 80 years of beer retailing. Meanwhile the question remains: how much longer will these two temporary structures survive? Will they go the way of their local counterparts or will they stand as a reminder of one of the city's solutions to its post war problems?

Having already endured beyond expectations, it is interesting now to note that in 1971 Peter Nissen's grandson, Richard, produced a new, very temporary, Nissen hut—designed for use in disaster areas. It is made of cardboard, can be erected in an hour and a half and should last for about a year. »Postscript

28th December 1985.

St Luke's Church

In 1827 when the Rev. Robert Hawkes, Vicar of Charles Church since 1784, died, the congregation naturally anticipated that the Rev. Septimus Courtney, his curate, would succeed him. Instead, however, James Carne was appointed and a large number of the congregation met at a public meeting in July 1827 where it was resolved that 'in consequence of Charles Church being insufficient to contain one fourth part of the parishioners which may be fairly estimated at 10,000 persons, it is essentially necessary for the support of the Established Church that a Chapel of Ease be erected in the same parish for the accommodation of the inhabitants'.

Donations were made, the foundation stone laid (1st March, 1828) and then, two years to the week after the resolution had been passed, the Chapel was consecrated by the Bishop of Exeter and Septimus Courtney appointed its first incumbent. Strangely enough, the Rev James Carne died in 1832, a victim of the cholera epidemic and Septimus Courtney then became Vicar of Charles Church and thereby gave rise to the speculation that, had he been appointed there in the first place, Charles Chapel might never have been built.

But built it was from the designs of Mr. Ball and at a cost of around £4,000 in what was then the western side of Gibbon's field. Then still a large expanse of land, within a few decades Gibbon's field had been completely enveloped by the maze of Victorian streets built between Greenbank Road and Tavistock Road. The corresponding increase in local population accompanying all this development led to the creation of a new parish here in 1874 and on 17th March of that year Charles Chapel became the Parish Church of St. Luke. Frederick Courtney, fifth Bishop of Nova Scotia, held the distinction of being the last Incumbent of Charles Chapel and in 1913 in memory of his wife, a stone pulpit was erected outside the Church. An unusual feature for any Church to have, it is only to be wondered now how much longer it will survive here.

After the destruction, in 1941, of Charles Church by enemy bombing, the congregation moved firstly here to St. Luke's for a month, then up to St. Mathias until its Vicar returned from active service.

As the Rev. J. F. Davies, Vicar of St. Luke's, had died in December 1941, Frank Green, Vicar of Charles Church since 1931, took charge of both parishes. Then on 22nd January 1946 in the ruins of Charles Church, the last Vicar of Charles was Inducted and Instituted. Eight years later, however, the two Churches were formally united with the creation of a new parish, that of Charles with St. Luke. As the then Bishop of Plymouth was quoted as saying of Charles, 'As a Mother Church she bore a Daughter Church, now the Daughter welcomes Mother home.' However, the new arrangement was short-lived and John Allen James 1954–61 was, as we read in his daughter's booklet on the Church, to be the only Vicar of this Benefice. In 1961, the year of his death, it was learnt that the City Council had earmarked this site for development and apart from baptisms, weddings and funerals, the Church and congregation, after Easter 1962, joined forces with St. Matthias. In March 1964 this move was consolidated with the creation of yet another new benefice, that of Charles with St. Matthias.

Thus the name of St. Luke has gone as perhaps may soon the building. Several artefacts from St. Luke's can now be found in St. Matthias although for the time being all the windows and upstairs pews are still here in Tavistock Place.

However, since 1966 the building has been used successively by Plymouth City Libraries and Devon County Libraries as administrative and support departments to relieve the very cramped Central Library. It once housed the Library's Bindery which has now moved to Cot Hill, Plympton; the space now houses many old journals, patents and a stack of some 40,000 books. Here too all new library books first go through the hands of Peter Bidgood who, along with many other Library staff, is looking forward to the extension to the main library across the road that has been 'on the cards' now for over 20 years.

5th October 1985.

Plymouth Museum

The Ashmolean Museum at Oxford is generally acknowledged as the first museum in this country to be opened to the public. Housed in a purpose designed building in Broad Street, its doors were officially opened on 6th June, 1683. The building was named after Elias Ashmole who, in 1675, had presented the University with 12 cartloads of exhibits which were roughly split into two categories 'Natural' and 'Artificial'. The Natural collection included all kinds of stuffed animals and birds (a Dodo being one notable exhibit), shellfish, insects, minerals and plants; while amongst the Artificial items were weapons, armour, costumes, household goods, coins and 'general curiosities'.

Ashmole himself, however, was not the man responsible for amassing this great collection. That had been done earlier in the century by John Tradescant of South Lambeth, who had willed his collection to the older Ashmole. In 1656 Tradescant published a catalogue to his collection under the title 'Musaeum Tradescantianum' and in those early days some private viewers had been admitted.

But it was to be another 100 years before the first national museum was established, (the British Museum 1759) and almost a further hundred before the establishment anywhere of a Municipal Museum (Sunderland 1846). Plymouth, in some respects, was slow to follow such leads although, in the buildings of the Plymouth Institution, the second oldest provincial literary and scientific association in the country, a museum had been established in 1829. Fifty years later, following the visit of the British Association in 1877, members of the Institution determined that even if the local authorities were not going to act they would and in March 1883 the Lord Mayor, himself a member of the Institution, opened their New Museum.

The following year proposals were aired for a Public Museum and in celebration of Queen Victoria's Jubilee a foundation stone was laid for such a magnificent building on the western side of Tavistock Road, not far from where this view was taken. The building did not materialize, however, and instead the new Museum and Art Gallery was opened in Beaumont House, in the building that currently houses the Chest Clinic.

Three years later the city's art treasures and science collections had outgrown this well-situated house and a publicly-subscribed building fund for the proposed premises on Tavistock Road, had reached nearly £6,000, almost half way to the anticipated cost of the Thornely and Rooke designed scheme. Later that year, thanks largely to a substantial grant from Andrew Carnegie, building on the Municipal Library and Museum building at last began. Scottish born Carnegie, manufacturer and philanthropist, made his fortune in America where he lived from the age of 13. At the age of 66 he retired and from 1901 until 1919, among a great number of other good deeds, he gave over ten million pounds towards building and equipping 2,505 libraries in America and Great Britain. The foundation stone for the present Plymouth Library building was laid on 16th October 1907, as was the stone for the Museum and Art Gallery. Three years later the museum was opened, since when it has been greatly added to and improved. New wings were added at the rear of the building in 1938 and two new galleries and offices were incorporated in 1975. Today there are nine main exhibition galleries, three or four of which are used for temporary exhibitions. Foremost among the permanent displays is the internationally regarded Cottonian Collection, which came to the museum from the Proprietary Library in 1916 where it had been housed since 1863, following the death of William Cotton. Cotton had given part of the collection 10 years earlier. However, impressive as it all is, the collection is but part of what his grandfather had inherited from his great aunt's husband, Charles Rogers, in 1784. His father, also William Cotton, had sold much of the Rogers' collection when he was in possession of it. Still, thousands of books, manuscripts, prints and other works of art from the sixteenth to the nineteenth century make up the collection today and it is hoped that soon a purpose-built, first floor, exhibition area will be constructed to better feature it.

The moving of this collection is one of many exciting and ambitious changes proposed for the museum over the next few years. Other plans include the installation of a proper shop and reception area in the main entrance hall and in new extensions at the back of the building, a restaurant and buttery and extra exhibition space. All this is part of curator Tristram Besterman's Museum 2000 plan as he hopes to help give the museum in the future, a new way of looking back.

6th February 1988.

Plymouth—Central Library

The idea of a library is virtually as old as portable recorded information. King Ashur-bani-pal, of Assyria, is believed to have set up the earliest surviving library around 640–630BC. At Nineveh great quantities of inscribed tablets and cylinders of baked clay were discovered in certain rooms of his palace. However, for over 2000 years libraries were almost invariably private collections with very few people having any opportunity to consult them.

In 1608 the civic authorities in Norwich established what is taken to be the first municipal library in this country, although this was principally for the use of preachers and it contained mainly theological works. So too did Chetham's library in Manchester which was started in 1653 thanks to the generosity of the wealthy linen merchant Humphrey Chetham. By 1684 there were sections within this library devoted to history, travel, law, medicine, topography and science. However, although Chetham's library continued to prosper, when the Select Committee of Public Libraries made their observations over 150 years later, it noted that this was the only important library in Britain fully and freely accessible to the public. Furthermore, it held around 20,000 books and was used by about 25 people a day. Out of the Select Committee's findings came the first of a number of Library Acts, the Public Library Act of 1850 which had largely been promoted by William Ewart MP who in turn had been encouraged and prompted by an assistant at the British Museum, Edward Edwards. In 1852 Manchester became the first authority to open a Free Public Lending Library under the Act and Edward Edwards became its first librarian. Over the next 20 years another 40 towns established libraries under the terms of the Act which permitted but did not compel local authorities to provide public libraries from the rates. Plymouth was one of them. But, although Plymouth had adopted the Library Act in 1871 (thanks largely to the enthusiasm for the project of the then Lord Mayor, Robert Coad Serpell), it was to be another five years before a suitable building could be found. In the event it was the old Guildhall that became its first home in February 1876. The building was completely empty, having been made redundant on completion of the present Guildhall in August 1874.

The old Guildhall, which stood on the site of at least two of its predecessors, was in Whimple Street and had been erected in 1800. W. H. K. Wright, a notable local historian was the first and only librarian here, a post he held until his death in 1915. By then, of course, his ambition to see the library in its own dignified and purpose built surroundings had been achieved with the opening of this building in Tavistock Road in 1910.

It is worth noting that Plymouth did already have other well established libraries before the opening of the Free Public Library, the Plymouth Public Library, which became Plymouth Proprietary Library soon after 1876 and that of the Athenaeum which was built in 1819. Both of these, however, were subscription libraries for members only. Today the Proprietary Library is situated at 111 North Hill, while the rebuilt Athenaeum stands on its original pre-war site. Many irreplaceable books and treasures were lost when the Athenaeum was bombed during the last war as, indeed, they were here when all but the facade of the library building was destroyed. 72,618 books were lost out of a collection of 93,510 of which well over 4,000 were

out on loan at the time of the bombing. The library was quick to begin operations again though and in August 1941 Lord Astor, the Lord Mayor, became the first to choose a book from the 'nucleus' library established in the Museum and Art Gallery next door.

This temporary home was to last 15 years until the library moved back onto its old site, but in completely new surroundings, only the facade and the large and attractive stained glass window above the main entrance being retained from the original. In May 1954, Princess Margaret unveiled a tablet commemorating the rebuilding of the central library and, on 22nd February 1956, it was opened by writer, artist, broadcaster and ornithologist, Peter Scott. Bill Best Harris was the then librarian who oversaw the move (he had been with the library since 1935), and with him as a junior member of staff at the time, John Elliott who, after a number of years in the Library Service away from Plymouth came back, in March 1974 to take over from Mr. Best Harris.

The major reference library west of Bristol, Plymouth Central (which was built to serve a population of 60,000 and now serves a catchment area almost six times that), now looks set for the next phase of post war building. As well as housing the reference library, there is the Scott lecture theatre, the local history section, the Naval history library moved from Mount Wise in 1962, a large and inviting children's library, with a jolly wall to wall mural by Wyn George, the music and drama library and the administrative offices. Space also has to be made for all the latest technological innovations. Today the library is about much more than just books and periodicals. Records, tapes, compact discs, some educational videos plus direct linking into computers and information sources around the world, are just some of the recent innovations to have appeared behind this old facade.

30th January 1988.

Sherwell Church

In the middle of the last century this area was described as being a little to the north of the Old Town Gate and just below Drake's Reservoir. The site was then occupied by an old and derelict mill. In 1860 a fire had broken out in the mill and although there was plenty of water to hand, the available hose was too short and the firemen had to make do with buckets. The mill was left a charred and unsightly ruin. Consequently, a year later the council decided to offer this 'most eligible site in Tavistock Road' for sale; an offer which came hard on the heels of a decision, made by deacons of the cramped Norley Chapel, to build a more commodious chapel. There can be no doubt that the council knew of the deacons desires as, just a few years earlier, 1850–53 had witnessed a run of three consecutive mayors of Plymouth, Derry, Rooker and Gibson, who were also deacons of Norley and in 1861 the son of one of these three, William Derry of Derry's Clock fame, was mayor.

Meanwhile, back in 1861 it was Rooker who was 'largely responsible for negotiating, with the Corporation, the acquisition of the site on which Sherwell Church is built' (Stanley Griffin, *The Sherwell Story*). The site here then was purchased for the sum of £1,675 and the completion announced, at the annual meeting of the Church on 9th October 1861. On 7th September 1862, David Derry laid the foundation stone; two years later, on 22nd September, Sherwell Chapel was opened and, in an after dinner speech at the celebrations, the Reverend Charles Wilson noted that 'Mr. Richard Derry had helped to build Norley, now his son (David) had helped to build their new sanctuary'.

Norley Chapel itself had been opened for divine worship in 1797. The incentive for building what was then called the New Tabernacle came when an ever growing band of local Congregationalists were prevented from using an earlier Tabernacle that had served them and their predecessors since 1745. This old Tabernacle had been built by Andrew Kinsman and until the bombing of 1941 it had stood in a garden behind properties now in Exeter Street, Bretonside and was approached by a narrow entrance between two shops opposite the Salvation Army's Exeter Hall. Andrew Kinsman was born in Tavistock in 1724 and was 17 when he discovered the writings of one of the founders of modern methodism, George Whitefield. Kinsman came to Plymouth two years later and set up a small grocery business in Bretonside and, after interesting others in his own sermonising, he soon decided to build a meeting house, capable of seating 400, in his back garden. Built by public subscription but regarded largely as his own, this Tabernacle served handsomely until his death in 1793. Two years later, however, his son, under an old statute, took legal, then physical, possession of the property and the church members were forced to look for a new place in which to worship. Norley Lane, later Norley Street and now gone, was the site chosen and the new building, like the old, stood until the Blitz. Norley Chapel closed, on the opening of the present church, but then re-opened as a daughter chapel of Sherwell in 1866.

When built Sherwell had another mill, 'Drake's', immediately to its north and the old 'Dartmoor Inn', now a small car park, to its south. On the other side of Tavistock Road stood Sherwell House, part of the large Sherwell estate that had first been acquired by the Sherwill family early in the seventeenth century. The Chapel, registered as a church in 1930, took its name from the estate happily enough as the Reverend Nicholas Sherwill was one of Plymouth's celebrated early non-conformists. Before the end of last century, Queen Anne Terrace had been built on the site of Sherwell House. However, as late as 1879 we find the church secretary instructed to ask the gentleman resident in Sherwell House to muzzle his peacock during church meetings!

Today, Sherwell is miles inside the city boundary and a falling inner city population makes it increasingly difficult for the church to maintain a large congregation. Nevertheless, Sherwell is actively involved with its local community, working closely with the Council for Christian Care and with Plymouth Polytechnic. Fridays are drop-in days here when anyone can come in and enjoy coffee and, at lunchtime, the singing of the Polyphonic Choir—just one of the attractions that the Reverend Michael Diffey hopes will cause this large and impressive haven to be used by more people, more of the time.

20th September 1986.

Plymouth Polytechnic

'Plymouth Polytechnic came into being on January 1st 1970. While to many people the only noticeable change in the progress from "College of Technology" to "Polytechnic" was the alteration of the neon sign on the College Hall, in fact many radical and far reaching changes have occurred, and many more should follow . . .'

So began a report written for the Students' Union just a few years after Margaret Thatcher, in her capacity as Secretary of State for Education and Science, had signed and sealed a document which designated this Institution as a Polytechnic. Such a change in title, however, had been anticipated since 1966 when Mrs. Thatcher's predecessor, Anthony Crosland, issued a White Paper with its central theme 'The Government believe that the best results will be achieved by developing higher education on Polytechnic lines wherever possible.' In other words there was to be a new emphasis on vocational learning with the development of industry orientated academics. Thirty Polytechnics were proposed in this plan and Plymouth was to have one of them. As Mr. Crosland had said the previous year, there was to be an end to the plans to create more universities. To a certain extent this would, doubtless, have pleased the architects of the 1943 Plan for Plymouth who considered then that all towns over 100,000 inhabitants should have the educational advantages of a university colony. Certainly they would not have been surprised by the scale or the site of various Poly buildings. As they noted in the plan, property had been bought in this neighbourhood from time to time with 'a view to extending the educational facilities for which a layout was produced some years ago.' The area they were referring to being 'roughly triangular in shape, bounded by North Road, Tavistock Road and Cobourg Street, and containing Portland Square and Drake's Reservoir and Gardens.' Public Baths, a Health Centre and the BBC Headquarters completed what the wartime planners envisaged as being a cultural precinct on this site.

Today, with all its integral parts, the Poly alone occupies by far the greater portion of this triangle. The eight storey block here, opened in March 1967, currently houses the Science Faculty, with the Main Hall standing out at right angles to it. Visible on the right, on the corner of Portland Place East, is the entrance to the Library, Learning Resources Centre and Students' Union, which was officially opened by the Duke of Edinburgh in June 1976. Further round in Portland Square is the large and impressive Faculty of Maritime Studies, with its own residential block. Behind all this there is also the Workshop Block, General Teaching Block, the Engineering Block (the four storey development begun in 1952 as Plymouth & Devonport Technical College became Plymouth College of Technology) and the newly acquired Cobourg Street building (formerly Public School for Boys and Public School for Girls). In addition to these main developments there are also various annexes in Endsleigh Place, Skardon Place, Kirby Place and Portland Villas (which chiefly house the Administration Offices and the Social Science Faculty). There are two principal departments which are outside this area altogether—namely the Civil Engineering Faculty in Palace Court and the School of Architecture, in the Hoe Centre, in Notte Street. With the attractively designed residential buildings—Gilwell House, in Gibbon Lane, and an increasing number of neighbouring houses being

acquired for student accommodation, the Poly is certainly rapidly developing into the sort of campus that was, perhaps, envisaged all those years ago.

A far cry indeed from the cattle market which, 100 years ago, occupied part of the area that was taken up by the 'Victoria Jubilee Memorial Science, Art and Technical Schools' which was begun on 30th September, 1889, completed 3 years later, and which stood, approximately where the car park cum pannier market is now to be found, until the new plans were effected in 1966.

Prior to its being here there was a Science and Art School in erstwhile Courtenay Street (which in turn grew out of the Mechanics' Institute founded in 1826 and which came to occupy premises in Princess Square). W. H. K. Wright, in his 1879 guide to Plymouth, observed that this school was very limited in its accommodation, adding that it was 'certainly no credit to the town that it has not long ere this founded a Science and Art School, worthy of some of its other establishments'. Small wonder then that in 1887, to celebrate Victoria's 50 years on the throne, the City decided to build the new college. In 1914, when the three towns merged, this Plymouth Tech merged with Devonport Tech (built to commemorate Victoria's 60 years as Queen). In 1937 the Art Faculty separated from the main college and it is still independent today. However, with the Poly gradually edging towards University status by degrees who knows what the future holds for college life in the City?

Certainly one thing is clear, Plymouth Polytechnic has already established a fine reputation for itself. Furthermore it is currently one of the largest employers in the area, with over 1,200 staff; it also has over 5,000 full-time students, all of whom generate a lot of spending in and around Plymouth, making it a financial, as well as a cultural, boon for the City.

Central Hall

There are few clues to the layout of Plymouth's pre-war city centre; the most obvious perhaps is the original part of the Western Evening Herald and Morning News Offices, opened in December 1938, which sit along the line of old Frankfort Street and at a definite angle to post war New George Street. However, there is another clue here at Central Methodist Hall. This building is a rarity in the city as it's neither pre-war nor post war. It was opened on May Day 1940 before the Blitz, before the thought of major reconstruction. The Hall, however, is a product of reconstruction itself as it was built on to the main structure of the Ebenezer Methodist Chapel which, in turn, was erected on this site back in 1817. The impetus for this conversion came after a terrible fire destroyed the Wesley Congregationalists Chapel in Ebrington Street on 12th September 1937. Once the loss had been accepted, it was decided to plough the money available for rebuilding into fashioning one large Mother Church for Plymouth Methodism. It was a fitting step to take; the national move for establishing a Central Hall in every major city had begun just after the turn of the century. Devonport already had its Hall and so Plymouth was already behind in this respect. Furthermore, the Ebenezer and Ebrington Street congregations had common ancestry as both had started out as societies based in the first purpose-built home of Plymouth Methodism, constructed in 1792 in erstwhile Buckwell Lane,

when the street was then known as Mud Lane. This Chapel still stood when Central Hall was opened; it had been deserted by the Methodists when the Ebenezer opened in 1817, repossessed 30 years later and then left once more 30 years on again in 1879 when the Ebrington Street Chapel was completed.

After the loss of this later building in 1937 plans were soon drawn up for a new Central Hall and on 17th April 1939 work began. The old Ebenezer, which had cost around £5,000 to build over a century earlier, was gutted, its balcony ripped out, its front wall taken down and moved forward a few yards nearer its impressive stone-pillared and iron-gated entrance in Saltash Street (more or less where the barrier gate is today). Inside the present structure one or two old rooms remain. The side windows are unchanged, but a large new balcony was constructed across the bulk of the hall and the scar of the old side seating was squared off.

In the war years that followed, Central Hall played a vital role in the spiritual and physical sustenance of its local and service community—up to 1,000 meals a day were served in the canteen. That the Hall survived the war was thanks, in no small part, to the efforts of the Minister, J. Leslie Nix, with students and helpers who between them threw more than 30 incendiary bombs off the building and fought flames that might have spread to it.

But survive it did and when it came to the celebrated *Plan for Plymouth*, Central Hall was singled out along with St. Andrew's Church and Charles Church, as important buildings that could 'be preserved in the plan and in no way would they prevent the realization of the full scheme' (page 77). And well might they say that, as the other two were but shells and, since the bombing of the Guildhall in 1941, the council had used Central Hall for the Lord Mayor Choosing Ceremony and other Civic occasions and, indeed, a plaque in the Hall foyer commemorates this association which lasted until the Guildhall was reopened in 1959. Central Hall was also used during this time for school speech days, concerts and other public events.

Its success in this area was doubtless due to the fact that Central Hall was completed partly through the money and influence of Lord Rank—J. Arthur Rank—a keen methodist who, in line with the notion that a Methodist Hall should be an inviting auditorium to witness sermons, also felt that the cinema could be used to convey the message too. It was his idea to make religious films and show them in halls such as this one and in addition to cinema style seating, Central Hall has a fully-strengthened projection room which, but for the course of the war, might have boasted fine projection equipment. As it has turned out the room has never been used. The Hall, however, has flourished and on its 30th birthday, 1st May 1970, the ancillary premises, with its fine multi-purpose hall, were opened. A lively and effective centre; current incumbent Jeffrey Sharp is sensitive to the irony of this modern world where he observes that, as people have tended to drift away from the Church as a whole, so society's problems have become aggravated, and yet he suggests timeless solutions to these problems are still being preached for those who want to listen.

10th January 1987.

The Noah's Ark

Two hundred years ago if you had found yourself standing just outside the north eastern door of Boots the Chemist in Old Town Street, you would have been right on the edge of town at the Old Town Gate. An ancient structure, this had been rebuilt in 1759 beyond it was just a handful of buildings marking out the original line of Drake's Circus, beyond them—nothing but the odd house or farm until you came to the first village to the north of Plymouth—Compton. But it was a situation that was not destined to last; the expansion of Plymouth was well under way.

By 1804 among the newer buildings in the town was an Inn called the 'Noah's Ark'. It stood just 30 yards or so to the north of the gate and its address was given as 'Old Town Without'. However, within five years, the Old Town Gate had been pulled down and, as development beyond this point went on apace, the area around Coburg Place (now Street) appeared on maps as New Town.

A little over forty years ago that same 'Noah's Ark' was still standing. It stood just beyond the end of the old Old Town Street, its address, number 2 Saltash Street. Today Saltash Street, of course, has gone and the area immediately to the east of it and for some distance to the west makes up the new 'New Town' centre of Plymouth. The original 'Noah's Ark' was just one of the many victims of the Blitz. However, its name was preserved here in one of the first post war pubs to be built in the City Centre. The present 'Noah's Ark', though, stands nearer the original Frankfurt Gate than anywhere else, and probably the nearest pre-war pub to its present location was the 'Fountain Inn' in Frankfort Street.

In all, six pubs have so far been built into Plymouth's modern shopping centre or at least that part of it which stands surrounded by dual carriageway. Those six, the 'Noah's Ark', the 'Newmarket', 'Trader Jacks', 'Silks', the 'Prince Regent' and the 'Good Companions'. (The 'Unity', in Eastlake Street, is still in its pre-war location). In that same area before the war you could have found over four times that number and, of that total, only two others were remembered by name in post-war Plymouth—the 'Newmarket', whose predecessor stood in Cornwall Street and the 'Barley Sheaf', which stood looking down the line of the present Raleigh Street. However, although a 'Barley Sheaf' (there were two, an old one dating back to the eighteenth century and a new one from the beginning of the nineteenth century) had stood on a site near here for centuries, the name was changed just a few years ago to 'Trader Jacks'. Likewise the name 'Silks' is also a recent change, that post war pub originally being known as the 'Eagle'.

But what of the dozens of pre-war city centre pubs? Certainly they didn't all disappear in the bombing, many were still standing and trading well into the 1950s. Pubs like the 'Bedford Vaults' in Old Town Street, the 'Welcome Inn' and the 'Revenue Hotel' in Richmond Street; the 'Lord Clarendon' in Summerland Place, the 'Sugar Refinery', the 'Albion Spirit Vaults' in Coburg Street. Then in Russell Street there was the 'Prince of Wales', the 'Druids Arms' and the 'Russell Arms', in Cambridge Street, the 'Red Lion', the 'Empire Inn' and the 'Cambridge Arms', in York Street, the 'New Town Hotel', the 'South Western' and the much loved 'Opporto', which stood well into the 1960s like its equally well remembered near neighbour the 'Harvest Home'. 'If you did not know the 'Harvest Home' you were

obviously a stranger to the City' noted Brian Moseley in his extremely valuable book *Vanishing Plymouth*, which contains photographs of so many of the city's treasures that have been lost since the war.

There is of course one major building inside this area that did in fact survive both the bombing and the planners—namely the Leicester Harmsworth building, which houses the offices and printing works of the 'Western Evening Herald' and the 'Western Morning News'. Set on the original street line of old Frankfort Street, this building would have been unique with its red brick facade contrasting sharply with the Portland stone facings that surround it, but then came the 'Noah's Ark' also built of brick and to a similar style as well.

However, it's a far cry from the original Ark which inspired the name of this pub and many others before it. This, if we are to take the dimensions quoted in Genesis (vi, 15), was about as big as a medium sized church, almost 500 feet long, 75–85 feet wide and 45–50 feet high. And if Noah did indeed build his ark strictly according to God's prescription, it would have had but one window and one door in the side. Plymouth did in the past have more than one 'Noah's Ark' hostelry, the other was on the Barbican and across the country generally 'Noah's Ark' is comparatively common as a public house name. This is doubtless due to the fact that Noah is not only credited with planting the first vineyard but is also said to be the first to sample its produce '. . . And he drank of the wine, and was drunken' (Genesis ix, 21).

5th December 1987.

Phoenix Way

What's in a name? After all the recent fuss over the naming of what is now to be the Copthorne Hotel at the top of Armada Way, it is interesting to note that on the 28th July 1947, Plymouth City Council rounded off their monthly meeting 'with an hour's "ramble" in search of inspiration for the names of the two main streets of the new City centre', names which were to be inaugurated by the King and Queen when they visited the City in October.

The prolonged 'excursion' began, we are told, when the Lord Mayor, (Mr. W. Harry-Taylor), presented the recommendations of the special sub-committee that the north-south road, from the Hoe Promenade to the junction of the east–west axis road, should be named Armada Way and that the east–west road should be named Royal Parade.

Of the 40 councillors left in the chamber to discuss the issue, it would appear from the report that everyone 'seemed to want a different "way" to those recommended'. Alderman H. M. Medland suggested 'Phoenix-way' and 'Hoegate' to little avail, then Alderman F. C. Roach proposed that 'Common-way' might be worth considering—'in appreciation of what the folk of Plymouth did during the war'—but few were impressed. However, the idea of commemorating the local spirit and gallantry was well received. Another suggestion, however, moved the focus to

national level as Alderman R. H. Baker suggested 'Churchill Way', only to find others countering this with claims for 'Attlee'. In the end Armada Way won through by 22 votes to 18! A second debate, this time on Royal Parade, prompted 'Commoners Way', 'Elizabethan Way', 'Hoegate' (again from Alderman Medland) and even a 'Sir Francis Drake Avenue', but once again the original suggestion held sway. Doubtless just as well too, as rumour has it that Royal Parade is a foot or so off its proper line and it's only having 'Royal' (or alternatively the name of a Monarch) in its title that guaranteed that it could stay where it was once it had been opened by George VI, thereby avoiding any readjustment.

One interesting observation of the above, however, is that Armada Way, as here defined, refers to the stretch south of Royal Parade and although the northern part had been planned it does not appear to have been named by then. Strangely enough, we later find that, according to H. P. Twyford in a 1949 revision of his 1945 account of *Plymouth in the World War* 'It Came to Our Door', he believed that—'In due course there will be a wide vista from the top of York Street', then he added 'this will bear three names, from North Road to the centre, partly People's Way, partly Phoenix Way and from Royal Parade to the Hoe, Armada Way'.

Today of course it is all Armada Way. However, in the early seventies when the North Cross was developed and the garden for the blind created, this impressive Phoenix was placed in the centre piece fountain of the garden and, risen from the ashes of the council minutes that voted against Phoenix Way, it looks down the great wide boulevard that is perhaps J. Paton-Watson's finest gift to the City. In the 1943 Plan for Plymouth that this great City Engineer produced with Patrick Abercrombie, he wrote 'The authors have permitted themselves one great decorative—even monumental—feature. Those who to-day plan a straight line, such as an avenue in a park and place something attractive to look at, at the end, are in danger of being labelled vista-mongers: the authors of this plan are not afraid of this label; they have boldly planned a vista from the station to the Hoe: not a Renaissance road, but a Garden vista—a parkway, making use, with terraces, slopes, steps, pools, avenue and other contrasting features, of the varying levels . . . Anyone entering Plymouth from the Railway Station . . . will know where they are.' Before the war such a view would have been impossible; today it is there for all to see and with the latest proposals for pedestrianisation, it will soon be a true 'People's Way' with a minimum of traffic. »Postscript

15th February 1986.

Armada Way

'Armada Way is one of the most precious assets of the City Centre . . . There are few finer urban vistas to be found anywhere . . . it is a major legacy of the 1943 Plan. . . . It needs to be made more attractive.'

These quotes are taken from a draft report from the City Planning Officer, Chris Shepley, for Plymouth City Council's Policy and Resources Committee and would, without doubt, have warmed the hearts of James Paton-Watson and Patrick Abercrombie who produced the 1943 Plan which itself was apparently the 38th version of the Plan, it having been preceded by 37 drafts.

Armada Way is indeed a monumental feature of the modern city centre, just as the authors of the 1943 Plan had hoped. However, it is perhaps not as decorative or as stunning as they may have wished. It does though, as Frank Wintle notes in his book on The Plymouth Blitz, 'help to make a wonderfully neat aerial photograph . . .' but he goes on to suggest 'how far do the ants appreciate the complexity of the anthill?' Ten years after the Plan had been produced, the Architects' Journal looked at its implementation, up to that time, and concluded that Paton-Watson and Abercrombie had been obsessed with their 'vista'. But is the vista, as it stands, as they wanted? Is it truly a 'Garden vista—a parkway, making use, with terraces, slopes, steps, pools, avenues and other contrasting features, of the varying levels'? (*A Plan for Plymouth*, 1943, page 6). Does it really 'afford a pleasant break in the shopping precinct' and 'provide a backbone to the whole of central Plymouth, and lead up to its climax in the Hoe and Sound'? Or is it rather, as Andrew Paterson observed in his 1983 dissertation (*The Price Paid for Plymouth's New City Centre*), 'so frequently interrupted by roads and so littered with parked cars and rather petty flower beds and fenced off lawns, that any association with the openness of the Hoe is destroyed'?

Plymouth's town centre is a major achievement despite the many minor, but taken together significant, changes from the Paton-Watson/Abercrombie Plan, but Armada Way, which was designed as the showpiece, has, in many respects, been abused and not used. Had it been created with a grand central walkway with the features highlighted by the original plan, it would undoubtedly take pride of place in any brochure or guide to the modern city. As it is Armada Way is seldom if ever included, except in aerial shots or views from the top of the civic centre. Royal Parade appears fairly consistently, as does the one truly pedestrian stretch of Armada Way, outside the Civic buildings, but the rest, precisely because the ant's eye view is so disappointing and consequently so unphotogenic, is generally ignored.

The 1986 'Plan' is being true to its esteemed predecessor; Armada Way does need to be made more attractive; 'pedestrianisation will transform it' and, if the new plan is followed and it is then 'generously landscaped following its closure to traffic', it may, at long last, bear the full fruit of the Paton-Watson/Abercrombie vision that the cynics call obsession.

James Paton-Watson was an inspired City Engineer and Surveyor, a post he had held since 1938, while Sir Leslie (Patrick) Abercrombie was the inspired choice of

Plymouth's last nonpolitical, Mayoral appointment, Viscount Astor (Mayor from 1939–44). Abercrombie came to Plymouth on the 19th of October 1941 at the invitation of Lord Astor and the fellow members of the Emergency Committee. It was to be the first of many visits and Paton-Watson has since been quoted as saying that 'his job in all their talks was to keep his poet-architect partner's feet on the ground'. But Abercrombie was no young idealist eager to make a clean sweep just to make a name for himself. Born in Liverpool in 1879, he was 64 when the plan was produced and it was fully 30 years since he had won the competition for replanning Dublin, in 1913. Professor of Civic Design at Liverpool University between 1915–35, and, subsequently, Professor of Town Planning at London University 1935–46, Abercrombie was already working on the County of London Plan of 1943 when he came to Plymouth and also worked on The Greater London Plan of 1944— both reports were very detailed and comprehensive and illustrated on a scale never attempted previously. Neither were his activities limited to these areas; he also worked on plans for Edinburgh, Hull, the West Midlands, Clydeside, Bath, Bristol, Sheffield and Bournemouth.

The pursuit of the 1943 Plymouth Plan ultimately led to the Council achieving the compulsory purchase of 172 acres of city centre land, something the city has long had cause to celebrate, and it would be especially fitting if by 1988, the Armada's 400th Anniversary, the city could at last see Armada Way in all its intended glory.

»Postscript

3th May 1986.

41

Frankfort Gate

There used to be a plaque on the wall of the Globe Tavern that read as follows '... Near this place formerly stood Frankfort Gate which, with others, formed the principal entrance into the town then enclosed by a wall erected for the greater protection thereof by the Mayor and Commonalty under the authority of the Charter of Henry VI. But in course of years, this mode of defence ceasing to be of any effect, the gate was taken down in 1783 and the street and avenues adjoining were considerably widened and improved. This tablet was put up by order of the Mayor and Commonalty 4th of June 1813'.

Sadly, it came down before the century was out when in 1899 the 'Globe Hotel' was demolished. 'Once a little, squat, humble tavern, with thatched roof and dormer windows' the 'Globe' was reconstructed, with the popularity of the coach, and was further extended in 1800, soon after the road was widened and became famous as a coaching centre and, later, as the political headquarters of the Conservative party.

Frankfort Gate was always the city's west gate and although it is difficult to put a date on when it was first constructed, it is known to have been substantially redeveloped in the 1650s. Theoretically part of the city's walled defences, very little building had gone on beyond it until around the time it was pulled down. Incidentally, before it was pulled down, it gave its address to the predecessor of Foulston's original Theatre Royal. The city's first major theatre stood opposite Frankfort Gate and had been built upon three partially completed houses. A great success at the end of the 18th century, the Corporation earmarked this site for

Foulston to build his theatre. However, the architect had his own ideas and opted instead for a clear space in front of what was George Place and is where the ABC Cinema and adjacent car park now stands.

Meanwhile, Frankfort Gate itself, which was thought to have been 'in a low and feeble state' before its demolition, would have stood roughly at the SW corner of the junction of Armada Way and New George Street, slightly out from John Colliers and adjoining Visionhire, opposite Dingles. In 1890 when the Royal Agricultural Show came to Plymouth, a handsome canvas reconstruction was made of it, along with the Hoegate and Old Town Gate and these dummies were so effective they almost look real in contemporary black and white photographs.

Today's Frankfort Gate, however, is the area seen here and pretty much occupies the old junction of King Street and Well street. Until the laying down of Union Street in the 1820s, King Street, which led into Stonehouse Lane, was the main route out of Plymouth into Stonehouse and Dock (Devonport). Indeed, to quote Whitfield (Dec 1900) once more, outside the Globe 'a quaint signboard depicted a traveller on horseback, and a Boniface of rotund proportions handing him the stirrup cup with which it was the custom of landlords to bid their guests a safe journey and underneath this illustration the words "Huzza, my boys for Doch-an-dorrach" ... A whimsical suggestion of the parting drink at the door, and an intimation that the traveller was now bound for Dock.' This King Street route ran north of the present Union Street, for this land was formerly part of Surpool, the inner reach of Millbay only reclaimed from the sea in the last 200 years. Although the western end of King Street still stands, from Western Approach to Frankfort Street it all fell to the city centre post war rebuilding plan. 250 families in this area alone were displaced by the construction of the Market in 1957. However, the area around Frankfort Gate and the Market boasts some of the only in-town residential developments above ground floor level and help give this part of the centre its own unique flavour. Also, well above ground level, we see the gentle curves of the roof of Plymouth Market, designed by Messrs. Walls and Pearn in association with the then City Architect Mr. H. J. W. Stirling, providing a welcome relief to the otherwise linear skylines of the modern centre.

22nd March 1986.

The Civic Centre

'The basic conception of this scheme is the grouping of a number of large public buildings in such a manner as to give a feeling of spaciousness and vitality at a focal point in the city centre and to present to the moving eye of the viewer a continuously interesting series of visual compositions both in height and depth.'

That is how H. J. W. Stirling, City Architect, opened an article on the 'proposed Civic Centre for Plymouth' in the November 1954 edition of the *Municipal Journal*. In the event the completed scheme, finished 8 years later, was a slightly amended version of this plan but 'the basic conception' remained the same and as such it was probably the first major departure from the 1943 Paton Watson and Abercrombie 'Plan for Plymouth'.

The earlier vision of the Civic Centre had been an altogether more traditional one without a 'tall building'. However one feature common to both was the preservation of some of the 'splendid trees' of Westwell Gardens which survived the blitz, trees which today still help to make this the most successful of the pedestrian areas in Armada Way.

While some of these old trees survived on this site, St. Catherine's Church, at the bottom of Lockyer Street, didn't. Opened in 1823 as a Chapel of Ease to St. Andrew's Church, St. Catherine's was one of the few remaining examples of Georgian architect John Foulston's city centre works and after various alterations and restorations over the years the church was ultimately able to seat 800 worshippers, about the same number of people as currently work in the Civic Centre itself. Situated roughly at the entrance to what is now the car park for this complex, St. Catherine's was demolished in January 1958. By this time the final piece of compulsory purchasing to clear the site had been completed, however such was the volume of local work then in the hands of the City Architect that it was decided to engage Messrs. Jellicoe, Ballantyne and Coleridge as architects to complete the design work of the Council House and Council Offices.

Their subsequent freedom 'to redesign the buildings in detail and to interpret the spirit of Mr. Stirling's proposals' resulted in various alterations. A butterfly roof now capped the building and the entrance on to Royal Parade was forsaken as were some of the buildings to the west of the 'tall building' where – for the time being – the car park is situated. The number of floors however in the Civic Centre remained constant throughout, fourteen, making it a very tall building for Plymouth – over 200 feet – but small fry when compared, say, to New York's twin towered World Trade Centre with over one hundred floors.

In the absence of a formal foundation stone, two years after work began here, a tablet, which stands in the wall of the Council House, was unveiled by His Royal Highness the Duke of Edinburgh, K. G. on the 18th March 1960 on the occasion of his installation as Lord High Steward of Plymouth. This title dates back to the fifteenth century and appears in the town's earliest municipal records. It is likely to date from the 1439 Act of Incorporation, the Lord High Steward being the agent of the authority of the Crown. As Mayors are appointed annually and Lord High Stewards generally for life, it is no surprise to learn that Plymouth has had several hundred mayors over the last 500 years but only twenty or so Lord High Stewards.

In the days of Elizabeth I Sir Robert Cecil held the title, while four of the last nine holders have been installed when they were Prince of Wales – all four later succeeding to the throne.

Of the many Mayors Plymouth has had, only the last fifty have been *Lord* Mayors, this dignity being conferred upon the City's chief citizen in 1935 following the designation of Plymouth as a City by Royal letters patent in 1928. James Pillar, who sadly died in office, was the first; George Creber is the only man to have held the title twice, while today sees the investiture of Plymouth's 51st Lord Mayor, Gordon Draper.

The new Council House incorporating the Chamber and the Lord Mayor's parlour was formally handed over to the Corporation on 21st March, 1962, the twenty first anniversary of the wartime destruction of the old municipal offices. A few weeks later Alderman Arthur Goldberg became the first Lord Mayor to take office here and it was he who had the honour of attending Her Majesty Queen Elizabeth II on 26th July, 1962, when she officially opened the building.

Since then the Civic Centre has been filled with the various departments that, during wartime, had of necessity been scattered all over the area and which had previously been squeezed into the old municipal buildings, only half of which remains in the form of the reconstructed Guildhall.

Today Housing, Treasury, Environmental Health, City Estates, S. W. Water, Planning, Personnel, Social Services, Education, Architects, the Chief Executive and Town Clerk are amongst the various departments occupying the 'tall building' and its appendages whilst the roof deck is generally open to visitors for 30 pence.

»Postscript

21st May, 1988.

Royal Parade

Under the terms of the 1944 Planning Act local authorities in bombed towns were empowered to control post war redevelopment and when, in February 1946, the local authority here gave preliminary notice of its intention to compulsorily purchase 178 acres of the city centre (at 1939 prices) it became the first to take advantage of those powers. However, it was another year before any substantial progress was made and it wasn't until the morning of Monday 17th March 1947 that the first kerbstone of the new city centre was laid in what was Raleigh Lane. Today it is to be found—'wrongly dated 21.3.47 in the edging of Derry's Cross roundabout' (Crispin Gill).

Over the next few months the great east–west dual-carriageway was mapped out and flagpoles were erected along the route that His Majesty King George VI and Queen Elizabeth were to take on the 29th October 1947. That was the day they came to dedicate the replica of Drake's Drum in which the Civic Flagstaff is planted, at the crossing of the two great axes of the Paton-Watson Abercrombie Plan, Royal Parade and Armada Way, and which were officially named in that same ceremony. This is, incidentally, also said to be the point from which distances to and from the City of Plymouth are measured.

To buy the land that made up the 178 acres and to negotiate the leasing of newly marked out sites, the city appointed a new Chief Officer, W. K. Shepherd, who became Plymouth's first Estates and Development Valuer. Creating a department as he went along, Shepherd stayed in the post 26 years. 'He did more for Plymouth than has ever been credited to him' (Crispin Gill, who then carried on to say) 'The first major decision was that the big stores, Popham's, Spooner's, Yeo's, Dingle's and the Co-op, should stand on Royal Parade roughly on their old sites' (Plymouth A New History Vol. 2).

First up, and ready for business from 1st September 1951, was Dingles. Designed by Sir John Burnet, of Tait and Partners, it was the first store in postwar Plymouth to have escalators installed. Dingles had been established as a general drapers in No. 30 Bedford Street back in 1880 by Edward Dingle who had been manager of Spooners. Dingle set up his shop with Thomas Baker and in time their sons Frank and Jack were to take on the running of the shop. In later years Wesley Brimacombe helped Dingles grow into a fair empire of West Country stores culminating in 1971, when the House of Fraser took them over.

A year after Dingles opened the Co-op was completed (November 1952) at the bottom of Royal Parade. It remains the only one of the big five still locally controlled. Yeo's reopened soon after the Co-op, over 80 years after John Yeo had first come to Plymouth and joined Joseph Pillman, Draper and Milliner, at 35 Bedford Street. A farmer's son from North Devon who learnt the business in London and Paris, Yeo bought out Pillman in 1871 and began running the shop on 'cash only' lines. In 1893 he was joined by his nephew John Beckley and once again respective sons took over the business. Edwin Beckley was the last family man in control here and in 1964 when he retired he sold John Yeo's to Debenhams, whose chairman at the time was a former manager of Spooners, John Bedford. Spooners themselves had been taken over by Debenhams back in 1929, just two years after Clarence Harty's Drapery Trust had acquired it. The business had been founded as long ago as 1837 by Joseph Spooner, who started trading in Whimple Street and moved to Bedford Street in 1858. Later, fronting onto a large part of Old Town Street as well as Bedford Street, Spooners, after a disastrous fire in 1902, became, eight years later the first store in town with a roof garden and 'an electric staircase'. They were also the first to use motor transport for deliveries. Although still known as the Yeo and Spooner buildings, the present stores were renamed Debenhams in 1977.

The one store, however, of which there is no reminder is Pophams. 'Where the West buy the Best' was one of their slogans and they were often referred to as the Harrods of the West. This enterprise had the longest pedigree of them all. Known as Popham and Radford until 1931, it had been founded by Elizabeth Radford around 1824 and later moved into the Bedford Street premises of the draper F. W. Lansdown. Last to reopen after the war in 1958, Pophams were also first to flounder. In 1962 Dingles took over all their assets and although they endeavoured to keep it running the magic had been lost. Today Argos occupies their old site, next door to Lloyds Bank, who are another pre-war Bedford Street business along with H. Samuel the jewellers. How these businesses will all be situated in a few years' time remains to be seen.

There's little change likely however for the award winning National Westminster Bank built by Humphreys in 1958, or indeed for Royal Parade's elder residents, St. Andrew's Church (re-consecrated and reopened on 30th November 1957) and the Guildhall (reopened by Field Marshall Lord Montgomery in 1959). While so far the only major changes in the immediate view from this 13th-floor window of the Civic Centre since it was built in 1962, are the subway, opened in December 1973 and the more recent addition of the St. Andrew's Cross Fountain, which was turned on on 10th April 1986.

28th November 1987.

Ark Royal Anchor

In 1621 when the Pilgrim Fathers reached North America, their first words are said to have been 'We anchor in Hope' an expression derived from the biblical use of an anchor to symbolise that which attaches 'Hope' to the 'soul' and gives life and a vision to Man. The inn sign for the Mayflower in Welling, Kent commemorates this piece of history.

In later years the sign of an Anchor generally indicated an inn patronized by sailors of the King's or Queen's navy, hence all the 'Crown & Anchor' pubs; meanwhile, along the road in Kingsbridge, or more precisely Hope Cove, there is the ancient 'Hope and Anchor', harking back to the earlier connotations.

Anchors have been with us ever since man was able to build boats either too big or too difficult to be safely and conveniently beached. There is evidence that, almost 5,000 years ago, the ancient Egyptians employed what is regarded as being the first type of anchor in general use, namely a large pierced stone (examples range from 100–700 kg i.e., approximately 16–110 stone) looking something like a large version of a stone pendant that might be worn on a neckchain. Following these large stones, or in some cases sacks of sand, came the iron hook, earliest examples of which are believed to be Greek and indeed the word anchor derives from the Greek 'agkura' meaning hook. Designed to prevent a vessel from drifting with the wind, tidal stream or current when in harbour, since the beginning of last century at least, perhaps the best known style of anchor has been that described as of the Admiralty pattern. This has an iron shank with two arms tipped with wide blades (flukes) and a wooden or iron stock at the top, running at right angles to the arms.

More recently anchor design has tended to follow the pattern of the one we see here, stockless, armless and with greatly developed hinged flukes. The hinging, which locks around 45 degrees, allows the flukes to grip the seabed whichever way the anchor falls. This particular anchor, now set in stone in Armada Way, was presented to the City (then represented by Lord Mayor Graham Jinks) by the Admiral of the Fleet, Lord Hill-Norton, on the 24th of April 1980. As impressive and aesthetic as (and undoubtedly more interesting than) a good many pieces of sculpture on public display today, the anchor came from HMS *Ark Royal* before it made its final journey to the breaker's yard.

Originally included on the Supplementary Programme of 1940 as the 'Irresistible', the great new aircraft carrier was renamed *Ark Royal* in 1942, the year before she was laid down at Cammell Lairds and eight years before she was launched by the Queen Mother. The renaming followed the sinking, in November 1941, of the third HMS *Ark Royal* which had been torpedoed by a U-boat 30 miles from Gibraltar. Disappearing 14 hours after being hit, only one rating out of her complement of 1,600 was lost. A principal participant in the sinking of the *Bismarck*, the third *Ark Royal* was the only one of the four warships so named to have been lost in action; of the previous two, only the second was a carrier. Commissioned back in 1914 as a seaplane carrier, in the early days of flight this *Ark* became part of the reserve fleet in 1923 and was renamed *Pegasus* in 1934, four years before *Ark Royal III* was commissioned. Sold after the war and renamed *Anita I*, the second *Ark* was finally broken up in 1950.

Meanwhile, to bring the story full circle, the first *Ark Royal* was sailing the seas when the *Mayflower* was around. Launched at Deptford in 1587 as the *Ark Raleigh*, this ship was in the campaign against the Armada and became the *Ark Royal* after its purchase by the Crown from Raleigh in 1592. Rebuilt and relaunched in 1608 as the *Anne Royal* (in honour of James I's wife), this *Ark* had the longest life of all of them to date, finally being broken up in 1636 after going aground in the Thames.

War Memorial on the Hoe

'At the northwest corner is the principal entrance and the Lodge, a neat structure where resides the Hoe Constable. This cottage is tastefully surrounded with flower gardens ... The Park is chiefly used by the youths of the town for purposes of recreation. Here they congregate in large numbers to indulge in the good old English game of cricket.'

Thus began a description of the Hoe Park written a little over 100 years ago for a Handbook to Plymouth, Stonehouse and Devonport.

A little more than 30 years later in 1914 those three towns merged, largely under the stress of what became the First World War, to ensure that the new Corporation could unify its services to cope with whatever might develop. As it transpired the war was more terrible than anyone could have imagined. The men who fought it 'endured unexampled hardship and methods of warfare more exacting and horrible than any the world knew'. It was estimated that over 8 million were killed in the war, around one million of them British citizens. The memorial here, on the corner of Lockyer Street and Citadel Road (formerly Windsor Terrace), is in memory of 2,000 local men and one lady who gave their lives in that war and it stands on the site of the old Park Lodge.

The war itself had had a simple enough beginning. In the heady atmosphere of European Imperialism the Continent was, to some extent, tense and already braced for conflict when, following the assassination of the heir to the Austrian throne, the Austro-Hungarian government determined to take political control of Serbia by open war. Germany, only unified into a single state in 1871 and already anxious to show itself as a world power, gave the Austro-Hungarian government unconditional support. Within six weeks those central powers (Germany and Austria-Hungary) were at war with Russia, France, Great Britain and its Empire, Serbia, Belgium and Japan. Others joined later.

For Plymouth of course war was nothing new. The Boer War had only just started when Whitfield published his *Plymouth and Devonport in Times of War and Peace* (January 1900). And in one of the most recent and certainly most comprehensive histories of Plymouth, by Crispin Gill, published some 20 years after the Second World War, we find the almost weary sentence '. . . August 1914 came to Plymouth as so many wars before had done' then he adds: 'The fleet was already at battle stations and the reserves mobilised.'

In all, some 30,000 local men served in his Majesty's Navy and Army between 1914–18. For many it was their last act of service. Between Mons 1914 and the Bois de Buttes 1918 thousands fell on *terra firma*, while at sea, of all the battles, Jutland in 1916 took the biggest toll. And although the Navy asserted its superiority that May, fourteen British ships were lost and almost a third of them were Devonport manned. It was also the first war to have major conflicts underwater in submarines and in the air in fighter planes.

For those who did survive, pay was poor, there was little home leave and great discomfort. Meanwhile, come the end of the war, the working population of the dockyard had almost doubled, from 10,000 to nearly 19,000, with substantial war bonuses and a great deal of overtime available. This contrasting situation inevitably

bred a certain amount of post-war resentment. Curiously enough, however, the establishment of this memorial to the dead, 'Plymouth's guerdon to the fallen', also generated 'differences and difficulties which hampered the project at every stage'. There was, amongst other things, controversy over where the memorial should be sited, what form it should take, and how it should be paid for. Indeed, it was completed with £1,000 still owing. But completed it was and on 19th May, Whit Saturday 1923, the memorial was unveiled by the erstwhile Secretary of State for War, the Earl of Derby. With its 8 foot 4 inch female figure, sculpted by Birnie Rhind of Edinburgh, Lord Derby believed that the memorial, designed by Messrs. Thornely & Rooke, would be more than a reminder of those who did their duty in the Great War. 'It should' he added, 'be a deterrent to war in the future that future generations should know what war means, and that each town and each parish should know the toll that war has made in our midst.'

Responsible for the famous Derby recruiting scheme during that war, the 17th Earl of Derby lived long enough to see the whole of the Second World War. However, he did not live to see this memorial become almost a lost corner of the Hoe Park. No longer is this 'park' approached by paths either side of the memorial. Instead, following the widespread destruction of the Second World War, the approach to the Hoe, with Windsor Terrace gone, has been relocated in line with the altogether larger and more spectacular memorial to the servicemen lost in those two grim wars. But will it, or any memorial, act as a 'deterrent to war' in the future?

17th January 1987.

Elliot Terrace

Towards the latter part of the last century John Pethick, a leading local Victorian property developer, erected Elliot Terrace—arguably the finest and most hand-somely disposed terrace ever built in the City of Plymouth. Small wonder then that when Waldorf Astor came to Plymouth in 1908, having been adopted as a Unionist Parliamentary Candidate, he should choose this block in which to base himself. Heir to part of the massive fortune amassed in America, by his German-born great great grandfather, a century before (estimated to be worth around 200 million pounds in 1890), No. 3 Elliot Terrace was a modest purchase in his terms—their other residences were much larger. However, it was one which was to prove ultimately very beneficial to Plymouth.

Successful in the second of the General Elections of 1910, Waldorf Astor was again returned in 1918, but a circumstance, unforeseen when he first became an MP, prevented his keeping the seat in 1919. In 1916 his father, William Waldorf, who had subscribed large sums to various war funds, was created a peer—Baron Astor, and Viscount Astor of Hever Castle the following year. Two years later at the age of 71 he died. Waldorf inherited the title and despite his efforts to change the legislation, as a member of the House of Lords, he was forced to surrender his seat in the Commons. A by-election resulted and after a little persuasion his wife, who had worked hard with him over the preceding nine years, agreed to stand in his stead. Born within two days of her husband, American Nancy Witcher Langhorne (married previously to Robert Gould Shaw II) had come to England in 1903.

By 1906 she had met and married Waldorf and thirteen years later she succeeded him as MP for Plymouth Sutton. Nancy Astor, therefore, made history as the first woman MP to sit in the Commons. Women had been allowed to stand in the 1918 Election and seventeen did, but the only successful candidate, a Sinn Fein member, refused the oath of allegiance and never sat in the Commons.

Over the years that followed the Astors did a great deal to help the city, both through public and private channels. They established the Astor Institute at Mount Gould, for the housing estate they built there and the Virginia House Settlement on the Barbican, named after the American State in which Nancy was born. They converted Manor Lodge at Devonport into a hall of residence and presented it to the Technical College. To open the latter, they invited their friend George Bernard Shaw to inaugurate the building. Indeed such was the Astors' standing in society that they brought great colour to the city at times. Charlie Chaplin was among the many celebrities to stay at number 3 Elliot Terrace and to tour the Barbican and Virginia House with Nancy. During the Second World War George VI and Queen Elizabeth had tea at No. 3 on 20th March 1941, leaving the city just hours before its first major blitz. A night when Nancy, on her way to help deal with an incendiary that had just landed on her roof, looked back across the blazing city and ruefully said 'There goes thirty years of our lives, but we'll build it again.' And, indeed, perhaps no-one was more instrumental in orchestrating the rebuilding than Waldorf Astor, the quiet diplomat with his influential contacts, who had been appointed, like Drake before him, Plymouth's Mayor without actually being a member of the council. Mayor throughout the troubled war years, it was Lord Astor who interested Sir Patrick Abercrombie (the most eminent authority possible who was already at work on a plan for Greater London), in coming to Plymouth to work with the City Engineer, James Paton-Watson, to produce the *Plan for Plymouth* (1943).

Lord Astor was Mayor for four terms, after which he virtually decided that Nancy should give up her seat and not stand for Parliament again, a decision she reluctantly accepted. Waldorf died in 1952, Nancy in 1964, but not before she had bequeathed No. 3 Elliot Terrace, virtually lock, stock and barrel with original books, pictures and furnishings, as a residence for future Lord Mayors. Today it is used for small Mayoral receptions, visiting dignitaries and circuit judges. This weekend four members of the Polish Embassy are staying here. Local visitors can look over the building by arrangement with the Lord Mayor's Parlour.

However, apart from their own contributions, very little exists to show the city's appreciation of the Astors' contribution to twentieth-century Plymouth. As John Grigg, in his biography of Nancy Astor, notes '. . . A statue on the Hoe would, surely, be the right solution . . .' no doubt placed in front of No. 3 on the Promenade, where the spirited old lady danced into the hearts of blitz-stricken Plymothians.

Whether or not such a thing ever happens, however, the Astor name could well soon extend what has been a long standing parliamentary association with the city. After Waldorf 1910–19 and Nancy 1919–45 came their son Sir John (Jakie) Astor who was MP for Sutton 1951–59 and today a grandson, David, is the SDP Prospective Parliamentary Candidate for Plymouth Drake.

1st November 1986.

The Hoe Watchtower

'Near the centre of the promenade is a small octagonal building called the Camera Obscura, where, for a small charge, the panorama of the surrounding scenery may be witnessed in miniature.' W. H. K. Wright, 1879.

Sadly, today it is no longer possible, for the price of one penny, to view Plymouth and the Sound 'with all the various shades and colours. . . . enhanced by the contraction of the view provided by a revolving periscope reflected onto a horizontal oval table . . .' as it was when the Camera Obscura was in operation. However, even when such a thing was possible, it was not from here, for this curious castellated, Victorian building does not house and indeed never has housed such a device. Rather it was purpose-built some time around 1870 for the benefit of the shipping firms who, in the days before radio communications, could watch from here for mail steamers making their way towards the Sound, so that arrangements could be made as soon as possible for tenders to be made ready to meet the boats and whisk the postbags and important passengers on to waiting trains at Millbay with all possible haste.

The camera obscura, meanwhile, stood at the top of the 'Bull Ring' and it was removed when this was rebuilt in the early 1890s to accommodate all three tiers and the colonades of the Hoe Belvedere that now stands on its site. Within these colonades there was now ample shelter for visitors to inspect the view comfortably and, besides, the increased availability of photography now rendered the camera obscura more of a quaint novelty than a genuine wonder.

By the same token ship to shore communication soon meant that this little watch tower, 'Tom Thumb's Castle', had outlived its original purpose and for many years it was used as a police and ambulance call centre (and less frequently as an 'on the spot' interrogation centre). However, for almost two years now it has enjoyed a new lease of life as probably one of Britain's few, if not only, limestone, Victorian, octagonal, deck-chair stores.

However, its superb location as an observation point for the coming and going of shipping in the sound, has not altogether been overlooked—and although the shilling-in-the-slot telescope has now gone from in front of it, the wonderful new Hoe Interpretation Centre is due to be constructed just below it over the next two years. This will, at last, provide the much needed details and displays of centuries of traffic in the Sound.

But what of some of the vessels this tower was designed to observe in the golden age of the screw steamship?

As early as 1832 HMS *Rhadamanthus* made the first Atlantic crossing entirely under continuous steam, stopping only, on its voyage from Plymouth to Barbados, to desalt its boilers. 50 years later P & O introduced many improvements to local servicing facilities and 100 years later Plymouth was enjoying extensive free, national advertising as the big shipping lines vied with each other for the coveted Blue Riband, the decoration due to the ship that made the fastest Atlantic crossing. Cunard's 50,000-ton *Mauretania* had held the honour throughout the 1920s, but in 1929, the German *Bremen* steamed into Plymouth, having crossed the Atlantic at an average speed of 27.83 knots. The French Liner *Normandie* topped 30 knots on the return leg of her maiden voyage in 1935, while the following year Plymothians were treated to the spectacle of Cunard's new *Queen Mary* returning to the Sound with a passage of 30.99 knots. That November *Normandie* was on top again, until the *Queen Mary* established a new record in 1938 that held good until 1952. The record, then established by the United States Liner *America*, still stands today. But today big passenger ships are more concerned with luxury than speed—commercial airlines put an end to all that. Pan-American launched their first transatlantic passenger flight, in 1939 and although Plymouth was used as a port of call by one or two of the major shipping lines until 1962, its decline had begun many years earlier. However, many are they who 'can still hear the tender's farewell salute on its foghorn, and the deep, booming reply from the liner high above', so vividly described by Crispin Gill in his fascinating look at *Plymouth As A Liner Port*.

5th April 1986.

49

The Hoe Dome

The 1880s witnessed great changes on Plymouth Hoe not least of which was the construction of Plymouth Pier. First opened on 29th May 1884 it quickly became one of the town's prime attractions.

Its entrance stood on the seaward side of the road just opposite what was then known as the 'Bull Ring' which in turn was situated just below one of the earliest of the Hoe's 'tourist attractions' the Corporation Seat. Erected to celebrate the passing of the Reform Bill in 1832, this feature was in 1891 made part of the more elaborate colonnaded Belvedere still there today. 1891 was also the year that the end of the pier was provided with a covered, almost dome-shaped pavilion. Until this time a small bandstand had stood in the middle of the end of the pier. With its new roof, exciting new possibilities opened up at the end of the pier. Here under the light of eighteen lamps of two thousand candle power, large crowds would congregate for boxing matches on certain evenings while at other times there might be a military band playing, a concert party, dancing or even roller skating.

Designed by E. Birch esq of London, the entrance to the pier was over 40 yards wide whilst its overall length was around 150 yards. Running around its perimeter were great long seats with elaborate cast iron arm rests made in the shape of dolphins. For almost 60 years the pier withstood the elements and, for the most part, the ravages of time. During the last war however it became one of the city's many blitz casualties and by 1953 virtually all traces of the pier had been removed.

When the pier first opened there was little else that was man-made around this section of the waterfront but by the time the pier had come to its untimely end all of Tinside and the interconnecting pools and paths had been completed. Also all of West Hoe had been developed. Had this area not been extensively quarried around the middle of last century it is possible that the land sweeping around to Millbay would still today look much as the main Hoe foreshore does. However, quarried it was and in the late 1880s it is thought that among the many projects that the limestone from West Hoe helped to realize was the building of the St. Levan Road railway viaduct which was opened to traffic in 1890. In use for some 70 years, this massive structure was finally pulled down last year and strangely enough this latest Hoe development—the Hoe Dome—has been constructed with the limestone from the viaduct, prompting the architect of this scheme, Tony Irish, to believe that this limestone now stands but a matter of yards from where it was originally quarried.

The use of indigenous materials is, according to the architect, one of the main features of this development which, in a curious way, from this angle at least almost echo some of the lines of the Victorian pier. The dolphin here, although much bigger than the armrests on the pier weighs only 6–8 lb, it being made of GRP (glass reinforced plastic) and painted in gold leaf.

Standing on the site of the short lived and uninspiring Mallard Café (which first opened for business on Tuesday 13th April 1965) the Dome complex was begun a little over a year ago and is due to open soon. Yesterday, around midday, the Queen became its first official visitor and unveiled a commemorative plaque marking the 400th Anniversary of the Armada. However, although the structure of the building is almost complete and, says the architect, still within its original budget of 1.3 million pounds, there is still a lot of work to be done on the fixtures and fittings of this 'Hoe Interpretation Centre' which promise to transport visitors back in time using the most advanced technology of the present day.

While the Dome has undoubtedly had its critics it's likely ultimately to be the work that Tony Irish will be best remembered for. A Plymothian who has worked for the last 21 years on City buildings, his previous notable works include the award winning Magistrates' Court and the very successful campus-style comprehensive school at Lipson. Of all the work he has been involved in the Hoe Dome is, he feels, the one most likely to improve with age as the copper roof gradually turns green and the limestone weathers naturally. There can be little doubt that this building will come to represent to the coming generation what the Pier did to those who knew it in the past.

21st July, 1988.

East Hoe

300 years ago this week, on 6th February, 1685, Royalists mourned the death of Charles II. Surviving Parliamentarians doubtless did not mourn however. Their cause by then had been well and truly lost and amongst the many acts taken by Charles II to ensure there was no repeat of the civil uprising that had unseated and beheaded his father was the building of this massive Citadel here on the Hoe.

Plymouth had, of course, taken up Cromwell's Parliamentarian cause and been one of the deciding elements in their subsequent success, and in designing this fortress Sir Bernard Gomme was instructed not only to place cannons overlooking the entrance to the Port but also over the potentially unruly Plymothians themselves. In doing this the King took, some say stole, choice land from the City and within a handful of years from his accession the building had been commissioned. Six years later in 1671 the King came to Plymouth with his brother to inspect progress, returning in 1677 by which time it was thought to be complete.

Little changed from the outside at least; it was some 200 years before the view from this vantage point altered substantially. In 1888 a road was made (Madeira Road) around the front of the Citadel. Before that grass and rocky slopes ran from the Citadel walls to the sea, although its easternmost corner had a protected rampart which ran down to the Tudor Artillery Tower. There was a landing stage and protected area behind the western seaward corner where now stands the Royal Plymouth Corinthian Yacht Club just visible on the right of the picture. The basin here had been built largely with convict labour in the early eighteenth century and was primarily designed for small men o' war and supply vessels to enable men and matter to pass to and from the Citadel's cellars by means of a tunnel which is still there today. The arrival of the Yacht Club here towards the end of last century reflected both the declining need for these strategically placed defences and the growing interest in sailing and racing on the waves. Charles II would undoubtedly have approved for he is credited with being the man who introduced the sport into England.

Whether he would have been quite so keen on the Victorian Marine Biological Association building obscuring the low but nevertheless imposing lines of his Citadel is less certain.

The Association was founded in 1884 after interest in marine biology had been stimulated by two Germans, Karl August Mobius and Victor Hensen, working in Kiel Bay. Hensen, working from the middle of last century, was particularly interested in the study of fishes used as food and this became one of the principal areas of research for the Plymouth laboratories. Plymouth was chosen largely because of the rich and varied fauna available in this region of the English Channel where the boundaries of cold and warm water communities meet.

Prior to the establishment of the Association there was no institution concerned specifically with marine biology in this country although a great deal of work was done on board HMS *Challenger* which between 1872–6 went on a round the world scientific cruise sponsored by the Admiralty and the Royal Society.

In the event the first true land base in this country was established in Granton in Scotland; while an investigative committee was set up in Liverpool in 1885, but Plymouth had the first major laboratory and the building here was opened on 30th June 1888.

Today most countries in the world have their own coastal marine biological stations. The expanded and ever improving Plymouth station however continues to lead research in many areas.

While most of its work is done behind closed doors the aquarium at least gives locals and visitors alike some idea of what life is like beneath the waves.

Boer War Memorial

The Boers had originally settled in South Africa in the mid seventeenth century and were principally of Dutch, and later Huguenot, extraction. The word Boer comes from the Dutch 'boer'—a farmer or husbandman. The Boer War itself centred around the Transvaal Republic and Orange Free State in South Africa; here were based, primarily, Boers who had trekked northeastwards from Cape Colony to escape from the British who in 1814 had bought Cape Colony from the Dutch East India Company. At this time there were around 26,000 Boers in South Africa and, according to law, they became British subjects. However, in 1881 the British were unsuccessful in attempting to enforce their rights in arms and, after being defeated in the Battle of Majuba Hill, they recognized the Transvaal as an independent republic.

The discovery of gold on the Rand in this area a little later however, led to many Uitlanders (foreigners to the Transvaal), settling in the area and fighting began again in 1899 after the Boers steadfastly denied franchise and other civic rights to these people, many of whom were of British descent.

Much of the fighting of the Boer War is recorded on this memorial which was unveiled on 8th August 1903 by Lady Audrey Buller, wife of Sir Redvers Buller—the first commander in chief of the War in South Africa. In December 1899 Buller, together with some 20,000 men, was involved in an unsuccessful attempt to relieve the besieged British in Ladysmith and this setback, together with two others in the same 'black' week, alerted Britain and its Empire to the serious nature of the task before them. In addition to the many battles fought, the British were besieged in Ladysmith, Kimberley and Mafeking. The latter, defended by Baden-Powell (later renowned for his founding of the Boy Scout Movement), was under siege the longest and news of its relief on 16th May 1900 after 217 days, led to such 'uproarious scenes' and 'unrestrained exultation' in the centre of London when the news arrived on the 18th of May, that a new word entered our language—to maffick meaning to rejoice with hysterical boisterousness.

Further consequences of the Boer War were a real start in the development of British gunnery; firing guns from concealed positions, where the guns could not see the target and from which the fire had to be directed accurately, and the general adoption of the khaki (literally dustcoloured), uniforms in place of the hitherto traditional 'sitting duck', bright-red jackets. Thus, ironically, in many ways the Boer War prepared the British well for the First World War.

However, a nation and its people can never really prepare for such emotional upsets and this memorial, paid for by a South African merchant of West-country descent, Alfred Mosley, and originally intended to be sited in Bristol (whose authorities could find no suitable ground for it), is a sobering reminder of the cost of such warfare.

19th October 1985.

Standing proud, opposite the north western corner of the Citadel on Plymouth Hoe, is this large obelisk, carved out of red Swedish granite and mounted on a base of green Swedish granite which weighs about 17 tons and contains four bronze panels. The base is 'surmounted by a flowing Greek wave, emblematic of the sea, beyond which fell the brave soldiers to whose memory this monument is dedicated.'

Those brave soldiers were men of the Gloucestershire, Somersetshire and Devonshire Regiments who fell in the Boer War. Fought between 1899 and 1902 in South Africa, at the end of the war the British had 250,000 men down there; 5,774 men had been killed in the fighting, 22,829 wounded and 43,616 sent home either maimed or sick. Of the various conflicts Britain has been involved with, in the last two hundred years, the Boer War was notable for the British actually losing more men than its conquered foe; the Boers lost around 4,000 men. However, some 40,000 Boers—men, women and children, were held captive in conditions that, due to much improvisation and mismanagement, gave rise to a great deal of hardship and suffering and brought into our language the term concentration camp. Held partly to prevent them from helping guerilla commando units of Boers who, in small bands, were causing problems for the established British troops, and partly to secure adequate food for the Boer women and children, these camps were fraught with troubles.

The National Armada Memorial

Writing from the Drake Chamber of Plymouth Guildhall in April 1888, a committee, chaired and led by the Mayor, Henry J. Waring, produced a document outlining their proposals for commemorating the 'three hundredth anniversary of the Spanish Armada'.

'Since the matter was first mooted,' they wrote, 'a considerable amount of attention has been brought to bear upon the subject, public opinion has been aroused, the press, both London and Provincial, has expressed approval of the scheme, and a large and steadily increasing section of the community has declared in favour of celebrating, in some appropriate manner the tercentenary of so great a crisis in our national history. Into the details of the history of that time it is needless to enter; it is sufficient to say that the significance of the event cannot be over-estimated, for to the providential deliverance of this country from Spanish invasion and foreign sway, the English-speaking race the world over, is largely indebted for the liberty and privileges it now enjoys.'

If this does now seem a little overestimated to us, almost 100 years later, it is worth remembering that back in 1588 Philip II, King of Spain, had been determined to conquer England. Pope Sixtus V had already, formally, made England over to him and eminent Roman Catholic soldiers from all over Europe were ready to help the Spanish King deal a mighty blow at Protestantism. 30,000 men under the Duke of Parma, had been poised in Flanders waiting for the support of the Armada, which itself, eventually, consisted of 129 vessels, manned by 8,000 sailors and carrying 19,000 soldiers, with over 2,000 cannon and enough provisions to feed 40,000 men for 6 months. Figures that are put into some sort of perspective when it is remembered that although the population of Plymouth almost doubled in these troubled times, it would still have been less than 8,000 in total.

So confident, then, were the Spanish of their invasion fleet that they dubbed it the 'Invincible Armada'—literally, the armed force that can't be beaten. But beaten it was of course, thanks largely to the seamanship of the British naval commanders, the improved manoeuvrability of their main fighting ships (the British fleet was only three fifths the size of the Spanish), and the untimely natural death of the Spanish admiral, Santa Cruz.

This memorial, therefore, honours those men, notably Howard, Drake, Hawkins and Seymour—the four chief commanders in the campaign; the monarch, Queen Elizabeth I, and the cities, towns and ports that provided the men and the means to effect the defence of the realm. In the end plague and poverty probably accounted for more death within the English forces than the Spanish themselves, whose shores only ever saw the return of 54 of their massive fleet of 129 vessels.

Designed by Herbert A. Gribble with bronzes by W. Charles May, the Armada memorial looks very similar to its original design. The two old-style mortars (kindly lent by the War Department from Her Majesty Queen Victoria's Royal Arsenal at Woolwich) on either side as we see it, were supposed to be temporary but the two 'symbolic figures of heroic proportions, one representing Valour, the other Vigilance' have never appeared. And so the massive figure of Britannia, eleven foot six inches high, alone looks down upon the ground where nearby, on Friday 19th July

1588, Drake was supposed to have completed his legendary game of bowls, despite being interrupted with the news that the long-awaited Armada had been sighted off the Lizard.

24th August 1985

St. Katherine Upon the Hoe

'Ther is a righte goodly Walke on an Hille without the Toun by South, caullid the How, and a fair Chapel of S. Caterine on it.'

So wrote Henry VIII's Chaplain and Librarian, John Leland, who travelled England extensively between 1534 and 1543, and who came to 'Plymmouth' around 1538.

Today some 450 years after the Royal Antiquary's visit, it remains true to say that there is still a right, goodly walk to be had on the Hoe and further, that a fair Chapel of St. Katherine still stands upon it. However, a contemporary sixteenth-century map illustrates just how much without the town this chapel was, for in those far off days the whole population of Plymouth, as it was then, lived in an area huddled around the north and west banks of Sutton Pool; Old Town Street being the most north westerly point and the present site of Friary Station the most north easterly point. The town's western boundary was marked, appropriately enough, by St. Katherine's Street—a name that the Victorian Plymouth historian Henry Whitfield states derived from its being the 'approach to the fair Chapel of St. Catherine on the Hoe'. Today it is just known as Catherine Street but it still runs from the tower of St. Andrew's in the general direction of the present chapel.

The present chapel, however, is not the one John Leland would have seen, as that was pulled down in order to clear the Hoe for the building of the Citadel in 1666. The St. Katherine's we see today was rebuilt on the site of the former chapel in 1668 and its official title now reads 'The Royal Chapel of St. Katherine the Virgin upon the Hoe within the Royal Citadel'. Immaculately maintained and substantially altered in

1845 the second chapel has now been standing for a little over 300 years, which means that it has only recently surpassed its predecessor in terms of longevity, the original St. Katherine's first being mentioned 296 years before the building of the Citadel; that reference appearing in Bishop Thomas Brantyngham's *Register* of 1370 (Vol. 1, folio 10). Indeed a second reference in February of the following year, shows that on the 17th of that month the parishioners of Sutton were granted 'Licence to celebrate Divine Service in the Chapel of St. Katerine on the Howe in Suttone for one year, provided that on Sundays and Festivals they shall attend the Mother Church' (St. Andrew's). 600 years later, with St. Andrew's still the Mother Church, most major services here are conducted by the Vicar of St. Andrew's and the public Sunday service at 11.00 is regularly conducted by the Reverend John Watson.

Quite why a chapel was ever erected here in the first place has long been a matter of great conjecture, with theories ranging from it being built 'to counteract the lingering pagan appeal of Gogmagog' or that provision was made for it by Edward the Black Prince (who passed through the town on a number of occasions, notably for the last time in 1371); his followers; the local people of Suttone; or the prior of Plympton. It is even possible that a much earlier church stood on this site. Hilltop churches were common among the celts. The medieval St. Katherine's, judging from available illustrations, appears to have been about the size of the present structure, but with a lofty tower and enclosed by a low rounded wall. It stood along an east–west axis, as did the building that we see here, until it was given its cross formation by the addition of the north and south transepts. These alterations were carried out, under the Governorship of General the Hon. Sir Henry Murray, KCB, in 1845. Sir Henry also presented a font to the Garrison Chapel.

St. Katherine's had become, in some respects, a garrison chapel long before the building of the Citadel, as the earlier building was similarly enclosed by the fort that Drake had built on the Hoe soon after the thwarting of the Armada. Unusual then, in many respects, St. Katherine's is 'one of a very small number of Royal Chapels existing in the Empire'. King George V reasserted its claim to the 'Royal' title back in 1927. Indeed, Royalty appear to have always had a strong interest in Sutton—it was a Royal Manor in Saxon times, and the Domesday Book notes that 'the Kinge holde Sudtonie . . .'. The Chapel is also unusual in being dedicated to St. Katherine with a 'K'. Although the name can be spelt either way it is more common, in this instance, to spell it with a 'C'. St. Catherine herself was a virgin of royal descent in Alexandria. Following a public confession of Christianity, at a sacrificial feast, she was put to death (*c.* 310) by being tied to a wheel like that of a chaff-cutter. According to the legend, as soon as the wheel turned her bonds broke and she was beheaded. In later years, the good lady was adopted as the patron saint of wheelwrights. We also get, from this, the Catherine Wheel as applied to certain types of window, firework and, of course, the reckless pastime of turning head over heels on the hands!

18th April, 1987.

Norrington's Fountain

In November 1880, Marianne Norrington wrote a letter to the local paper expressing the hope that a fountain would be placed on the Hoe in order that tired and thirsty children might refresh themselves.

Mrs. Norrington had been a regular visitor to the Hoe with her own children—she had four sons and five daughters—and had often observed how hot boys and girls became in their play and how distressed they would get for want of water.

There were too, the 'girls who had perhaps dragged up some heavy baby from Higher Street or Briton Street' and 'had no means of satisfying their thirst'.

100 years ago the Hoe was as popular a place as it has ever been. Most people whiled away their leisure hours within walking distance of home and the Hoe was the nearest attraction for all Plymothians, but prams were not commonplace and iced lollies or cans and cartons of drink unheard of and anyway would be expensive for children, so a drinking fountain was a good solution.

Sadly, though, its protagonist passed away only months after her letter had appeared in the Press. Her husband, however, 'being desirous of raising some memorial to one so much lamented,' thought he could do no better than carry out what was her own wish.

Consequently, on one hot sunny day in June 1881, this fine fountain was 'unveiled' and as the plaque reads, 'Presented to the town of Plymouth by Charles Norrington in memory of his wife, Marianne Norrington, 1881. Thirsty and ye gave me drink.' The latter being taken from St. Matthew, chapter 25, verse 35. Charles Norrington was a keen churchman.

Born in Plymouth in 1820, Norrington was pretty much the self-made, Victorian gentleman, was much loved and respected locally and was a truly great philanthropist. Tragically his first son, Charles Henry, had died at the age of 25 in 1877 and in his memory Norrington presented a carillon and Westminster chimes to St. Andrew's Church and these could be heard ringing at the fountain presentation ceremony in 1881.

That year also saw the death of his second son, Harold, and in his memory, Norrington gave an aisle to the Church of St. John, Sutton-on-Plym, where he had earlier been a regular member of the congregation.

As a young man Charles Norrington had shown an interest in agricultural chemistry and had learnt much from both books and practice at his father's farm, Lamerton, in Tavistock. He went on to become a master of the science of artificial manures, often lecturing on the subject to local farmers.

In 1846 he set up the first artificial manure manufactory in the West of England, starting out on Commercial Wharf, later setting up extensive works in Cattedown within the newly created parish of St. John.

He entered Plymouth's Town Council in 1852 and later changed his Church allegiance to Emmanuel when, like so many of his peers, he moved out to the growing Victorian villa suburb of the town, Mannamead, to his presumably, purpose built residence, Abbotsfield, in Seymour Road.

In 1863 Charles Norrington was made Mayor of Plymouth and, like his predecessor William Derry, was given the unusual privilege of being allowed to

retain the office for a second consecutive term. Derry was made Mayor again, in 1879 and attended the presentation of Norrington's fountain and no doubt Norrington had been at the presentation of Derry's Clock back in 1862.

Derry's Clock was also supposed to have been a fountain but as no money had been available for a clock, it was decided to construct a fountain with a clock on it. Water was never run through Derry's fountain, however, but for many years it did through Norrington's although sadly the flow has not been 'perpetual', as promised by Mayor Francis Morrish in 1881.

Charles Norrington died in June 1900. His obituary in the *Western Daily Mercury* was headlined 'One of Plymouth's Greatest Philanthropists' and spoke of his popularity among the rich and poor alike, his many interests in general welfare, his setting up of a soup kitchen in the east end of town and his efforts in establishing a House for Incurable Cripples in Wyndham Square.

It also spoke of the time he had received the famous red-shirted Italian 'liberator', Garibaldi, when he passed through Plymouth in 1864 and the time he hosted the Prince and Princess of Wales at a ball where French and English officers met socially for the first time since the Battle of Waterloo!

Today, however, he is best remembered for this 20-foot high memorial to his wife on the Hoe, topped by an almost lifesize sculpture of Rebecca of the Well, crafted by Samuel Trevenen. Until 1982, almost hidden for 20 years by the Hoe Theatre, it now stands restful but dry, with its own place in local history.

24th April, 1986

Blitz the Dog

There are memorials on Plymouth Hoe to those soldiers, sailors and Royal Marines who died in the 1939–45 War. There is soon to be an RAF memorial, but there is no such token of remembrance here for more than a thousand citizens of Plymouth, who lost their lives in the 59 bombing raids that were carried out on this city, in that period. There is, however, a simple cross that by rights should hang on the tall tree by the Hoe putting green, erected in memory of 'Blitz', the dog mascot of Mill Street Rescue Depot.

The original cross (it has been replaced several times after being removed by vandals), was put up some time in the late forties. Blitz had been adopted by the Mill Street Rescue Squad in January 1941 after running into their post one night after an air raid. Thought to be a stray or perhaps an 'orphan', Blitz, as he was christened, was cared for by the men of the squad and from then on where the men went—Blitz went. At night the little light tan mongrel would sit in an old rocking-chair and keep an eye on everyone, and if after a hard day's work a few started to doze,

Blitz would wake them up with his barking, at the slightest sound of trouble outside the depot. Whenever the squad were mobilized the agile animal would leap up on the lorry and head off with the men who, in turn, used to discuss who would look after the dog when the war came to an end. Sadly, however, for Blitz that moment never came for on 26th August 1942, he was run down by a heavy service vehicle in Union Street, where he was with the squad on demolition work. William Wood, a carpenter and one of the Depot men, later made the first cross and Edward Butler, another squad member, signed an agreement with the corporation that the cross would be hung on a particular tree every day thereafter. Unfortunately, in the interests of safe-keeping, the cross is now kept inside the little hut on the edge of the putting-green. The reason for choosing this site, incidentally, is because during the war the putting-green site was used for allotments and here the Mill Street men 'dug for victory' with Blitz alongside them. As Pat Twyford, the local journalist who kept a detailed diary of Plymouth during those grim days, notes it was 'probably the first time in history' that vegetables were grown on the top of the Hoe. All in all, this site, and others in the various corporation parks and even in the grounds attached to local hospitals, yielded many, many tons of potatoes each year.

In those days of course, this is where the Hoe Park properly began—south of Citadel Road. Now the approach to the Hoe (Armada Way) starts way back beyond Mayflower Street part of which, around the area of the 'Good Companions' public house, covers the site of Mill Street, now just a name from the past, like so many other pre-war parts of the city centre.

At the beginning of the war, Plymouth was a tightly packed, busy and thriving place. With a population not dissimilar to that of today, it occupied about half the acreage of the present city. After many thousands of high-explosive bombs had been dropped and an estimated quarter of a million incendiary devices—'one for every man, woman and child of the pre-war population' (Frank Wintle *The Plymouth Blitz*) the two main shopping centres had been destroyed; so had 26 schools, 41 churches and 100 pubs. In addition to these, a number of other public buildings went, as did 3754 houses and more than 18,000 were left in need of major repair. Of the 4448 adult and child civilian casualties, 1172 were killed.

Six years ago a memorial bench and plaque was unveiled, in Portland Square, where 72 people lost their lives in a direct hit on an air raid shelter. As yet, however, there is no Hoe memorial for blitz victims other than that for Blitz the dog. André Savignon, who produced an account of his days in the city *With Plymouth through Fire* (1940–41), would doubtless be amused. Walking through Ebrington Street, at the height of the troubles in 1941, he recorded this passage 'Here is Ebrington Street. Near the Catholic Church . . . a monster poster that reads: "Plymouth Society for the Total Abolition of Vivisection STOP VIVISECTION! It is UNSCIENTIFIC, IMMORAL, ILLOGICAL"', then he adds 'though mercy on mankind be out of fashion, in England some people still take pity on the animals'.

23rd May 1987.

The Naval War Memorial

'It has been the British destiny to venture greatly at sea, in peace and in war, and the time is not yet in sight when this long history will be ended'.

So runs the opening sentence to the Introduction to the Registers of those 15,608 men and 6 women who 'have no other grave but the sea' and whose names are recorded in the bronze panels set in the winged extensions to the earlier Naval War Memorial, here on Plymouth Hoe. The original memorial is one of three identical monuments each with 'an obelisk, supported at the four corners of the base by buttresses . . . each of the four buttresses carries a sculptured figure of a lion couchant, looking outwards.'

The two other memorials are sited at Portsmouth and Chatham and, together, the three commemorate 'the names of those Officers and Men of the Navies of the Empire' who fell in the First World War and 'who have no other grave than the sea'. Around 48,000 naval personnel of the Dominions were lost in the First World War, of which nearly half died on land. The Plymouth memorial commemorates 7,268 of those lost at sea. It was unveiled in 1924 by one of George V's five sons, Prince George (later the Duke of Kent who died in active service in 1942). The design for the original three monuments was the work of Sir Robert Stodart Lorimer, the Scottish architect famous for restoring ancient, Scottish buildings and drawing up the Scottish National War Memorial in Edinburgh Castle.

The main enemy menace to the British Navy during the 1914–18 war was undoubtedly the German submarine campaign, a campaign which peaked in 1917 when submarines sank 1,134 British ships, representing a tonnage in excess of 3 million. At one time one in four ships leaving British ports failed to return and in one month alone, April 1917, 196 ships were lost. Improved anti-submarine weapons and the introduction in May 1917 of the convoy system helped combat the submarine threat at sea, but in 1918 the decision was taken to block the two ends of the Bruges canal, Ostend and Zeebrugge, which was being used as a German submarine base and which, because of its location, posed a major problem for British shipping in the English Channel. The subsequent daring raid on Zeebrugge when the Navy approached under cover of a smoke screen, invented by Wing-Commander Brock (who lost his life in the engagement), was hailed as a major success. It was certainly the most famous of the contributions by the Marines to the Great War effort, as they stormed the mole or outer harbour wall to divert enemy fire from the three old cruisers, *Intrepid*, *Iphigenia* and *Thetis*, which were sent in as blockships, full of cement and explosives, to seal off the canal. Zeebrugge and Ostend are among those actions recorded on the fourth panel of the original memorial.

Like its Chatham and Portsmouth counterparts, the Hoe memorial was also intended to serve as a 'Leading-mark' or 'Sea-mark' for ships entering the port. However, what no-one could have envisaged in 1924 is that twenty years later, in the aftermath of the Second World War air attack on Plymouth, this obelisk would be used as a landmark by the principal architects of the rebuilding of Plymouth's city centre. It is perhaps hard for the City's post war generation to appreciate that, as late as 1954 when the Second World War extensions to the Memorial were unveiled by Prince George's niece Princess Margaret, Windsor Terrace, running along the line of

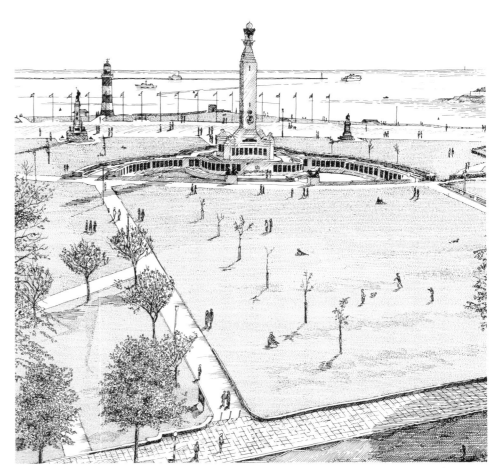

Citadel Road, would completely have obscured this view. Today, Armada Way, running north from this pivotal point, is a little too readily taken for granted and, perhaps, pedestrianisation of more northern stretches will enhance and focus attention on this wonderful boulevard, bestowed on the City by James Paton-Watson and Patrick Abercrombie. But it is a shame that there is no central walkway to this monument, as envisaged in the original plan and in the later drawings of Sir Edward Maufe, who designed the extensions to the Memorial. Although similar to the Portsmouth extensions, Maufe (who also designed Guildford Cathedral) had the problem in Plymouth of trying not to intrude on the lines of the Hoe and so he came up with the idea of sunken memorial gardens, which come but a few inches above the level of the paved platform of the original memorial. In addition, the many names recorded here are also graced by some fine bronze sculpture by M. W. McMillan (Neptune and Amphitrite) guarding the northern entrance, and the haunting sailor and marine stone statues by McMillan and Charles Wheeler. Of the many inscriptions one now stands out above all others—

'All these were honoured in their generations, and were the glory of their times.'

14th March 1987.

Plymouth Hoe

While there are, doubtless, still those who mourn the passing of the Hoe Theatre, there can be no denying that it was good to regain a large green area of the Hoe. Plymouth Hoe is a delightful wide open space with a view that has changed little down the years. Hopefully, it will long remain that way; however, already houses in the Staddiscombe area are marshalling like troops just beyond the ridge, seemingly poised at any moment, to break across the skyline and deface the natural beauty of the eastern side of the Sound. Mount Edgcumbe to the west, is for the foreseeable future, safe from the developers, but is only part of the frame of this wonderful harbour and, like any well framed scene, all sides are important.

Certainly, in recent years the City has done well to remove some of the less aesthetic man-made intrusions on to the Hoe itself. The Hoe Theatre, which was never intended to be a permanent structure, nevertheless stood for 20 years until it was pulled down five years ago. The massive blimp that was the Hoe Café also long outlived its original purpose and even the poor old Mallard Café could hardly be described as a major contribution to the appearance of the Hoe. It remains to be seen whether or not the building that replaces it will add to the general scenery; hopefully it will.

Up until the 1880s there had been little development of the Hoe outside of the Citadel but in that decade the Hoe promenade and adjoining paths were laid out and a rash of memorials, monuments and major constructions appeared. In addition to the building of the Mountbatten Breakwater and the cutting of the road in front of the Citadel, that decade witnessed the erection on the Hoe of Norrington's fountain (1881), Smeaton's Tower (1882), Drake's Statue (1884), Plymouth Pier (1884), the Hoe Lodge and formal gardens (1887–8), the Armada Memorial (1888)

and the imposing Marine Biological Association buildings (1888). With the exception of the bathing facilities on the water's edge around Tinside, it's probably true to say that there were more changes made to the appearance of the main part of the Hoe in those ten years than there have been in the hundred that have followed it. For the most part, these later additions have been war memorials; the Boer War, the 1914–18 War, the Naval Memorial extended to commemorate both wars and the Royal Marines' Memorial, situated in front of the south western corner of the Citadel. The latter, just visible here, was unveiled in 1921. Sculpted in bronze by W. C. Storr-Barber of Leominster, the figures depict St. George slaying the eagle of militarism and underneath is the inscription 'Erected by the Plymouth Division Royal Marines (Past, Present and Relatives) to the memory of their comrades who fell in the Great War 1914–1918', to which has been added '1939–45'. There is also a quotation from John Bunyon's *Pilgrim's Progress*, on the front 'So he passed over and all the trumpets sounded for him on the other side'.

Norrington's Fountain, which stands adjacent to the site occupied by the Hoe Theatre, has itself been moved from the other side of the Hoe. Originally it stood in the area of the Hoe bowling green. The formal gardens and Caretaker's Lodge, meanwhile, have altered little since they were laid out 100 years ago; one major change being the erection of the Prejoma clock, which stands on a pole in the middle of the gardens. This replaced a modest fountain and was provided for under the terms of the will of Preston John Ball, who bequeathed £2,000 for a clock to be known as the Prejoma Clock, in memory of his parents John and Mary Ball; the name of the clock deriving from the first letters of each christian name.

2nd May 1987.

Bowls on the Hoe

'There is time enough to finish the game and fight/beat/lick/thrash the Spaniards afterwards. . . .' So runs one of the most widely accredited quotations of all time. The man who is supposed to have uttered those words, or words very much like them of course, is the man whose statue has, for over 100 years now, looked out on the scene of his many comings and goings—Sir Francis Drake.

Over the years there have been many who have doubted that Drake would ever have said such a thing, but his biographers and most of those who have studied him are sure enough that such a gesture of bravado, guaranteed to dispel any mad panic around him, is typical of this brilliant and intuitive sea captain. Besides which, all the evidence suggests that at the time, on the 19 July 1588, when Drake would have received news of the sighting of the Armada (which he had been looking for in Spain), the winds and the tide were so set against him that it would not have been possible for him to manoeuvre his fleet out of Sutton Harbour for five hours or more. Even then it would appear that it was necessary to tow the ships out of the harbour one by one across the Hoe to the shelter of Rame, an operation that ran long into the night, making the most of the outgoing tide. Thus on the morning of the 20th July, the English fleet were out in the Sound, just beyond the island fast becoming known as Drake's Island, ready and waiting to 'fetch a wind'. Then it was that Drake chased after the Spanish, who had undoubtedly erred in not trying to bottle up the English fleet and in allowing Drake to get down wind of them.

Indeed throughout the rest of the July campaign it is probably true to say that the Spanish were not so much defeated at sea as thwarted by the winds, superior English seamanship and ultimately a lack of water and provisions.

But what of the game of bowls itself? The first written record of it comes from a pamphlet published in Spain in 1624, in which the Duke of Braganza is quoted as saying 'Did we not in '88 carry our business for England so secretly . . . as in bringing our navy to their shores while their commanders were at bowls upon the Hoe of Plymouth?' But is it really likely that it was played here on top of the Hoe as Lucas's famous painting suggests, with the Island and Sound behind him? Certainly on this score, the evidence suggests that Drake and his officers were more likely to have been on the Eastern side of the Hoe where the fleet, in Sutton Harbour, could have been clearly viewed. This in turn condemns the idea of Drake playing bowls in Charles Kingsley's 'Pelican Inn', to the realms of artistic fantasy. However, the idea of a 'little terrace bowling green behind the 'Pelican Inn', as described in Canon Kingsley's *Westward Ho!*, is typical enough of Elizabethan England. Such bowling alleys were extremely popular in the sixteenth century and indeed the game, frequently linked to 'gambling and dissipation' and to the decline in standards of archery, had been the subject of acts of Parliament outlawing it since the days of Edward III and Richard II early in the fourteenth century. It wasn't until Henry VIII's time though that bias was introduced into this ball game, when according to legend, Charles Brandon, playing a game in Yorkshire, split his wooden ball then ran off to the nearest house and cut off the top of a newel post. When he came to play with this unbalanced ball, flat where it had been cut, he found he could curve his ball around his opponents', reaching positions previously covered. Delighted, the said

Mr. Brandon gave a £5 reward to the house owner for his troubles and his mutilated staircase. Henry VIII, however, passed an Act forbidding anyone to play bowls unless they were 'wealthy and well to do'. The Act (which wasn't repealed until 1845!) also forbade anyone to 'keep, have, hold, occupy, exercise or maintain any common house, alley or place of bowling'. The legislation was not very effective and in 1579 Common Bowling Alleys were said to 'eat up the credit of many idle citizens, whose gains at home are not able to weigh down their losses abroad' and consequently 'their wives and children cry out for bread, and go to bed superlese ofte in the yeare!' As Shakespeare's Hamlet said 'Ay, there's the rub'. Shakespeare used many bowling metaphors in his plays and these would not only suggest that the game was very popular in his, and Drake's, day but that the great bard himself may have been a player. Certainly, by the time of James I, the game had grown high in Royal favour and Charles I and II were both enthusiastic players.

Today bowls is one of the largest participation games in Britain—there are well over 1,000 registered players in Plymouth alone and in recent years the impact of television has done much to increase interest in the game among the young and old— indeed age is no great bar to this game at all. There is record of one American who was playing the game daily well after his 103rd birthday!

One hundred years ago, for the Armada's tercentenary celebrations, a game was played within the walls of the Citadel and thousands turned up to witness it, although most of them drifted away when they couldn't see the play. Neither side was local. Today there are many local teams and, in recent years, the Hoe Public Bowling Green has been one of the City's most popular 'stop and watch' places on the tourist circuit.

28th March 1987.

No Place Inn

'Where have you been all the day?'
'No Place!'

Signboard of inn.

So reads the second line of page 18 of the Appendix of Henry Whitfeld's 600-page history of Plymouth and Devonport published in 1900. Whether we are to deduce from it that both the question and answer made up the signboard or that the inn was simply called the 'No Place', is unclear. The situation is further confused when we read W. H. Wright's 1879 *Walkabout tour of the Three Towns*; 'Here,' he says 'we are now at "No-place" and it will be noticed that the inn at the corner bears the name "No-place Inn", while a signboard gives an artistic definition of the title, which we will leave for our friends to decipher to the best of their ability.'

However what is clear is that on street maps from 1830–1880 the terrace of houses stretching 100 yards or so eastwards from here was marked as 'Noplace' whilst the street directories variously gave the address of the Inn as North Place, Stoke Lane, Stoke Hill and Eldad. In those days of course you could have stood outside the door here and looked right across Stonehouse Creek to Penlee Gardens with only a handful of isolated buildings standing in the view. North Road was growing in a somewhat disorderly way on the south side with very little building at all having been completed on the north side.

By 1885 the story was different; Five Fields Lane, Four Fields Lane, Densham Terrace, Torrington Place, Hundiscombe (sic) and Clarendon Terrace had all joined up and merged into one long road—North Road. The No Place was no longer 1 North Place but 156 North Road—later 353 North Road. In the previous decade North Road Station had opened, some 30 years after the great railway engineer Isambard Kingdom Brunel had recommended nearby 'No Place' as the best site available for a station for the Three Towns. Had the station been constructed here, the 'No Place Inn' might have enjoyed a very different history. However despite Brunel's dismay at the jealousies between the Three Towns which he referred to even then as 'one long straggling community', the first local terminus was sited at Millbay.

The 'No Place' has thus endured a much quieter neighbourhood than might otherwise have been the case and from the 1840s through to the 1920s at least the Inn was in the hands of the Dodd family. John Dodd was here as owner/licensee for many years initially: after the mid 1850s however a variety of licensees held the pub. Such is not to say that no member of the Dodd family was here as licensee thereafter but it was not generally the case. Nevertheless, the Inn stayed in the family well into this century when it was eventually bought by Charles Blundell's local brewery, which was then operating from pre-war Westwell Street.

Around this time the 'No Place' went through a great number of landlords; there were seven in the twenty years between the wars. The arrival of Fred Philpott in 1941 however marked the beginning of a new period of stability and with two exceptions at the dawn of the 1950s all subsequent 'No Place' landlords have stayed 5 years or more, as Jack Darlington was followed by Fred Polden, then Jim Cookson, Barry Phillips and since February last year, Mick and Rowena Smith, for whom the pub is a first.

The Pub has had minor alterations inside in the last twelve months; the old off sales snug area is now part of the lounge bar. From the outside though little has changed, either with regard to the Pub or its neighbours. The long, high wall of the Royal Naval Hospital has forever dominated its western aspect while behind it can be seen a rare brick Victorian sewer-gas chimney outlet and the tower of St. Peter's Wyndham Square. Built around the former Eldad Chapel (begun in 1828) and described by R. N. Worth last century as being built in the first field of 'Noplace Lane', this further adds to the mystery surrounding the coining of this name.

Finally, and to further confuse matters, Mick and Rowena say they frequently get 'phone calls and taxis intended for the 'Nowhere Inn', behind the main library, beside the Co-op Dairy—but that's another story!

4th January, 1986.

Corporation Grammar School

According to C. W. Bracken, author of a history of the Corporation Grammar School and its headmaster between 1909 and 1929, this school building was the last home of what was in its day the City's oldest school. It was, after all, his contention that the Corporation Grammar was a direct descendant of the school founded by the Mayor and Corporation and Townspeople in 1561 and known in its earliest years as the Latin School and the Free Grammar School. He further adds that 'about 1823 the name "Corporation" was prefixed to distinguish it from the New Grammar School, a private venture then established'.

Today it still says 'Corporation Grammar School' on the front of the building, but this summer marks the 50th anniversary of the school's closing. Frank Sandon was its last Head and if we are to go back to 1561, Thomas Brooke was its first. His brief then, to freely teach all the children, native and inhabitant within the Town and to 'teache no other but gramer and writinge'. For this he was to be paid ten pounds a year.

Interestingly enough, this move took place a little more than 20 years after Henry VIII had dissolved the monasteries and chantries which up until then had served a very useful educational role within communities. It also antedated, by more than ten years, the Letters Patent of Elizabeth I requiring the establishment of free grammar schools.

For the next three hundred years, during which time many of the City's influential citizens from one generation to the next passed through its doors, the school was conducted in the Almshouse Chapel and in the purpose-built schoolhouse in the Orphans Aid quadrangle off Catherine Street, on part of the complex later pulled down to make way for the New Guildhall and the Municipal buildings. In 1858 the school was moved to Alfred Place, then in 1866 on to Princess Square, before moving again to Park Street in 1885. In the last two moves the school joined with, and nominally took over, existing schools (the New Grammar School and Park Grammar School respectively). In January 1909 the school began a very brief sojourn in the old Plymouth Technical College before finally coming to rest here in North Road.

Built in the 1890s by the local School Board set up in the wake of the 1870 Education Act (which locally revealed some 2,000 children were receiving no education at all), it was one of 18 Board schools to have been completed in Plymouth by 1903. That year, however, School Boards disappeared, local education authorities were set up and schooling was now split into primary and secondary education. Indeed the move to the Technical College had involved the Grammar's amalgamation with the Municipal Secondary School which was not only the first of its kind in Plymouth, but was also 'mixed'. C. W. Bracken was its Headmaster. For the best part of 30 years then, the Corporation Grammar had its home in North Road. Once again, many eminent people passed through it, including the author of the two volume 'Plymouth A New History', Crispin Gill, whose work admirably superseded Bracken's own 'History of Plymouth'. Many other former pupils became Headmasters or Headmistresses themselves, many are still alive today and most still bitter about the local authority's decision to close the school in 1937. 'Professional jealousy'

is how Stanley Goodman, another prominent old boy, described this act of execution. The official excuse at the time was that the buildings were 'unsuitable for educational purposes' but strangely enough that's all they've ever been used for since, Public Primary School having their home here until 1961, when the then head W. H. Wilmot retired. The school was then used for a while by Public Secondary and the Technical College. More recently it has been the home of the School of Chiropody and, although it is also used by the Languages and Travel and Tourism Departments of the College of Further Education, it is the Chiropodists who will be taking over the whole building from next year. Then the present 'temporary' buildings at the back will be demolished to make way for a car park and the old buildings will be refurbished to accommodate what is the only School of Chiropody west of Bristol and one of only thirteen in the United Kingdom.

Properly understood to include both hands and feet, chiropody, as recognized by the British Medical Association, is the 'treatment of malformed nails and superficial excrescences occurring on the feet (such as corns, warts, callosities) and bunions'. An estimated 80% of the population will need the services of a chiropodist at some time or another yet it was only with the 1960 'Professions Supplementary to Medicine Act' that this art or science reached full professional status. A disproportionate number of 'patients', and there are already over 5,000 on the books here in North Road, will be women whose foot problems are all too often associated with their footwear! Consequently, health education as well as remedial work is an important part of the students' work. There are about sixty students here and few, if any, will have trouble finding work as nationally there is a greater demand than there is supply of qualified people in this unfashionable area of health care. Although, as the School's Head Lewis Russell points out, Plymouth itself is quite well off for chiropodists and certainly the facilities at the 'School' would surprise many, as a number of minor operations can be performed here, as can the expert fitting of foot pads as well as countless other means of alleviating pedestrian problems.

27th June 1987.

St. Dunstans

1848—Miss Lydia Sellon came to Plymouth after reading of the Bishop of Exeter's appeal for help to relieve the spiritual and moral destitution of the Three Towns, with particular reference to the need for the education of children.

Miss Sellon began her educational work with a friend, in a room in Milne Place, Devonport. Her efforts were instantly successful and Bishop Philpotts of Exeter came down early in 1849 and sanctioned the establishment of the Sisterhood, then known as the Devonport Society. And in Devonport it might well have stayed had it not been for the terrible outbreak of cholera in the Three Towns that summer. Stonehouse Lane–King Street was one of the main problem areas. The Reverend George Rundle Prynne at St. Peters, in whose parish it was, records how Miss Sellon visited him and offered her services and those of her fellow 'Sisters of Mercy'. A temporary hospital was promptly erected in the fields above the Mere (the 'marshy boulder-strewn inlet which in older days was Stonehouse Creek') and in the three months that this hospital was open, records show 121 patients died and 177 were discharged. Many more died without reaching the hospital.

The following year Lydia Sellon bought the land on which the hospital had stood and here, founded St. Dunstan's Abbey, named in honour of St. Dunstan of Glastonbury, who had connections with the West country and was noted for his educational work and his attempts at reviving the monastic discipline in the Anglo-Saxon church. There appears though, to be no proper grounds for using the title 'Abbey'. However, that is the name that has stuck through the many changes here.

On 5th October 1850, following the Consecration of St. Peter's Church, a procession of clergy, choristers and scholars (belonging to several charities) joined the Sisters of Mercy on the Abbeymere site and laid the foundation stone of a 'House of Religion and Charity'. The Rev. Henry Philpotts officiated at this ceremony, which was said to be the first occasion since the dissolution of the monasteries that a Bishop of the Church of England had blessed the foundation of a religious house. Dr. Edward Pusey, a friend and patron of Miss Sellon, was also at the ceremony. Pusey had founded the small 'Community of the Holy Cross' in London, and this undoubtedly influenced Miss Sellon, who was a visitor there in 1845. This community was the first true revival of religious life in the English Church since the Reformation and through Pusey it was closely linked to St. Dunstans. The Plymouth Sisters kept a small room above the entrance, shown here, for Dr. Pusey's use. The strong 'Anglo-Catholic' attitudes of Pusey and his followers, including the Sisters and the Rev. Prynne at St. Peters, provoked much local opposition. There was trouble with rioters on 5th October, and it is said that the walls of St. Dunstan's were built high to deter hostile persons.

Designed by William Butterfield, who was also a follower of the Anglo-Catholic Movement, the architect made no charge for his designs for St. Dunstan's. A celebrated church architect, Butterfield was also responsible for Keble College, Oxford, founded by another Anglo-Catholic champion, John Keble.

Although the original plans were never fully completed, St. Dunstans soon took shape. However, in 1907 the Sisters of the Holy Trinity (as they had become in 1856) decided to discontinue their work in Plymouth, in favour of expanding a later base at Ascot, where they are still to be found today. Fortunately though, through the efforts of the then Vicar of St. Peters, Father Downton, the Community of St. Mary the Virgin, Wantage, was persuaded to take on the lease of the buildings and add the school to their list of 'Wantage Schools'. These ladies themselves later pulled out of the school after almost 50 years, to concentrate their efforts elsewhere and once again the school was threatened with closure.

Developed by this time to Public School status, it appeared to be an uneconomic proposition to take on a fully paid, qualified staff. However, again thanks to the initiative of one man, parent governor Harold Gambrell, sufficient support was obtained to launch the school on these lines as an Independent Church of England School for Girls with a lay headmistress. To date, since the reopening in September 1956, there have been only two headmistresses; first Mary Tamplin, then Hazel Abley, who took over in 1970.

With the same motto as Oxford University—Dominus Illuminatio Mea—The Lord is my Light—St. Dunstan's Abbey School today welcomes pupils of all creeds. It is intentionally a small school, around 40 girls in each year, and it has impressive academic results. This year the fourth side of what has always been known as the quad has been completed. Sympathetically designed to blend with the existing listed structures, this is the new sixth form centre and it will have its official opening on the 19th May, St. Dunstan's Day. A day which promises to be rather special as 1988 marks the 1,000th anniversary of the death of this former Archbishop of Canterbury and patron saint of Goldsmiths—St. Dunstan.

23rd April 1988.

Plymouth Cathedral

'This lofty structure is situate in Cecil Street, and is one of the finest structures of the kind in the West of England. The building which is in the Gothic style, is 150 feet long, 50 feet wide, and 77 feet across the transept. The walls are of rough ashlar, and the doors and windows, etc., are finished with worked Bath stone. The building will cost in erection £5000, and is fixed to be open for public worship on the 4th of August in the present year.'

That 'present year' was 1857 and work had begun on the building the previous year, the foundation stone having been laid by the Rev. Dr. Vaughan, the new bishop of the Roman Catholic diocese, in June 1856. However, the Cathedral did not open on the appointed day in August for, in the event, the unforeseen happened; in the current booklet on the Cathedral we read 'After many vicissitudes the Cathedral was opened on Lady Day, 25 March 1858'.

The most notable of these 'vicissitudes' occurred in June 1857, just before the authors of our Guide of that year went to press, hence we find the following post script . . . 'Since writing the above, a catastrophe has happened, showing the utter fallibility of human calculations. The lofty structure described above has become nothing more than a heap of ruins. About 3 o'clock on the afternoon of Wednesday, the 3rd June, about 70 feet of the western end of the building fell in, owing it is said to defective materials; and on the following Tuesday the whole of the remaining portion gave way, leaving only the asp, about 8 feet in length, and the outer walls (which were materially damaged) standing.'

The roof had not long been completed, however, when on Tuesday 2nd June the builder, Mr. Roberts, had noted certain defects which gave him cause for concern and he telegraphed the Architect, who was in Bristol and who immediately made his way down to Plymouth. On Wednesday morning the architect inspected the work and found that the Bath stone columns had proved to be too weak to support the weight on them and had split; consequently the arches would have to be shored up before the defective work could be removed. Unfortunately, however, there wasn't enough time for this and realising that the structure was about to collapse the architect cleared the building of the 40 or 50 men who were working on it and finally made his own exit, but not before a piece of falling masonry caught and bruised his arm.

Needless to say the disaster caused a great sensation and large crowds came to view the scene. Happily though, it was all put right and the main building has stood now for 130 years, surviving some damage during the Blitz, but without further major incidents, which is what you would expect of a building designed by Joseph Aloysius

Hansom. A celebrated architect and a Roman Catholic himself, Hansom was responsible for many English churches and public buildings, including Birmingham Town Hall. But he is, perhaps, best remembered as the man who invented the Hansom 'safety cab', a design he patented in 1834 and which earned him the princely sum of £300. Hansom also, incidentally, founded the trade journal 'The Builder' in 1842.

The Cathedral was eventually opened on the same day that the Virgin Mary is believed to have told Bernadette at Lourdes in France—'I am the immaculate conception', so it is an auspicious day in the Roman Catholic Calendar.

Dedicated to St. Mary and St. Boniface, the Cathedral in Plymouth was founded by the man who was appointed Bishop of Plymouth by the Pope in 1855 and who, although then in semi-retirement, was still in office in 1902 when he died in St. Augustine's Priory, Abbotskerswell. This 47-year tenure stands today as being the longest of any English bishop.

The Cathedral of Bishop Vaughan is not, however, Plymouth's first 'Cathedral'. This distinction belongs to a small chapel, St. Mary and St. John the Evangelist, in St. Mary Street, Stonehouse near the Royal Naval Hospital. This was erected in 1806 by a French refugee, M. Guilbert, and this was where the Roman Catholic Bishop of Plymouth, Dr. George Errington, came following his appointment in 1851. Technically, a Cathedral is that building which houses the 'cathedra', a Latin word which describes the chair of authority or the Bishop's throne.

Clearly this small chapel was hardly suitable as a centre from which the Bishop was to guide and rule his diocese and this was Bishop Vaughan's reasoning when he arranged the purchase of a large area of meadow land just up from King Street West, which was, we are told, in the middle of last century 'the favoured resort of the Irish population' and also 'the rallying ground of beggars, tramps, costermongers and other "professional" characters.'

Within ten years of the main body of the church being completed, the impressive spire, said to be the tallest in Devon, it is around 210 feet high, was added.

Today the Cathedral is the Mother Church of some 130 Catholic parish churches or chapels of ease, covering a diocese that embraces Devon, Cornwall and Dorset; a large area, but one which has a catholic population a little under half the national average, which is about ten per cent of the population.

The present Bishop, the eighth, Christopher Budd, was enthroned early in 1986 following Cyril Restieaux who retired after 31 years in the chair.

16th April 1988.

Wyndham Lane Sewer Gas Chimney

Among the gases found in sewers are methane, carbon dioxide, coal gas and hydrogen sulphide. Nowadays every house has its own sewer ventilation outlet; back in the 1880s when most of Plymouth's sewerage system was originally laid, they did not and, apart from drains and manholes, the solution to the problem of noxious gases took a variety of forms. On the Barbican, where the build up of such evil fumes was particularly bad, there is still to be seen a lamp-post which was once lit with sewer gas. Meanwhile here in Wyndham Lane, this 100 year old, 60 foot high, red-brick chimney still ensures that any sewer gases are dispersed well above head and house height.

In the darker days of Victorian England, before the passing of the 1875 Public Health Act, the whole question of sanitation had become a major issue for the first time. It had been brought to a head by overcrowding, inferior water supplies and the increased use of an object we now all tend to take for granted – the water closet. Sir John Harrington produced one of the earliest designs for the 'W. C.' back in 1596, but it wasn't until 1778, when Joseph Bramah patented his first water closet, that its development really took off. Even then up until 1820, liquid sewage was generally disposed of in cesspools, the main purpose of sewers being to drain off storm and excess rain water to stop the lower levels of a district flooding. As A. Hamilton-Bampton wrote in a lecture he delivered at the Athenaeum in Plymouth in 1849—

'Sewers have only been used to carry off the contents of house-drains since the introduction of water-closets, and the abundant use of water generally'. Then he added 'At no distant period it was an indictable offence in London to permit the filth from a cesspool to overflow into the public sewer ... There is a restraint of this nature in one of the districts of Plymouth'.

Plymouth in the 1840s did not present, overall, a very pretty picture. Investigations by the Unitarian minister W. J. Odgers revealed that 27 streets (containing 3,300 inhabitants) had no sewers and a further 53 streets (with 9,996 inhabitants) were 'very imperfectly sewered', while there were many more living in houses, either badly drained or with no drains at all. At this time W.C.'s were rare in most areas and even privies were few and far between in certain places. In one street just off King Street, there was one privy to every sixty-six inhabitants, a fairly staggering statistic especially when taken in conjunction with Hamilton-Bampton's observation that 'The excrement and other solid refuse of each adult is usually assumed to be one ton annually'. On that basis, 60 adults would be generating over one ton per week. Small wonder that visiting Inspector Robert Rawlinson from the General Board of Health found, after a lengthy inquiry into 'the sanitary condition of this Borough', that Plymouth 'ranks amongst the most unhealthy towns of Great Britain'.

Not that the other major towns were that much better, concern having been highlighted by Edwin Chadwick's enquiry into *The Sanitary Condition of the Labouring Population in industrial towns*, published just a few years earlier in 1842. It was this report which introduced the word 'sanitary' into our dictionaries and led to the passing of the first Health Act in 1848. Indeed the story goes that Parliament had to suspend a sitting of this Bill because of the stench of the sewage from some 11 outlets that had accumulated in the Thames. The London Embankment now houses a major interceptor sewer which runs the offensive material down the river to treatment works. In those days it was thought that the vapours or noxious effluvia associated with such deposits was a direct source of disease. Before long though, the true source of such dreadful infectious diseases as cholera, which decimated the population of many areas, was found to be a poor or contaminated water supply. However, because these devastating outbreaks generally occurred among the 'poorer classes', there were many who initially opposed the introduction of the 1848 Public Health Act, despite Hamilton-Bampton's pleas for the improvement of the 'sanitary and therefore the moral as well as physical condition—of the poorer classes who,' he said to his distinguished audience 'have the strong claims of nationality and fraternity to your sympathies'.

Although a number of improvements were subsequently carried out, it took the establishment of the Local Government Board (1871) and the 1875 Public Health Act to really get authorities moving, and Plymouth witnessed a great period of activity between 1880–1890, when mile after mile of sewer was laid around the city. This particular ventilation chimney is the only one of its kind left in the area but it still services, as it did then, what is known as the Dead Lake Sewer for Compton (Peverell) and what 100 years ago was West Plymouth, the area around Wyndham Square to the middle of Union Street.

30th May 1987.

The Odeon

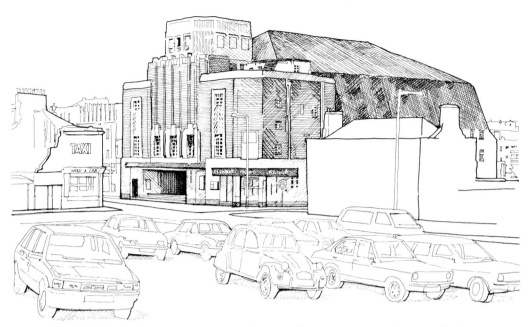

On Monday 16th November 1931, the Gaumont Palace was officially opened by the Mayor of Plymouth, Alderman G. P. Dymond, JP. The programme for that night, and for the following five days, was *The Ghost Train*, the screen adaptation of Arnold Ridley's play, starring Jack Hulbert and Cicely Courtneidge. Preceding the main film were Sydney Howard and Nelson Keys in *Almost a Divorce* and live on stage, Leslie James 'Britain's greatest cinema organist' on the mighty Compton Organ; Eddie Windsor, raconteur and musical entertainer, plus 'An entirely Original Stage Presentation featuring the world famous Sidney Firman and his band of BBC fame'. Also present at the gala ceremony was Plymouth's much-fêted MP, Lady Nancy Astor, who took the opportunity to make a 'strong plea' and one which still echoes around the various corridors of power, namely for 'clean wholesome films'.

At that time talking pictures had barely been around for three years, the first, *The Lights of New York*, having been shown in New York City on the 6th of July 1928. Nevertheless, there was no shortage of films in the new medium indeed few silent films were being made by now, and forthcoming attractions at the Gaumont included: Edward G. Robinson in *Smart Money*, and Maurice Chevalier in *The Smiling Lieutenant*, a production later nominated for best film in the 1931/32 Academy Awards.

The Gaumont Palace stands on the site of Horace Andrews' purpose built picture house which, in 1910, eclipsed all the many little penny-gaff picture houses that sprang up towards the end of this century's opening decade. In its turn the 2,300-seater Gaumont was not alone in spelling the end of these strongholds of the silent movies for, the week after the Gaumont opened, the Regent in Frankfort Street, billed as Plymouth's Mightiest Cinema and one of the ten largest in Europe, opened its doors to potential houses of 3,500 patrons for each performance. And a little before both of them the 2,500 seater Electric Theatre at Devonport had been opened.

There was no disputing the popularity of cinema-going then and Gaumont manager Reuben Eady reported capacity attendances for his opening four days; and with adult admission prices ranging from two shillings to sevenpence in the front stalls—that must have represented a fair bit of income!

Sadly, however, for cinema managers and proprietors alike, the advent of television made large inroads into the cinema going population. The Regent, after being bought and renamed by the Odeon chain in 1940 and then surviving the Blitz, was closed in 1962 and later demolished as the City centre was redeveloped. Meanwhile, the Gaumont was itself renamed and it now became the Odeon. However, in 1962 more than just a name change took place here as the new Odeon was considerably smaller than the old Gaumont and an elaborate reconstruction now meant the stalls had become part of the 'Majestic Ballroom'.

With its large screen and luxurious atmosphere the Odeon, now with only 1,040 seats, continued showing films until 9th April, 1980. On that night it closed; 149 patrons paying between them £220.20 to see its last screening—Robert De Niro and Meryl Streep in *The Deer Hunter*. By November 1980 the Odeon was in business again, although its new role as a Rollerena lasted less than two years. Downstairs fared better and after a string of different names, as the 'Majestic' became the 'Top Rank Suite', 'Implosion', 'Oceans' and 'Waves', it survived as a disco dance hall until this year.

Currently closed, this massive building, now owned by Whitbread Westcountry, who are about to sell to a Plymouth businessman, still occupies a prime site. The question now remains—what will it be next? »Postscript

7th September, 1985.

The General Moore

The construction of Union Street in the early part of the last century prompted a great deal of building on either side of it. Streets, terraces and workplaces sprang up around and about the length of it. West of here, however, the independent town of East Stonehouse had already been moving towards this road that had long since run North from Millbay before bending to cross the Tudor Millbridge. South of Union Street this road, since 1830 at least, has been known as Phoenix Street. To the North, this particular stretch was for many years called Twickenham Place, and in 1844 we find Thomas Glass listed as being here as a retailer of beer. Why it was ever called Twickenham Place is not known, as is the case with so many street names. In 1840 Twickenham was a substantial village (pop. 5,000) in Middlesex on the bank of the Thames, 12 miles west south west of St. Paul's. Today of course, it is part of the Greater London Borough of Richmond-upon-Thames and famous for Hampton Court Palace, Bushy Park and the English Rugby Football Union Ground and has a population well in excess of 100,000. But Plymouth no longer has a nominal link with it. In the 1870s Twickenham Place was renamed Manor Street and added to the rest of Manor Street, the western half being in Stonehouse the eastern in Plymouth. No. 23 Manor Street, however, was known as Twickenham Cottages for many years afterwards.

Meanwhile, by 1850, John Rogers was selling beer here and was duly succeeded by, presumably, either his son or brother with the somewhat unusual name of Orpheus Rogers, around 1860. (In Greek legend Orpheus was the poet who went to the infernal regions when his wife died and so charmed Pluto that she was released from that place, but only on the condition that Orpheus did not look back until they reached Earth. When he was just about to set foot on Earth, however, he did turn back and his wife vanished instantly.) Orpheus Rogers, on the other hand, with or without a wife, was here for many years and it was while he was here that we first find No. 7 Twickenham Place referred to as the 'Crown' (1862), although it was perhaps known by that name since it had first opened its doors. Today there are over 1000 public houses in England with this name, which is generally a compliment to the monarchy and an assertion of loyalty—although sometimes it can refer to the old coin worth five shillings (current equivalent the 25 pence piece, last produced for the Royal Wedding in 1981).

'The Crown' in Manor Street, however, no longer contributes to this statistic as in 1982 the pub was renamed the 'General Moore' in honour of Major-General Sir (John) Jeremy Moore KCB, OBE, MC. Known throughout the corps as 'J. J.', he had joined the Marines in 1947 at the age of 19 and in 1979 went out to the Falkland Islands as Commando Commander there. Later, as Commander of the British Land Forces in the Conflict, he accepted the Argentine surrender there on the 14th of June 1982.

Plymouth thus becomes one of those rare places to have not just one but two pubs named after contemporary figures. Strangely enough, the other change was from a 'Crown' too, the old 'Crown and Anchor' on the Barbican, now (since 1967) the 'Sir Francis Chichester'. Both men visited their 'memorials', 'J. J.' Moore and his wife Veryan spending a very pleasant evening here as guests of Flo and George Bold. George Bold first came to the 'Crown' in 1975 and began a nine year stint here as licensee in 1977. It had been George's idea to change the name of the pub for some time, so that it would in some way honour the Royal Marine service, and as so many of his customers had been in the Falklands fighting under 'J. J.' it seemed appropriate, once the permission of the man and the brewery had been obtained.

Not that the pub, in comparative terms, has that long been in the hands of the brewery. Whitbread currently have it after Starkey, Knight and Ford had originally bought it from the Parkers, who were licensees here for nearly 50 years.

George Bold is an ex-marine himself and in his time in the 'General Moore' amassed a vast collection of Royal Marine artefacts, many of which still decorate the pub. Indeed, so well has the pub been adopted by the corps that NP (Naval Party) 8901, who were based in the Falklands when the trouble first broke, have made the General Moore the official venue for their annual reunion, which this year takes place today. Hosts for these proceedings will be new licensees Mark and Linda Taylor, and among the guests the local ex RFA Merchant Navy chef hopes to entertain will be Rex Hunt, ex-governor of the Falkland Islands.

12th April 1986.

The Talbot

The imminent proposals for the Stonehouse end of Union Street spell, amongst other things, the final curtain for number 122, the 'Talbot Hotel'. Closed in anticipation of these developments a couple of years ago now, in losing the 'Talbot' the city will be losing its last substantial links with an era whose memory is still cherished by many older Plymothians; for here, between 1906 and 1929, was the man they called the Guv'nor, Harry Jenkins. Born in Wolsden Street in 1876, Harry Jenkins brought professional boxing to Plymouth on a scale it had never seen before and has never seen since. The venue, for all but a few of his promotions, was an enormous barn of a building in neighbouring Mill Street, once known as 'Hancock's Winter Gardens' and later re-named the 'Cosmopolitan Gymnasium' or the 'Cosmo'. Here the legendary pre-Ali black heavyweight champion of the World, Jack Johnson, made his only appearance in a British boxing-ring. Here too almost every boxing champion of the day fought at one time or another. The 'Cosmo' had been set up by three local sportsmen in 1907 and the Talbot was a regular meeting place for them. Soon after, these three became four and, as the story goes, Jenkins' involvement with them grew out of a need to avoid deadlock disputes with having an odd number round the table. Before long the 'Guv'nor' had become the principal figure in the running of the 'Cosmo' and continued as such until dwindling audiences finally compelled him to call it a day—a decision he took on the 26th December, 1924; one Boxing Day that proved to be a very unhappy one for the sport locally. Jenkins claimed that, as much as anything, it was the growing success and interest in Plymouth Argyle that was responsible for draining his patrons' finances. They couldn't afford both boxing on a Friday and football on a Saturday.

Harry Jenkins stayed at the 'Talbot' for five years after closing the 'Cosmo' and, strangely enough, one of his immediate successors at the pub was one of Argyle's most respected defenders, and their most capped player, Welsh International Moses Russell.

But what of the 'Talbot' itself, where and when did it acquire its name? After all there are many 'Talbots' around the country, including a 'Talbot and Falcon' and most of these owe their names to that, now extinct, breed of hunting dog known as 'Talbots' and said by Blaine, in his 1870 *Encyclopedia of Rural Sports*, to be 'the original stock from whence all variety of the scent hunting hounds are derived'. Large and white, with long, hanging ears and heavy jaws, the 'Talbot' is in turn thought to have gained its name from the ancient English family name 'Talbot'; around 1449 John Talbot the first Earl of Shrewsbury is referred to as 'Talbott oure goode dogge'. An acclaimed fighter himself on the battlefield, John Talbot is believed to be the first known person to have been slain by a shot from a hand-gun (1453, the Battle of Chatillon). Incidentally, despite his untimely death, John Talbot nevertheless founded what has become the oldest Earldom in the country (est. 1442) that has descended in the male line only.

Later, famous Talbots include Mary Anne (1778–1808) the celebrated Englishwoman, who served in both the Army and the Navy disguised as a man; and William Henry Fox Talbot, the English physicist, who greatly advanced the process of photography in the 1830s and 1840s. However the Talbot from whom the pub undoubtedly took its name was James W. Talbot, recorded as a beer retailer of 112 Union Street in 1862 and as licensee of the 'Talbot Arms' in 1867 (becoming the 'Talbot Hotel' within ten years). Here until the late 1880s, the eponymous James W. Talbot and Harry Jenkins share the honours for the longest tenure here and, now that the 'Talbot' is awaiting demolition, it's an honour no-one can ever take away from them.

14th September 1985

Edgcumbe Street, Stonehouse

In 1812 Edgcumbe Street was right in the middle of Stonehouse, Durnford Street only just reached the end of the Royal Marines Barracks, Fore Street (now High Street), to the north, stopped at the entrance to the Royal Naval Hospital, the Victualling Yard had not yet been built and there was no Union Street. Indeed a new road had only just been made to Plymouth and this was 'by way of Stonehouse Hill'. This new road followed an old 'path for foot passengers which formed a pleasant promenade for the inhabitants of Stonehouse, but this path now being converted into a road for horses and carriages, its pleasantness as a walk is now lost'. The writer then went on to add, 'it was indeed an object of some importance to Stonehouse, to obtain a better access to Plymouth, and from thence with the roads to Exeter, Tavistock, etc. but it was gaining it at too great a sacrifice to give up this promenade, especially as the same convenience might have been more effectually obtained on the other side of the hill.'

That new road was Caroline Place leading into Millbay Road and within 10 years it was indeed superseded by a road on the other side of the hill. That road was Union Street. Work towards its realisation actually began in 1813, for in that year Edgcumbe Street was demolished possibly for the first but certainly not the last time. Prior to its rebuilding, it ran in a southerly direction from Stonehouse bridge, now it was restructured to run eastwards straight into Plymouth, across the marshes above Millbay into Union Street. Today what little is left of Edgcumbe Street runs from the roundabout before the bridge, to the Wesleyan Chapel which was established here in 1813. In recent years this stretch has been incorporated into the numbering of Union Street; however, by the end of the year it seems likely that there will be nothing left of Edgcumbe Street at all. The reason?—so that the road can be widened. Already all but two premises on the south side of the street have gone, although the tiled wall and floor of Luscombe's butcher shop can still be seen, as can the remains of the mosaic entrance step to number 29, Eastman's butchery, the wording still clearly discernible. There were, in fact, several butchers in this stretch, most of them trading since the middle of last century, Cleave's at number 42 perhaps being the oldest of them all. Of a similar vintage was Solomon Stephens bakery, at numbers 38 and 39, where baking was carried out 100 years ago by John Bone. Another long-established business on this side was Dawes the Pawnbroker and of the two buildings still standing, one housed, for most of this century, Herbert Ford's plumbing operations, the other was a Co-op store.

Of the grand edifices still standing on the other side, the Lloyds Bank building has recently been deserted. One of the oldest banks in the city, 100 years ago it was the Three Towns Banking Co. Ltd., later becoming the Devon and Cornwall Bank before being taken over by Lloyds, soon after the turn of the century. Next door, the Stonehouse Social Club saw a few years as the Conservative and Constitution Club and was the Kent Unity Hall for many years before that. Until comparatively recently you could find the India Tyre & Rubber Company in Market Street and before the war the ancient 'Market House Inn' was also there. Stonehouse Market itself was housed, for a large part of the nineteenth century, on the site next to the 'Queens' here. Along from there Westlake's Funeral Services are still operating today after having seen many generations come and go in the area. Right next door to them is the 'United Services' public house, formerly the 'Edgcumbe Inn', probably named after an earlier 'Edgcumbe Inn' in the original street and known to have been standing in the eighteenth century. The Wesleyan Chapel, at what was the end of Edgcumbe Street, still stands but, like most of the 'Queens', it is boarded up, desolated and deteriorating from the inside out. Part of the 'Queens Arms', as it used to be known, is still open for custom, however, and licensee George Crabbe is determined that he won't move out until the demolition men move in, a sentiment that warms the heart and quenches the thirst of Bill Luscombe the butcher and Jack Ling the tobacconist, who've both seen their places go and now drink here to see how long these condemned buildings have left to stand.

A major complaint of the 1812 guide to Stonehouse was 'the great want of good shops'. Today it looks as though that want is here again, while further echoes of those words of 175 years ago leave one wondering whether the proposed new road here will, once again, be gained at 'too great a sacrifice' for the people of Stonehouse.

»Postscript

25th April 1987.

East Stonehouse

At the northern end of Durnford Street, only a few yards from Stonehouse Bridge, on a piece of wall of the old Plymouth Brewery, we find this carefully preserved curiosity. For many years obscured by, what one observer called, 'a particularly hideous iron convenience', it was revealed and restored by the brewery in the late sixties. The wording East Stonehouse essentially harks back to way beyond the days when Stonehouse, East and West all belonged to the Durnford family, hence the name Durnford Street. Then it stood 'in contradistinction to the hamlet of West Stonehouse which stood on the opposite shore of the harbour near Cremill and Mount Edgcumbe until burnt by the French some centuries ago' (White's *Devon*, 1850). The Durnfords owned the manor of Stonehouse from 1368 to 1493, when it passed to the Edgcumbes by the marriage of Sir Piers Edgcumbe to Jane, the heiress of the Durnford family. The Durnfords in turn had acquired it in 1368, by the marriage of Durnford to the heiress of the Bastard family, who had held the manor since Domesday, 1086, when the name Stanehus (Stonehouse) first occurred. At that

time the manor had but a single farmer, however the very name Stonehouse suggests the pre-existence of a reasonably substantial, stone building and 100 years ago Plymouth historian R. N. Worth speculated on the possibility of there being a Roman villa somewhere in the area. Just a few years before (1882) the remains of what might have been a Roman-British burial site were found at the back of 23 Newport Street. Newport Street, a small quay, a large manor house and a few other houses, had been built in East Stonehouse by 1493, with a total population of around 50.

By the time of Henry VIII, Stonehouse had expanded slightly but then changed little for almost 200 years, extending maybe a hundred yards or so in any one direction from this point. It was not until the latter half of the eighteenth century that major and rapid development took place as the Edgcumbes sold, leased and built on great areas of East Stonehouse. The Long Room, the fashionable assembly room that for a short while stood alone on the peninsula, appeared first in 1756. Then followed a series of important building projects, chronicled in Cynthia Gaskell-Brown's *History of Stonehouse*. The government was the biggest single buyer purchasing land for the Royal Naval Hospital (1758–62), the Royal Marine Barracks (1781–83) and later the Royal William Victualling Yard (1826–32).

Meanwhile, Lord Edgcumbe and Sir John St. Aubyn had linked their estates and with them Stonehouse and Devonport, with the construction of Stonehouse bridge. On the domestic front, Durnford Street was begun the year the bridge was completed, 1773. Initially the street did not extend this far north, the original northern tip being known as Chapel Street which met here at this junction with Edgcumbe Street. This in turn later became the western end of Union Street.

Whilst the naming of Durnford Street went back many generations, the newly constructed Emma Place was named in honour of the then Lady Edgcumbe (some time later neighbouring Caroline Place was to remember her grand-daughter). Lord Edgcumbe also had his share of honours. In 1781, the year after he had sold the land for the Marine Barracks and partly in compensation for the disruption to his land caused by the building of new local defences around 'West Stonehouse', Admiral George was created Viscount Mount Edgcumbe and Valletort. Then in 1789 he was made the 1st Earl of Mount Edgcumbe. Not surprisingly then, it is the Edgcumbe Arms we find here beneath the words 'East Stonehouse', together with the family motto *Au Plaisir Fort de Dieu*—'*To the powerful pleasure of God*'.

And long may it please the Almighty to preserve this attractive and unusual reminder of the past.

31st May, 1986.

The Globe Theatre

'Shortly after the Barracks were built in 1783, a small racket court or ball court was built about 1788. This court was really too small to be of much use and it was adapted for use as a theatre in 1848. The present theatre is the result of a skilfully designed enlargement and rearrangement of the old theatre and the straw yard which existed at its back.'

So wrote Colonel R. D. Ormsby CBE, RM, back in 1930. The Barracks he was referring to are the Royal Marine Barracks, Stonehouse and the theatre—the Globe. Harvey Crane, in his book *Playbill, A History of Theatre in the West Country*, dated its change of use from a racquets court to 1820, when after years of disuse it was turned into a theatre 'for the recreation and instruction of the men of the battalion'.

Whenever the change was effected though, it seems to have been well received and in 1864 the Admiralty provided a grant for a major conversion. The barracks thereafter had what was described in a contemporary press report, as a 'pretty, bijou theatre' capable of accommodating 400 persons.

In 1887 the builders and carpenters moved in again and by 1889 the theatre looked, structurally, much as it does today. Described then as being compact and well arranged, the theatre could now hold 600–700 patrons. Contemporary reports praised its fire and safety features but, as new standards for such considerations came into force this century, the auditorium was refashioned once more and in 1928 the seating capacity was reduced to 252 and so it still is today. Seventy of these seats are upstairs in a Circle that almost lives up to the name, being more than semi-circular. Redecorated many times over the years, the Globe today is undoubtedly the oldest and arguably, from the inside at least, the most attractive in the area. From the outside it could hardly be more unassuming, tucked away in a far part of the Barracks.

Unassuming as it might appear, it was in this delightful little theatre during the last war, that one of the many servicemen to pass through the city wrote the score for his musical *Bless the Bride*, composing his tunes on the Globe piano. He was Lt. Vivian Ellis RNVR, responsible for many hit musicals and *Bless the Bride* with lyrics by A. P. Herbert was one of the biggest, opening in London in 1947 and running for nearly 600 performances.

Always known as the Globe, it is likely that the name was arrived at as a clever link between the Marines' Badge and the Elizabethan Globe Theatre of Shakespeare's day, said to be the most famous theatre in history.

It was George IV who directed, in 1827, that the new distinguishing badge of the Marines would be the 'Globe encircled with the Laurel'. This was, according to his Majesty, the most appropriate emblem of a Corps whose duties carried them to all parts of the Globe, in every quarter of which they had earned laurels by their valour and good conduct.

Globes as we know them with post Christopher Columbus geography, were first made in this country by Molyneux in 1592, exactly 100 years after Columbus had sailed the ocean blue, but only a few years before William Shakespeare became a part owner of Richard and Cuthbert Burbage's Globe Theatre. What better name for the man who claimed that 'All the world's a stage'. Built in 1598, the Globe stood on the banks of the Thames opposite James Burbage's 1576 structure, simply called 'The Theatre', which had been the first theatre to regularly stage plays in this country. The Globe opened with Shakespeare's *Henry V* and estimates suggest that the theatre held audiences of between 1,200 and 2,500. Here in the years that followed, Shakespeare's greatest plays were performed as were many of Ben Johnson's works. According to Johnson, admission to the Globe could be had for sixpence if you wanted to join the groundlings in the general auditorium, or if you wanted a gallery seat or a seat on the stage, one shilling or half a crown. Sadly this Globe was destroyed by fire in 1613 when the thatched roof was ignited by a cannon, discharged at the entry of the King in Henry VIII and, although rebuilt, it was later razed in 1644 and no trace now remains.

However, should you wish to visit this Globe theatre you can do so next week for the princely sum of two pounds. There to entertain you from Wednesday to Saturday will be *Plymouth Presents*, presenting a new play written by Chris Savery, a young Plymothian who won his green beret with the TA's. His play, strangely enough, is an historical piece, reminiscent of the Shakesperian play and is about Oliver Cromwell—and it picks up where the first Globe left off back in the 1640s!

13th December, 1986.

Thomas Hardy's Residence?

At the Southern end of Durnford Street in Stonehouse, stands one of the finest examples of Georgian architecture in Plymouth and on its wall is a simple plaque which bears the following inscription: 'Here reputedly lived Admiral Sir Thomas Hardy, Bart, GCB. Born 1769, Captain of Fleet at Trafalgar 1806 and witness to Nelson's immortal dying words aboard H.M. *Victory* 'Kiss me Hardy' First Sea Lord 1830–1834 Governor Greenwich Hospital 1834 Died 1839'.

Mounted in 1975 as part of the local effort in recognition of European Architectural Heritage Year, the idea for a plaque here had been mooted back in the thirties, on the 200th Anniversary of Hardy's death; however, nothing transpired. Then the initiative for this small memorial had come from the Navy and it would appear, from their interest, that they knew something about the property and Hardy's involvement with it, that is by no means general knowledge.

Thomas Masterman Hardy was born at Kingston Russell, between Dorchester and Bridport in Dorset, on 5th April 1769 and it would seem that between then and his marriage, he regarded his parents' home at Portisham, Dorset as his base, returning there regularly during the early years of his naval career. After his marriage in 1814 to a nineteen year old colonial girl he spent most of his shore time living in style in

London, although there is a reference to him joining his wife and daughters in Florence in 1823. The last years of his life were spent at Greenwich, where he died in residence as Governor.

Evidence of his links with Plymouth and particularly Stonehouse are few but like his namesake, an earlier Admiral Sir Thomas Hardy and any other long serving naval officer, he undoubtedly made many visits to the port. This earlier Hardy operated here around the early part of the eighteenth century and around 1709–12 did much to purge the channel waters of privateers and French men o' war, much to the relief of the local merchants.

Back to the Hardy who joined the Navy at the age of 12, then left to go to school and later rejoined, first coming to serve with Nelson in 1795. A celebrated team in Naval history, Hardy and Nelson were involved in many notable incidents in the Napoleonic Wars and back in Plymouth in 1801 after another successful campaign, Whitfeld records that: 'Nelson was received with magnificent hospitality and was greeted with almost reverent affection in the streets. His stepbrother and his friend Captain Hardy were his invariable companions and the figures of the trio became more familiar than ever to the grateful populace.' Nelson is known to have been a visitor to Stonehouse's then fashionable Longroom, patronized also by Royalty, and it may well be that, around that time, Hardy used this Durnford Street house as his port residence, in which case, who knows who else might have visited here?

Graham Knight, who was born here and in whose family the house has been for over 70 years, is doubtful that Hardy ever owned the property, but thinks his mother may have done at some time. Certainly in those days, this part of Stonehouse was very little developed. Foulston had yet to arrive in Plymouth and make his mark in this area of Durnford Street and this property, part of a pair, had been standing many years. Classically Georgian and thought to have been built in the latter half of the eighteenth century, the two properties were originally slate-hung front and sides, as part of the side of the adjoining property still shows. Sadly, this slating, along with original railings (taken like so many others unnecessarily 'for the war effort' in the forties) has now gone but in all other respects the house is a fine example of its period. Essentially just four main rooms with the rest servants' quarters, the house has been well preserved by its present owner. The windows have been rebuilt and many internal features carefully restored.

To return to the inscription. Properly titled Vice Admiral (from 1837) Hardy had been created a Baronet (Bart.), the year after Trafalgar and the month after Nelson's funeral (February 1806), and made a KCB, Knight Commander of the Bath, in 1815. He was awarded the GCB, Grand Cross of the Bath in 1831. Controversy will always surround Nelson's dying words; whether it was 'Kiss me Hardy' or 'Kismet (fate) Hardy', or whatever—according to David Howarth in his book on Trafalgar, Dr. Scott, Nelson's chaplain, distinctly heard him whisper 'Thank God I have done my duty' last of all. However, one historical question that may well be a lot easier to solve is whether the man Hardy, who would amuse his friend Nelson, when going into battle, with stories of his eccentric aunt, ever did live here in this house in Durnford Street.

6th September, 1986.

78

Victualling Office Tavern

Of all the many thousands of public houses, inns, taverns or whatever, kept by licensed victuallers in this country, only one has the word victualling or victualler in its title and that one is here in Stonehouse. Until comparatively recently there was a 'Victualling Arms' in Portsmouth but that is now closed. However, if we are to go back a little further in time, we find that around the middle of last century, Stonehouse had two 'Victualling Office Taverns', the one here and another at the Ha'penny Bridge end of High Street. But the second establishment, despite apparently being every bit as old as this one, did not last and 100 years ago it had become a general store, providing victuals of a different kind. Of course it is a slightly different kind of victualling again that gave rise to the names of both Taverns in Stonehouse and indeed the one in Portsmouth. For in both cases it is their proximity to institutions dealing with the victualling of Royal Naval ships that has provided the inspiration for these unusual pub names.

The Royal William Victualling Yard at Stonehouse was completed around 1835. It was a massive undertaking involving the annexation of almost all the land in Stonehouse known as Cremill Point, plus several acres of land reclaimed from the sea. The building also took a number of years and, so the story goes, the site office for this major development was a fifty year old cottage which until then had stood in virtual isolation overlooking Stonehouse Pool. That cottage, built in 1776, still stands and it is immediately behind the Victualling Office Tavern, which was built on to its side in 1846, soon after the new yard was completed. The cottage, set well back from the road, sits at right angles to it and can be seen from the small beer garden at the rear of the pub; a garden which also just manages to afford a reasonable view of the water off Freeman's Wharf.

Prior to the building of the Royal William Yard, victualling of the Navy locally had been conducted at Lambhay, not far from where Cromwell had first instituted local Commissioners of Victualling back in 1654, but in those days of course there was no dockyard and indeed, no Devonport. When victualling operations were moved to Stonehouse the old Office at Lambhay was converted into one of the country's major Emigration Depots.

Changes also followed at Stonehouse and before long Durnford Street had extended well beyond the Marine Barracks to its present length and the address of this pleasant little Victorian public house had settled down to 10 Cremyll Street. Earlier variations put it simply as Cremill Point, then Dunford Lane, then Point Street . . .

Inside the pub changes have taken place but they tend to be slow and slight. Landlady Margery Jeffrey and her husband Edwin have been here twenty years already and the large picture of Queen Victoria in the corner has been there as long as anyone can remember. Indeed, apart from a turbulent spell in the mid-sixties, the licensed victualler here has tended to be a remarkably consistent figure as, for thirty years down to 1962, Edgar Bartlett ran the 'V.O.T.', as it's sometimes known. Before him a man called Brewer was landlord here, an apt name for a publican, especially one in charge of a pub with a name so closely linked with licensed victualling.

The expression 'licensed victualler' incidentally, is only a little older than the tavern itself, first appearing in print around 1824, although the requirement of having a licence to keep a victualling house dates back to Tudor times. Originally of course, victuals simply referred to 'whatever is normally required, or may naturally be used, for consumption in order to support life' and hence 'food or provisions of any kind'. And knowing where we all, temporarily at least, store such provisions having consumed them, it comes as no great surprise to find that even in the eighteenth century the term Victualling Office was being used in boxing slang to refer to the stomach. 'He . . . found it impracticable to smite his antagonist upon the victualling office', Smollett 1751.

One thing all boxers find indispensable of course, is courage and you'll certainly find plenty of it in this Victualling Office! »Postscript

11th April, 1987.

The Royal William Victualling Yard

In the early part of 1824 the south-western tip of the Stonehouse peninsula was split in two. One half was left much as it was, the other half was blasted, quarried, levelled and extended out over the sea. In this way about six acres were won from the Hamoaze and a total area of some 15–16 acres was created upon which, over the next ten years, these impressive buildings, known as the Royal William Victualling Yard, were constructed.

300,000 tons of rock and limestone were removed, most of which was used in the formation of the embankments, although much of it was probably used for the buildings themselves, which are substantially limestone with granite detailing. The principal architect of the whole scheme was the man who had taken over the construction of the Breakwater following his father's death in 1821, John Rennie. As Jonathan Coad observes in an article on Historic Architecture of H.M. Naval Base Devonport—'Plymouth Breakwater was rightly regarded as one of the engineering wonders of the age. It was logical that the engineer-in-charge of this should be asked to undertake the nearby victualling development.'

Three years passed before the site had been sufficiently cleared and well enough settled for building to begin. The first contract issued in November 1827, was for the present Clarence Wharf, Stonehouse at the western end of the yard. Named in honour of the then King's younger brother, the Duke of Clarence, the King, George IV, was himself ultimately not so honoured despite the original intention being to name it the Royal George Victualling Yard. George died in 1830 and upon completion of the complex it was named again in honour of the Duke of Clarence, now William IV.

The most impressive block of the development though, is not named after a royal but rather the second Lord Melville who, between 1812 and 1827, was First Lord of the Admiralty. The Melville Block, which incorporates the striking clock tower, was also begun in 1827. The clock, which has no fewer than 1,393 pieces, was made in 1831 by Vulliamy of Pall Mall.

By the end of 1830 contracts had also been placed for the cooperage, the slaughterhouse, flour mills, bakehouse, warders' quarters, officers' residences and the main gate.

In those days of course, the nature of Navy Victuals was quite different from that of today. Then the emphasis was very much on bread, beer, meat and biscuits. Reading L. W. M. Stephen's History of the Yard we learn that the: 'Mills and Bakery were capable of converting 1,000 sacks [270 lb each sack] of flour into biscuits each week and that up to 100 cattle per day could be slaughtered in the Slaughterhouse while the massive brewhouse was built to brew 120 tuns [250 gallons per tun] of beer daily'.

The first change to affect the output of the yard came just a few years after it had begun operating. By 1840 the general issue of one gallon of beer to all naval seamen was stopped, resulting in a dramatic drop in requirements. The meat business, on the other hand, flourished. However, as the century wore on, a new Office, 'the Director of Navy Contracts', was created and increasingly, supplies were brought in from outside, although chocolate, mustard, pepper, oatmeal, cooperage items and biscuits continued to be produced 'in house'. Navy biscuits in fact, came to be very highly regarded as they were deemed to be vastly superior to commercially available alternatives.

In time though, as Navy rations widened in range so more and more food supplies came from outside, the legendary Tickler's jams first appearing on the ration at the turn of the century. Increasingly therefore, the William Yard, and its nineteenth-century counterparts the Royal Victoria, Chatham and the Clarence, Portsmouth, relied less and less on their own food produce and instead spread their range of interests, as directed, to cover all naval clothing and mess gear requirements. Free kit on entry and the issue of manufactured cigarette tobacco in $\frac{1}{2}$lb tins, were among the 'reforms' introduced at the beginning of this century.

Today the victualling side of activities here accounts for only about one third of the use of the Yard, which is now shared with 539 Raiding Squadron of the Royal Marines and an area used for conventional armaments. However, by 1992/93 all is set to change radically as then it is anticipated that the Royal William Yard will be handed over to the City Council and the Navy will move out. At present there are a number of ideas in the air for the future of these buildings; undoubtedly one of the most fitting would be to transform the complex into what could be, one of the most handsomely constructed and best situated Maritime Museums in the world.

30th April 1988.

Drake's Island

Some time around AD 1135, Walter de Valletorta granted this Island, then called St. Michael's Island, together with all its rabbits, to the Prior of Plympton. It appears that during the Middle Ages the cult of St. Michael was popular in this country but before long the little chapel that stood on the summit of the Island was rededicated to St. Nicholas and it is by that name that, until comparatively recently, the Island was best known.

Sadly no trace of this little chapel, thought to be the first building ever erected on the Island, can be found today. However, four years ago in November 1983, the Rt. Rev. Kenneth Newing, in his capacity as Bishop of Plymouth, crossed over to the Island and conducted a service of dedication in an old gun casemate which had been especially converted into a chapel. This new chapel is dedicated to St. Michael and St. Nicholas and is, apparently, the first chapel known to the Island records since the original building was pulled down 435 years earlier. It is somehow quite fitting that a military installation should have been converted in this way for it was in order to fortify the Island in the first place that the earlier chapel was pulled down in 1548. Not that the local authorities seemed overkeen to get on with the job, as a letter from the Privy Council to the Mayor of Plymouth and his colleagues earlier that year 'marvelinge of their unwillingness to proceede in the fortefyinge of St. Michaelles Chappele to be made up a bulwarke, when the suretie of so small a thinge might assure them againste all attempts . . .' shows. However, the following year an indenture was drawn up between the King (Edward VI) and the Corporation for the building and maintaining of a fort on the Island and by 1551 the Privy Council had made a payment to the municipality which allowed for paying the 'wages of 4 gonners one at 8d by the daie and thothers at 6d by the daie serving in the forte of St. Nicholas Ilande for 2 hole yeres . . .'.

Having established the Island in its new role as a defensive position, it is no great surprise to find, thirty years later, that a petition was sent to London from the City requesting that one man be appointed 'captain of the isle of St. Nicholas'. That man being their 'verie ffriend and neighboure Sir Francis Drake', and whilst it is on record that John Sparke and his fellow petitioners succeeded in establishing their right to appoint a governor or captain for the Island, it is not recorded whether or not Drake ever accepted the title. We do know though that Drake himself urged the government to build a fort on the Island and offered £100, 'for his parte at leaste, towards the cost. Whatever Drake's actual involvement, in the absence of any substantial chapel it is perhaps not surprising that from around this time we first find his name linked with that of the Island. Although it was still being referred to as St. Nicholas Island hundreds of years later, Drake's Island is the name by which most recent generations of Plymothians have known this 'lozenge-wise' lump of hard volcanic rock which reaches a height of 96 feet and has an area of around six acres.

Much developed and redeveloped as a military defence down the years the position of the Island became particularly important once the Navy moved out of Sutton Harbour and around into the Hamoaze. Today however, while the various structures visible on the Island illustrate different eras in its defensive history, they are now home for the Drake's Island Adventure Centre—a title which was conferred back in 1974; eleven years after the War Department had, at long last, released the Island, modern weaponry rendering its strategic role obsolete.

A registered charity, the Adventure Centre lease the Island from the City, and are responsible for it. At present there is no recognized public access here, despite a promise from the City to run 2 ferries a day to the Island throughout July and August this year, with an accompanying guide. But superb views of the Island can be enjoyed from Devil's Point, certainly the closest vantage point without taking to the water. The landing pier was constructed in 1939, at the beginning of the last war. The largest building seen here is the barrack block which, like the smaller Commanding Officer's House, dates from the early 1830s. Today the Adventure Centre staff occupy the latter, while up to 100 young people can now be 'garrisoned' in the renovated barracks.

With excellent local facilities for sailing, canoeing, rock climbing, orienteering, caving, marine biology and a variety of expeditions, Drake's Island has perhaps never been manned by a happier bunch, except perhaps those rabbits!

15th August, 1987.

82

Milton's Temple

'Through another leafy avenue and we arrive at the Amphitheatre a very fine assemblage of trees rising tier above tier, to a very considerable height, and displaying the most beautiful variety of form and foliage. Amongst the trees may be found the Tulip tree, a fine specimen of the Cedar of Libanus, several large Planes with abundance of foliage, and a Cardina Poplar, of great height and beauty. At the right of our path, close under the shade of these woods, stands a small temple, dedicated to the poet Milton. It consists of a little dome, supported by four Ionic pillars, and is enclosed within iron railings. Within the Temple is a bust of the poet, and an inscription consisting of the following lines from his *Paradise Lost* which are admirably adapted to form a description of this enchanting spot. It is currently reported that this place was a favourite resort of the poet, and probably suggested the ideas of the lines themselves:

> "... over head up grew
> Insuperable height of loftiest shade,
> Cedar, and pine, and fir, and branching palm,
> A sylvan scene, and as the ranks ascend
> Shade above shade, a woody theatre
> Of stateliest view."'

That account, still largely applicable today, appeared in W. Byer's *A Walk Around Mount Edgcumbe* in 1836. The poet's bust and the railings have gone but the poetry and the prose hold good. Indeed so well do Milton's lines describe this area that at least one 19th Century guide assumed that the poet had written his piece in the Park. John Milton, however, composed his epic account of the 'Fall of Man'—*Paradise Lost*—over a six-year period, 1658–64. It was first published in 1667. Milton was then 59 and had been blind for over 16 years. The lines above come from the beginning of Book IV (of XII) and are lines 137–143. Among English poets, Shakespeare aside,

John Milton is generally recognized as the undisputed head, and of all his work *Paradise Lost* is the greatest and most complete. In it Milton proposes that pride is the greatest sin and that humility is true Christianity, and when Satan seeks out Adam and Eve in Eden it is here, in Paradise, that he finds them.

It is doubtful that Milton ever did survey this 'Sylvan Scene', however it is likely that, like many other members of the landed gentry, the Edgcumbes, probably George (1721–1795) the first Earl, strove consciously to recreate Milton's Paradise within the estate. In Milton's day it would appear that the Amphitheatre was a formally laid out garden, possibly a kitchen garden which it is believed was transferred to Empacombe around 1780 when George and his wife Emma created a lawn here and planted yet more great banks of trees around the sides. The temple itself is thought to date from around this period.

George's father, the 1st Baron Edgcumbe, had begun restructuring Edgcumbe after his retirement from politics in 1742, some 203 years after Henry VIII had first granted Piers Edgcumbe license to empark part of the Rame Peninsula. Land he had inherited on his marriage to Joan Durnford. A classically trained scholar, Baron Richard Edgcumbe modelled his efforts after the 'Natural Style' which took its lead from Alexander Pope's notion that 'gardening is landscape painting' (1734) and, like many of his peers, George turned to poetry and painting to provide images for working models.

Today Mount Edgcumbe Country Park stands as a supreme example of the spirit and society of that time. Here at the Amphitheatre the only significant change since then has been the reappearance of the stream and the creation of this pond. Believed to have been diverted by pipes prior to the eighteenth century, it was apparently rediscovered during the second World War after the pipes were broken by the heavy American Army vehicles that were temporarily based at Barnpool.

1st February, 1986.

Stonehouse Creek

'Anthony. 25th April 1813 . . . My Dear Fanny—You may now congratulate me on having lost a companion with whose company I have long been oppressed.

I went to the Military Hospital at Plymouth on Saturday, determined to submit to any operation that might facilitate the extracting the ball. After much pain and many trials the black gentleman was pulled out by the forceps without an incision. I look forward to my recovery now with delight, and hope I may bid adieu to pain and mutilation . . .

Your most affectionate J.Colborne.'

John Colborne, one of the Duke of Wellington's principal officers, who later became Field Marshal, Lord Seaton (hence Seaton Barracks), had been on his back suffering his wound for some 15 months. When his arm was eventually operated on, the pain was extreme and this brave soldier was reduced to allowing the surgeons just five minutes' exertions at a time, and it was three or four days before they 'wrenched the bone from its ossified bed' and were able to extract the ball of shot.

Colborne's letter to Frances Bargus, a lady he knew as a 'sister' was written from his brother-in-law's house in Anthony, from where he had travelled to the Military Hospital doubtless by boat, and landed somewhere to the left of the view as we see it here. By 1813 this hospital, barely 16 years old, was already only partly in use; however, given the role of this city in time of war, one contemporary account did not feel that this large establishment was a white elephant. 'The arrival of the troops from Corunna (1809) when 500 men and upwards were immediately received here, proved that the money expended in the erection of it was well laid'. Earlier in this same account we find reference to the colonnade 'admitting convalescents as soon as they can quit their beds, without experiencing the fatigue of descending and ascending stairs, to walk on a delightful terrace, and enjoy a fine sea air and exercise'.

That sea air has now to travel a little further to reach the noses of the current occupants of these buildings as, in 1972, Stonehouse Creek was filled in. The original line of the hospital sea wall can be seen on the right here, in front of the hard-surface playground.

Just before the last war, the water levels here were not great and many remember the 'stinking mud flats' of Stonehouse Creek but, over 100 years ago, the tidal flow went much further, beyond the old Mill at Millbridge right up to Pennycomequick. In the 1890s a great deal of development took place in Plymouth and all the consequent rubble and surplus material was then used to infill the upper part of the creek. By 1905 this work had been finished and Victoria Park had been laid out more or less as it appears today. During the war a coffer dam was constructed across a part of the remaining creek, west of Millbridge, to hold a static water tank, holding back a 12 foot head of water. In the early 1960s as many as a hundred boys a week from Devonport High School and Tamar were using this expanse of water for sailing. However, when it looked unlikely that the council were going to maintain the dam at its full height, parents from both schools, fearing the reappearance of the 'stinking mud flats', campaigned for its infilling.

At first no suitable way of doing this could be found. An early offer, in 1964, of 400,000 tons of quarry waste, from the Billacombe gas works project, came to nothing as the city were reluctant to pay the three shillings and sixpence per cubic yard that the South West Gas Board required for moving the material. In the end it was British Rail, with their generous offer of old railway ballast from all over Devon and Cornwall to be dumped free of charge, who brought the change.

Over 600,000 tons of ballast and rubble were used, ultimately, to provide what is now 19 acres of playing fields and public open space that runs between the Royal Naval Hospital and the old Military Hospital. In addition to British Rail's contribution, waste material came from Devonport Dockyard, excavated surplus from Crownhill underpass and Pennycomequick Hill road-improvement schemes, and also the two old railway bridges that had once spanned Wolseley Road.

27th December, 1986.

Tamar High School

Valentine's Day 1939 was a Tuesday, it was also the day that four Plymouth schools were officially instituted into the newly converted Military Hospital off Stonehouse Creek. Those schools were Valletort Senior School for Boys, Stoke Senior School for Boys, the Junior Technical School for Boys and Tamar Central School for Boys.

Plymouth Education Authority appear to have acquired the Military Hospital five or six years earlier and had been operating a Boys Junior Instruction Centre there along with a Remedial Treatment Clinic. The site had cost the Authority £12,040— a modest sum when compared to the bill incurred for the alterations and additions to the building, the construction of playing fields and playgrounds and the various professional fees which totalled £84,774.

The Military Hospital took these changes well, however, and looks in good shape to celebrate its 200th birthday in 1997. It had been built not long after the outbreak of the Napoleonic Wars in 1793. Extensive early campaigns in the West Indies had led to great numbers of sick and wounded soldiers flooding into Plymouth in 1795. The Naval Hospital, completed over 30 years earlier, would not take soldiers and many were dying in the cramped and inadequate temporary hospital set up at Friary. So it was that in 1797, Blocks A, B, C & D of the new Military Hospital were erected on the North Bank of Stonehouse Creek, directly opposite the Royal Naval Hospital. The four small blocks were all connected by one long and impressive colonnade. A fifth block was added in the 1860s. The Military medical practitioners were still facing great problems, however, and in 1809, one thousand of the sick soldiers, brought back from the retreat from Corunna, died of fever in a converted barn in Friary, and a further 3,000 Plymothians became infected and subsequently died.

With the development of civilian hospitals and the falling military role in Plymouth the Hospital gradually became superfluous in the years after a late period of intense activity during the First World War. However, it was the outbreak of the Second World War that immediately put paid, albeit temporarily, to the plans to develop this site for the purposes of local education. The schools were evacuated after only a few months in situ.

On Saturday 10th May, 1941, 93 boys from Block A—Tamar Central School— 'under the supervision of Mr. F. E. Sanders and two temporary members of staff, left North Road Station for an unknown destination. This later proved to be Truro . . .' (H. W. A. Warren). Those boys who stayed behind were moved first to North Prospect School then, in June 1941, they joined with the boys of Public in Coburg Street in what was dubbed the Emergency Central School. While at North Prospect the boys had had their school meals from a field kitchen set up in the playground of the old Johnston Terrace School, the school out of which Tamar had grown some ten years before.

Johnston Terrace Boys' School had first been reorganized as a boys' central school in 1928, although it was not until 1930 that the boys took over the whole building from the girls. Mr. A. E. E. Cook was first head of this new school but soon after, was succeeded, on his retirement in 1931, by Tom Willcocks. It was during Willcocks' time that the school name was changed to Tamar Central (although Devonport Central and Scott Central were both considered). That was in 1933, the year of the first Speech Day. On that occasion Dr. A. B. Rendle was guest of honour and in his speech quoted from Robert Browning's *Rabbi ben Ezra*, including the lines 'Grow old along with me, The best is yet to be'. For the new Tamar Central School, 'The best is yet to be' was singularly appropriate and the phrase duly became the school motto.

After the war, the returning evacuees went to Mount Street, moving to Durnford Street (in the ertswhile Durnford Hotel) in 1946. Now with J. E. (Eddy) Ellis as their Head they waited to move back into both A and B Block of the Military Hospital. War damage and death watch beetle ensured it was not a short wait. It was not until November 1956 that the boys of the school were all united on one site.

Today, 30 years on, Tamar High School remains a selective school, proud of its academic and sporting achievements. Of Plymouth's four remaining grammar schools, it is the only one that is co-educational; girls were first admitted in 1972 and, although few would like to speculate on Tamar's long-term future, current Head Ray Rose, is in no doubt that the school motto is as pertinent today as it was 50 years ago.

Ray, who taught for many years at Sutton and before that at Honicknowle is, incidentally, an old boy of Devonport High School which occupies Blocks 'C' and 'D' of the Old Military Hospital—but that's another story! »Postscript

. 15th November, 1986.

Devonport High School for Boys

For older old boys of Devonport High School for Boys this is not what they will know as their old school. Despite these premises having been built more than 100 years before most of them were born, these buildings were, until the mid-thirties, blocks C, D and E of the Royal Military Hospital. Indeed, they were used as such again during the Second World War.

For pre-1939 old boys then, it is the imposing building in Outram Terrace that is their Alma Mater. Presently the Albert Road annexe of the College of Further Education, that building has seen a variety of educationally linked uses. It was built in 1878 to house the newly constituted Devonport, Stoke and Stonehouse High School for Girls. In 1898–9, on completion of Devonport Technical College, the girls moved out and into part of that new building. At the same time, boys from Devonport Naval and Civil Service College moved into the Outram Terrace buildings. Founded by all accounts, a couple of years earlier, 1896, by Alonzo Rider, this new school was soon better known as Devonport High School. However, the epithet 'Naval and Civil Service College' remained linked with the school for many years.

Alonzo Rider was well known in local educational circles. He had, for a long time, been headmaster of Stoke Public School, having arrived there in 1863. Stoke Public School stood for 90 years (1819–1909) at Keppel Place until it was knocked down and replaced by the building that, until recently, housed Stoke Damerel High School for Girls who, in later years, used Outram Terrace as an annexe themselves. The schools' library services were also based there until they moved to Chaucer Way a few years ago.

Head for some ten years at the new school, Alonzo Rider moved into the old caretaker's house, 'Outram', adjoining the school, when he retired from the post and lived there till his death in 1921. Neither was he the only one living here, as the school started out with a large number of boarders. Arthur Tresider became the school's second Head soon after it was taken over by Plymouth Education Authority in 1906 and under him, a number of specific objectives were added to the school curriculum, notably—preparation for the Civil Service Executive; Customs and Excise; RNC Dartmouth and mathematical professions.

In addition to its boarders, the school used to have a preparatory department and until the passing of the 1944 Education Act fees had been charged at DHS. By this time Henry (H. A. T.) Simmonds had been appointed the school's third Head and more boys than ever before were going on to University, after leaving the school.

The outbreak of war in 1939 saw a large part of the school evacuated to Penzance, where they were described, at one time, as being the 'best looked after schoolboys in England'. Admittedly the title was not immediately appropriate since their first major billet was the Madron Workhouse, but they were soon after distributed, where possible, in more comfortable surroundings. Boys from Grenville House spent some time in the newly-built Royale Hotel, while 'Ponsandane', home of a branch of the Bolitho family, housed the Drake boys. Amongst the other places used at one time or another were Mount's Bay Hotel, Marine Hotel, Mount Prospect Hotel and two other large, private houses in their own grounds; 'Tredarvah' and 'The

Rookery', home of the late Lord St. Levan, at Marazion. Classrooms were dotted about the town in seven different buildings, with Richmond Sunday School as the main base. Meanwhile, those day boys who remained in Plymouth joined up with the boys of Sutton to form 'Emergency High School'

When the school reformed after the war, it didn't move back into Albert Road; those premises were now too small for the growing school. Instead they moved here, into Blocks C, D and E of the old Military Hospital.

Since then, 1945, the school has seen three heads—Stephen Baker, Dr. J. L. Cresswell (here for over 20 years until his untimely death in the mid Seventies) and current head J. G. W. Peck. A full history of the school is due out soon from former master Henry Whitfeld. Meanwhile, although the school is firmly set to continue well into the 1990s, its long-term future is unknown. Taking its lead from the school motto (which like the school badge is that of Devonport itself, the Arms having been granted to the town in 1876) *Prorsum Semper Honeste*—Forward Always Honestly, the prevailing mood is that here is a school not only with a fine tradition but still a great future. »Postscript

22nd November, 1986.

Stuart Road School

In 1893 a new school opened in Palmerston Street, Stoke—Stuart Road Higher Grade School. Instituted by the Devonport School Board, this was a school where very high standards were expected both from the staff and from the pupils. The school, with a curriculum that was far more broadly based than that in the local board schools that were being established locally under the terms of the recent Education Acts, quickly established a fine reputation for itself. In the event, however, it did not have long to prove itself for, within a few years, a Queen's Bench ruling in London effectively put an end to any attempts made by local school boards to provide anything more sophisticated than 'Elementary Education'. Any breach of this was considered to be an illegal use of the rates. Stuart Road Higher Grade School was then 'downgraded' to the level of an ordinary board school.

A later ruling in 1900 allowing for the creation of a new system of Higher Elementary Schools came too late for Stuart Road, and anyway with amalgamation of the three towns looming, the slightly newer Regent Street Higher Grade School (which became Sutton High) was better placed to accommodate the demand for such an institution.

Stuart Road was already split into infants on the ground floor, girls on the middle and the 11–15 year old boys on the top floor, allowing them no room to expand along the lines set out in this latest ruling.

So it was that Stuart Road's 'Brief Glory' came to an end, or at least that is how one old boy of the school saw it in 1961 when he was looking back on his years at the school between 1893–1898. Those were the days, he said, when the school took a

more enlightened look at education than was generally prevalent at the time 'interpreting that word in its true meaning—to educate(educe)—not to cram in but to draw out—latent capabilities and personality'. Perhaps he would be more impressed with the current curriculum at Stuart Road which, albeit for infants and juniors only now, is, in common with other schools, far more enlightened today than it has ever been.

Back in the 1890s free education for all was still very much a novel concept and one which was imparted with an air of great seriousness. There was little in the way of in school recreation, only 'physical drill' once a week in the boys' playground, supervised by one of the School Board Attendance Officers. School Team sports were little known outside the 'more favoured senior schools' and holidays were few and far between; the Queen's (Victoria) Birthday, Bank holidays and one month at Midsummer.

There was also very little in the way of reading material other than the standard text books. Printed matter generally was thin on the ground and there was no school library. Some of the equipment that the original school did have—benches, apparatus etc. from the laboratory—was moved when the school's status was amended, the said items being moved to the new Devonport Technical School which was opened in 1899.

And so, as our 'old boy' records, the existence of the original school 'is now only visibly recognized by the defaced remains of lettering on the outer wall of 'Stuart Road Higher Grade School' beneath the present designation of 'Stuart Road Council School'.

Even this wording, however, belies the various changes that have taken place since the turn of the century. For many years it was a Girls' Secondary Modern School with juniors and infants below. Then in 1955 following the opening of Penlee School, the older girls moved out and the youngsters took possession of the whole building. And at that time there were certainly plenty of young children here; following the post war development around Maker View the great influx of young families meant that numbers at the school doubled during the fifties—declining only as the new population settled down and the children grew up and moved away.

During the war itself Stuart Road School, like so many others, faced difficulties. Bombing early in 1943 saw the school close for five months for repairs while five neighbouring properties, 34–38 Palmerston Street, were damaged beyond repair.

Miss E. E. W. Cain was junior school head during these troubled times and she was succeeded by an energetic lady, Gladys Long, in 1950 who was head here for 16 years and who today still lives in Plymouth. Miss Long's successor, Ron Thorogood, just pipped her 16 years at Stuart Road by holding the headship from 1966–1983, while someone well acquainted with both is Margaret Dyer who, apart from a few years break, has been teaching here since 1955.

With a school roll currently around 120, the mood amongst Stuart Road's pupils today suggests that their brief stay here will be as glorious as it has been for any old boys or girls.

7th May 1988.

Stoke Damerel Church

'Here stands a church where a church has stood for the greater part of a thousand years.' So run the first lines of Patricia Gray's entertaining and thorough *History of Stoke Damerel Church*. A church which has written record, so far discovered, stretching back to the thirteenth century and which structurally in part, dates back to the fifteenth century.

Henry le Megre appears to have been the first rector here, although his incumbency was a brief one (1310–12), but then the first ten years documented here show six different rectors in charge of Stoke Damerel, an unparalleled turnover in the church's history. Indeed, if you go back over the twelve appointments leading up to the arrival of Gordon Cryer the current rector, you end up in the eighteenth century, demonstrating the stability that has been a feature of Stoke Damerel since Charles II came to the throne. A situation emphasized by the fact that between 1660 and 1940 only two incumbents resigned from the post, the others all remaining until their death.

The church itself is unusual in many respects, its squat, fifteenth-century tower being dominated by a disproportionately large clock (erected in 1811). The main extraordinary feature, however, is that since 1751 the width of Stoke Damerel has been greater than its length and this makes for a very strange, spatial quality inside the building. When first built, or rebuilt, in the fifteenth century the church just consisted of the tower and a simple nave, small but perfectly adequate for the population it then served. In those days this would have been a fairly isolated spot, although it was not to be long (1525) before Sir Piers Edgcumbe constructed the nearby mill and bridge over the erstwhile tidal creek, thereby increasing the traffic and then the quality of the surrounding roads.

However, it was the arrival of the Dockyard that really changed the nature of this rural 974-acre manor and, despite the building of a separate chapel in the yard itself, led to the expansion of Stoke Damerel. It was in 1691 that work began on the Dockyard and although the chapel appears to have been completed by 1700, by 1715 Stoke Damerel had been extended by the addition of an aisle on the Northern side of the nave and then in the 1750s the whole building, apart from the tower, was re-styled essentially to accommodate a southern aisle. However, as this proposed new aisle was to be wider than its recent counterpart, other adjustments were made which resulted in the central axis of the church moving southwards. Thus, from that day to this, the tower has been off-centre from the main body of the church. Although this new work destroyed the old line of the building, many of the original fifteenth-century features were moved around and incorporated into the fabric of the new layout, most notably the large, granite arch in the north wall.

Other ancient items in the church to be refashioned in the eighteenth century were the four bells which were known to date back at least as far as 1553. In 1789 they were taken down and recast with additional metal, into a peal of six. Then almost 200 years later, these six became eight, returning to the tower in 1977 after a six-year absence. In between this last change Stoke Damerel was blessed with its first stained-glass windows, an attraction it had done without until 1863 and still today many windows are clear. Fortunately, during the blitz Stoke Damerel's damage extended little

beyond a few panes being blown out and it survived the war as the only unscathed church in Devonport.

By this time nine separate parishes had been carved out of Stoke Damerel, the oldest, St. Aubyn's (1771), being named after one of the principal land-owning families and not dedicated to a specific saint as all the succeeding churches have been. But then the same is true of Stoke Damerel itself which takes its name from the ancient manor title of *Stoches*, which at the time of the conquest belonged to the Saxon, Brisma, and afterwards was given, by the Conqueror, to Robert de Albamarla hence—Stoches de Albamarla-which became Stoke Damerel as the French name was Anglicised over the years. *Stoches*, *stoc* or *stok* itself denoting either a dairy farm, when used on its own, or lands belonging to whoever, when used as a prefix.

At the time of *Domesday* the population of this manor was 25, not overly large you might think, but in those days there were only seven people said to be living in Sutton, around which Plymouth later grew. Today of course many thousands live around this delightful church. However, walking through the larger, rambling churchyard with its old and towering trees, it is hard to believe you are in the middle of such a densely populated area, No longer the 'haunt of grave-robbers and murderers', the churchyard was cleared, some twenty years ago, of many of its graves and the headstones were ingeniously used as paving stones. Currently maintained as public open space by the Corporation, this is now an idyllic spot.

13th June, 1987.

Devonport Market

JAMES ST.

'The history of the growth of Devonport is the history of the extension of the Government Establishments connected with the town . . .' so wrote R. N. Worth in his 1870 *History of Devonport*. Referring later to the 'extraordinary recent growth' (mainly since 1850) of Stoke and Morice Town he suggested that the 'increased activity of the Government establishments consequent on the Crimean War, largely contributed'. Then adding that such growth 'has now been checked by extensive reductions made in the Dock and Keyham Yards during the past and present years'.

'Peace' said Worth almost philosophically on the next page, 'is most favourable to Plymouth; war and its arts to Devonport'. And for his next example he cited the seven years after the downfall of 'Buonaparte' when the effects of the cessation of war were felt dramatically and recorded thus in 1823.'Numbers of houses are at this time

shut up, and the town affords a melancholy proof of the assertion that peace has come unattended by its usual blessings; instead of being all life and bustle as heretofore it is now quite the reverse; little business is in progress, no employment presents itself to the poor, who are thus without the means of sustenance for themselves and families; the workhouse overflows with tenants, and the number of distressed objects applying for relief is incredible.' Moved by compassion, in the absence of a welfare state, back in 1823: 'Some humane and charitable individuals, in order to alleviate these distresses, have at various times since the peace promoted subscriptions for the purpose of supplying food and labour for the industrious.'

A century and more later, as twentieth-century man endeavours to push forward the frontiers of civilization, a war more devastating than any the world had known before resulted in much of Devonport being razed to the ground. However, when looking in the 1943 Plan for Plymouth we find little evidence today of the grand plans then laid out for Devonport; rather, part of the area earmarked as a section of a tree-lined way running straight on from Morice Street to Mutton Cove has instead been taken over by the Dockyard. No great surprise when, at the beginning of the Devonport section in the Plan, Worth is paraphrased and brought up to date in the sentence 'The future of this city, and particularly of the Devonport area, is dependent upon the maintenance of a Grand Fleet . . .'

In 1956 the South Yard of the already massive Government Establishment took over what had been St. Aubyn Street, most of Fore Street, Cherry Garden Street, Market Street, Barrack Street, Catherine Street and Tavistock Street. It also took Devonport Market.

Originally based in Fore Street, there had been a market on this site since the 1760s. Prior to its construction this area had formerly been a pond which had been filled in and converted 'in a very commodious Manner'. Hoxland, in 1792, describing Devonport market, said that 'the plentiful supplies of every Kind of Provisions which are poured into the Market here three Times a Week, viz, on Tuesdays, Thursdays, and Saturdays, are a Matter of Astonishment to Strangers', and in the 'Mackerel and Pilchard Season, the Quantities exceed all description short of ocular Demonstration'.

The present Market building, designed by J. P. St. Aubyn and erected in 1852, is currently a Sale Store for the Principal Supply and Transport Office. A covered area on two floors it is a listed building of a type we are told is becoming increasingly rare. With its 124 ft high Italianate tower making it still quite a noticeable landmark, perhaps it is not impossible to think, in the light of present circumstances, that one day it may be handed back for civilian use, particularly as Devonport appears not to have fared as well on the shopping and commercial front as the architects of the Plan for Plymouth had apparently intended.

10th August 1985

New Pier Inn

Throughout the nineteenth century James Street, Devonport was a thriving thoroughfare full of a great variety of commercial enterprises that occupied virtually 100 separate premises. Begun in the 1770s, by 1886 James Street boasted schools, churches (St. Michael & St. Joseph's, St. Mary's and a Moravian Chapel), four grocers, two butchers, a chemist, a shoemaker, nine shopkeepers or general dealers, two furniture brokers and a host of other businesses. There were also six or seven public houses including the 'Royal Naval Stores', 'Queen & Constitution', 'Royal Exchange' (on the corner with Pembroke Street), 'Navy Arms' (formerly the 'Oporto'), 'Britannia' and the 'Impregnable'. And there had been more: 'Duncan's Victory', 'Lord Nelson', 'Country House Inn' and the 'Newcastle Tavern' at 50 James Street, an address that, in 1885, had been taken over by a butcher called Mr. Beer!

Today however, of all these busy little commercial enterprises, only a couple survive and one of those is no longer situated in James Street as its line has been re-drawn, placing the 'Queen & Constitution' (known in pre-Victorian days as the 'King & Constitution') firmly in Duke Street. So we are left with one public house, the erstwhile 'Blue Anchor', built at the beginning of last century, renamed the 'Naval Inn' around 1857 and known since the early 1890s as the 'New Pier Inn'. Why the name was changed from the 'Blue Anchor' is not clear. Neither are the reasons why it was recorded variously in street directories between 1857 and 1890 as the 'Naval Inn', 'Royal Naval', 'Royal Naval Stores' or the 'Royal Naval Spirit Stores'. Nevertheless it was. More obvious though, was its second renaming as the 'New Pier Inn', for around this time the little stone, T-shaped pier was constructed off the earlier stoneworks at Mutton Cove. In those days of course, Mutton Cove was virtually a village in itself, with many houses, shops and inns of its own. As it was described in 1879, Mutton Cove was the 'chief place of embarkation and debarkation of seamen and others to or from the ships in the Sound, and also the nearest point to Cremyll on the Mount Edgcumbe shore. Consequently, the watermen of Mutton Cove made a good living ferrying their clients to and fro'. The names of two Mutton Cove Inns telling their own story—one the 'Waterman's Arms' another the 'Mount Edgcumbe Inn' which stood for a century but was no match for its Cremyll namesake. Thus the New Pier at Mutton Cove, which made landings easier irrespective of time and tide, was a boon for trade at this nearby hostelry. Quite how it has come to survive the decline in commerce and the relentless redevelopment of this area (mainly block upon block of flats) is doubtless due, in no small measure, to its proximity to the dockyard wall and the slight kink in the same which leaves this plot awkwardly situated for redevelopment. However, the Inn is on the market as Courage intend to sell it as a free house and the day that happens, current licensees Wendy and Andy Gay will give up the trade after some 16 years which have been shared between here,

'Diamond Lil's' and the 'Western Belle'. 'Wilks' the barman may stay however. Wilks has lived in Devonport all his life and well remembers the last pub to close in James Street, the 'Impregnable' ('that which cannot be moved, or impressed or shaken'), which was pulled down in the course of flat development in the fifties. As well as the 'Impregnable', Ash and Sons, Wine Merchants, were still in business in James Street in the fifties. They too were in the street 100 years ago and as a business, had been founded by Alexander Ash, cork cutter and licensee of the 'New Pier Inn' (when it was the 'Blue Anchor'), from the 1830s through to 1850.

Today then, James Street, although still well populated, is but a shadow of its former self and while the recent Devonport Carnival, organised by the 'New Pier Inn', the 'Crown & Column' and the Red Ribbon Majorettes, was agreed to have been a fair success, it was the first for 15 years. For many years now though, the biggest all year round attraction in the street has been, and continues to be, Bogey Knight's Government Surplus Store! »Postscript

9th August, 1986.

King Billy

At the southernmost tip of the south yard of Devonport Dockyard stands this larger than life, wooden form, affectionately known as King Billy and believed to be the figurehead of the 120-gun, 3-decker fighting ship, Royal William.

Launched on the 2nd of April 1833 from Pembroke Dockyard, 'in the presence of thousands of spectators', the Royal William 'glided past the vessels after taking the water rapidly and would have reached the other shore but her speed was soon checked by letting go her ponderous anchor'. Lady Owen, wife of Sir J. Owen, MP, the Lord-Lieutenant of Pembroke County, conferred the name and cut the ropes. Described then as magnificent, and costing £94,971 to build over 150 years ago, the Royal William was later converted to steam at Devonport and undocked as a screw ship with 72 guns on the 9th of February, 1860.

As Ken Burns tells us in his book *The Devonport Dockyard Story*, 'conversions often necessitated the ship being lengthened by"cutting asunder"—cutting the ship in half—separating the two parts and adding a new section'. At the same time there would be substantial alterations to the fore and aft end of the ship to improve the ship's entry through the water and make room for the screw. And it is at this time that it is thought that the ship's figurehead took up residence in the South Yard. Certainly a photograph from an 1884 edition of the *Navy and Army Illustrated*, shows King Billy here, standing proud in front of the 'last intact eighteenth century building slip in any Royal dockyard' (Jonathan Coad).

Subject of minor controversies through the years—various sources have suggested that King Billy is, not a figurehead but a statue, that it was made by the Dockyard for Devonport Column, or alternatively, that it was the full-size model for Sir John Rennie's statue of King William IV, designed in 1832 and still standing above the entrance to the Royal William Victualling Yard. However, it is listed as a figurehead in early Admiralty catalogues of 'Figureheads, Models, Relics and Trophies etc.' and Peter Norton, in his 1976 book on Ship's' Figureheads, cites it as being 'one of the last full length figureheads in the Navy'.

An unusual, extremely varied and very ancient craft, the creating of figureheads for sea going vessels has been accredited to several different fears and anxieties to which sailors worldwide, are prey. Giancarlo Costa, in perhaps the most comprehensive account of figureheads yet written, tells us that 'the birth of the figurehead and its survival down the ages is to be found in that superstitious element which may be found in superficial religions coupled with a soupçon of the seaman's innate idolatry which endeavours to endow ships with faces, souls and personalities, as in the case with every living thing which is kept or loved'.

The most primitive form of figurehead itself is believed to be a simple, large eye painted on the bow of the ship, possibly in an imitation of a big fish to scare off others or, possibly, just a symbol to protect sailors from the evil spirits and the perils of the sea. After all, when man first took to the sea he thought the world was flat and there was always the fear that if he sailed far enough he might just go too far and fall off the edge of the earth.

Morice Yard

In 1736 the 'West Prospect of His Majesties Dockyard' near Plymouth was drawn-up in fine detail for Sir William Morice, Third Baronet and owner of the Manor of Stoke Damerel, by his 'much Oblig'd and very humble Servants—Samuel and Nathaniel Buck'. Prolific and proficient, the Bucks provided a key to their engraving which included the following description of what is now the Morice Yard of the Devonport Dockyard complex . . . 'To ye north of ye Dock Yard is ye Ordnance Wharf (ye Magazine for Stores of war as ye Yard is for Naval Stores) a Beautiful Pile, built about 12 years ago'. Clearly visible in this particular section of the engraving is the western prospect of this gateway with these two adjacent houses forming then, as they do now, part of the wall of this yard.

The gateway and the houses date from 1722, two years after work had begun on the site and it is thought that the houses were probably designed by the overseer and clerk of the works at the site, Andrew Jelfe, who had been appointed in January 1720. The main buildings comprising this 'Beautiful Pile', however, were more likely the work of the local senior officer, Colonel Christian Lily, and his draughtsman, Mr. Schutze. It has, in the past, been suggested that the great playwright and architect of Castle Howard, Blenheim and Woodstock fame, Sir John Vanbrugh, may have been responsible for the impressive terrace and storehouses here, but Jonathan Coad, in his very thorough paper 'Historic Architecture of HM Naval Base Devonport', suggests it was perhaps just Lily attempting to copy Vanbrugh's style. Certainly, it is quite possible that Sir John cast his eye over the designs; he was after all 'Comptroller of the King's Works' at the time and all plans would have been sent up to the Chief Engineer for approval.

Although properly titled Ordnance Wharf for over 200 years, it was more commonly referred to as Gun Wharf until it became integrated into the Dockyard around 1941, when the Army authorities finally gave it up. It has since been known as Morice Yard in honour of the man who leased the land to the Crown in the first place. That man was Sir Nicholas Morice, 2nd Baronet, father of William, and second son of the 1st Baronet, also William. (Nicholas's older brother was a William too but he died before his father). Morice Town takes its name from this first William who, in 1660, had become Governor of, and Member of Parliament for, Plymouth and played an important part in the Restoration of Charles II. It was he who had arranged the meeting between the emissary of the King in exile, John Grenville, and General Monck from North Devon, whose role in the restoration was ultimately a vital one. For his services Morice was knighted, created baronet (1661) and appointed the King's Secretary of State. Grenville incidentally, was made Earl of Bath and it is his name that appears on the foundation stone of the Citadel dated 1666. Clearly aware of Plymouth's future as a defence base, William Morice shrewdly purchased the Stoke Damerel estate from Sir Edward Wise in 1667 for the princely sum of £11,600. Unfortunately, however, he died and was buried in February 1690, just before the first major new phase of the development of the Stoke Damerel estate took place.

In December 1690 a contract was issued for the building of a stone dock at Point Forward. This of course became the First Yard (South Yard as it is now) and was land

then owned by William's son, the teenaged Nicholas Morice, whose guardian, a 'bad tempered and obstinate Hamburg merchant', said they would require an Act of Parliament before they would sell the land. The Admiralty had after all, signed the contract with the builder before consulting the landowner. In the event the land was leased, and indeed parts of the Dockyard remained leasehold until 1857.

The seeds for Plymouth Dock had been sown back in the days of Cromwell who had established, in the Cattewater, a hulk from which to service and repair naval ships. While subsequent Parliaments and successive Monarchs capitalized on Cromwell's reorganization of the army and navy, in 1683 Charles II effected a thorough reorganization of the Ordnance Board, making it a civil department of state charged with the provision, inspection and custody of all naval and ordnance stores. Thirteen years later, the newly reconstituted Ordnance Board rented part of South Yard as a gunwharf—to supply ships with guns, powder and shot. They soon afterwards moved out, however, to Mount Wise, but attempts to expand there met with hostility from landowner 'Mr Edgecombe', who also wanted an Act of Parliament before he would sell, and so it was that in 1718 the War Department leased this site here, from Sir Nicholas Morice, for a Gun Wharf. Their terms—the same as the Dockyard's, £11.17s.6d. rent per annum.

Today, much added to since the 1720s, the Gun Wharf or Morice Yard, stands as 'not only the earliest but also the most complete ordnance yard left in the country' (Jonathan Coad).

16th May, 1987.

Raglan Barracks

On the 15th May 1976 Admiral Sir David Williams opened the new naval married quarters known as the Raglan Estate. It stands on the site of the old Raglan barracks, of which all that is left today is this impressive Doric-style main gate, built in limestone with granite dressing, between 1853–6, by Captain Fowke. Raglan Barracks themselves, constructed between 1854–8, in turn replaced four of Devonport's original six barracks buildings erected 100 years earlier under a scheme sponsored by George III, in 1757. Before this time British troops, unless they were based in fixed fortifications like the Citadel, tended to be billeted or quartered in private houses or ale houses, a situation not always welcomed by the private individuals thus imposed upon, and certainly not one conducive to general discipline.

To help ease such problems, young Prince George and his advisors produced a scheme to provide buildings that were to be used just for living accommodation for the army. Four one-storey developments were then erected in Plymouth Dock and were christened George, Frederick, Cumberland and Ligonier Squares; Ligonier being named after John (Jean Louis) Ligonier, later Field Marshall, Earl and Military Governor of Plymouth 1752–60. A British soldier, born of a French Huguenot family, Ligonier was knighted by George II on the field, under the royal banner at the battle of Dettingen in 1743. As such he was quite possibly one of the last men ever to be honoured in this way as Dettingen was the last occasion on which a British King personally led his troops to battle. At that time the Duke of Cumberland was Commander-In-Chief of the British troops, and Ligonier, who later succeeded him in that post, was acting as his staff officer.

Frederick Square was possibly named after George III's father, who had died in 1751 nine years before his father, George II and thereby missed becoming the first, and to date the only, King Frederick of Great Britain. George Square, we must assume, was named after the patron of this new-style service accommodation. The new North and South Raglan Barracks, when built, could accommodate two entire regiments of the Line, or 2,000 men and 80 officers. 'A principle and novel feature' of Raglan being the introduction, via more than 1,000 separate jets, of gas lighting. The barrack buildings themselves were set back some 240 feet from the gatehouse and on either side of this feature spread the massive parade ground, some 860 feet long.

Over the years that followed there were odd additions and improvements to Raglan but then in 1937 the War Office decreed that the Barracks were out of date and plans for their demolition were set in motion, with the intention then of handing the site over to the Admiralty. Work on the razing of South Raglan had just begun when war broke out and put a halt to the proceedings. After the war, Raglan received a certain amount of repair and went on to house a Civil Service department and act as headquarters for some of Plymouth's Territorial and Auxiliary Force units. However, when the phasing-out of the Territorial Army began in 1967, Raglan's future again looked doubtful and, despite the various plans for its revival that had appeared since the war, it was eventually pulled down.

Many famous Regiments had been based here in its long history. However, it's not clear whether the great Raglan himself ever visited. Born Lord Fitzroy James Henry Somerset in 1788, Raglan began his military career in 1804 and was in the Peninsula War and Flanders under the command of the Duke of Wellington. At Waterloo he was standing beside Wellington when he was struck by a bullet in the right elbow and had to have his arm amputated on the battlefield, without an anaesthetic. He bore the operation without a word, but when it was ended he called to the orderly 'Hallo, don't carry away that arm 'till I have taken off my ring', a ring which his wife had given him.

Between 1827 and 1852 Somerset was Military Secretary to Wellington, who he then succeeded as Commander-in-Chief of the Army. He was also made Baron Raglan and was appointed head of the British forces in the Crimea. Victorious at Alma, he was present at Balaclava when the Light Brigade made their disastrous charge, and the following month, successfully held off the enemy at Inkerman. After the fearful winter of 1854 in the Crimea, Raglan died in command in June 1855. He was 67.

Today, apart from this one area of Devonport, Raglan is remembered as the man who gave his name to the overcoat without shoulder seams . . . a feature first identified in 1864. This is the raglan sleeve we know now although in 1881 another source described a 'raglan' as being 'a waterproof light overcoat without sleeves.'

25th October, 1986.

Brickfields

'Brickfields—site of clay pits and bricks manufactured: upper part known as Brickfields and lower as Parsonage fields—now all Brickfields.' Such is the description that appears in Henry Whitfeld's book on Plymouth and Devonport, written at the turn of the century. A few years later, another authority claimed that the 'Brickfields are to Devonport what 'the lines' are to Chatham—the scene of frequent military reviews, troops pouring out from adjacent barracks in amazing fashion'.

It is difficult to find any reference to brickworks in this area at any time. The ownership of the land by the Crown, however, has long been established. Indeed the reason the neighbouring Devonport Park was created in the first place, was to end the situation whereby 'persons deviating from the public right of way across the fields' were forever being prosecuted. So it was that in 1858–9 the Public Park was, to quote R. N. Worth, 'formed out of the Brickfield—the north-eastern glacis of the fortifications'. The park then came under the control of the Town Council, while the rest of the Brickfield remained Crown Land. Running through this land and forming the east and north boundary of the old town of Dock, was a massive defensive ditch. Anyone familiar with the Brickfields today can, presumably, get some idea of the scale of this ditch by the drop behind the grandstand which effectively separates the two great, flat recreation areas. It is not all that clear though when the Brickfields first became a recreation area, particularly as our whole idea of recreation has changed a great deal over the years.

In 1857 a Mr. Joll was reported in a newspaper article as saying that he had been a lessee of this Ordnance Land for 20 years and that for 'five times 20 years a way had been enjoyed across them' and further, 'He was convinced of the value of them to the labouring population as a means of healthful recreation, which was as necessary as healthful education, ... It was preposterous', he went on, 'to think of depriving the labouring population of the Town—densely crowded as they were within the fortifications—of the only place of recreation open to them.'

As we have seen, one outcome of all this protest was to free part of the land which became Devonport Park and of course nowadays Mr. Joll would doubtless be quite delighted to know that the rest of the Brickfields was also regularly being let for recreation. However, back in 1857 there were not only no football, hockey or rugby clubs in Devonport, there were none in the County or Country. Indeed, it is doubtful whether organised cricket had made much impact in the area and certainly unlikely that athletics had gained any real foothold in the town, as Britain's oldest athletics club, Exeter College AC, had only just been formed in Oxford seven years earlier.

The second half of the nineteenth century, however, saw all these sports take off as they developed rapidly through the Services, the colleges and the public schools.

In the Plymouth area one of the first great sporting groups was Argyle Athletic Club, formed in 1886, which in the early days had its social headquarters in a basement under a shop on Mutley Plain. Here people actively interested in all branches of sport would meet. There was a Rugby section, which struggled to raise a side strong enough to compete with other local teams, a cricket XI and the legendary athletic club Argyle Harriers. It was, however, the football section that went on to

flourish most successfully. So much so that by 1903 they were able to raise a professional side, an achievement they marked by changing their name to Plymouth Argyle.

Argyle Athletic had already, by this time, acquired the lease of Home Park and on Whit Monday 1901 they staged an athletic sports meeting. That summer they widely advertised that motor cycle racing, whippet racing, pony trotting, running and hurdle events were being promoted to attract the public to the ground during the close season.

Today of course, all the city's major running and hurdle events take place here at the Brickfields. Schools, not only from Plymouth but also in neighbouring parts of Devon and Cornwall, hold their sports days here and in 1983 the English Schools Championships were staged at this venue.

Still run and leased by the Navy, it is now more than 30 years since the Doidges Annual recorded that Devon athletes were 'now fortunate in being able to enjoy the facilities of the Services' well-equipped athletic ground at the Brickfields . . .' In those days Plymouth had a handful of athletics clubs. Plymouth Spartans were among the front runners as were Devonport YMCA, who later became simply Devonport Athletic Club and then a few years after the Spartans folded, it was decided that there should be one main City of Plymouth Athletic Club and so, sometime around 1969, that was the new name adopted by Devonport AC. With their base at the Brickfields, the club currently has training evenings four times a week and last year they had their own clubhouse erected on the site. Never before has the ground been so well equipped as it is now, the top track in Devon and Cornwall, it was blessed with a new grandstand earlier this month—erected in just three weeks by 2 Troop 59 Independent Commando Squadron, Royal Engineers.

With the City, County and the Sports Council putting money into the new granular-rubber track and facilities for different events, the future looks very 'healthy'. It is perhaps just a little sad that the pavilion, incorporating restaurants and bars and providing panoramic views of the track and the area, put forward many years ago by the Nuffield Trust, never got off the ground. It does, after all, have the potential to be one of the finest athletics grounds in the country.

29th August, 1987.

St. Joseph's Church

One hundred and twenty four years ago the Church of St. Michael and St. Joseph was solemnly opened in James Street, Devonport, chiefly to service the needs of those Roman Catholic troops of both the Army and Navy stationed in the Three Towns. The sight of the band leading the soldiers to the 9.30 morning Mass would evidently attract quite a crowd and was dubbed by the *Western Daily Mercury* (the *Herald*'s forerunner), the 'Sunday Morning Spectacular'.

As the years passed and Plymouth (now incorporating Devonport and Stonehouse) became less of a garrison town, so the Church catered increasingly for its civilian congregation. However, with the changing face of Devonport, particularly in the wake of the Blitz, the church and the neighbouring school of St. Joseph's were left increasingly out on a limb.

First to move to this more accessible location, was the school in 1972, then last year, work began on the new church. At the same time the old church was demolished, the money from the sale of the site being used to pay for the new building. Today 48 flats have been built just up from Mutton Cove where the church once stood, and tomorrow, the Rt. Reverend Cyril Restieaux, the Roman Catholic Bishop of Plymouth, will conduct a dedication service here in the new church.

Soon to retire, Bishop Restieaux has started some 63 churches in the Diocese of Plymouth (which includes Cornwall, Devon and Dorset) and his 31 years as Bishop have only previously been surpassed by Bishop Vaughan, amongst whose achievements was the setting up of the original church of St. Michael and St. Joseph in 1860.

The second Roman Catholic Bishop of Plymouth, Bishop Vaughan, held his post for 44 years and such is the record of his successors that in 130 years there have only been 6 men to have filled that role. For Bishop Restieaux, however, tomorrow will be the last public function of this nature that he will perform.

Thirteen years ago the Bishop opened the adjacent St. Joseph's Primary School in Raglan Road and it is ironic that both are now hard by the old Raglan Barracks that once housed so many of its congregation.

The new church is also right next to the earliest post-Reformation site of Roman Catholic worship in the City as it was in a room over a stable of the erstwhile 'George Inn' in Fore Street that the first resident priest in the area, the Irish Franciscan Father Michael Flynn, set up a chapel in 1793. In 1806 another Chapel was established in Stonehouse near the Royal Naval Hospital, but apart from the Cathedral which only antedated it by 5 years, the original Church of St. Michael and St. Joseph had the distinction of being the oldest Roman Catholic Church in the City.

Today the newest St. Joseph's has been built from the inspired designs of Christopher Bilson. Incorporating parts of the old church, it includes one stone used as the foundation stone, and several original windows which have now been incorporated in the foyer area which stands as an affectionate memorial to the old church and contains a small lending library and shop. There is also here a window presented by the Anglican Bishop of Plymouth, the Rt. Reverend Kenneth Newing from the old All Saints Church in Harwell Street. The windows in the main body of the building, however, are new and were designed by Christopher Bilson's colleague, Peter Reading and together they are responsible for all the fixtures and fittings of the church; all of which greatly enhance the simple, yet tremendously successful design of the building. A design which instantly communicates everything Father Bartholomew Nannery hoped it would. Practical and warm, incorporating a great deal of wood, unlike so many modern religious buildings, St. Joseph's looks like a church from the outside and feels like one in the best traditional sense, inside. Employing a basic A frame design in both its superstructure and in many details (the windows, whilst not unduly elaborate, all look as though they belong in a church), St. Joseph's is a very good example of how modern architecture can be inexpensive (it cost £250,000 to build), unfussy yet impressive.

9th November, 1985.

St. Aubyn's, Chapel Street

'... but a small Part of St. Aubyn's Street was built towards the Year 1770. The like may be observed of Chapel Street, and the other Streets in that Quarter down to the present Market. The Date on the Chapel, on Mr. Nelson's Buildings at the South End, are Proofs of its modern Foundation.'

So said Hoxland in his Guide to Plymouth Dock published in 1792.

Originally a Chapel of Ease to Stoke Damerel, St. Aubyn was built, 'under the Authority of an Act of Parliament' in 1771–2 at a cost of £7,000 and Hoxland went on to describe it thus ... 'The exterior of the Chapel is in the Style of modern Architecture, on which we shall not enlarge. It has a Dial Plate to the West, to shew the Time to the Inhabitants; and on its small square Tower, which contains but one Bell, a neat and plain octagonal Spire is erected, surmounted by a Vane to discover the Current of the Wind. It is surrounded by a Wall and Balustrades; and has three Entrances all at the West End, to the several Iles and to the Galleries.'

If the appearance of the Chapel failed to impress its contemporaries it seems that time has failed to give it any charm; writing in 1879, Historian W. H. K. Wright said of St. Aubyn's '... It has no feature either of architectural style or decoration worthy of note'. The spire, according to Wright, was 'ill-proportioned' and the portico was 'heavy'. Possibly a later addition to the Chapel, this 'Doric' portico, were it still standing, would have taken the middle and main entrance to the church right out into this busy road. However, like the original pillar to pillar railings that once enclosed the front of St. Aubyn's, it has long since gone. As has the top of the spire which was taken down after damage sustained during the last war had made it unsafe. It is unlikely now that the spire will ever be replaced. The original timepiece, which was destroyed by enemy action in the Blitz, was replaced after the war with a clock given by Lord St. Levan (a title first conferred upon John St. Aubyn his grandfather in 1887). Sadly, despite being restored and repaired in the 1970s, this clock has not kept time for several years.

However, while the exterior of the church has suffered a little over the years, inside the picture is very promising as the current incumbent, Tim Deacon, who followed Ivor Marsh here four years ago, has great plans for the existing two galleries with a third to be re-erected inside the main entrance. Furthermore, the nearest of the two blocked side entrances is about to be reopened with a ramp, especially constructed by workers with the Community Programme Agency, for the benefit of those attending the church in wheelchairs. As Churchwarden George Austin (who has been associated with St. Aubyn's for 35 years including 15 as Verger) observes, the future looks particularly healthy for the oldest and only surviving Anglican church in Devonport. From the 1850s through to the 1940s there had been four others in the area; St. Paul's (1851) in Morice Square, St. James (1851) in Duke Street, St. Mary's (1852) in James Street and St. Stephen's (1858) on the corner of Clowance Street and George Street. St. Mary's, although it survived the war, was later demolished, the Church authorities decreeing that one church in the area would now be enough and so St. Aubyn's it is that has survived. The four later churches, incidentally, were all designed by the man who was also responsible for Devonport Market—J. Piers St.

Aubyn. As an architect J. P. St. Aubyn was based in the Manor Office adjacent to the church and separated from it by a small grassed area which currently sports a fine variety of cherry tree and which is preserved by yet another Act of Parliament to be a green area 'for all time'. The Manor Office is made up of six small cottages, which were constructed in 1775 and which were leased out by the St. Aubyn Estate. In 1867 Edward St. Aubyn junior was appointed agent to this Estate and immediately he moved into one of the cottages (No. 9 Chapel Street or Green) and established his offices and accommodation there. Long used by the Estate Agents, today nos. 9, 10 and 11 are occupied by the offices of Atkey Goodman the Accountants, while nos. 12 and 13, facing Chapel Street, are currently occupied by James Piers St. Aubyn (nephew of Lord St. Levan) who is a financial consultant.

The St. Aubyn family acquired the Manor of Stoke Damerel, upon which Devonport is built, back in 1749 upon the death of the last male member of the Morice family, Sir Nicholas Morice, who left the Manor to his elder sister's son, 23-year old John St. Aubyn. Originally a French family, the St. Aubyns are said to have come over with the Conqueror. The family seat is St. Michael's Mount and, although the bulk of their estate is in Cornwall, the ground rents of several hundred properties in Devonport are still paid to them.

Beyond Manor Office and these cottages, south of Barrack Street were many other fine 18th century buildings which survived the Blitz and which stood for a good ten years or more thereafter. Sadly, however, there is today but one survivor, the 'Brown Bear'. Opened in April 1774 as just 'The Bear', it was so named with good reason as then a large bear pit in the cellar was used for live bear fights and doubtless a wild time was had by all. Today licensee Rod Jordan runs a much more orderly establishment, with a large and attractive restaurant due to open next month.

21st November, 1987.

The Forum

From the little that remains of Fore Street today it's hard to imagine that this was ever 'The shopping dormitory of the West' and 'remained so up to the outbreak of the second World War' (Pat Ghillyer). Large and impressive it was, however, running from the Dock Gates to Granby Barracks and housing over 100 businesses. These included Tozers, Woolworths, British Home Stores, Boots, Timothy Whites, Marks & Spencers, Liptons and Hepworths, almost a dozen hotels or public houses, an imposing post office and three cinemas—The Electric, The Tivoli and The Forum.

Sadly, little of Fore Street survived the Blitz or the redevelopment and replanning that followed it and today most of it would stand inside the new boundary wall of Devonport Dockyard. Strangely enough, one of the few pre-war buildings that has survived is the old Forum Cinema. Not that it was old when war broke out in 1939 because it had only opened the previous year.

Standing alone today, the Forum, when opened, was flanked by Singers on one side and Hockings Musical Instrument Warehouse on the other. The complete block ran from St. Aubyn Street to High Street; the Forum screen itself set back from Fore Street, virtually backed on to High Street or 'Coal Racket Ope' as it was known in the middle of the last century. At that time George Hearle's Printing and Stationery Premises occupied the site now taken up with the Forum's main entrance, while 100 years ago A. H. Swiss & Co. Printer and Bookseller and sole Devonport agent for Eyre Bros., who published *The Plymouth, Devonport etc. Directory* from which this piece of information was taken, occupied this site. Indeed that was the name that was last advertised on the outside of the building before the Welsh-based firm that set up

the Forum, placed their tiled facade over the top of the earlier Victorian frontage. A picture in the *Evening Herald* of 16th November 1937 showed the Swiss & Co. frontage, stating that it had 'been bought with the intention of building a kinema'. It went on to add that the 'site has considerable depth and includes the former Princess Street Chapel'.

Princess Street was then perhaps better known as the home of the Hippodrome, a 2,000-seater cinema that had opened in 1908 as a music hall. Sadly, the Hippo (as its roof proclaimed) disappeared along with the Electric nearby in the 1941 Blitz, whilst the Tivoli had never been the same after the passing of its well loved manager of many years standing, Harry Harcourt. After losing its nearest rivals, the days of the postwar Forum were very busy ones. Ron Wilson, a projectionist at the Drake Cinema since it opened in 1958, served his four-year apprenticeship at the Forum and recalls how well business went, even in the 1950s. Only two weeks behind the major Plymouth cinemas with its programmes, the seats were cheaper and, like its counterparts, the programme changed every three days with a different bill again on Sundays. Meanwhile, the weekly Movietone newsreels were shared with the old Gaumont (later the Odeon) which showed them on Mondays, Tuesdays and Wednesdays before passing them over to the Forum. Telford Davey was then manager, whilst Robert Liddicoat saw out the 1950s and the end of the Forum's days as a cinema at the beginning of the 1960s.

By 1961, however, the Forum had been cleared of all cinema seats, and boxing, wrestling, roller-skating and bingo were now the order of the day. In 1965 there were plans, reported by Angela Rippon in one local newspaper, to convert the Forum into an 1,800-seater theatre. However, they never bore fruit and today the building, having passed from the Devonport Cinema Company to Mecca to Top Rank, thrives under manager Hugh Dorliac as a plush Bingo Hall, although it is still just possible to imagine how the old cinema might have looked inside.

26th October, 1985.

Belisha Beacons

It was in Kensington Road, London, in the summer of 1934 that the first yellow globes mounted upon distinctive black and white banded poles first appeared on Britain's roadsides. Designed to draw attention to pedestrian crossings first established in 1926, the globes were originally made of glass, easy prey for small boys; they were soon replaced with painted aluminium globes. In July 1952 the now familiar plastic beacon with winking light appeared. The beacons were the brainchild of the then Minister of Transport, Leslie Hore-Belisha, the sitting Liberal MP for Plymouth, Devonport. The name Belisha-Beacon was suggested in a letter to the 'Times', of 13th October 1934, in response to an earlier suggestion 'Beleacon'.

A former journalist with a keen sense of the power of the media, Leslie Hore-Belisha had only been appointed Minister of Transport in June 1934 and he lost little time launching a campaign against what he called, 'mass murder on the roads'. His beacons were just one of the valuable measures introduced by him that summer. However, coming as they did during the Parliamentary recess when politicians traditionally take their summer break and Fleet Street enters a lean period for stories, generally dubbed the silly season when all sorts of nonsense can make the headlines, he encountered a lot of flak from certain quarters who claimed it was a publicity seeking ploy of 'great vulgarity, as was to be expected of a Liberal'. Whatever his critics may have said, however, there was no disputing the fact that during 1935, although the amount of motor traffic had increased substantially, the number of deaths on the roads had fallen by 822 and the number injured had fallen by a staggering 12,805. This of course, did not mean that these peculiar roadside lollipops were not fair game for the cartoonists and music hall and radio personalities, all of which helped ensure the popularity of the Belisha Beacon pencils and cigarette holders which followed. And indeed the popularity of the man himself, among whose other 'achievements' at the time were the successful introduction of the 30 miles an hour speed limit in town, the silent zone between 11.30 pm and 7 am when the sounding of motor horns was prohibited, and for every new driver, a driving test which would then cost seven shillings and sixpence.

Such was Hore-Belisha's skill in organizing and his energy in pursuing his aims that he was quickly singled out for political advancement. In 1935 he was made a Privy Councillor and by October 1936 he had been given a seat in the Cabinet. He

was then 42. Like his Devonport counterpart today, Dr. David Owen, Hore-Belisha had won this Plymouth Division seat and entered Parliament while still in his twenties. Many, at one time, would have tipped Hore-Belisha to become Prime Minister, but after a very encouraging start as Minister of War, soon after he had completed a brilliant job of overhauling the Army both with respect to recruitment and promotion from the ranks, Hore-Belisha's upward drive ended rather abruptly, after he was dropped by Neville Chamberlain in a cabinet reshuffle in January 1940. Although he continued to sit for Devonport until his defeat by Michael Foot in 1945, the Devonport born Hore-Belisha never held high office again and although there were rumours of his attempting to return to the Commons, his last involvement with Parliament was in the Lords after he had been created Lord Hore-Belisha of Devonport.

Meantime Devonport, along with the rest of the country, continues to reap the rewards of improved pedestrian safety generated by Belisha beacons. Plymouth alone has 35 sites with beacons like this one here, situated near the top of Albert Road, Devonport, in the heart of Hore-Belisha's old constituency. Zebras, Pelicans and Pandas have arrived on the scene since, but still, 50 years on, the old Belisha beacon is being put up in new places.

21st December, 1985.

St. Levan Road Viaduct

The railway line that ran across this viaduct was opened officially on the 30th May, 1890. Ninety-seven years later all that remains of it are photographs, drawings and memories.

Demolition of this St. Levan Road, or Ford, Viaduct was completed earlier this year after almost 23 years of disuse, the last trains calling at Ford Station on 6th September 1964. Like King's Road Station at Devonport, which closed at the same time, nothing now remains of this once busy stop. However, right up to its closure, no less than thirteen trains a day serviced commuters to Plymouth, with a fourteenth being added on Saturdays. The Sunday service, on the other hand, saw only three local runs, all after midday, although there were also morning trains to Tavistock and Exeter. For through train passengers arriving from London or bound for London, this meant either finding yourself on the platform just after 7 o'clock in the morning after an overnight trip from Waterloo (the 1.15 am passenger and news train), or travelling the other way, waiting for the 12.05 pm.

Built to service an area of housing that had largely been constructed to accommodate the growing dockyard workforce in the second half of last century, the station remained an important stop for 'Dockyardies' until its end. An end which was foreseeable once Southern Region lines west of Salisbury were transferred to the Western Region in the wake of the Beeching Report published in 1963. Desperately unpopular in many rural areas, the closure of this line to Tavistock was just part of the many casualties of the Beeching axe. This axe, wielded by the first Chairman of the newly constituted British Railways Board, Richard Beeching, had to have the effect of making the railways pay, or at least lose less money, and he sought to do this by concentrating on main lines, at the expense of half the country's smaller stations and about a third of Britain's total route mileage which, it was argued, were a huge drain on resources and only contributed about 2 per cent of the total revenue. In

some places of course, the situation was worse than others, particularly as the old rivalries between the old separate Railway bodies had, in the past, created duplications and complications. Here at Ford for example, Station Road had, between 1904 and 1941, a station at either end of it; the one serviced by the Great Western Railway—Ford Halt, bombed in 1941 and never rebuilt, and the other Southern Railways, aforementioned, Ford (Devon) Station 1890–1964. It was called Ford (Devon), incidentally, to save confusion with Ford (Sussex) which still operates just outside Littlehampton. However, as Bernard Mills noted in one of several of his memorable 'Back Track' Herald pieces about this area '... Just to complicate matters, Sussex Road and Sussex Terrace are almost adjacent to Ford (Devon)!' Lamenting the passing of Ford, 'a classic example of the wayside Station', he elsewhere expressed the hope that the viaduct might 'be maintained for some useful purpose'. Sadly, that was not to be and, within a matter of weeks of that article, it was announced that the City Council, who had bought the viaduct many years earlier, now intended to demolish it.

Now that massive, seven-arched construction has gone for ever, no longer does it span the 135 yard gap across St. Levan Valley or tower a maximum 83 feet above the ground. Today a massive scar cuts across the valley, but soon the southern site, adjacent to the St. Levan Inn, will see a 39 dwelling City Council housing development (14 flats, 25 houses). A difficult site to plan for, by 1990, when the viaduct would have been 100 years old, it will be hard to imagine it was ever there at all, although at present no details have been decided on the development of the northern site. It is interesting to note by the way, that some of the stonework from the old viaduct will be used in the construction of the new dome on the Hoe.

The earlier Keyham Viaduct, or bridge, of course, is still in use and it originally dates back to a time when Keyham Lake still reached up to this point and there was no housing at all in the area. Timber built, in 1859, to take the railway into Cornwall, this bridge has been rebuilt twice since, first around the turn of the century and then again in 1937. The word viaduct, incidentally, first entered our language in 1818, when such constructions were first erected for train traffic, albeit horse-drawn traffic. The word itself is based on the Roman 'aqueduct', typically, huge man-made ducts often borne high on brick archway bridges and examples of which survive from before the time of Christ. A time, incidentally, that we have to go back to for the derivation of the name St. Levan, for if we are to believe the authority of one former incumbent of St. Levan Church, near Porthcurno, there was no real St. Levan as such, rather St. Levan comes to us via 'Selevan' the Celtic way of saying Solomon. Porthcurno, evidently, was a favourite haunt of Selevan. However, why the name St. Levan Road was ever given to a road once known as Keyham Lake Road appears to be a mystery which even local folklore cannot explain.   »Postscript

31st October, 1987.

St. Levan Gate

The Royal Dockyard was begun over 150 years before Keyham Steam Yard was founded. In those distant days the idea that steam would ever replace sail was unthinkable. However by the middle of last century already over a quarter of the ships in the Royal Navy had steam power. Furthermore Her Majesty's fighting ships were now bigger than ever and the existing Devonport wharfage accommodation could no longer cope with the demands being made upon it.

An appropriate site for a new 'Steam Yard' was sought – on both sides of the Tamar. In the event the land chosen was just half a mile up river from the original Dockyard. Comprising of 43 acres of foreshore and 38 of land the site was purchased from the Trustees of the St. Aubyn estate.

On 12th September, 1846, the First Lord of the Admiralty, the Earl of Auckland, laid a massive nine ton 'foundation stone' which was, in turn, incorporated into the South Lock entrance to the basin. Eight years later the new yard was complete. However had Parliament known just how expensive the project was going to be, in the beginning, it is possible that they would never have approved the work. Initially they were told about £400,000 was to be the likely cost but within a few years almost one million pounds had been added to that figure. Still, built it was and although it was only a short distance away from the Dockyard, the Steam Yard was operated as a distinctly separate entity with different hours of work, rates of pay and conditions. In 1853 it was even granted its own Police Force.

The geographical separation was soon blurred however with the construction, between 1854 and 1856, of an interconnecting tunnel. At first this was only for pedestrians and horse and cart traffic; but then in 1876 it was turned into a railway tunnel and, in the same year, the two yards became fully integrated in all other respects.

The main land entrance to the new steam yard was, for general convenience, situated at the southern end of the site. Soon dubbed the Albert Road Gate this imposing edifice served until midnight on 4th September, 1966. The grand old towers remained and the old Dockyard clock was moved from the one tower to the other to be nearer the road. But the entrance itself was walled up. Albert Road was not the only gateway to the steam yard though – a second had been opened at the northern end in 1869. 30 years later it was moved a little to its present location opposite the bottom of St. Levan Road.

The move came as Keyham was in the process of a massive extension, which almost doubled the existing area of Dockyard acreage, from 140 to 270 acres. All this was good news for the proprietor of the 'Avondale Arms'.

Said to be named in honour of a Scottish Duke who had men working in the yard at some time, the 'Avondale Arms' was originally known as the 'Sportsman Arms' and appears to be contemporary with the Keyham Yard itself. In recent years the

'Arms' have been dropped by landlord Arthur Squire who arrived here in 1950, the year Starkey Knight and Ford bought this pub which was previously owned by William Williams. Quite when the inn was bought by William Williams is unclear but there was a W. J. Williams here in 1880. Certainly consistency has always been a feature of this pub and Arthur Squire is probably the longest serving licensee in one pub in the city today. Born and bred in the trade (his father started out in the 'Valiant Soldier' in Notte Street in 1909) Arthur came here after a few years in the Army. His customers however have almost invariably been Naval personnel or dockyard workers. In his early days here he reckoned on a balance of trade that was 90% Navy 10% dockyard. Today he says those percentages have just about been reversed. The overall figures though have declined quite considerably – the results of a smaller fleet, a smaller dockyard workforce and a smaller lunchbreak for that workforce.

Ship's lunches today, of course, are generally that much more palatable than they were in days of yore and the issue of rum instituted by the Navy many moons ago in order to give the men a better appetite for what was often rotten food, was finally stopped in 1970. However to keep this old naval tradition going, the Avondale has served tots here twice a day ever since. These 'tots' of 100 proof rum while not given away are half price at the appropriate times and Arthur Squire says that on a good day in the past his 'men' would get through up to 15 bottles of rum in half an hour!

Perhaps it's just as well they made the St. Levan Road gate much wider in the late 1970s.

11th June, 1988.

Ford Palladium

Situated opposite the bottom of one of the city's steepest major roads, Ford Hill, is Palladium Limited—Builders Merchants and Home Improvement Centre, better known, perhaps, to many locals as the old Ford 'Bug House'.

However, it is now twenty-one years since the screen of the Ford Palladium has shown any films. The last performance took place on the 15th November, 1964; a date that appears to have eluded other chroniclers and at least one regular, as a sad little story from a local paper at the time noted. According to this account, one veteran, female cinema-goer walked through the door of the Palladium on the 16th, made her way to her favourite seat and settled down for one of her usual 'quiet afternoons' of cinema viewing, whereupon, true to form, the lights went out but the screen remained unlit. When the dear lady came back out into the foyer she met the proprietor, Mr. Cyril Charters, who told her 'I'm afraid it's all over, the Palladium has closed for good . . .' 'Economic reasons' had forced Mr. Charters to call it a day and so it was that one of the oldest cinemas in town joined the growing list of kinematic emporiums to fall by the wayside.

It had first become the Ford Palladium back in August 1912 after a three month period of refurbishment and renewal. It had previously enjoyed some years as the Theatre Metropole, home of melodramatic and music hall entertainment, and opened, according to one source, in 1893. At some time activity here literally raised the roof by six feet and this was quite possibly at the time of its conversion to a combined picture and music hall. When it was first built the theatre stood overlooking acres of lush farmland with the newly built terraces of the growing Ford Estate behind it. In the middle of last century Keyham Lake would have reached up beyond this point to the top of what is now St. Levan Road and all of this area was open fields. However, this was a time when the development of the Steam Yard at Devonport was creating a lot of work in the dockyard and there was a great need to establish some housing in the area. So it was that when, in 1855, the area known as Ford, one of the few pieces of freehold land left in the borough, was put on the market, it was readily bought up and developed for 'working class' accommodation by the Devon and Cornwall Freehold Land Society.

Within a few years a 'new road to Ford' had been built along the edge of Keyham Lake from what was then Brandreth Road and is now Keyham Road. Today St. Levan's road stretches from St. Levan's Gate to just below Milehouse. The new way, when first constructed, however, was called Keyham Lake Road. The oldest crossroads along its length is undoubtedly this one and the north south route, along here across Keyham Lake at the ford (hence the name Ford) had been a comparatively busy one since the Tudor development of the road from the mill bridge over Stonehouse Creek was built by Piers Edgecumbe.

The approximate size and scale of Keyham Lake can still be appreciated by looking at a street map and working inland from number 4 basin and following the green expanses along the north side of St. Levan Road. That the water still comes up this far was verified when the extension, last year, to Palladium Limited was carried out and the new building was created on a kind of floating pontoon, there being a great deal of water just below the surface here at high tide.

Today it is just possible to imagine how the 400-seater cinema might have looked when walking around the inside of this old building, but it's hard now to imagine there being such queues outside on a Saturday morning that many children would be turned away.

14th December, 1985.

St. Marks, Ford

In his *History of Devonport,* published in 1870, R. N. Worth chronicled the rapid expansion of the early Victorian parts of Stoke and Morice Town then wrote '. . . To the extraordinary recent growth thus showing the increased activity of the Government establishments consequent on the Crimean War, largely contributed . . .' he then added: 'it has now been checked by the extensive reductions made in the Dock and Keyham Yards during the past and present years.'

It is from that same burst of development, based on a busy dockyard, that we find origins of the new suburban district of Ford after the former little estate was bought and divided into allotments for building in 1855, the year after the erection on the Saltash Road of the Devonport Workhouse. When first built the Workhouse, now converted and better known today as Wolseley Home, would have stood almost entirely on its own. Within a few years, however, the new young suburb of Ford sprang up east of the Saltash Road.

By 1881 the following roads had appeared on the map; Sussex, Adelaide (now Auckland), Alexandra, Kent, Cambridge and Alfred plus Clyde Street, Bedford Street and Seaton Place. All this meant that the area now boasted a sizeable population. Small wonder then that certain of their number felt that their parish church of Stoke Damerel was a little too far away and that it was time Ford had its own church. So it was that in the 1870s a band of determined Christians managed to raise £520, a lot of money in those days and sufficient then to buy a plot of land in Cambridge Road and to start building. They began with the chancel and the Bishop of Exeter laid the foundation stone on the 3rd of January 1874. However, building did not properly commence until October 1875 and, although the chancel was completed the following year, it was not until 1882 that the nave and aisles were built; the work only proceeding as money became available.

By this time though, it had long been used for services. These started here two years before the Bishop of Exeter consecrated St. Marks, on St. Stephen's Day—26th December 1879. Designed by Alfred Norman, the architect also responsible for the Workhouse, the whole project cost between £3,000–£5,000 (£1,000 of which was contributed by the Three Towns Church Extension Society). In 1885, St. Marks became a separate parish and has now become mother church of three offspring; The Good Shepherd Mission (which is now St. Thomas the Apostle), Renown Street, Keyham, erected in 1908, itself becoming a separate parish in 1929; St. Anne's Swilly, a temporary wooden structure put up in 1930 which served until the transfer of War Damage funds from the blitzed St. James-the-Less at West Hoe made possible the building of St. James-the-Less at Ham; and thirdly, St. Clement's in Warleigh Avenue which had been built in 1913 but which was destroyed in the 1941 Blitz. Back in the early days at St. Marks, however, before the church was complete, J. W. Gaud was vicar and among those who regularly attended his services in the late 1870s was young Robert Falcon Scott, one of the first and, undoubtedly, one of the most famous choirboys to have sung in St. Marks. In those days Scott lived with his family in Outland House. He left Plymouth before the church was finished in 1880 when he was just 12 years old, to join HMS *Britannia* as a naval cadet. Outlands remained the Scott family home for some time. Sadly, it was pulled down after sustaining damage

in the last war and St. Bartholomew's Church now stands on that site. Now while St. Bartholomew's has a piece of a tree in which Scott carved his name, mounted and preserved in a glass case, St. Marks has a half lifesize, wooden carving of 'Scott of the Antarctic' within its walls. The statue is the work of David Weeks and was unveiled in 1956, at a service attended by the naturalist, Peter Scott (son of the great explorer) and three of Scott's ex-comrades. St. Marks also has a Processional Crucifix made out of wood, from HMS *Rodney*. Kenneth Thompson, who was wartime vicar here, also served as the Chaplain of HMS *Rodney*. The present incumbent, Brian Whitehead, has been at St. Marks for seven years but although he'll still be here for the Easter services, he will have moved up country by the 25th April—St. Mark's Day. St. Mark or John Mark, to whom the church is dedicated, was the author of the second gospel and for some peculiar reason the eve of his day, 24th April, is associated with two strange superstitions. One has it that all persons fated to die in the coming twelve months will have their ghosts pass into the church that night. The other concerns brides to be and was thus described in 'Poor Robin's Almanack' of 1770, 'On St. Mark's Eve at twelve o'clock, The fair maid will watch her smock, To find her husband in the dark, By praying unto good St. Mark'.

4th April, 1987.

St. Nicholas HMS Drake

On the 18th March 1905 Sir E. H. Seymour, Admiral of the Fleet, laid the foundation stone for this Church in the Royal Naval Barracks, Devonport. A little under two years later on 18th February 1907, the completed church was dedicated by the Right Reverend Archibald Robertson, Bishop of Exeter.

The Church is dedicated to St. Nicholas who is amongst other things the patron saint of all seafarers. Not surprisingly this is a common dedication around our coastline and of course, the little chapel that stood for centuries on Drake's Island was, for most of that time, known as St. Nicholas' Chapel, indeed the island itself was long known as St. Nicholas' Island. In time strangely enough, both the island and the barracks were renamed in honour of Sir Francis Drake and here in the church, as in the rest of the barracks, there are several Drake mementos.

A large model of the ship in which Drake circumnavigated the globe, the *Golden Hind* (originally the *Penguin*), hangs in the Nave. Under a later Captain, Thomas Flemyng, the Golden Hind was the first ship to sight the Spanish Armada and Flemyng it was who interrupted the legendary game of bowls upon the Hoe. The *Golden Hind* model was made by ratings based at HMS Drake. A silver replica of this ship stands in *Drake* Wardroom; there too they have a replica of Drake's Drum. The church, on the other hand, has a silver replica of the Drum. This drum has a somewhat chequered history. It was presented by the men of Devon to HMS *Devonshire* in 1904. Thereafter it was handed down through subsequent ships of that name until in 1929 it was installed aboard the last HMS *Devonshire*. A number of strange and unfortunate incidents then occurred on board and superstitious members

of the crew put them all down to the presence of the drum. It all began on 26th July, 1929, when one of *Devonshire*'s gun turrets mysteriously blew up. It was followed by 'a spate of men falling down ladders, then two officers were fired on by the Turks'. Drake's spirit resented the Drum being where it was, said the men, and they asked the captain to remove it, but he wouldn't.

Some time later, when the *Devonshire* was taking part in a fleet regatta, the Captain ordered the Drum to be brought up and beaten in triumph after his ship had won the first race. His order was duly executed and the Devonshire won no further races that day! The final straw, however, came in November 1936 when the *Devonshire* was re-commissioned. Ten days after the ceremony a telegraphist fell down from the main mast and, once again, the Drum was blamed. This time the new Captain was persuaded to write to the Commodore of the Royal Naval Barracks to ask if the Drum could be landed, at least until a less superstitious crew should man the ship. And so the Drum came to St. Nicholas' Church where, doubtless, even the most superstitious sailor would not have attributed the bombing of the church, on the night of 21st/22nd April, 1941 to the presence of the Drum. An incendiary bomb fell into the centre aisle of the church that night and a few windows were broken. But the damage was slight compared to the losses elsewhere in the barracks. One after another the Gunnery School, the Signal School, the central reading room, the Drill Shed, the Commodore's House, the Mechanical Training Establishment and the Boscawen Block were hit and set ablaze; 113 lives were lost in the barracks that fateful night.

A small patch of newer oak blocks in the floor of the church is the only obvious sign today of the repairs done to the damage sustained here that night. In 1953 the Church was redecorated and in the process a number of White Ensigns taken from famous ships of the First World War were taken down, many in a very bad state of repair, and these were replaced by a number of Ships' Badges taken from vessels which served in the Second World War.

On the pillars in the Nave are badges from ships commissioned from the West Country Division RN, while in the chancel are the badges of some of those ships that were lost in action.

Also in the church today is the Armada section of Tom Mor's New World Tapestry, which is currently being worked on by a number of people. There will be a special Drake Armada service in St. Nicholas on 10th July and there will be readings from the 1552 prayer book that Drake would have used.

For Chaplain Tony Ross it will be one of his last services. Like his 36 predecessors his stay here is limited to around $2-2\frac{1}{2}$ years. Rather like a rural dean, the Drake Chaplain is the co-ordinator of the whole western area of naval chaplaincies, stretching from Culdrose to Yeovilton. However, his flock is by no means restricted to naval families, St. Nicholas is also open to civilian worshippers.

26th March, 1988.

HMS Drake

There have been 23 sea-going 'Drake's' in British service named, for the most part, in honour of Sir Francis Drake. The last of these was launched at Pembroke in 1901. An 18-gun, twin-screw cruiser, she was 14,000 tons and was capable of a speed of 24 knots. Her first captain was Admiral Sir Francis Bridgeman who, just before the First World War, became First Sea Lord. This *Drake*, unfortunately, became a casualty of the Great War when it was torpedoed by a U-boat off the north coast of Ireland in 1917. It did, however, manage to reach harbour before sinking in shallow water.

The first *Drake* was also lost in action 329 years earlier. This was the *Thomas Drake*, a 200-ton merchant ship, crewed by 80 men and owned by Sir Francis Drake. The ship was commanded by Henry Spindleow and served under Sir Francis against the Armada. Indeed, the *Drake* took part in the confrontations off Plymouth, Portland and the Isle of Wight, but her most important role in the campaign was also her last. At Calais she was sent in on the tide, with all sails set and fully ablaze, amidst the Spanish ships at anchor. So successful was this drifting fire ship that many of the Spaniards cut their cables and tried to escape only, as the history books recount, to be defeated.

On 31 July 1933, in the wardroom of *Vivid* (as the Devonport Royal Naval Barracks were then known), a Drake Dinner was held in the Mess, to celebrate 'the victory over the Spanish Armada and to do honour to the memory of Sir Francis Drake and his companions in that great battle . . . A game of bowls was played on the lawn afterwards'. This Drake Dinner was a great success and became an annual event. It is perhaps more significant though, that as a result of a suggestion made at that dinner, the name of the barracks was changed from *Vivid* to *Drake*. The name *Vivid* had come from an earlier Commander-in-Chief's yacht—HMS *Vivid*—but the new name became effective from 1st January 1934.

With the new name came new cap ribbons and a new ship's motto and badge. The motto—*Sic Parvis Magna* ('thus from small things to great things')—is taken from an inscription on the original Drake's Drum, a replica of which was presented to HMS *Drake* in 1963. This replica was made in London in 1917, for the Commander of the Drake Battalion of the Naval Division, Cdr. Walter Sterndale Bennett, who then used it to drum his men into action.

The badge of HMS *Drake* also relates to Sir Francis as it features a 'Wyvern passant red, armed and tongued blue'. Now while no wyvern or dragon appears in the arms granted to Drake in 1581, it is known that he liked to use one in his arms and of course, the name *Drake* is derived from the Latin draco, meaning dragon.

Another feature of Drake's coat of arms is the visored helmet, which denotes his knighthood, and this is one of the features engraved upon the blade of a two and three-quarter pound sword which belonged to Drake and which today has pride of place among the trophies in the wardroom of HMS *Drake*. The sword was transferred here from Portsmouth when the barracks changed its name in 1934. It is on permanent loan from the Williams family in whose ownership it has been for the past 100 years.

The Wardroom has one other period Drake artefact, the 'Coconut Cup', a cup

made from a coconut that Drake is said to have brought back from his travels and which has been finely mounted, strapped and topped in silver, while the shell has been engraved with the Royal Arms, the Arms of Drake and those of the Courtenay family (into which Drake's widow married in 1597). In those days, amazingly enough, the coconut would have cost more to acquire than the silver it is mounted in! Another similar cup, mounted in gold, is believed to have been given to Drake by Elizabeth I.

One of the Wardroom's best known trophies must undoubtedly be their silver replica of Drake's ship the *Golden Hind*. This model was made in London in 1936 as a display piece and for fifteen years the jewellers would not sell it. However, in 1951 they did finally agree to part with it and it was purchased by the Mess. It later became very well known to Westward TV viewers when the station used the model as its emblem for a number of years.

The Wardroom itself was not completed until the barracks had been in operation for some 14 years, by which time the clock tower had seen seven years service, having been completed in August 1896. Interestingly, for the first years of its existence the clock tower was surmounted by semaphore arms which were used to communicate directly with the Mount Wise base. These were soon rendered obsolete, however, by the introduction of 'electrical communication' in 1897. Today communications are very sophisticated, but certain traditions remain to convey a sense of timelessness, like the Drake Dinner. This year's dinner, however, will be a very special one—marking the 400th anniversary of the Armada—as it will be attended by Her Majesty Queen Elizabeth II; a fitting beginning to a series of celebrations that will culminate, next year, with the 100th anniversary of the establishment of the naval barracks here.

The Submarine

In 1825 it would appear that the Reverend C. T. Collins-Trelawny of Ham erected the 'Camel's Head Inn' for the benefit of those men involved in laying the new road from Plymouth. Ironically, 160 years later, this same inn is to be pulled down in order to further develop this same road. In those days, Camel's Head creek, or Weston Mill Lake as it is properly known, ran right up to Weston Mill and even at the turn of the century this route alongside the inn was negotiable for travellers on foot only. A small tram depot on the western side of the swamp, crossed here by a footbridge, appears to have stimulated the development of the embankment capable of carrying trams and other vehicles and turned this road into the very busy thoroughfare it is today. However, that it is a very old route is obvious from the ancient and recently painted milestone that stands in the wall of No. 17 Brooklyn Terrace opposite and just along from the erstwhile 'Camel's Head Inn', and which informs the traveller that Plymouth is still two miles away!

In 1978 the 'Camel's Head' was rechristened and the large facsimile camel's head, which for years had been in the alcove above the door, disappeared with the name. Such is not to say that the name has gone altogether. It has only gone from the Inn, but the very presence of a carved camel's head raises one of the favourite local questions—why was the area called Camel's Head in the first place? Certainly it seems unlikely that there ever was a spur of land or a stretch of water around that was shaped like a camel's head, although any trace of it would doubtless have long disappeared anyway and the legend does persist here and there. Nevertheless, it seems far more plausible that the name is a simple derivative from the name of the family who, in medieval times owned this land—the Kemylls or Kemells as they were variously known. Indeed, C. W. Bracken in his *History of Plymouth*, put it thus: 'In

Edward I's reign (1272–1307) John Kemyll held land there. Keame, Came and Keyham are variant spellings of his name, as is the slightly altered form 'Camel's (Kemyll's) Head''. Whatever the derivation though, on 8th March 1978, the name of the Inn here was changed to the 'Submarine'. This new name was chosen in recognition of all the submarine work and activity that occurs on the built up mouth of the creek. It is particularly apt for a hostelry in this town, as Plymouth has been associated not only with some of the very latest developments in submarine technology, but it also has links with the very early stages of submarines in this country. After the pioneering work of the Dutchman Cornelius Drebell in the seventeenth century, it is invariably John Day's adventurous and ultimately fatal experiment of 1774, conducted between Firestone Bay and Drake's Island, that is cited at the beginning of any history of submarines. Day, a millwright turned inventor from Suffolk, had intended to take his vessel *Maria*, a converted sloop, over 100 ft below the surface for at least 12 hours. However, the experiment appeared to fail as the craft went under, but neither the Maria nor its 'captain' were ever seen again, although it was almost salvaged some weeks later. One early vessel that was recovered, though, was the Holland I, the Royal Navy's first official submarine built in 1901. Due to be scrapped 12 years later, she foundered just off the Eddystone on the way to the breaker's yard. She then lay on the seabed for nearly 70 years when she was discovered by a diver and, in 1982, was rescued and brought to Devonport Dockyard prior to renovation and removal to the Submarine Museum at Gosport. A significant find since most major navies in the world began with Holland I-type craft and none have kept back or restored an example. It is interesting to note that our navy were not great early pioneers in this field. Indeed the Royal Navy were already several years behind France when they declared submarines as being 'underhand, unfair and un-English . . .' Furthermore, the official role of the Holland I, when it was eventually built under great secrecy in 1901, was to give British destroyer captains practice in combating submarines.

With an underwater range of 20–25 miles at a speed of 7 knots, it is evident that this form of seagoing vessel has come a long way in 80-odd years. So too has the quality and quantity of surface traffic using this road. So much so that if you want to know what this particular 'Submarine' looks like inside you have only tonight and tomorrow to do so, for after that it is closing for good, prior to demolition in order that this old road can be widened.

Going down with it, the old cinema next door. It served as a police station during the last war and latterly saw life as the Star School of Dancing. Soon, however, it too will be just a memory.

3rd January, 1987.

108

HMS Defiance

On 28th January, 1596, Sir Francis Drake died of dysentery near Nombre de Dios. The town had only recently been captured by the English expeditionary forces who had been sent out to contest the Spanish possessions in the West Indies and Central America. It proved to be an expensive outing for the English as the other great naval leader on the trip, Sir John Hawkins, had died a couple of months earlier.

Deprived of its two commanders, the expedition set sail for home after Drake had been buried at sea from the ship that carried his flag – the *Defiance*.

Launched in 1590 this 92 foot long 500 ton ship had a complement of 150 seamen, 30 gunners and 20 soldiers. In 1612 she was taken to pieces and rebuilt, finally being sold out of the service in 1650. The second *Defiance* was built at Deptford in 1666 and down the years, apart from the occasional period, there continues to have been a *Defiance* in service to the crown.

The most recent was commissioned on 26th March, 1981, when the Fleet Maintenance Base here in Devonport Dockyard was given that name. The Fleet Maintenance Base was opened three years earlier on 21st April, 1978 by Prime Minister James Callaghan. It was at this time that the name *Defiance* was last dropped from use. In June 1971 *HMS Forth*, the 13,000 ton submarine support ship, came back to Devonport after five years in the Far East. There then followed a short refit and in February 1972 the *Forth* was renamed *Defiance* as a fleet shore establishment at No. 13 Wharf. (This was also a local revival of the name as prior to 1959 *Defiance* had been the name of the torpedo and anti-submarine school based in Plymouth.)

However, just as *HMS Tyne*, *Forth*'s predecessor, had become inadequate after a few years (it had been the base for the Captain, Fleet Maintenance from 1967–72) so this new ship was quickly stretched beyond its capacity. Hence the need for the new on-shore Fleet Maintenance Base which now stands adjacent to the Submarine Refit

Complex. Situated on the north eastern corner of what was No. 5 or the 'Prince of Wales' basin, this area has been greatly altered since it was opened by the then Prince of Wales, the future George V, in 1907. In 1980 it was, appropriately, the great grandson of George V, Prince Charles, also Prince of Wales, who officiated at the opening of the most dramatic new extension to this area. This was the Submarine Refit Complex which is situated predominantly to the rear of the nine-storey Management Office Block and which, in turn, is overshadowed by the massive 80-tonne crane.

Capable of lifting 80 tonnes at a maximum radius of 72 metres and to a height of 46 metres, this giant cantilever crane stands on four massive concrete columns and lifts the used core packages (which weigh 72 tonnes) from the nuclear submarines across No. 14 dock to a waiting rail-transporter.

Like the management block the submarine support facility block next to it is also nine storeys high, the difference here being that four of the storeys are below what appears to be ground level.

Also based on this site are the Headquarters of the 2nd Submarine Squadron. Just after the turn of the century, when the first Prince of Wales came here, submarines were in their infancy. With a decade or so of the century still to run the changes, of course, have been dramatic. The submarine seen here to the right of *HMS Active* is the *Swiftsure*, the first nuclear submarine to have been refitted here, 1980–83.

272 foot long with a displacement of 3,500 tons when on the surface, this type of craft would doubtless have been inconceivable to our Tudor forebears even to a man with the vision of Drake who could never have imagined that one day a vessel like this would be capable, as it is, of circumnavigating the world, submerged, without needing to refuel.

30th July, 1988.

Ferry House Inn

On the night of 23rd October 1961, five sky rockets were fired across an inky-black sky above the River Tamar to mark the last ever trip of the Saltash Ferry. At the bar of the 'Ferry House Inn', Irish licensee Mike Goulding was quoted as saying that the Inn would keep its present name. 'It will remind people of the good old days' he said. In one form or another, ferries had been carrying passengers across the Tamar here on a regular basis for some 600 years. In the early days they followed the line that was taken by the Brunel Railway Bridge but, for well over 100 years, the ferry's landing point on the east bank of the Tamar was on the ramp just below the 'Ferry House Inn'. This change apparently occurred some years before the bridge was built and was a consequence of the launching of J. M. Rendel's chain-guided 'floating bridge' from here at the end of 1832. Rendel had already been responsible for improving the traffic flow over the Plym with his iron bridge at Laira. Funded by the Earl of Morley, this five-arched bridge replaced a variety of ferries, including an early version of Rendel's 'floating bridge'. It was completed in 1827.

Five years later the Earl of Morley, together with Mr. A. Edgcumbe, Sir William Molesworth and other local notables, obtained an act of Parliament authorising them to buy the ferry rights from Saltash Corporation and set up a steam powered, floating bridge here. An action that was partly prompted by the instalment of a steam ferry at Torpoint in 1829. Unfortunately, although this new service started in a blaze of glory, its trial run taking but four and a half minutes, within a year or two it was taken away for renovation and replaced by the old horse-boats. However, as the new higher toll charges continued to be levied, local dissent grew and Saltash Corporation made moves to regain control of the ferry rights. By 1839 they had succeeded, but it was to be another 11 years before a steam ferry bridge replaced the horse boats. In the same year, 1850, the 'Ferry House' was converted into a coaching house.

By this time work had begun on Brunel's Rail Bridge and when it was eventually completed in 1859, the former 'Devonport Inn' at the eastern side of the old ferry's path, changed its name to the 'Royal Albert Bridge Inn' in honour of the bridge's proper title. However, it appears to have been business as usual at the 'Ferry House', where Thomas Skinner had been licensee for many years. John Sole was recorded as landlord here as early as 1812 but, as the original house itself is said to date back to 1575, it has doubtless provided travellers with food and shelter for several centuries.

In these 'good old days' of course, the crossing was quite a different proposition from that of more recent years. Although it is some way up the river, in the years before the building of the Breakwater conditions would at times have been much rougher. In 1724 the well known writer and novelist Daniel Defoe (author of *Robinson Crusoe*) wrote, 'The Tamar here is very wide, and the ferry boats bad; so that I thought myself well escaped when I got safe on shore in Cornwall'.

Just a few years later, on 29th May 1733, the ferry boat was 'cast away' with a loss of 29 lives, 9 of them Plymothians. Later in the century, a graphic account of the rigours of this crossing appeared in a letter from the wife of a Mr. Russel who, together with her husband, was visiting Captain William Trelawney at Coldrenick. They arrived, she said, to make the trip without a carriage ('for no carriages can go') and waited nearly 3 hours for the boat '. . . but by the time it came there the market people came so fast upon us that we were quite jockeyed, for it holds but 9 horses and 16 wanted to get in. We strove for a little while but both men and women were so brutish and dexterous at it that though they each had panniers they leapt in like dogs on their horses; sometimes their panniers went over the other side and their horses down, it became quite a battle who could get in first either by fair means or foul . . . This deterred Mr. Russel from venturing ourselves among such Westcountry brutes . . .'

In the end, the Russels were transported across by a friendly eight-oared, naval man-o-war's boat and they left their horses with their men to bring them over on the next ferry—which by all accounts was just as difficult, and so the delayed party was forced to dine at Saltash.

Mrs. Russel was writing in October 1760; exactly 201 years later then the Saltash ferry ran for the last time, superseded at last by the Tamar Road Bridge. Carriages now have a very simple crossing and soon of course they will be able to pass through Saltash quicker than ever before!

9th January, 1988.

Budshead Manor

At the time of the Domesday survey, Bucheside, or Budshead, Manor had just passed from the hands of the Saxon, Alwin, to its new owner the Norman lord Alured Brito (the Breton). The land was shown as supporting 4 serfs and 5 villeins and comprised around 320 acres of ploughland, about 4 acres of meadow plus a small wood. There were undoubtedly buildings on this land then, but exactly what they were and where they stood is not certain.

The area Budshead had of course acquired its name from the Breton saint Budoc, who is said to have come here in AD 480 to establish one of his many small religious communities and it is believed that baptisms were held by a great cross hauled to the bottom of a fresh water spring at a point nearby where it ran into Tamerton Creek. The French pronunciation of St. Budoc has given us St. Budeaux, while Budshead itself is a corruption of Budoc's hide—that is, the land belonging to Budoc. Apart from the information gleaned from the Domesday Survey of 1086, little is known about this area until 1241 when we find its ownership ascribed to Alan de Buddekeshid—Alan of Budshead. Surnames were not common at this time, but it appears that Alan's family adopted the name and it survived through a great many variations as it was passed down over the next three or four centuries via '14 descents'. Thus in 1285 we find reference to William de Bodeshid and in 1346 Thomas de Bodekishide. Twelve years earlier, on 3rd March 1334, we find an early record of the private chapel in Budshead Mansion, as the Bishop of Exeter granted the Priors of Plympton authority over the 'Capella de Buttockiside' and the taxes in respect of it.

The following century a licence renewal appearing in Bishop Lacy's Register, shows us that this 'capella' was licensed for divine service on 17th February 1421 to 'Wm. Buttock-Kysyde and Joan his wife' and that it was 'situate in their Mansion of Buttockyside'.

However by this time the local population was growing and there was mounting pressure on the Bishop for this small St. Budeaux chapel to be elevated to a position whereby all church offices could be performed here—including burial. This was finally granted by Bishop Courtenay, in May 1482, who also decreed that a cemetery should be created adjoining the chapel and that a chaplain should reside here in a house (30ft by 16ft) especially provided for him. Thomas Aclinn duly became the first chaplain here and, until the building of the 'new' St. Budeaux Church in 1563, this was the parish church.

After 1563 it fell into disuse; however it stood, gradually deteriorating, for another three hundred years, and it was not until 1885 that it was finally pulled down altogether. By this time Budshead Manor House had passed through many different families. Soon after completion of the church the long occupancy by the Budokeshids came to an end, the house then passed through 2 or 3 generations of the Gorges family, through the Trevills, then Trelawnys (Sir William Trelawny laying out fine gardens and many rare trees here in the mid eighteenth century) and then on to George Leech who sold it to Richard Hall Clarke in 1798.

Clarke it was who had the old house and the old Budshead Mill House pulled down. The Manor House he had rebuilt on a smaller scale in 1810, incorporating many of the elements of earlier constructions.

It was not long, however, in comparative terms, before the house ceased to be used as a mansion and became instead the home of local tenant farmers, one of whom in 1885 determined to grow grapes on the site of the Chapel and had it pulled down. He then began building a large greenhouse and, sinking deep pits to accommodate the roots of the vines, was quite unprepared for his finds—the remains of people buried almost 400 years earlier!

The site of the chapel today is covered by a recently erected Community Building, which stands to the right of the second archway shown here. The lintel of the first arch incidentally is thought to come from the old mill house and was another of Mr. Risdon's efforts in the 1880s.

The old Budshead buildings were last used for farm housing in the early fifties. Then Plymouth City Council acquired the farm and had the Ernesettle Housing Estate built on land to its south. Of the buildings here the great 16th century barn, at the bottom of this path, was converted by the council to a branch library for the estate and opened in 1952. In 1959 the library was moved to the school in Biggin Hill, 'a more accessible site' and for a while, until vandalism became too much of a problem, it was used simply as a book store. The barn was then adapted for use by Ernesettle Youth Association, but tragically in December 1975 a mysterious fire gutted the building.

It was estimated that it would cost £50,000 to restore this great barn. The insurers generously offered £42,700; however the County Council, who had taken over responsibility for it in 1974, eventually concluded that the best they could do would be to pull down the charred remains and level the ancient walls to a height of 3'6" so that some idea of the scale of the barn could still be obtained.

So in 1982 this work was done and sadly another piece of our local heritage all but disappeared. However some sense of history undoubtedly still lingers in this delightful spot on the south bank of Tamerton Creek.

14th May, 1988.

112

The Blue Monkey

Names of animals have provided countless public houses with a title and a sign and more than 50 different species have been so honoured. The trusty horse alone occurs in some 50 variations.

The monkey however has traditionally not been such a favourite; there is the Drum and Monkey in Brownlow, Salop, and here in St. Budeaux we have the 'Blue Monkey' said to be the only one of its kind in the country. 'Officially', the 'Blue Monkey' has only been known by this name since 1939–40 when the change was recorded first on the property deeds then on the records held in Plymouth Magistrates' Court. However the various theories put forward for the derivation of the name all suggest that the change took place several decades earlier, that is some time between 1895–1915, since when locals have always referred to the pub as the 'Blue Monkey'. In much the same way as the 'Eagle' at Cattedown has been known to locals as the 'Screeching Cat' for nearly seventy years without any official change as yet. But whilst the original 'Screeching Cat' is clearly identified with a former landlord's wife, the original 'Blue Monkey' is apparently a matter of some debate.

St. Budeaux historian Marshall Ware favours the story endorsed both by locals and another eminent local historian, H. Montagu-Evans, 1842–1930, with whom Marshall Ware, himself a lively octogenarian, was well acquainted, and this story revolves around a real, live monkey. Supposedly brought home by a merchant seaman, who lived in Agaton Road off Ernesettle Lane, this little monkey escaped one day and was later seen on the roof of the pub by the then landlord, James Silas Alger. A sight which reputedly prompted the said Mr. Alger to change the name there and then from the 'St. Budeaux Inn' to the 'Blue Monkey'. As noted before however this name change was not registered until Henry Pengelly took over from the Algers in January 1940. As Alger and son had been at the Inn since 1897 it is difficult to date the story and a change of name on the deeds by Alger, from the 'St. Budeaux Inn' to 'Ye Old St. Budeaux Inn' in 1937, only adds to the confusion. As does the story extracted from an undated clipping from the *Western Evening Herald* probably written around 1940. This account, framed and hanging in the lounge bar, talks of an incident, about 45 years ago, when a dispute arose between the men of the North and the South Staffordshire Regiments, then stationed at Devonport and fresh from firing-practice in Ernesettle. The dispute, a simple argument over a glass of beer, threatened to get nasty until William Dunsford, the landlord, 'a man of massive proportions' intervened and knocked one man to the floor. The man picked himself up, turned on the landlord and burst out 'You . . . blue monkey' and ever afterwards, the story goes 'the public house was known as the Blue Monkey'.

More recently however, the brewery decided against acknowledging either of these 'anecdotes' and chose instead to replace the blue monkey and the basket sign with an image depicting a Naval Blue Monkey Boy. That is, a powder monkey boy—generally a young lad whose job it was to feed ships' cannons in the Napoleonic Wars with gunpowder. A job which, due to the resultant smoke and flashback, gave the young men's complexions a somewhat blue hue. This, in turn, leads us to yet another theory familiar to some of those who have heard an Audrey Hosier local history talk on the subject. Still with 'blue' powder monkeys, these she says were men who would drink in the Inn, having worked with explosives in the neighbouring quarries that stood a little to the south east of the pub on the other side of the road.

However, if this change of name did take place around the turn of the century, one perhaps can't discount the influence of the best known Blue Monkey at that time, the Marquis Luis Augusto Pinto de Soveral who, between 1884 and 1909, enjoyed an almost uninterrupted spell as Portuguese Ambassador to London. A close friend of King Edward VII and noted for his wit, discretion and prowess as a story teller, the Marquis was a notable figure in Edwardian society. He was dubbed the Blue Monkey on account of his swarthy complexion and blue black hair. And whilst he may have had nothing to do with this St. Budeaux Inn he undoubtedly popularized the nickname around this time.

Whatever the true story may be, however, there can be no doubting the antiquity of this hostelry, known originally as the 'Church Inn'. For obvious reasons too, as just a small village green separates the Inn from St. Budeaux Parish Church, the church in which Francis Drake married his second wife, Mary Newman, on 4th July 1569.

Quite when Church Inn was built is unclear, however, old inns are nothing new to current licensee Russ Randal who moved here with his wife Judi a couple of years ago. Russ's parents and grandparents before them kept the Dolphin at Kingston in the South Hams, and whilst there discovered Latin deeds to the property dating it back to 1550!

7th June, 1986.

114

Ham House

It was erected on the site of an earlier dwelling in 1639. Portions of that earlier edifice were incorporated in this rebuilding. During the Civil War Cromwell's soldiers set fire to it and partially destroyed it, but it survived. In 1759 it was remodelled, and further restoration work was carried out towards the end of the nineteenth century.

At the outbreak of the Second World War, exactly 300 years after it had been built, Ham House was still in the hands of the same family, the Trelawnys. A couple of years later it was again the victim of war damage when a German incendiary bomb devastated part of the East Wing. In 1947 the Rev. W. T. Trelawny-Ross sold the property to Plymouth City Council. The council at this time were steaming ahead with their post-war housing development, but all the money being spent went into new housing and this grand old house at Ham was left unrepaired. Opening part of the building as a library for the area did little to improve the situation. Local vandals, however, did much to aggravate it. For some thirty years it stood forlornly on the edge of Ham Woods with steel sheets fastened across its doors and windows, its great roofs patched up with chicken wire and tar paper. Members of the Old Plymouth Society campaigned for its salvation. Back in 1947 the then secretary, G. W. Copeland, presented a fine potted history of the place and wrote that 'its historical associations and its architectural value warrant its preservation, particularly as Greater Plymouth has now sprung into being, making Ham virtually a Plymouth building'.

But little was done and in 1971 Stanley Goodman, of the Old Plymouth Society, attacked the City Council in the light of its wanton destruction of the 'Old Ring of Bells' in Woolster Street, Widey Court at Manadon and Devonport's Ker Street Chapel . . . adding that if nothing constructive was done for Ham House in the next few years the place would 'moulder away'. His words came to the attention of the younger brother of the last private owner of the house, the Rev. S. M. Trelawny-Ross, who was living in Yorkshire. He promptly rang his brother's widow and she and he agreed it would be kinder to pull the house down than to let it just crumble away. She also suggested, however, that it would make a fine old people's home. That same summer of 1971 the World of Property Housing Trust, a non profit making organization, approached the council with a view to converting Ham House into flats—but they were turned down. In 1973 Bill Best Harris, the then City Librarian, announced that following the 'worst ever' act of vandalism there, he had taken steps to remove £150,000 worth of books and documents and further added that he would be making strong comments indeed to the Libraries' Committee about the future use of Ham House as a Library.

In 1976 the council at last approved in principle a scheme to turn Ham House into flats for the elderly. Four years later on 22nd April 1980 Ham House, restored and converted by WPHT and the Anchor Housing Association, was officially 'reopened' by Lord Mayor Graham Jinks, the Mayor stating that he had been trying, himself, to see Ham converted for council housing since first becoming a member of the City Housing Committee 25 years earlier.

For seven years now Ham House has enjoyed its new lease of life and hopefully its principal architect, Robert Trelawny (himself a Lord Mayor of Plymouth and son of a three times mayor), can now rest a little more easily in his grave.

Robert Trelawny had bought the Ham site in the year of his Mayoralty, 1633. The Trelawnys had lived in Plymouth since 1578 and could trace their lineage back some 16 generations to Edwin de Trelone, who was around in 1041. (There was, incidentally, a member of the family at the 1980 reopening). Robert Trelawny lived in Looe Street until his brief move out to Ham in 1639—the date was carved above the front door and can still be seen today. In 1640 he was elected MP for Plymouth. However, his support of the Royalist cause in those troubled times, led to his expulsion from the House of Commons and imprisonment in Winchester and, although he was later released and returned here to Ham, further Royalist support (he gave the King £2,000 worth of plate and jewels) saw him imprisoned once more. In 1644 he died in Winchester 'for want of ordinary relief and refreshment', but not before he had heard of the premature death of his 'faithful and loving' wife and the partial destruction of his new country home.

Today that country home is not without some of its former dignity. However, the surrounding Ham Woods, littered with broken furniture and rubbish, are a testament to the fact that this corner of the City still suffers from local neglect and lack of council care.   »Postscript

28th February, 1987.

Burrington

From Domesday to the dawn of the twentieth century, Burrington changed little. In 1086 there were three farms squeezed into this small manor, then said to be worth ten shillings. Fifty years ago there was still little more than that to be found in 'Buretona'. The ancient name itself means 'boors', or 'peasants', 'tun', that is farm. (There is another Burrington in Devon, a small and very old village just outside Chulmleigh). The principal dwellings here before the war were Burrington Farm, Burraton Farm, Burrington House, Burrington Lodge and Burrington the third and smaller farm.

At the time of the Norman conquest, 1066, the Saxon, Alwin, owned the Manor of Burrington. As the country subsequently passed into the hands of the successful invaders, so Burrington, by 1086, was recorded as being the property of the Judhel, the Norman Baron of Totnes, who held a great deal of land in the South West, including the Manors of Weston and Manadon and East Whitleigh which, like Burrington, he leased to another Norman, Odo. From then on little is known of Burrington until the seventeenth century when we find, in the Registers of St. Pancras, that 'John Reed of Burrington' was married in 1658. Soon after this, it would appear that Burrington House was either built or rebuilt on the site of the old manor house. According to Dr. J. T. Trelawny-Ross (writing in the 1920s when he was living at Ham House) there was, on the wall of Burrington, a small shield bearing the date 1661 and the initials J. R. (John Reed). Other key dates being; 1793, which was carved above the gate to the walled garden that stood by Ham Brook, just below the house; 1825, the date the house was given a new frontage; 1941, the year another would-be invading force made its presence felt here, by dropping a bomb on the house in its blitz of Plymouth; and 1945, the year Dr. Andrew Scotland, Director of Education spotted the derelict site of Burrington House and earmarked it as an ideal plot on which to place the housing estates which were then planned and which have now long since been completed.

In the event it was another 16 years before the school was opened, in September 1961; 39 year old Bill Button was its head and 'Conabar'—'I will try' was its motto. The school also adopted a coat of arms which, like the motto, is taken from those of the Were family, who lived in Burrington House until 1778. The Weres had come to Burrington many years before that, when Thomas Were married Joan Reed, only daughter of Dorothy and John Reed referred to earlier, and there is quite an elaborate memorial to the Were family in the chancel of St. Pancras. Planned to cope with the post-war population explosion, almost as soon as it had been opened it was realised that Burrington was too small. In 1969 the City announced its intention to enlarge the school by providing additional accommodation for 450 children. This led to the building of the ROSLA Blocks which were designed in part to cater for the extra pupils at the school following the Raising of the School Leaving Age (ROSLA).

Currently there are about 800 pupils on the school roll and there are yet more building works in hand. These began late last year and include a new gym, drama studio and workshop.

However, even this is supposed only to be part of a further phase of expansion as Burrington awaits the Government's approval of the County Council's proposals for the restructuring of the secondary schools in West Plymouth. For years now, it has looked certain that neighbouring Honicknowle and Burleigh will close, having already apparently outlived their usefulness as post-war baby-boom schools, but successive Government Ministers have refused to give the go ahead that will make Burrington a major comprehensive school.

Whatever happens though, the school looks set to survive for many years yet. Currently under only its third head since 1961, following Geoff Rees, who has just moved out to Ivybridge Community College after two years at the school, Kenrick Barter arrived at Burrington this term and became the third consecutive head under forty to be appointed here. Successful academically and on the sports field, Burrington is fortunate to have a close association with the YMCA's Kitto Centre, just across the very busy and at times dangerous, Honicknowle Lane.

With excellent indoor sports facilities available to an open membership, the Kitto Centre was built in 1973 to replace the Kitto Institute that served the Barbican area between 1884–1970. Named after the celebrated, self-educated, local, biblical, scholar, John Kitto, the Kitto Centre stands on the site of the birthplace of another celebrated local figure, Lt. John Rousse Merriott Chard, one of the two principal heroes of the defence of Rourke's Drift when 80 men of the 24th Regiment kept 4,000 Zulus at bay in Zululand, in January 1879 (not, incidentally, 1897 as it states on the memorial plaque!). »Postscript

6th June, 1987.

Woodland Fort

Woodland Fort takes its name from the adjacent Woodlands Estate. Here the manor house 'Woodlands' once stood in isolation a little to the north and west of the fort. The fort of course, is a comparatively recent addition to this ancient manor and its site is properly part of the original 'Witelie No. 2' manor (West Whitleigh). However, today it is more clearly identified with Honicknowle. Honicknowle library and Community Centre are both housed within the fort's densely overgrown stone walls and traditionally it has housed a local annual gala. Honicknowle's original manor house appears to have stood on the site of Warwick Park House opposite the western end of Dickiemoor Lane. Hanenchelola or Hanechelole as it was called around the time of Domesday, belonged to a Saxon named Wado or Wadelo at the time of the Conquest (he also held West Whitleigh). Afterwards it passed into the hands of the Count of Mortain, the Norman lord who leased it to Reginald de Valletort. Thereafter the manor passed through a variety of hands down the centuries and, by the middle of last century, had changed little from its Domesday appearance. The line of Crownhill Road which forms the approximate northern boundary of the Honicknowle estate is, incidentally, believed to be of very great antiquity, H. Montagu Evans showing it as a 'supposed Roman Road' on the map he prepared just before the end of last century. Apart from the two manor houses already referred to, little else appears on his map in the immediate area. Woodland Cottage and Woodland Wood are marked as is Little Dock Lane and Butt Park Terrace, which was the first major housing development in the area. Also shown are the Brick Works, Bogers Farm and the Manor Farm which was simply marked as a ruin. Woodland Fort itself is not shown, but then neither are the other Victorian fortifications constructed along, or just off, the Crownhill Road at Agaton and at Crownhill.

These forts made up part of the North Eastern line of defence around Plymouth and the Dockyard, as drawn up by the Assistant Inspector General of Fortifications, Major Jervois, on the instructions of the Palmerston administration who feared a French invasion. Jervois' superior, Sir John Fox Burgoyne, was not originally in favour of a string of detached forts, preferring the idea of a continuous line of defensive works around the area to be protected. He was swayed ultimately by Jervois' insistence on the ever-improving quality and range of artillery, which meant that positioning the forts about one mile apart would adequately cover all the open ground in between.

Originally, the line of forts inland of Plymouth, between the Tamar and the Cattewater and known as the 'North Eastern Position', was intended to run along the following sites, 'St. Budeaux, Burrington House, Quarry Pound, Tor House, Mount View, Wellington Villas, the Borough Gaol and Cat Down' with three additional advanced defensive works. In the event of course, 'Ernesettle, Agaton, Knowles, Woodlands, Crown Hill, Bowden, Egg Buckland, Forder, Austin, Efford and Laira' were the chosen sites. Of these today, all but one remain—Forder, having never been more than a simple earth rampart open battery in the first place, has long since been cleared and levelled. The site now houses a television transmitter. Of the others, Ernesettle is used by the Royal Navy as an ammunition depot; Agaton has been adapted by the Ministry of Transport as a heavy goods vehicle testing centre; Knowles houses Knowle Primary School; part of Crownhill, the principal fort of the whole development, is being restored to its former glory by the Landmark Trust; while Bowden is occupied by a garden centre. Eggbuckland Keep (said to be the last fortification erected in this country to be be called a keep) is now a DIY centre; Fort Austin is a base of Plymouth City's Direct Labour Organisation and Cleansing Department; Efford houses the Showman's Guild and the Laira battery is used by a transport company.

All the forts in the North Eastern Position were designed by one man, Captain Du Cane. He was also responsible for Stamford, Staddon, Brownhill, Polhawn and, partly, for Tregantle.

Less than half the size of Crownhill Fort, Woodland cost £28,500 to construct (a little over a third of the cost of Crownhill), and in 1929 it was sold to a local builder at a public auction for £600. At that time the building had been adopted as tenement dwellings and was let in eight, two and four roomed tenements, which yielded a gross weekly rental of two pounds sixteen shillings. The road then stood out much further from the entrance and it still had a drawbridge. At the beginning of this century a company of Bugle Boys were housed here and after a period of disuse it was re-opened as married quarters for Scottish troops. A Jewish Battalion and a section of the Portuguese Labour Corps were stationed here in the 1914–18 War and for a while it also served as a military hospital. In addition to its civilian tenants, between the wars the fort housed various artillery units, the Horse Guard, Civil Defence, Fire Service Detachments and the First American Army during the last war, after which it passed into the hands of the Corporation where it has since remained. A year or two earlier, in the 1943 Plan for Plymouth, the area at Whitleigh Hall between Honicknowle and Tamerton Foliot was earmarked as an 'area capable of easy development as a suburb of particular use to workers at the Devonport Dockyard'. A proposal to which, forty pages later, the optimistic postscript was added 'Honicknowle . . . and other small settlements should not lose their identity by the expansion of urbanization around them'.

18th July, 1987.

Crownhill Fort

'Palmerston's Follies ... is the name given to the imposing, expensive and quite useless ring of forts built around Plymouth between the years 1862 and 1870'. So says John Babbs (*Military Fortifications of Plymouth and District*, 1980) in a critical account of the planning, building and subsequent history of the defences constructed around the city and, more specifically, Devonport and the Dockyard, last century.

On the other hand, we find David Evans stating, in a piece entitled 'The Victorian Defences of Plymouth' (October 1986), that 'with the completion of this ring Plymouth was furnished with some of the most theoretically advanced defences in the world'. He then adds that this 'has been effectively obscured through the label "Palmerston's Follies"—a description which a very slight amount of knowledge shows to be false'.

The truth it would appear, contemporary political issues aside, lies somewhere between these two views. Certainly Crownhill is an unparalleled British example of the state of the art of fortification around 1870. The biggest (it is on a similar scale to the Citadel), the most expensive and the least altered of the nineteenth century ring of forts, Crownhill stands some 400 feet above sea level and, although partly hidden by trees and massive earthworks, nevertheless commands a superb view of the surrounding lands. It was completed in 1872 at a cost of around £76,000 and included barracks for some 300 men, with ample provision for artillery stores. For well over 100 years it was in the hands of the military and consequently, as David Evans notes, it survived any of the structural alterations that affected the other forts as they were sold, let for commercial use or simply left to deteriorate. Headquarters in recent years of the 2nd Infantry Brigade, then 43 Wessex Brigade and, more recently, 59 Independent Commando, in 1981 there was a lot of talk about this fort being adapted as a wartime administrative HQ for the city. Andrew Forbes Watson, the city's Chief Executive, was quoted at the time as saying that 'it has been apparent for some time that Plymouth has no effective war-time administrative headquarters and steps to remedy this failing are currently being taken'. Reg Scott (who was Lord Mayor the following year), said such a plan could only push people one step nearer the brink of a nuclear war; 'I am not going to be a party to this great load of codswallop and to pretend that the people of Plymouth can get any protection from a nuclear bomb' he said. For which he was duly accused, by a Conservative councillor, of ostrich-like behaviour—'When there's danger he sticks his head in the sand'.

Such a debate would doubtless have amused and amazed William Gladstone, who ultimately followed Palmerston as a Prime Minister of this country and who almost brought Palmerston's Cabinet down with his bitter and determined fight against the 'Fortification Loan', which funded the building of this fort and the ring of defences here and around Portsmouth and Gosport. Henry Temple, the 3rd Viscount Palmerston, was 75 when in 1859 he formed his second government and began formulating his proposals to fortify the two major, south coast dockyards against an imagined French invasion. The plan, with its nine million pound budget, was typical of the man who, one biographer describes, as 'loud, self-confident and imperious' and who set out to make 'the greatness of England felt whenever a slight was to be

avenged, freedom to be asserted or weak defended against the strong'. The irony of the defensive chain around Plymouth, however, is that there is little evidence to suggest that, in the late 1860s when the French invasion was deemed imminent if not inevitable, these local forts had any substantial weaponry between them. Furthermore there was a great hole in the chain at Saltash where none of the three proposed forts had been constructed. Twenty years later a report from the Deputy Adjutant General showed little improvement as he noted that 'the land forts are practically without guns'. By that time, however, although nuclear weapons were still inconceivable, these forts had already become largely outdated as defensive structures against the latest developments in weaponry.

However, it remains true that Crownhill fort is the most advanced and impressive of the fortifications either here or in Portsmouth (where many have already been restored). As part of the largest scheme of fortification ever undertaken in Britain it is, therefore, a great thing for the city that last year this fort was acquired by the Landmark Trust who, over the next three years, hope to restore it completely to its original appearance. Already, with assistance from the Community Programme Agency, much work has been done clearing the massive ditch which surrounds this 15-acre fort, and it is heartening to know that one day soon this massive structure with its miles of underground passages, galleries and walkways will be open to the public.

11th July, 1987.

Lord Seaton

'Few men are like him; indeed, except the Duke of Wellington, I know no officer in the British Army his equal.' So wrote Sir George Napier of Sir John Colborne in 1828.

John Colborne was born in 1778, educated at Winchester and by 1799 was serving as a lieutenant in the army in North Holland. In 1801 he was in Egypt. Four years later he participated in the Battle of Maida and that of Corunna in 1809. Badly injured at Ciudad Rodrigo in 1812 Colborne, despite his wound, led his men to success. He was, however, subsequently out of action for some time and it was 15 months before the ball of shot, which gave him great pain, was removed from his arm; an operation which took place in the Military Hospital in Plymouth in April 1813. Back in the fighting for the 1814 Campaign, perhaps his greatest moment came at Waterloo the following year, leading the 52nd Light Infantry.

'No man can point out to me any instance, either in ancient or modern history, of a single battalion so influencing the result of any great action as the result of the battle of Waterloo was influenced by the attack of the 52nd Regiment on the Imperial Guard.' General Sir J. Shaw Kennedy.

Colborne's first major non-combative assignment was as Lieutenant-Governor of Jersey. Then, from 1828 to 1836, he gained much respect as only the second Governor and Commander in Chief of Canada. Whilst there he founded the

country's first English-style public school—Upper Canada College and even now they say a daily prayer for Sir John. From 1843 to 49 he was Lord High Commissioner of the Ionian Islands and based on Corfu. (These Greek Islands were a British Protectorate between 1815–64).

Like all military figures involved with the Napoleonic Wars, Colborne frequently passed through Plymouth. His personal links with the area however began with the marriage in 1806 of his half-sister Cordelia with the Rev. Duke Yonge of Anthony, near Torpoint. The latter's cousin, Elizabeth, lived in the family house of Puslinch, built in 1720 by James Yonge, surgeon, local diarist and Mayor of Plymouth in 1694. Her father, also James Yonge, was then rector of Newton Ferrers. On 21st June, 1809 Colborne visited Puslinch and met, for the first time, Elizabeth Yonge, 'the beauty of Devonshire'. Four years later to the day, they were married and, when the couple returned to this country in 1839 after their time in Canada, they chose to settle in this area and moved to a country house—Lyneham, near Plympton.

On his return it was announced that Sir John was to be created a baron and the title was to stay with the two generations after him (the third and last Lord Seaton died in 1955). Sir John Colborne chose the title Seaton because he had intended to buy a property near Seaton. However such a move did not transpire and in 1841 Lord and Lady Seaton moved from Lyneham to Kitley and then in 1856 to Beechwood at Sparkwell. Members of the Colborne family still live there today and their 7th cousins, the Yonges, still occupy Puslinch. Beechwood itself still houses the swords of Sir John Moore, the Duke of Wellington and Sir John Colborne. In 1863 the great man died at Beechwood and within three years this fine statue, commissioned by friends and comrades, had been unveiled at Mount Wise, in the grounds of Government House. (It had been offered to the town council for placement on the Hoe, but it was turned down in the interests of keeping the Hoe as clear as possible; Drake, the Armada Memorial and Smeaton's Tower were still many years away.) Moved once while at Mount Wise in 1904, the statue, designed by Mr. G. Adams, was moved again at the beginning of the last war to the Army barracks at Crownhill, which then took the name Seaton Barracks. Government House, Mount Wise, had long since become Admiralty House and the presence of a soldier—no matter how dignified—was a little out of place there.

Barracks had first been constructed at Crownhill in 1891–2 and followed the earlier building of Crownhill Fort, one of Palmerston's Victorian follies. In the early 1930s these barracks were renamed after the Torquay born Field Marshall, Lord Plumer. With road extensions and the building of Crownhill flyover most of the old Plumer barracks were pulled down in the late sixties. However back in 1964 Seaton Barracks had undergone an extensive rebuilding and looks set to serve as service quarters for many years yet. Ironically though the statue of Lord Seaton, moved for the third time in the redevelopment, no longer surveys the coming and going of army personnel as the barracks are now in the hands of the Navy and the Royal Marines, and today 59 Independent Commando, of the Royal Engineers, are stationed here and Commando Logistic Regiment are barracked here. »Postscript

4th October, 1986.

Notre Dame School

One hundred and twenty eight years ago, six Sisters of Notre Dame arrived in Plymouth from their Mother House in Namur, Belgium. They had been invited to the town by Bishop Vaughan on 28th July 1860 and on their arrival they were taken to a former priest's residence in Stonehouse which became their convent.

'The locality' we read 'was not a very tempting one but the Sisters came to work for the poor, and gladly took up their abode in the midst of them'.

Bishop Vaughan came to say Mass for the Sisters the morning after their arrival, in a little chapel they had set up in their new residence. A day school was opened soon afterwards in the convent and it is from these humble beginnings that the modern Notre Dame Comprehensive School for Girls, on its 20 acre site in Crownhill, has its origins.

The Congregation of the Sisters of Notre Dame of Namur was founded by Blessed Julie Billiart (1751–1816) and, prior to the arrival of the six Sisters in Plymouth, an earlier six had gone to Penryn in 1845. These were the first Sisters of Notre Dame to come to England. Their work in the area however aroused a certain amount of local hostility and they were later withdrawn from Penryn to Clapham at the request of the Redemptorist Fathers. Today there are Notre Dame Convents and schools in almost every country in the world and central guidance for the Sisters lives still emanates from Namur.

Three years after their arrival in Stonehouse, the Reverend Mother General visited the convent and advised a move from Stonehouse. Eventually, after a search for alternative premises, it was decided to build a convent on a large plot of land near the Cathedral. This was begun in 1864 and opened in October of the following year. Meanwhile a boarding school had been established in one of two buildings purchased in Westbury Terrace, North Road. From the mid 1860s onwards, education came to play an increasingly large part in the work of the Sisters and around the same time (1863) a Catholic Boys' school was established in neighbouring Melbourne Street— out of which St. Boniface College ultimately grew.

Not long after the turn of the century, as part of a general movement towards improving local education, Notre Dame Secondary School was recognized for the Higher Grant by the Board of Education and a number of free places were awarded. In 1936 the Presbyterian Church adjacent to the Convent was purchased and within two years an extension linking the two buildings had been completed. The outbreak of the Second World War however was soon to herald an early end to the use of these new premises. At first school and convent life generally followed the routine pattern but then on 21st April 1941 the recently acquired hall was set alight by enemy incendiaries. The Sisters and others worked hard to stop the fire spreading any further and although they were successful, the following night further bombing set the Convent ablaze from end to end. After this, like their contemporaries all over the city, the children and the High School Sisters were evacuated. For the remaining years of the war Notre Dame High School was based in two large houses in Teignmouth—Ashleigh and Buckeridge Tower.

After the war the school re-opened in Wyndham Street; the Convent however was not rebuilt and the Sisters moved instead into a house in Seymour Road,

'Trenley'. This new home was always going to be too small for the Sisters and there was certainly no room for a school there, so a new site was sought and soon found, here at Crownhill. However although the site was acquired in December 1946, it was not until April 1954 that work began on moving the Convent out here.

Within a few years of the Convent moving, playing fields were laid down and girls were brought out in the school bus for games. But it wasn't until 1964 that building work started on the new Notre Dame School and it was a further two years before the school was opened.

Mr. R. C. Clark was the architect, Staverton's the contractors and the Rt. Rev. Mgr. Cyril Restieaux, the Roman Catholic Bishop of Plymouth, the man who opened the new grammar school. Sister Margaret Xavier (Margaret Sheridan) was headmistress and also on the staff then was Miss Chris Bowly, the current head of P.E., Music and Dance. Present headmistress Sister Kathleen—Kathleen Bulley ('not a good name for a headmistress' she laughingly says) was not here at the time of the move, although she was here when the school turned comprehensive in 1981 and indeed she is an old girl of Notre Dame itself, having spent a year as a pupil of the school 'some time' before the move.

Today Notre Dame is bigger than it has ever been with over 700 pupils on its roll. Of these girls about 100 board during the week, as they come here from a wide catchment area that stretches from Penzance to Barnstaple to Exeter. Unique in the West Country as an all girls' Catholic Comprehensive School, Notre Dame is beautifully situated. It stands in the grounds of an old country residence—'Alwin' and many of the old and rare shrubs and trees planted by former occupants can be found around the school, providing the biologists with a wonderful natural resource.

On the side of the School Hall, visible here, is a representation of Notre Dame— 'Our Lady'—that is the Virgin Mary, the Madonna and child.

20th February, 1988.

Kings Arms Tamerton Foliot

Over the years Plymouth has gradually spread its boundaries and incorporated a number of once 'distant' and very much detached villages. One of the most interesting and undoubtedly one of the oldest is that which by all accounts grew around the ancient port of Tamerunta and which has, for centuries now, been known as Tamerton Foliot.

Situated at the head of Tamerton Creek, some two miles from the point at which the creek opens out into the Tamar, it is thought that the Phoenicians may have used its quays in their tin-exporting operations, and that the Romans after them may well have used the port. Towards the end of the sixth century we read that the Celtic saints, Indract and Dominic, arrived at Tamerunta and certainly the first church on the site of the present one was thought to be dedicated to St. Indract and was built well before the Norman conquest. It would appear that a Norman building replaced this earlier edifice and in 1318 it was rededicated to St. Mary. The tower of the church, clearly seen here and from many other points around the village, dates from the eighteenth century, when the church was again largely rebuilt. After yet more alterations in the nineteenth century, in 1922 a wooden hut was erected near to the 'King's Arms' and for many years it served as the church hall. Also nearby were the 'King's Arms' cottages, now gone, which like other neighbouring buildings in the lower part of the village were occasionally prone to flooding. In one of these cottages once lived Mary Jane Luscombe, a crippled lady without legs, whom P. S. Bebbington, in his booklet on Tamerton, describes as being 'more than once found in her house surrounded by hens and floodwater, waiting to be rescued'.

Once several miles out of Plymouth, an old granite milestone in the village bears the legend 'P & D VI'—6 miles from Plymouth and Dock, communications with the outside world were greatly improved with the arrival of the railway. The next few decades also saw a great improvement in road transport and the pre-war, horse-drawn Vicary's van was followed by various private bus ventures, Took's, Facey's and the Pioneer, before the arrival in the 1920s of the Devon Motor Transport buses. However, as the links with Plymouth improved they also got shorter and in 1951

Tamerton became part of Plymouth and twelve years later the railway station closed.

1951 also saw the publication, in a major national magazine, of an article by singer and entertainer, Donald Peers, describing a visit by him to the King's Arms. In it he wrote '... I stood in the public bar ... and watched the fresh-faced six foot tall landlord draw beer for his customers, who are his friends ... As I stood watching I thought of the many times he had caused thousands of goal hungry fans to cheer vociferously as he would guide the ball home with head and foot'. The man in question was Ernest or Pat, as he was better known, Glover, who remained landlord here until 1968. Six times capped for Wales, Pat Glover had come to Plymouth from Grimsby in 1939, a year that saw him play two games for Wales and only three for Argyle, for on August 26th he was a member of the last side to play at Home Park before war broke out and ended the league programme for several years. Future Argyle manager Jimmy Rae was also in the side which went down 3–1 to West Ham United; 1939 had also seen the inclusion of the King's Arms in the list of licences controlled by the Plymouth Authorities.

Whilst Pat Glover would appear to be the longest serving licensee here this century, the honours for last century must almost certainly go to the Northcott brothers, James and Richard. As well as setting up their local building business the two were, between them, licensees here for over 30 years until local assessor and assistant overseer, Henry Huxham, began an almost 20 year spell in the early 1880s.

Dates and names of earlier landlords are hard to come by. Fred Flint, who took over here from Graham Lanning three years ago, says the present pub was built some time between 1620 and 1670. Deceptively spacious inside, the pub now incorporates the adjacent cottage and Fred Flint has just added a very attractive children's lounge with soft drink optics and an ice-cream counter. Next month will see the opening of a pets' corner in his enormous beer garden. In it will be 50 rabbits, guinea pigs, hamsters, ducks, chickens, finches and budgies. A Derbyshire man, Fred says that Midland pubs are very good at catering for families, but not so much down here—a situation he hopes to change.

22nd February, 1986.

St. Mary's, Tamerton Foliot

'With nine companions and his sister Dominica, he [Indract] set out on the voyage calling at Britain on the way, where they landed at a port called Tamerunta and lived there a most strict life in the service of God for a long time, and built an oratory in which to pray.'

Indract or Indractus was, according to the historian William of Malmesbury, the 'son of a certain king in Ireland' and, forsaking the pleasures of the King's court, he chose to go on a pilgrimage to Rome. From William's account, written in the early part of the twelfth century, it would appear that the pilgrims then stopped here at Tamerton before carrying on to Rome. Having successfully reached his goal Indract returned to Britain and made for the shrine of St. Patrick in Glastonbury where, unfortunately, he was murdered.

However, if this account of events that took place 500 years earlier is accurate and Tamerunta is indeed Tamerton, then it means that Christians first worshipped here twelve hundred years ago.

Of such an early building there is no sign today but, as P. S. Bebbington notes in his well researched history of St. Mary's, 'it is fairly certain that a church or chapel of some kind existed here and the site of the present church seems its most likely location—on a pitch of rising ground, close to a settlement of people and communication routes, not far from the head of the creek'. The first reliable documentary evidence of a building here is found in a letter written in 1186 by the Bishop of Exeter, to Prior of Plimton Convent. It concerned earlier grants made in respect of church property and so clearly the church had been established some time before then. No church was recorded here in the 1086 Domesday survey, but by no means all churches were recorded by that survey.

Until the 1890s evidence of a structure, believed to date back beyond the thirteenth century, existed in the form of a small, rectangular building which is thought to have had two square headed windows in its side walls. This is reckoned to have been added to around 1292 and together these parts formed the complete north aisle of the church, that is until it was decided that the best way to increase the seating capacity here was to widen this aisle to bring it up to scale with the main body of the church.

The wide nave and seventy-eight foot high tower were added around 1440 and at the same time the south wall of the original church was taken down and a row of pillars and arches put in its place. The south aisle, which was five feet wider than its northern counterpart, dates from around 1500 and here the pillars are of Roborough stone (moorstone) rather than granite. Patronage of St. Mary's rested with the Priors of Plympton until the Reformation and it's interesting to note that the church at Plympton, which is contemporary with the original Tamerton building, was also dedicated to St. Mary. The 'Seven Stars' public house at Tamerton also dates from this period and here we find the likely source of the Inn's name for, not only was the sign of the Seven Stars a popular one at that time, but it represented the seven starred, celestial crown that generally appeared on figures of the Virgin Mary.

Another thirteenth century Tamerton Foliot building was the original vicarage, a reference to which is found in 1279, which is also the date from which the list of recorded vicars of St. Mary's dates. To date 49 names appear on that list spanning 700 years and 12 of them are the names of incumbents who have been here this century. A century that has so far seen the church survive the Death Watch beetle, the Blitz and a fire which, in 1981, might easily have destroyed the whole church but for the actions of the local people, fire brigade and the vicar himself, Christopher Goodwins. The Rev. Goodwins came here in 1969, following a man whose name appears on the official lists as Archibald R. Leggate but whom everybody knew as Colin. Colin Leggate arrived at St. Mary's, in 1963, from St. Paul's, Newton Abbot. The second son of a medical missionary working in Manchuria, he was automatically christened Archibald after his grandfather, his elder brother taking his father's name. However, his mother was not overly happy with Archibald and wrote home to her seven sisters asking them to send out their favourite boys' names and from the list she chose Colin!

An impressive old church, it still stands in a delightful rural setting with its present 200 year old vicarage across the road on its south side and its new (1974) church hall on its northern side. And, apart from the widening of its oldest aisle, one of the few major changes in the last 400 years has been the introduction, or perhaps reintroduction, of stained glass windows, a process which began in 1868.

2nd January, 1988.

Church of the Holy Spirit

'From Whitleigh I turned right, in the rain, for Southway' writes an *Evening Herald* staff reporter. 'The name is destined to become still better known, for Southway is one of the principal ways in which Plymouth is shortening its current waiting list of 8,000 applicants for council homes . . . Southway is planned to be the City's biggest housing estate, with a total of 2,300 dwellings. The first 300 are already occupied'.

So ran the first two paragraphs of a newspaper report entitled: 'Southway's "Pioneers" settling Down' and dated 6th September 1957. Three years earlier Tony Tremlett had left school, at Plymouth College, and embarked on a successful career in road transport management; at that time Southway was still a scattered collection of farming properties. It was an area little known to Tony Tremlett, although he had once cycled past it on the road from St. Budeaux to Tamerton Foliot. Today, some 30 years on, Southway is indeed a massive housing estate; a parish in its own right with a church which, until October last year, also doubled as a hall. The Vicar of this recently restructured church, dubbed from the first Southway Community Church, is the newly ordained Tony Tremlett. Faced with a financially-rewarding move to London with a directorship, or the alternative of following up the beginnings of his

work towards entering the church, he chose the latter, arriving first as a curate, at Tamerton, then coming to Southway in 1981 as Priest in Charge, until his ordination two years ago. In his time here he has seen his congregation grow quite dramatically and with the completion of a new adjoining hall and the redesigning of parts of the church, that congregation looks set to grow still further. But the picture here has not always been a rosy one. In 1979 the church was nearly closed down and the neighbouring vicarage demolished. In 1971 Southway Parish had been carved out of that of Tamerton, perhaps a little belatedly as it had already long since outgrown it in terms of population, but the arrival in 1972 of the Reverend Charles Abbott failed to mark a new prosperous era for this church. The congregation dwindled and after his departure in 1978 the Tamerton Vicar, Christopher Goodwins, resumed responsibility for the parish.

For any number of reasons Southway has in the past been an area with its problems. A number of facilities and traditional community-based buildings, pubs, halls, shops, have been slow to arrive in Southway. Despite its wide open spaces and well disposed housing stock, Southway is still poorly catered for if you consider that twenty years ago it was already housing more people than lived in Tavistock, and today almost as many people live in Southway (over 15,000) as live in the City of Truro. The situation has improved. In 1966 in an article entitled 'Paradise or Purdah' reviewing the state of Southway, Michael Miller noted that: 'For baby clothes, a choice of knitting wool, curtain material, a birthday present or a pint of beer, people have to travel off the estate . . . It's hardly surprising' he added 'that there is a lack of community spirit.'

Today however there are signs of a growing community spirit but like so many other 'new' estates, one wonders how long it takes for a place to achieve a sense of identity. With many young families moving out here in the late fifties and early sixties, perhaps it takes around 25 years (the time it takes, so we are told, for one generation to succeed another) for people to settle. Now the first major wave of Southway's children are growing up and having children of their own. 'And,' says Tony Tremlett, 'most of the people who live here like it here.' Few people with influence over, and authority within, the area actually live in Southway, so sentiments may not always, in the past, have been expressed in the 'proper' way.

The Church of the Holy Spirit was preceded by the sterling Sunday school work of Norman and Elspeth Sitters and built using the funds available in respect of the wartime loss of St. Chad's, Devonport. It was dedicated—to the renewing work of the Holy Spirit—on 4th June 1960. Now more than ever before its prospects look extremely healthy, and it is Tony Tremlett's hope and belief that the same can be said for his parish as well.

25th January, 1986.

The George, Roborough

Until comparatively recently, in historical terms, the main road out of Plymouth towards London was via Tavistock and the road which runs north through the city to Roborough Down, just a little beyond the George Coach House, known as Tavistock Road, follows, from Mutley Plain at least, the ancient Bronze Age route that began at the top of Sutton Pool.

As with any busy thoroughfare in the days before motorized transport, there were a number of inns along this way providing rest and refreshment for tired and thirsty travellers, some providing accommodation and rest facilities for horses. Today of course the motor car is designed not to get tired, as a horse might have done, but it still gets thirsty and so we find petrol stations being constructed where we might, once, have found an inn; some of which will make provision for servicing the needs of the human travellers.

'The George', always a large inn, was fully equipped with stables and beds. Today it can still offer accommodation but the stables have since been incorporated into the general refreshment area and in 1962 an extension to the front line of the building joined the old stable block to the main building. Thought to be basically a Georgian building, it was most likely constructed towards the end of the eighteenth century. However as there was an uninterrupted period of 116 years when this country had a George on the throne (between 1714–1830), it is difficult to say precisely which king the inn was named after although, like its namesake in Plympton, it was probably George III. Of course, there is also a long tradition of 'George' hotels, inns and taverns in England and many of the very old ones take their name from our patron saint, who fought the legendary dragon.

One name many people currently associate with this particular 'George' though is Louis Roseman, licensee here for 28 years until his retirement three years ago. In the trade for well over 50 years, Louis started out at the Falcon Hotel when he was just 16. In those days, he said, magistrates weren't as bothered about your age as they were your suitability and with an uncle well established in the business he was deemed fit and proper. His second pub in fact was one his uncle Sam had kept—it was Cousin's, later Heath's Hotel, next door to Genoni's Swiss Restaurant and opposite the ABC Cinema. A blitz survivor, the hotel was eventually pulled down in 1958.

Meanwhile after 6 years in George Street at Cousin's, Louis, with his new bride Eileen, moved in 1938 up to the Mount Pleasant and together they stayed there until moving out to the 'George' in 1955.

At the 'George', although the days of Baskerville's horse drawn buses from Roborough were long since a thing of the past, until fairly recently horses still met

here before a Dartmoor Hunt. While across the road, transport of an entirely new variety was taking off and landing with increasing regularity. Louis remembers in his early days at the pub being asked to leave certain lights on, on days of poor visibility, so that the aeroplanes could use the 'George' as a reference point for landings.

When Louis Roseman retired he was followed by another man well-established in the trade, Don Vellacott. Don started out at the Ford and, after 14 years there moved to another pub along the old northern route to Tavistock, 'the Tamar' at Crownhill, where he spent seven years. Strangely enough his parents, Dick and Ena, kept a pub in Tavistock itself for many years, the Duke of York, leaving only when Dick finally retired at the age of 74.

Very much a family pub, as Don Vellacott is assisted at the 'George' by his wife Peg and his son and daughter-in-law, Paul and Karin, just recently the Inn has been extended once more and transport continues to be a relevant theme. This time however, a large part of the lounge has been fitted out just like the lounge of a 1930s luxury Atlantic liner!

23rd August, 1986.

Derriford Hospital

'It is suggested that a site sufficiently large to permit of the ultimate concentration of the whole of the city's hospital facilities should be reserved in the proposed green belt area, just outside the city boundary where the services of specialists in each and every department would be readily available . . .'

'The site proposed is that occupied by Derriford House, and the surrounding lands just north of Crownhill and comprising an area of approximately 150 acres.'

So ran part of the text in the closing paragraphs of Chapter Four of the *Plan for Plymouth*, published in 1943. A chapter which was concluded thus: 'It is realised that a proposal of this magnitude, considered separately, might be thought too utopian to be practicable, but considered in its proper framework, as part of the plan for a reconstructed and enlarged city, it assumes its correct proportion and the necessity for reserving the site in a suitable position would appear to be obvious and essential.'

The site was purchased, doubtless as a result of this recommendation, although a reference in council proceedings two years before the outbreak of the Second World War, back in 1937, suggests that even then Derriford was being considered as a potential hospital site. In the event, however, it was to be another 30 years before any working plans were drawn up and several more before any actual groundwork began in 1974. At that time the plan was for an ambitious three-phase development giving Derriford an ultimate bed total in excess of 1600. No sooner had work begun on phase 1 though, than phase 3 began to look much less certain. Opinions in the Health Service began to change and, in the same way as Educational Authorities started backpedalling on the idea that bigger schools meant better schools, so a similar logic was applied to hospitals. Currently the 'best' number of beds for any one acute hospital to service is thought to be around 600. By 1992 Derriford, with phase 2 now approved and under way, will have almost 1,000 beds. Strangely enough, by 1992, in terms of the bed usage on which the projected figures of phase 3 were based, this represents considerably more than 1600 beds. In 1974 the average length of stay by a patient in an acute hospital like Derriford was around 10 days; now the figure is a little under 6 days. So virtually the same amount of work can be achieved with roughly half the number of beds.

This is thanks to advances in all aspects of health treatment; technological advances, differences in operations, reduction in size of some machinery enabling hospitals to afford and accommodate more equipment and an increase in the scale and complexity of work that can be done via outpatients. Projecting forwards who knows what innovations may take place before the end of the century? It is even feasible that major operations could be done at home. However it would not be for the same reasons that they were last century, when patients were often so frightened of going into hospital that operations would be conducted in their own homes, often under very unsanitary conditions.

Today of course most houses are clean, comfortable and fairly healthy environments. A little earlier this century though such a generalization was often far from the truth and it was because of the poor condition and backgrounds of so many of the conscripts of both world wars that the idea of a National Health Service was first conceived. As Phil Sanders, Assistant General Manager, Planning and Performance, at Derriford notes, it was not originally conceived as an 'Ill-health service', designed primarily to deal with the sick and injured, but rather to help promote a Healthy Nation. However, once improved sanitary conditions, better water supplies and an effective vaccination campaign had helped to reduce the problems of the once-common diseases like TB and polio, so the emphasis began to change. Even now though there are new initiatives to help improve our individual health by promoting low fat, high fibre diets, no smoking and more exercise. The 'I love my heart' slogan is to remind us that heart troubles are still the biggest single cause of death in this country.

The beauty of most simple exercises is that they don't cost anything—unlike hospital treatment which is very expensive. 100 years ago the average maintenance cost for each patient at the South Devon and East Cornwall Hospital was ten shillings a week (50p). Today the cost of keeping a patient in a bed at an acute hospital in the area is around £140 per day. Overall running costs of the local health authority exceed £80 million a year (excluding G.P.s). On top of this, the estimated cost of completing the next phase of Derriford is over £26 million.

When complete, Plymouth will have one of the top hospitals in the country within its boundary. The city though is fortunate in that it has always enjoyed a good reputation for its health services and now, as in the past, many of Britain's top medics in their chosen fields are based here.

West of Bristol, Derriford is the only hospital with departments in Neurosurgery and Plastic Surgery.

Completion of Derriford also spells closure for Greenbank, most of Freedom Fields (excluding Radiography) and parts of Mount Gould. Most of the new development here will be adjoining the main block and to the west of it and the tower; 73 metres high, the massive chimney tower of Derriford is regarded almost as a toy by the Dutchman who came over to supervise its construction—it's one of the smallest he has ever had to build!

One only wonders what the old occupants of Derriford House would have made of it all. The house, rebuilt around 1820, is long since gone but parts of the garden walls and an old ornamental pond still serve as reminders of the old estate. As does, to a certain extent, the farmhouse next to this massive high-tech hospital, for the farm has no mains electricity, despite being only a hundred yards or so from an incoming supply of some 11,000 volts.

12th March, 1988.

Plymouth Airport

The idea of man taking to the skies had long been the stuff of myths and legends in this country until just over 200 years ago when, on 15th September 1784, Vincent Lunardi flew 24 miles from London in a hydrogen balloon. It was almost a year to the day since a sheep, a cock and a duck had been sent up into the air in front of Louis XVI at Versailles outside Paris. The fact that these animals suffered no apparent ill-effects greatly encouraged men to follow suit. However despite much experimentation by a number of adventurous balloonists, there was little mass development of this mode of transport. Balloons were, and still are, a rarity and when in 1825 a couple of famous balloonists, Margaret Graham, described then as the only female aeronaut in England, and her husband, came to Plymouth some 50,000 people turned out to witness their demonstration flight. A flight which started out from Stonehouse Market Place and ended, fourteen minutes later and ten miles away, in the water between Stoke Head and Yealm Point. Unable to take off again, the couple were rescued by a boat and no sooner had they left their balloon than it took off and disappeared towards France never to be seen again.

It was not until this century that anyone produced a machine capable of sustained and controlled, power-driven flight. First to demonstrate the viability of such a machine were two brothers, Orville and Wilbur Wright, both bachelors because, as the one of them put it, they had not the means 'to support a wife as well as an aeroplane'. Their historic breakthrough took place in North Carolina USA, at 10.35am on 17th December 1903. Few people then, however, would have believed that such a device could ever, ultimately, travel as far as and faster than, a ship or a train, and in Britain only one paper, the *Daily Mail*, carried a reference to the Wright Brothers' achievement of that day.

It was to be another five years before a British citizen flew in a powered plane, and he was a guest passenger of Wilbur Wright in France. Within another three years paying passengers had become a reality in this country and suddenly a whole new transport system had been created. Civilian development of the airways however was in some respects curtailed by the First World War although at the end of it great leaps forward in aviation had been made. In 1914 Britain had around 300 service aeroplanes—by the 30th November 1918 the newly formed Royal Air Force (created out of the RFC, Royal Flying Corps and RNAS, Royal Naval Air Service) had 22,647 aircraft. After the war air records fell in quick succession; the first crossing of the North Atlantic took place in 1919 and terminated just off the Barbican on 31st May.

In the City visionaries within Plymouth's Chamber of Commerce recognized that air travel and services could attract much business to the city and in 1923, together with the 'Western Morning News' and 'Western Independent', two demonstration flights were sponsored out of Chelson Meadow to show how mail, picked up from liners in the Sound, could be delivered to London and Manchester in a few hours. However despite attracting a great deal of publicity and inspiring the Ministry of Civil Aviation to inaugurate an experimental service for passengers and parcels between Plymouth, Birmingham, Manchester and Belfast, little ever came of the enterprise and the scheme was dropped.

In 1928 the Chamber of Commerce inspired a fresh initiative and the following year the Air Ministry approved a decision to purchase this site at Roborough. Although used earlier it was officially opened by the Prince of Wales on 15th July, 1931. For many years afterwards development here was spasmodic. In 1933 the Great Western Railway Company began an air service between Plymouth and Cardiff and two years later a service to Jersey started. Still there was no drive to establish a major airport in Plymouth, although the Chamber of Commerce continued to press for such an establishment. In 1957 night flying was allowed at Roborough but this site was still considered too small for significant development and in 1960 Plymouth went to the Polls to vote on the development of an Airport at Harrowbeer, Yelverton, which had been set up by the RAF during the Second World War. In the event only 10 per cent of the population bothered to express an opinion and, although it was almost 2:1 in favour of Harrowbeer, the subsequent 'Harrowbeer Airport Bill' was rejected by Parliament the following year. And so the Roborough site, which includes a former Polo ground, retained its position as Plymouth City Airport. However it is only in the last decade or so that it has begun to develop in any significant way. This development has taken place entirely under the auspices of Brymon Airways. Formed in 1972 at Newquay Civil Airport (RAF St. Mawgan) as Brymon Aviation, the infant Airline arrived in Plymouth in 1973. Starting out with a staff of 3 it now employs around 200 personnel. In 1976 Brymon laid the first tarmac runway at Roborough and today, having expanded their route structure, Brymon have increased their annual passenger traffic from 2,500, in 1972, to around 150,000 last year.

Today Brymon is succeeding where Mayflower Air Services, Westward Airways, Air Westward and even Dan Air have tried before and Plymouth Airport now has 2 tarmac runways, 2 Twin Otters and 3 Dash 7's (one of each seen here on the right and left respectively). With the prospect of the development of a short take off Airport in London's dockland being handled by Brymon Airline the chances are that, for Plymouth Airport, things will continue to grow from strength to strength.

7th December 1985.

Fursdon Barn

One of the oldest surviving structures in Estover today is this granite rubble barn which, it is believed, was constructed between 1820 and 1825. Part of the Fursdon farm complex for the next 100 years or so, this substantial structure was used as a store and as a shelter for cattle, who gained access via the five semi-circular arches which were then open to the elements. The major vehicular access—for horse and cart—was through a massive arched entrance, which now leads through to the latest extension, seen to the right of this picture.

Inside the barn there was one floor which stood just above the top of the five arches. A truly massive storage area, it was ventilated by the two rows of square holes that run along the whole length of the wall on this side just below the roof. Fursdon Farm itself today houses 'Fursdon Cat and Dog Boarding Kennels' and stands only yards away from the barn on the other side of Blunt's Lane; the lane itself being a fairly ancient thoroughfare, which ran north from here beyond Plymbridge Road until it met the Tavistock Road out of Plymouth.

Until comparatively recently the layout of what we now call Estover had changed little over the centuries. In the fifties the farm was still being used and the nearest neighbours were at Derriford Barton to the north west, Thornbury Cottages, Estover House, Mainstone and Briarleigh to the east, and Bowhay Cottage and Poole Farm to the south. Among the early casualties of the new Estover housing estate was Briarleigh House. Known simply as 'Rock' until the 1920s this pleasantly disposed Georgian building dated from around 1780 and was thought to have originally been a farmhouse. As late as 1965 it was occupied; then the Corporation bought the land and would have demolished the house almost straight away had it not been discovered that it was a building scheduled as of architectural importance. However after twelve months had elapsed this 'problem' was countered by the suggestion that the building should now be demolished 'because of its present state'. In 1967 it came down and little now stood in the way of the development of Estover, a process which led to the establishment of many factories (Fine Tubes were first, then in 1970 came Wrigleys), to the north with a huge sprawling housing scheme below it.

In 1976 there was a civic opening of the Estover Housing Estate and soon the residential population had exploded from a few to many thousands. However, unlike some of the city's former rural areas, Compton, Eggbuckland, Pennycross and St. Budeaux, Estover, rather like Southway, was allowed to grow without the traditional village core upon which to build. Estover started without a church, a pub, a shop or an office, bank or community centre. It had the population of a small town with very few of the facilities. Labels like 'a planners' desert' and 'municipal madness'

were invoked to describe the area and there was criticism of the way in which Plymouth, since the war, had reportedly been allowed to double in urban area, while the population had only increased by 15 per cent.

Anxious to secure a suitable focal point for this new estate, plans were put forward, in 1978, to convert Fursdon Barn into an all purpose assembly hall with a committee room, workshop, coffee bar, kitchen and cloakrooms. These plans however came to nothing and it was another four years before John Smith and Tony Tucker bought the grade II-listed barn and began the long job of clearing out the dung and debris and putting in an extra floor. By 1983 the Fursdon Leisure Centre had been opened here; much of the surrounding site had been levelled and an all weather playing surface laid. A gradual process of expansion has witnessed a number of interesting developments and extensions around this building. There is currently still work in hand but already the wonderful transformation of this erstwhile redundant building has provided the area with a valuable asset.

Today of course Estover has most of the basic community requirements—Thornbury Junior School, Estover Comprehensive School, Christ Church which, unusually, serves as an Ecumenical Centre for Anglicans, Baptists, Methodists and Roman Catholics. There is also that odd little outpost, built on Plymbridge Road in 1882, formerly known as Estover Baptist Church, later the Pentecostal Church and now North Plymouth Community Church. There are shops, notably Asda, and a pub situated just off one of the city's longest residential roads, Miller Way, and named, optimistically enough, 'The Jolly Miller'.   »Postscript

4th June, 1988.

Windmill, Leigham

The Domesday survey of 1086 recorded the Manor of Leigham as having a value of 10 shillings and showed it as being made up of two farms, eight acres of wood and three of meadow—a far cry, you might think, from the Leigham of today, but not from the picture presented just twenty years ago.

In 1066 a Saxon named Saulf held Leigham. However in the wake of the Norman conquest, he was dispossessed and, while he may have remained as a tenant farmer, the ownership of the land passed into new hands. Over the next 900 years there was little change in the appearance of this land. A substantial manor house, dating back at least to Tudor times, established Leigham as one of the principal country seats in Devon.

'Passing the bridge (Plymbridge) the vale expands into a rich meadow, through which it flows to the delightful mansion of Leigham. The lawn, whose graceful curvature discloses pleasing views of the river and the grounds of Saltram, is surrounded by plantations above which appears Estover, residence of H. Julian esq.'

That account appeared in John Sandford's guide to the area, published in 1830. Around that time, a gentleman named Addis Archer occupied the House and amongst its more notable earlier owners was Captain John MacBride, later made Admiral, an MP for Plymouth who is remembered for the Barbican piers which he is credited with instigating and the adjacent public house which bears his name. MacBride is also said to be the one who had Leigham tower erected; a fine, octagonal edifice in grey stone, two tiered, with a window in each face and built, so the story goes, for his second wife with whom he lived at Leigham.

For much of the later part of the nineteenth century, the capital four storey mansion house with its handsome dining room, library, breakfast room, housekeeper's room, large kitchen, wine, beer and coal cellars, drawing room, seven bedrooms, servants' quarters and variety of other rooms was in the hands of the Elliott family; although, at one time in the 1850s, Charles Norrington, Lord Mayor of Plymouth 1863–5, lived here. Norrington himself perhaps being best known for the fountain memorial with the statue of Rebecca of the Well, which he presented to the city in memory of his wife, on Plymouth Hoe. This century Godfrey Courage, Cholmondeley Vere, Walter Toogood and E. Huish H. Edye are amongst those who had Leigham Manor as their home. However, in 1966 after 900 years in which little had changed, the Council began developing Leigham for the newest phase of their housing programme. It was a bold plan and one which promised the best in modern planning, based on the Radburn principle of 'keeping people and traffic apart—sane living in which children can play out of danger and homes are free from the noise and smell of passing cars.' One of the earliest reports of the plan described it as being as far from the popular conception of a council estate as one could imagine. However, the same writer went on to beg the question 'Will Leigham be out of date in 20 years?'

That was in 1965—now, more than 20 years on, with most of the promised facilities, schools, shops, pub etc., all installed the answer would certainly seem to be that Leigham is not out of date; unlike the post war prefabs of Lipson and Efford, from which many people moved to set up home here in the late 1960s, early 1970s. Why even the 'Windmill' pub—barely 15 years old—has already seen a substantial refit in the last eighteen months that makes it one of the most modern inns around. Now called the 'Windmill Sports' pub, it boasts two football teams, five darts sides, a netball team, two pool teams and sports club 'chairman'/landlord, 'Tye' Harding, says cricket and rugby teams could be on their way.

The decor of the 'Windmill' definitely reflects this sporty image. Gone now are all the Dutch touches that were designed to complement the pub's original title, although quite why it was ever called the 'Windmill' appears to be a mystery. So Leigham isn't out of date then, certainly not.

But perhaps all this modernity is tinged with sadness, for the last twenty years have also witnessed the disappearance of lower Leigham House and Farm. Leigham Tower has been all but knocked down in order to provide little more than a windbreak for the vandalised benches now to be found inside; and last year, the grand old manor house of Leigham itself was pulled down, thereby ending one of the last man made links of the area known in 1318 as Leyham and in 1086 as Leuvichestona.

21st March, 1987.

Efford

In December 1945, work began on the city's first major post-war housing development. Its heart is here in Torridge Way, Efford, for it is here that we find the traditional centres of any local community—shops, the post office, the church and the pub. And in the time honoured style of the Great British village, the church and the pub are next door to each other . . . and which came first? In a way it was neither, for although the pub was opened in July 1958 and the church was completed six years later, they were both preceded by the church hall—the simple, high-roofed, red brick building which stands to the north of the church and was built in 1952.

Initially conceived as a daughter church to Emmanuel, St. Paul's, Efford was built with money made available in respect of the war-damaged St. Paul's, Devonport. Costing £30,000 to date, the church has had just one vicar—the present incumbent Ian Lovett who took up his post on St. Paul's day just over two years ago. Just a few months before this the first landlord of the 'Royal Marine', Jack Sorrell, had left the pub. He had been there, apart from a year's sabbatical in London, for 27 years and was very much part of the modern Efford scenery, indeed he and his wife Ruth provided the font for St. Paul's.

Before he came to Efford, Jack Sorrell had spent fourteen years at the 'Standard Inn', Queens Street in Devonport but his involvement with the licensing trade however, goes back much further than that to 1927 when, as a ten year old boy, he moved with his family into the Swan at Devonport. His father Alfred then ran the pub for the next 21 years. Alfred Sorrel had been a Sgt.-Major with the Somerset Light Infantry and his son insists that the naming of this new pub in Efford was certainly nothing to do with him. The name arose because David Simonds of the Simonds Brewery, had been well treated by the Royal Marines when he was in Plymouth and he felt that the 'Royal Marine' would be an appropriate name for a city pub. It had at first been mooted that it should be called the 'Chester Cup' for that was the name of the blitzed inn by the old Market in Radford Place, from which the licence for this hostelry was transferred. However, it was not to be and it was a Marine Major General who formally opened the 'Royal Marine' in 1958 and over the years Jack Sorrell built up a fair collection of marine memorabilia. Guns, muskets, badges and flags all helped to decorate the walls of this pub with the panoramic views, which is visited by marines from all over the country.

Although Jack Sorrell left the 'Royal Marine' nearly three years ago and, although he is now in his seventies, Jack hasn't yet given up the trade altogether—he still runs his two Wills Wine Stores in Albert Road and Stuart Road. He is also still very much involved with the Licensed Victuallers National Homes charity which helps to look after publicans who retire from their pubs only to wake up to the fact that, after all those years, they now have no roof over their heads. So active has he been for this charity that in Kingsteignton a recent development of 14 bungalows and eight flats was named Sorrell Court in his honour.

Of course St. Paul's on the other hand, is named in honour of St. Paul—the patron saint of preachers (and tentmakers) and who was originally called Saul. According to tradition, his name was changed in honour of Sergius Paulus of Paphos whom Saul converted. His undoing, again according to tradition, came when he converted one of Emperor Nero's favourite concubines in Rome around 66 BC. Nero promptly had the good man beheaded whereupon, as legend has it, milk instead of blood flowed from his veins.

There are two St. Paul's in Plymouth and coincidentally they are both situated in manors which were given to Robert le Bastard after the Norman Conquest. The other manor was Stonehouse which, at the time of Domesday, was not as important as Efford. However over the centuries Efford did not develop on anything like the scale of Stonehouse and indeed in the early part of this century Efford had changed little from its medieval appearance.

Today though this is the hub of a vast population. St. Paul's parish covers a population of 5–6,000 and that number looks set to increase by about another thousand in the next year or so with all the new housing developments in the area, development which includes the building of Efford's first vicarage. However the community still has no doctor's surgery or even chemist of its own, a situation the Reverend Ian Lovett, chairman of Efford's recently formed Community Council is very anxious to see remedied. However, it's not only his parishioners who need attention. The 500 year old bell that hangs in the church tower is cracked and although a replacement has been found for this historic bell, it will cost almost £1,000 to effect the changeover.

2nd April 1988

Widey Court School

This year marks the twenty-fifth anniversary of the establishment of a junior school here at Widey. Although it was not completed until 1964, it was actually opened in April 1963 as an annexe to Manadon Vale School. There were then forty pupils and they were under the charge of Margaret Smith who subsequently became deputy head of the school, a post she relinquished in 1972 when she went on to become head of Torpoint Infants and where she still is today.

One of the most pleasantly situated schools in Plymouth, Widey Court Primary has grown considerably over the last 25 years but many are they who remember the view that would have greeted the eye from this spot in the early fifties. For here for over 300 years stood the impressive Widey Court, the title 'Court' being conferred after the visit of Charles I during the Civil War. Much added to over the years, Widey Court dated substantially from the seventeenth century, although it was undoubtedly rebuilt on an earlier, Tudor, dwelling.

Had it not been for the last war, this fine 32-roomed mansion might still be standing today. That it isn't, however, is not so much due to the fact that it was damaged during the blitz but rather because the outbreak of war in 1939 thwarted plans to convert the buildings into a first class residential hotel. In the event Widey was requisitioned by Plymouth Corporation in 1941 and used by the City Police Force for accommodation and classrooms for the War Reserve Police—in case Greenbank was put out of action.

At this time both Widey Lodges were still standing, one at the Widey Lane entrance, just a few yards east of this spot, the other at Manadon. Both were occupied, the former by a Mrs. Fitzgerald widowed during the war, and the latter by Mr. and Mrs. Humphries and their son. Both are, sadly, now demolished—the Manadon Lodge site being buried under the massive new roundabout and flyover— although, thanks to the efforts of Stanley Goodman and the Old Plymouth Society, the original lodge gate posts have been resited within this complex. Today only Widey Grange, dower house to the estate, remains. Currently a residential home, during the war this was used as an emergency telephone exchange.

The real break up of the Widey Estate, however, came in 1921 when John Yonge Anderson-Morshead put it up for sale. It was offered as a whole, 358 acres including Coleridge Barton, Bowden Farm, Higher Widey, South Widey and other lands and buildings, or as 24 separate lots. Lot number one was Widey Court itself together with 53 acres of land. A large, well-disposed, manor, Widey had passed from the hands of the Saxon Wadelo to the Norman Robert d'Albermale after the Norman Conquest.

Owned by Yeoman Heale (Hele) at the time of the Civil War during Cromwell's Protectorate, Widey passed into the hands of the Morsheads, through whose descendants the estate passed until the early part of this century. For much of this time the room Charles I had stayed in was supposed to have been left undisturbed. In the early part of last century William IV became the second king to visit Widey Court.

Widey, unfortunately, did not altogether avoid war damage and this—together with various acts of vandalism, old-age and weathering—left Widey in a ruinous state once it had formally been de-requisitioned in 1949 and after the last occupants had left the house in March 1950. That year, a Compulsory Purchase Order was confirmed by Plymouth Corporation and the site was earmarked for use by the Education Authority.

As it transpired, Widey Technical School was the first to be opened in the area. Heralded as the 'School of the Future' when it opened in September 1959, it changed its name to Widey High in 1972 while, sadly, 1988 has become its last year and the site is soon to go for housing. Housing schemes have also threatened Widey Woods on more than one occasion since the Primary School opened. However, thanks to local opposition, and even at one stage intervention from the Prince of Wales' office, such plans have come to nothing.

So it is that Widey Court School comes to celebrate its Silver Jubilee under only its second head, Geoff Burley, with the outlook to the south still little changed. True, a swimming-pool, built during the time of the school's first head, Brian Stephens, stands where there was once a lawn but many of the grand old trees survive, as several great oaks, a famous yew and the odd willow can be seen around the school. Incidentally it was the presence of willows that caused the area to be named Withy or Widey in the first place.

9th July, 1988.

Prince Maurice

On Sunday 3rd December 1643, Prince Maurice led his Royalist troops into what turned out to be one of the bloodiest and most decisive of the Civil War encounters in this area. Based at Widey Court, Prince Maurice had rallied his men, billeted at various points in the neighbourhood, including here at Eggbuckland, for an assault on Plymouth. Setting out under cover of darkness, 400 of his musketeers were guided across Lipson Creek by two 'traitors' from Plymouth, Henry Pitts, a wine merchant and Moses Collins, a lawyer. After easily taking a small outpost at Laira Point they advanced towards the town and successfully held off an initial charge of cavalry and musketeers that had stormed out to meet them. By now Prince Maurice himself had arrived on the scene with his main force. They approached along the northern slopes of Mount Gould above Lipson Creek and then cavaliers managed, in part, to break through the defence force and ride right up to the town walls. However, none went further and most were killed or captured. The Royalists, nevertheless, held their newly-won ground for many hours. Eventually, they were out-manoeuvred and, under heavy fire from a gun sited in Freedom Fields, they retreated, suffering heavy casualties. Colonel Gould, who had not long since taken full command of the Plymouth garrison, was chiefly responsible for Prince Maurice's failure and, although Maurice had on more than one occasion promised his men that they should eat their dinner in Plymouth on Christmas Day, it was not to be. Although, on the 20th of December, he led another successful night attack on a position due north of the town, he was again, eventually dislodged and by Christmas Day Maurice moved out into the country, driving all the cattle in the countryside with him. Plymouth of course, survived the siege; there was, however, a good deal more bloodshed but even the arrival of King Charles I himself with his main army of 15,000 men in September 1644 and a last desperate fling by Grenville with some 6,000 men, in January 1645, could not take the town. On the 18th January, Parliament won back Dartmouth, earlier captured by Prince Maurice, and on that same day the Royalist seige of Plymouth ended. Two months later, Cromwell and Fairfax came into the town and '300 pieces of ordnance were discharged to welcome them thither'.

Three hundred and nineteen years later Prince Maurice was remembered, here in Eggbuckland, as the very old 'New Inn' changed its name to the 'Prince Maurice'. A nephew of Charles I and brother of Prince Rupert, Maurice's likeness hangs on a sign copied from a portrait in the possession of one of his descendants. The sign itself stands on the site of the old village shop, long since disappeared. Much of Eggbuckland village, however, is still as it was at the turn of the century. The view we see here is little changed although, immediately in front of the pub was once the village green. Behind and to the side the village pump has gone, the well has been filled in, the bakery is now a hairdresser's and the village now has a fish and chip shop, but otherwise, change is slow. While buildings have shot up all over the

surrounding Eggbuckland neighbourhood, since the main road passed this part by, so has much other traffic.

Even the landlords of the Inn tend not to move on very quickly. Harold Dear has been here over 24 years already, and he's still going strong, keeping his pub as he always remembers a pub, with a separate bar and lounge and no juke box in either. His predecessor, Wilf Goss, had been here many long years too, and he had come to the pub by marrying Ada Coombes, daughter of Samuel Coombes the previous licensee, who arrived at the 'New Inn' some time during the First World War. Eggbuckland then of course, was a separate parish altogether, a status it held until 1939. That year, Eggbuckland Parish Council met for the last time and a newspaper report noted that while they 'had fought very hard for their existence . . . the scales were weighted against them'. The fight to preserve independence from this growing city is a familiar enough one even now, but Eggbuckland's struggle had been a long one, lasting throughout the 1930s and largely led by Richard Townsend 'shoeing smith, wheelwright, motor tyre agent and farmer' (Doidges farm), long-serving member of Eggbuckland PCC, and then Chairman of Plympton St. Mary's Rural District Council. Today one of his sons, Tubby, now in his seventies, still lives in the village and drinks in the Inn. Saddened by some of the changes, for the most part he's philosophical. 'It's difficult to stop the Corporation having its way once they get going' he says.

6th December 1986.

RNEC Manadon

As ships have become more complicated, so have the training and recruitment requirements of the men and women who wish to serve upon them. Once upon a time, to sail a ship meant simply propelling a vessel across the surface of the sea, either by manpower with oars or windpower with sails. There were hundreds of possible combinations of one or other or both, but no real alternative. Then came the industrial revolution and with it the steam engine and with that came the engineer.

In 1820 the Navy ordered its first steamship, *Comet*. Seven years later, *Lightning*, *Echo*, and *Meteor* became the first commissioned HM ships. In these very early days 'engineers' were usually supplied by the engine builders, along with the engines themselves. However, as engines became more commonplace but at the same time more complex, so did the problem of finding capable and suitable engineers. As early as 1831 Lieutenant Robert Wall published his *Suggestions for the Establishment of a Naval University with some observations on the formation of a Corps of Naval Engineers*. It was a vision that was to take many years to realize—despite the rapid acceptance into the navy of these new vessels; 27 of the navy ships were steam driven by 1836 and so the following year, almost reluctantly, engineers were admitted into the ranks, 'next below carpenters', placing them on the lowest rung of the officers' ladder. By 1842 the number of naval steamships had trebled and so in 1843 at Woolwich, the first move to provide a training establishment was taken as the barque *Sulphur* was requisitioned for the accommodation of trainee engineers. It was around this time too that dockyard schools were founded and here many engineer boys would receive their theoretical education. But in many ways the engineers' progress in the middle of the last century was a slow one, as Geoffrey Penn observes in his entertaining *Story of the Royal Naval Engineering College Keyham and Manadon 'HMS Thunderer'*—'In a sailing navy of tall ships, white sails and raking masts, in which smartness in seamanship and success in evolutions were the only criteria of excellence and cleanliness value far above godliness, the engineer, with his dirt, coal, oil and smoke was far from welcome.' Then he added 'In rates of pay, status and promotion engineers lagged far behind the "military" officers . . .'

In 1876 the Navy made its first serious attempt to recruit engineers from the 'officers rather than mechanic class' and two years later HMS *Marlborough* was established as the first Engineering College base, albeit a floating one, in Portsmouth. In 1879 the first permanent accommodation was erected at Keyham. It was opened on 1st July 1880. These wonderful buildings, only recently demolished, served until 1958 by which time Keyham's resources had become far too limited and as an Engineering College at least, it was closed down. A little earlier that same year, the Duke of Edinburgh arrived here to officially open Manadon. The 100-acre site had been in use since 1940 and the college had been mainly housed in a variety of temporary buildings. In 1951 the instructional block and factory was completed and in July 1956 Earl Mountbatten laid the foundation stone of the new accommodation block and wardroom seen here. The Portland stone figures flanking the main entrance steps are the work of Mr. J. Woodford RA, and show a figure of Thunderer on the left and Marlborough on the right, both in the form of figureheads. Keyham and Manadon were christened HMS *Thunderer* in 1946 taking the name then of a steam picket boat which was, in turn, the Navy's seventh HMS *Thunderer*. The fifth, incidentally, was one of the Navy's first three iron-clad, no sail power, turret ships. Launched in 1871, Prince George (later King George V), served on it for a time as lieutenant. The third HMS *Thunderer*, meanwhile, took part in the action leading up to the Glorious 1st of June 1794, alongside an earlier HMS *Marlborough*. Marlborough himself, curiously enough, was a soldier not a sailor, while Thunderer is generally shown as Thor, god of thunder. The college badge is based upon an old tampion from HMS *Thunderer* and shows Thor rising out of a cloud charged with lightning. The old college motto, once dropped but reinstated, *Eripimus Jove Fulmen* reads 'We grasp the thunder from Jove'.

With its now completed accommodation block (1966), its own large lecture hall cum cinema/theatre, impressive sports facilities and its own chapel (a converted seventeenth-century tithe barn) HMS *Thunderer* or RNEC Manadon is today, doubtless, very much the type of college or campus university that Robert Wall may well have envisaged 150 years ago. Although he could not have foreseen the sophisticated engineering and technology used by the modern navy. With its excellent educational and research facilities it clearly differs from other degree awarding bodies in that its successful students (being also officers in training) are guaranteed work after graduation and are required not only to wear uniform but also to attend lectures. However, there cannot be many educational establishments where the Queen has consented to present the academic awards as she did here on 22nd July 1983 when she visited with the Duke of Edinburgh. This was the Duke's third visit here; Prince Charles has also been to Manadon. He came in May 1980 and when here noticed that the female figurehead which previously had been assumed to have come from HMS *Adelaide* in fact was a representation of his great, great, great grandmother Queen Victoria. Subsequent enquiries revealed that the figurehead indeed originally came from the *Victoria* laid down in 1844 and broken up in 1908. It came to Manadon in 1970 and last year, having been beautifully restored, was unveiled by a great, great grandson of Queen Victoria, the Duke of Kent.

23rd January, 1988.

Manadon House

There can be few more impressive sights within the city boundaries than Manadon House. Substantially a seventeenth-century building, it has traces of an earlier sixteenth-century development while the Manor of Manadon itself is known to date back before Domesday.

'Colbert' we are told, 'held "Manedona" on the day on which King Edward was alive and dead' (5th January 1066). After the Norman conquest Judhel (Juhel of Totnes) held the Manor and he let it to Odo. The present house is situated on one of the most likely sites for any early building. Few clues to the original dating of the Manor are to be found in the name Manadon itself. In *The Place Names of South Devon* we find that the 'Man' element is explained, possibly, as deriving from the Old English 'maene'—'common' or 'general' referring either to some natural feature or some particular object marking the boundary between two or more estates. Certainly at the time of Domesday, Manadon was, and indeed still is, encircled by the manors of Witelie, Buretone, Hanecholole, Weston, Widei, Torre and Colrige. Another explanation of the name suggests that 'Man' may have been a personal name, while C. W. Bracken offered another alternative in 1935; 'man' he wrote 'may mean "stone", as in "menhir", hence "the stonyhill".'

Whatever the true derivation of the name, it appears that the manor itself later became the property of the Buzun family who also acquired the manor of Weston. In 1228 Weston went to Hugh Peverell of Ermington while the Buzuns held Manadon until 1285, when it passed to Robert de Bloyo. When Hugh Peverell's daughter married Nicholas Carew, Weston was given as her dowry and that manor then was handed down through ten generations of the Carew family until, in 1620, John Carew mortgaged Weston to John Harris. Manadon meanwhile, which had passed into the Carew family by 1469, was acquired by Harris in 1628.

By this time Manadon must have been very well disposed. There appears to have been major building or perhaps even rebuilding around 1567 on this site and, before the end of the century, Drake's leat had been cut through part of the estate and, as at Ham and Whitleigh, the necessary land was given to the Corporation in return for a free water supply. Manadon estate therefore, would have been one of the first places in the Country to have such a direct private water supply. Reading David Hawkings 'Water from the Moor', we learn that this supply was drawn off by a 'simple sluice', generally a flat stone or slate in the bank of the leat, in which a hole known as an 'ox-eye' regulated the flow. The size of the hole regulated the flow of water. The Manadon 'ox-eye' was 2 inches in diameter and known as the Manadon Water-course. It was not until 1901 that this was replaced by iron pipes!

Back in the seventeenth century though, it appears that around 1681 Manadon was enlarged to appear much as it does today, although without the porch and perhaps 3 or 4 of the dormer windows. By 1737 we find Robert Hewer in possession of Manadon, probably the same Robert Hewer who took over as Mayor of Plymouth in 1735–36 after William Strong had died in office. Hewer had earlier been mayor in his own right in 1732–33, in addition to which either he or his father also served in

that position in 1708–9 and 1717–18 when again he followed a man who died in office. Earlier still it is also likely that John Harris, who was Mayor in 1663–64, was living at Manadon at the time he was in office.

By the middle of the 18th century, Humphrey Hall gained Manadon from the will of Robert Hewer and when Hall in turn died in 1801 he bequeathed his lands and his home jointly to his three daughters, Elizabeth, Jane and Letitia. Predictably enough, the three women and their husbands soon started squabbling over the estate and an action was heard at the Court of Chancery before, finally, the property passed into the hands of the youngest daughter Letitia whose husband was John Alexander Parlby. From then until 1935 Manadon remained in the hands of the Hall-Parlbys; in that year it was bought by the St. Levan estate and in 1938 it was acquired by the Admiralty.

In 1940 the Royal Naval Engineering College HMS *Thunderer* was opened on the Manadon estate. At first the House was used for accommodation for staff officers and a flat for the captain. The top floor was unoccupied, derelict and rat infested (eventually some 332 rats were eliminated!) When the first new accommodation block was completed, the House was used for a while as the senior mess. Today it serves as the Captain's house and, as the current occupant Captain Ian Pirnie observes, it is probably the finest Naval residence in the Country.

16th January, 1988.

Tramway Offices

Two large and well-maintained plaques visible here on this impressive redbrick edifice at Milehouse, tell the world that this is, or rather was, the Plymouth Corporation Tramway Offices and one sign is dated—1923.

The Plymouth Corporation Tramways Department had been formed back in 1892. Prior to 1923 their administration had been based at Drake's Circus; the expansion of Milehouse was prompted by the acquisition, in 1922, of the Plymouth, Stonehouse and Devonport Tramways Company. However, the Corporation had been using Milehouse since 1914 when the three towns merged and when they bought out the Devonport and District Tramways Company and it was this company who first opened the Milehouse depot when they formed in 1901. In time, as trams were phased out, the Corporation title became Plymouth City Transport until, that is, D-Day last year—D-Day being D regulation day when, as a result of the 1985 Transport Act, all local authority bus companies across the country were privatised. Today it is Plymouth City Bus Limited who occupy the Milehouse depot, with a fleet of over 200 buses which carry almost 20 million passengers a year. A far cry from the humble beginnings of public street transport in the City which began properly 115 years ago with the founding of the Plymouth, Stonehouse and Devonport Company who started out with 8 open-top trams, each pulled by two horses.

The three towns, like many others, had had private horse-buses operating in the area for at least forty years when Parliament passed the Tramway Act of 1870. Plymouth, Stonehouse and Devonport Company were first off the mark locally and their first route was from Derry's Clock, through Stonehouse to Cumberland Gardens, Devonport.

Over the next three decades the horse-tram established itself as the principal means of local public transport, although an attempt was made in 1880 by another company to establish a tram network hauled by steam locomotives. However, they gave up

and sold out after just one year, because of 'numerous complaints of excessive noise, black smoke, obnoxious smells and bad timekeeping'. In 1889 Plymouth Tramways Company who took them over, introduced new horse-bus routes but, because of the difficulties negotiating existing horse traffic in the City's narrow streets, they too gave up. It was, though, the sale of this company that led to the setting up of Plymouth Corporation Tramways Limited in 1892.

Extension of the services began immediately with routes to the Hoe and Compton. Car sheds and stables were established at West Hoe and in Lower Compton Lane. A number of small private horse-bus operators (Baskerville, Wills, Mills, Smith, Andrews) continued to operate at this time, most services originating at Derry's Clock but, once the City gained Royal assent to introduce electric traction, the days of horse-drawn public transport were clearly numbered, although it took a motor-bus service of the Great Western Railway from Millbay to Roborough, to finally kill off the horse-bus. In 1901, two years after the opening of the first City electric tramline (from Theatre Royal to Prince Rock) there were still 47 horse-trams and 127 horses on active service on lines not yet converted. However, by 1907 six single-deck, one-man operated trams were introduced on the West Hoe route and an era ended. Even horse-drawn Hackney cabs began to disappear around this time as the petrol engine began to make its presence felt.

Until the advent of the pneumatic tyre, there was little threat posed to the old open topped, two-deck electric trams. Plymouth Corporation was granted permission to operate motor buses in 1915 but it wasn't until 1921 that they were able to find suitable vehicles. Painted canary yellow and white, with 'Plymouth Corporation Buses' in pink and gold lettering, these new motors were soon nicknamed 'yellow devils' or 'boneshakers'. Their great solid tyres were not conducive to a smooth ride, and the accidental killing of two pedestrians didn't help their popularity. Still, herein lay the future of public road transport and in the wake of the First World War, a number of ex-servicemen and a few civilians started operating one-man charabanc businesses from as central a position as they could find (generally around Princess Square). Within a few years, such was the improvement in omnibus design and comfort that the new tramways manager was recommending complete phasing out of the tram, in favour of the double-decker motor bus.

In the event, the last tram in Plymouth ran in 1945 and, but for the war, it might have been five or six years before that. The dreadful devastation of both the Corporation depot at Milehouse and the Western National base at Laira during the war, led in 1942 to the establishment of a city wide, joint services network which still exists today, albeit on a less formal basis. At present it is little more than a gentleman's agreement that determines who runs what route as, under the 1985 Act, anyone with an operator's licence is eligible to run a bus route, provided they give six weeks' notice to the council and have satisfactory financial and mechanical backing.

But certainly, the future looks bright for the City Bus and especially for these offices, which were recently granted a stay of execution, as latest plans mean a change in the road line, but not the wholesale demolition of this fine building.

14th November, 1987.

The Far Post Club

Whilst there are possibly fewer public houses in Plymouth today than at any other time this century, there are undoubtedly more social clubs and sports clubs with affiliated licensed premises; one such club is the Far Post Club. This year celebrating its 10th Anniversary, the Far Post is the Club set up for supporters of Plymouth Argyle F.C., and was a personal triumph for Argyle's commercial manager Bill Pearce who arrived at Home Park back in 1972 and, in no time at all, transformed the Argyle financial set up with lotteries, draws and other highly successful money-generating ventures.

Bill Pearce first saw the Far Post, as he later named it, in the car park of Exeter's newest hospital. The structure had been used as an overflow unit and had corridors running down its inside, with rooms and offices off to the left and right. It was bought by Argyle with a loan from Watneys, brought down to Plymouth, gutted, then refitted exactly as it stands today. Originally, says Gordon Ward its manager throughout, the then Club Chairman, Robert Daniel, gave the structure a lifespan of 5 years, after which time it was thought a new, perhaps more permanent, structure would be built. For one reason or another those plans have not yet come to fruition. However the Far Post still stands and is in very good shape, something which apparently can't be said for the Exeter hospital in whose service it started out. Evidently this big new building has concrete cancer and will have to be pulled down and rebuilt!

The Far Post initially opened with the occasional licence held by the late Charlie Casterton for his pub, the Edgcumbe Hotel, in Millbridge. The Club soon had its own licence, however, although it came on condition that Argyle stopped selling alcohol on the terraces. With its first pint officially pulled by the famous Liverpool manager Bill Shankly, the Far Post kicked off with a regular programme of live entertainment and its Pool, Darts, and Football Teams were very soon off the mark. By 1977 Watneys had been paid off and the Far Post has been a free house ever since. A private members' club set up 'almost to the day' on the 50th anniversary of the founding of the Plymouth Argyle Supporters Club back on 22nd January 1925, the Far Post is administered by a management committee still chaired by Bill Pearce.

With all guests being signed in by members, just as with the Vice Presidents Club at Home Park, it was hard to see initially why the ban, applied to the sale of alcohol at grounds two hours before and one hour after the match, should be imposed on members clubs. Members are all known to the club and in many respects this represents a step towards the Government's preferred identity pass system for major league football supporters. What is more, the general claim that real supporters don't cause trouble appears to be well founded at Home Park. The Far Post has an excellent record and its fixtures and fittings are all original. Indeed in ten years even the carpet has remained unchanged and free of cigarette burns and beer stains, whilst its lavatory graffiti has been minimal . . . a state of affairs that doubtless many publicans would envy.

Regularly frequented by all the players, who often come down for a drink and to face their critics and fans alike after a match, win or lose, the Far Post has served many famous footballing faces over the last ten years and since 1977, on the Argyle side, I have drawn all those who have played at least half a dozen games for the Pilgrims. Currently no less than 66 player cartoons appear mounted above the bar with only John Uzzell and Chris Harrison surviving from the first 18 that appeared seven years ago. »Postscript

28th September 1985

139

Plymouth Albion RFC

Rugby football, 'a game for ruffians played by gentlemen' is said to owe its origins to a boy at Rugby school, William Webb Ellis (later the Rev. W. W. Ellis) who, one day in 1823, instead of catching the ball, dropping back a couple of paces and kicking it as the rules of 'football' then allowed, simply caught the ball and ran forward with it in his hands towards his opponents' goal. It was not long before this handling and running, although considered to be of dubious legality, became an accepted part of the game at Rugby school and its popularity spread as 'old boys' introduced it to Universities and Colleges around the country.

Blackheath, founded in 1862, is generally recognized as the oldest established club side. On 26th January, 1871, twenty-one clubs attended the meeting which inaugurated the Rugby Union after which the Laws of the Game were drawn up, principally by three old Rugbeians. In March that year the first international took place between England and Scotland, in Edinburgh. There were 20 players on each side. By the mid 1870s the number of players in an international side had come down to 15 and Rugby Union itself had come down to the Three Towns. It also reached Australia and New Zealand around the same time.

1876 was the year a number of dockyard apprentices first got together and formed the Albion Club (Albion is the old and poetic name for Britain). The 'Albion Hotel' had just been built a year or so earlier near the old Millbay Station. The hotel still stands and is the oldest part of the 'New Continental Hotel'. The new rugby club played at Devonport Park and for some years was known as Devonport Albion. They played in blue and black shirts. Ten years later they amalgamated with their great rivals the Keyham Club who played in blue and white. The time had come for expansion and Albion took up an offer of a field at Bladderley and in 1887 moved to Beacon Park for the first time. The Bladderley pitch was actually a few hundred yards to the south west of the present ground, roughly where Ayreville Road is today.

Spectators for these early matches paid threepence, of which one penny went to the owner of the field, Mr. Long. Even the players paid a penny each. The whole question of money was becoming an important one in the game and the debate as to whether players should be compensated for the loss of their working time raged hard. In the end the Rugby Union took a vote on the issue in 1893 and found in favour of keeping the game completely amateur. As a result 22 Yorkshire and Lancashire sides left to form what is now the Rugby Football League.

Meanwhile in Plymouth the pennies were mounting up. Total attendances for the 1891–92 season topped 27,000. In 1893 Albion moved again, this time to Home Park, home of Argyle Athletic football and rugby clubs. Albion's stay at Home Park was brief, as was their return to Bladderley in 1895, and the following year they were to be found playing at the Rectory Ground. Still known as Devonport Albion, the club, in 1898, supplied a number of the leading players into the Devon side that won the English County Championship that year. These were successful times for the club. However, with the advent of the First World War, the local rugby scene faded greatly and by the end of the war the recently formed Plymouth Rugby Club had virtually folded and the Rectory had been taken over by Devonport Services, formed just before the war in 1912. It looked as though Albion would be wound up, when the decision was taken to amalgamate Albion with the Plymouth club to form a new side—Plymouth Albion, its new colours 'cherry and white with the Borough Arms of Plymouth as a breast badge'. The three towns of Plymouth, Devonport and Stonehouse had, of course, themselves amalgamated in 1914.

In 1919 the new club premises were found at Beacon Park and a 'Million Penny Fund' was started soon after to raise money for facilities. Home players had been changing in town and visitors provided with changing accommodation in the Co-op jam factory, just along from Beacon Park. The 1920s was a golden era for Albion. The All Blacks arrived on a tour from New Zealand, the Waratahs from New South Wales played a trial game here and on one remarkable occasion in the late twenties, five Albion players represented England in an international side.

Today the Albion is still probably the best side west of Bath and it is among the top 30 clubs in the country. It almost certainly travels further than any of the other established teams. It has one of the oldest supporters' associations in the country and also one of the longest established juniors' sections. As local schools put less input into the game, so Albion have felt it incumbent upon them to put more effort into encouraging youngsters and skilled, dedicated and unpaid coaches work every Sunday, with large numbers of young aspirants to this fine game. A game in which the glory still lies in playing well and enjoying it with no question of the sort of financial remuneration that is in danger of crippling Association Football, both for the player and for the fan.

14th February, 1987.

Torr Home for the Blind

'The gay new houses with their cream coloured walls and red and green roofs that lie in an irregular circle about Torr make the old house behind the trees look very grey, but their nearness cannot rob it of its dignity, although they have denuded it of its rural surroundings.' Written barely 50 years ago, in May 1937, by Patricia O'Neill in a *Herald* series on 'Old Homes Around and About Plymouth', the thought of Torr in rural surroundings is today quite a difficult one to envisage. However when it became Plymouth's new home for the blind in 1929, having moved from Devonport, that is just how Torr appeared.

Set on one of the highest pieces of land in the Plymouth area and commanding excellent views in all directions, an earlier house at Torr was always painted white and was apparently used as a landmark by those entering the Sound. Built in the eighteenth century and named Tor Grove, this house was nearing the end of its life when purchased, around 1874–5, by Robert Bayly. Before Bayly had got around to building this present edifice immediately behind the old Tor Grove House, however, he entertained the famous Scot, Alexander Graham Bell in August 1877. Bell's telephone, the first capable of sustained articulate speech, had been patented by him on 9th March 1876 and had first been demonstrated in September that year in

Glasgow. But the first permanent installation of a telephone in this country took place here at Torr when the inventor fixed up one of his telephones between the old house and the gardener's house because Mrs Bayly felt nervous in 'such a lonely place' which was 'deep in the country'. Queen Victoria was evidently not amused—she had wanted to have the first private connection and although some sources credit her with that honour her first telephone at her Isle of Wight summer house was not installed until January 1878. The Plymouth phone was given, many years later, to the city museum by Miss Mary Bayly, who later became Plymouth's first lady Councillor and who was just six years old when Bell visited her family home. She also remembered the great man demonstrating to her his latest development, the microphone, as he placed a device against her ear and she was able to hear a fly, which Bell had placed in a pill-box, 'walking about like a man walking on a wooden floor with hobnailed boots on'. It is perhaps fitting that these inventions which, in one way or another, give so much pleasure to Torr's present inhabitants—the blind and partially sighted—should have had such early introductions here.

Robert Bayly built the present Torr House in 1882. A grand, spacious residence with an enormous hall and magnificent mahogany staircase, it was home for the Baylys until it was sold by the family a little while after Robert's widow died in 1920.

Standing on a site that still bears its Ancient British name—Tor—a number of finds in Torr Lane itself show both the antiquity of the area and the road. 100 years ago 2 palstaves and a celt (both Bronze Age axe like implements) were found in an old bank of the Lane. Variously spelt through the years, in recent times a double 'rr' was favoured. However after a lorry collided with one of the few Torr Lane signs about three years ago it was replaced with a Tor Lane sign and the others were altered to suit. Cannon shot finds within the grounds of Torr itself show another aspect of its past, that of a fortification during the Civil War. Meanwhile a stone near the gardener's present quarters acknowledges the spring that still bubbles up around here and that for many years was the principal water source for the Stonehouse Leat, which began here and fed the recently infilled Stonehouse Reservoir off Peverell Park Road. While the spring still runs away to the south-west of Torr, to the north a little stands what is left of the once extensive wood, known today as Blindman's Wood, where for almost 30 years Plymouth's scouts have had their headquarters. However whether this wood takes its name from an association with the home for the blind that antedates the scouts' arrival here by some 20 years (when indeed the woods would have run up to the then rural Torr) or not, still appears to be a matter for conjecture.

What is certain, however, is that Torr Home, registered as a residential home for up to 60 men and women, provides a comfortable home and sympathetic care for its blind and partially-sighted occupants, many of whom are elderly and infirm. Further, that it is still set in relatively expansive and undoubtedly attractive grounds and it is managed by a voluntary committee, who do their best to run this 100-year-old building to modern standards with whatever financial assistance and donations that come their way.

28th June, 1986.

Pearn Convalescent Home

'It is the custom among people of certain schools of thought on social questions to rail against capitalists and to argue that the accumulation of great wealth in the hands of individuals is not good for the community. It may be so when the riches are obtained by oppression and hoarded for selfish purposes or squandered in indulgence. But no one will dispute that wealth is an excellent thing when wisely used. The power it places in the hands of men of large hearts and good sense of blessing their fellows is immense.' So said an anonymous columnist in the *Western Daily Mercury* almost 100 years ago. The exact date, 25th February 1892, the same issue carried a strange review of Oscar Wilde's latest London stage appearance. The man whom this particular article was eulogising however was Edwin Alonzo Pearn whose 'munificent gift' to the South Devon and East Cornwall Hospital and the Royal Albert Hospital had been announced in the previous day's paper. Sadly Mr. Pearn died before his gift had been completed, but completed it was in 1895 and here it still stands today, 'to be known at all times as the Pearn Convalescent Home'.

The Convalescent Home was a Victorian 'Invention', the first one had been built in 1840, the Pearn however was the first in Plymouth and remains the only purpose-built convalescent home in the city. At the time this building was in many ways long overdue, the Hospital Authorities had been desperate to obtain the provision of such an institution but the funds were not forthcoming. E. A. Pearn's gift, which was the whole of his estate, included, for the nurses, his own house of Compton Leigh (recently demolished) plus a great deal of land and provision for the setting up of allotments and almshouses. (These were later built in the 1920s and are still in use today in Higher Compton Road—numbers 79, 81 and 83). The value of the Pearn gift was said then to be around £96,000, a great deal of money now but worth so much more last century. A quiet man, 'whose purse was ever open to the poor',

Edwin Pearn with 'characteristic modesty . . . always sought to do his good works in directions free from publicity'. Consequently very little appears to be known about him except that when working in the 'pursuit of commerce he worked as hard as any man in the west' and was 'entirely the architect of his own fortune'.

A Devonian, Pearn bought Compton Leigh (just off Eggbuckland Road and behind Mannamead Tennis Club, who lease their land from the Pearn Trust) from the man who had it built, W. Luscombe. Pearn had obviously lived here some time before his death. In 1882 he and his brother commissioned a William Morris window for Emmanuel Church, dedicated to his mother, Mary, while the year earlier he received the highest number of votes of 20 candidates in Compton Gifford's first poll for a Local Board of Government. Clearly a popular local figure, Mr. Pearn is undoubtedly still popular today with all those who have cause to benefit from his generous endowment. Today of course, Convalescent Homes are not quite as essential as they were last century when poor folk were frequently dying of infections contracted in hospital and were barely strong enough to survive medical treatment. Early annual reports from the Pearn regularly stress how patients, although only here for a few days or weeks at most, nevertheless registered great weight gains. One man alone putting on $33\frac{1}{2}$ pounds during a one-month stay in the Home's first year.

Little changed from the outside, the 30-bed home has recently had a facelift internally, which cost more on paper than the initial value of the bequest—over £100,000. The Pearn Trust now provide better than ever, subsidised accommodation for recuperating adults, who would be hard pressed to cope at home after a stay in hospital. And whilst residential homes and hospices have perhaps become the new social requirement, the Pearn will stand as a significant contribution to Plymouth's medical history and a classic example of Victorian philanthropy.

143

11th January, 1986.

Sir Francis Drake Bowling Club

On 19th July 1888 on the occasion of the 300th Anniversary of sighting the Spanish Armada, a game of bowls was staged at the Royal Citadel. There were, at that time, no local bowling organisations, so teams were drawn from Torrington (Devon) Bowling Club and Leeds (Yorkshire) Bowling Club.

This was not a particularly sad reflection on the state of the sport in this town for there were few Bowling Clubs at all in the country 100 years ago. Indeed, although the origins of the game go well beyond the days of Drake, by the middle of the nineteenth century, because of its associations with 'pothouses', gambling and general drunkenness, the game had fallen into disrepute. Its revival was sparked largely by the formation of bowling associations in Australia (1880) and in Scotland (1892). Throughout the late 1890s and early 1900s similar bodies were formed in the Midlands, around London and the Southern Counties. In 1903 the English Bowling Association was established and two years later a higher controlling body—the International Bowling Board—was founded. A founder member of this august organization was the famous cricketing hero Dr. W. G. Grace, a keen bowls player, who was also the first president of the English Bowling Association.

However, despite all this activity from 1888 elsewhere across the country, it was noted by 'Erimus', in a piece which appeared in the *Western Daily Mercury* of 12th January 1907, that 'The town of all England, indeed all Britain, which should possess a bowling green, has none. That is Plymouth.' These remarks did not go unheeded and a few weeks later a letter was written to the paper by B. Priestley-Shires and J. Pidsley, 'inviting gentlemen desirous of joining the proposed Bowling Club for Plymouth' to write to them.

Later that same month, March 1907, a committee of eleven gentlemen was formed to start a club in Plymouth. They then approached the Hoe and Recreation Grounds Committee for a site on the Hoe and on the 14th May this committee earmarked a plot of land for such use. In October work began on clearing a Hoe green and by 16th November 1907 this had been achieved, although it did not come into use until 7th May 1908. On that date the town Mayor, Sir Charles Radford, opened the Hoe Green and the Plymouth (Sir Francis Drake) Club hosted a series of games with visiting clubs—a list which once again included Torrington.

All this is not to say, however, that the members of the newly-formed Plymouth (Sir Francis Drake) Club had waited just over a year before they began playing—far from it. Their first game had, in fact, been held on 12th June 1907, on part of the grounds of Plymouth & Mannamead College, Ford Park, leased for a year.

The first specially constructed green to be laid out and opened, meanwhile, came into service a couple of weeks or so before the Hoe Green, at Thornhill Road in April 1908. The houses in Thornhill Road were but a few years old at this time and by 1908 the road was only just nearing completion. However, the green, opened to relieve anticipated pressure on the Hoe green, was not greatly used and in August 1908 Thornhill Road green was closed. Before long though, another green was opened in this area, once again on land at Ford Park. This venue was in use from July 1907 until September 1917 when it too folded. The Plymouth (Sir Francis Drake) Bowling Club then transferred its headquarters to the Hoe Bowling Green.

This situation was evidently not entirely satisfactory, however, and on 20th May 1922, a new green was opened on land purchased here in Whiteford Road. With a green constructed with Cumberland turf and graced with a fine wooden pavilion which still stands today, the Club marked its move here in 1922 by severing its connections with the Hoe Bowling Club. The name Plymouth (Sir Francis Drake) was retained, however, and the next few years truly were glory days at Whiteford Road. Bob Jack, the former Argyle player and manager, was a member here and in 1926 he won the English Singles Championship retaining the trophy, in fact, for the club as Harold Webber had taken the title in 1925. Webber later went on to co-write one of the standard books on how to play bowls.

Traditions at Whiteford Road die hard inside this charming pavilion (extended in the 1930s at the front and subsequently at the rear and side). You will still find one of the most civilised tea intervals in the country, adding greatly to the charm of a game where players in their eighties can compete on level terms with players a quarter their age.

By the way, although the story of Sir Francis Drake's game of bowls on the Hoe on 19th July 1588, is well known across the world, the result itself is not so well recorded. Legend has it that in fact Drake lost to Hawkins who, having won, turned to the famous seafarer and said;'There, Vice-Admiral, you're beaten, and that's the rubber. Pay up three dollars, old high flyer.'

2nd July, 1988.

Peverell Park Methodist Church

In 1893 Peverell Park Road was nothing more than an unnamed footpath that ran from its present eastern fork, where it meets Western Park Road, to just north of Pounds House, where it now meets with Outland Road. Little in the way of housing development extended beyond Hyde Park. The few terraces that did exist suggested a strong evangelical element in the area; Wesley Avenue and Wesley Terrace had been laid out and at number 18 Elim Terrace a Wesleyan Mission room had been established. This house, originally owned by Isaac Foot senior, could evidently accommodate 60 people and the need for such a meeting hall had arisen out of the successful work of the Mutley Mission in this area. Indeed such was their achievement that on the 3rd November 1893 discussion began on the desirability of establishing a new church in the area. Three sites were considered, with the final choice being settled here 'on the corner of two new roads in a growing part of Plymouth'. This land, between the top of Westbourne Road and Glendower Road, was one of the first pieces of the Pounds estate to be sold by the Chapell-Hodges. Stretching from Outland Road to St. Gabriel's Avenue, for most of the nineteenth century it had been surrounded by open countryside but in 1891 Devonport extended its boundaries to their doorstep and in 1896 Plymouth re-drew its territorial lines to include Compton Gifford, in which parish this part of Mutley was situated. William Buller Chapell-Hodge, a keen horseman, decided soon after to sell off most of the estate and in 1898 it was conveyed to the builders Shillabear, Shears and Shillabeer. Two years later William, the last of the Chapell-Hodges, was killed fighting in the Boer War.

Meanwhile the New Iron Church, described as being in Peverell Park Road, although at this time there was very little of it, was operational by the end of the summer of 1896. The first service on the site, however, had been an open-air one on the 27th May, true to the spirit of Methodism's founding father, John Wesley, (1703–91) who, in 50 years travelled about 250,000 miles, mostly on horseback, and preached nearly 50,000 sermons. These included several open-air sermons in Plymouth Dock (Devonport) and the Barbican.

The Iron Church, built by C. L. Duke, was a great improvement on 18 Elim Terrace which incidentally was soon after renumbered and is now said to be number 2, home of two Peverell Methodist members Rosalind Jones and her husband, the popular Peverell milkman, David. It was not long however before discussions had begun again with a view to further expansion and, with help from the '20th Century Fund' and various loans and gifts, it was resolved to build a school/church of stone.

Research by Plymouth historian and Peverell expert Barbara Marlow reveals that, after the Ceremonial Stone laying on 4th May, 1904, a public luncheon took place, tickets for which were two shillings (10p) followed later in the day by a public tea which cost the princely sum of sixpence. A year later, 17th May, 1905, the church was opened. That same year trams ran for the first time along the recently completed Peverell Park Road, and in one of the new smaller Park Roads, Broad Park, at number 14, Ted Prosser was born and from that day to this a Prosser has lived in that house. However, a luncheon held earlier this week for Ted Prosser's widow, Win, closes one chapter and opens another in a story that, to date, has been part of the story of Peverell Park itself.

Winifred Hexter, as she was born, moved into Broad Park Road, with her parents and brothers Stan and Harry in 1923 and used to wave at young Ted across the road from her bedroom window. They later married. Ted, a carpenter and joiner, later did his bit in the expansion of Peverell by working on the building of the 'railway houses' on Weston Park Road. A generation later their son and two of brother Stan and sister-in-law Lil's daughters all met their future partners here at Peverell Park Methodist Church youth club. Now, next month, Win leaves Peverell to join Stan and Lil, who recently emigrated to Canada to join their daughters and are now living in accommodation built by their son-in-law Peter, one of the Youth Club's old boys and her own daughter, Pam, who moved there nearly 30 years ago and broke form by marrying a Canadian!

Meanwhile, whilst the Prossers and Hexters complete their move from Peverell to Canada, John Lusty, the present minister here at Peverell Park is himself travelling across the Atlantic this summer. His destination however is Richmond, Missouri, 20 miles from Kansas City in the USA. This move though is just a temporary one, a six-week exchange with an American minister, one of around 300 such exchanges which take place each year.

A circumstance again that John Wesley would have applauded, having first ordained preachers to serve in America as long ago as 1784! »Postscript

24th May, 1986.

St. Gabriel's

'In thirty years the population of the Three Towns increased from 80,000 to over 220,000 due to the great Dockyard extension. This influx of men, women and children found accommodation in suburbs which grew up in what had been a country of hill and valley. A church extension scheme became necessary, and an effort to build ten churches was inaugurated under Dr. Robertson, the Bishop of Exeter . . . One of these was the Church of St. Gabriel'. (From a newspaper report dated 8th November, 1924.)

It was in 1906 that this work got under way but there had long been felt a need to build a church in the Hyde Park area. As early as 1893 a Mutley Mission had been established in connection with Emmanuel, on the corner of Ford Park Road and Mutley Plain. Today there is a travel agent's on the site, but then it was the home of a Dr. Price. In March that year the gathering moved to the Plymouth College gymnasium and the Reverend N. N. Lewarne, curate of Emmanuel, took charge of the proceedings. For over 15 years the old gym (demolished in 1933) witnessed regular services. On Saturday nights it would be converted into a church and on Sunday nights it would revert to being a gymnasium again. From April 1895 to January 1907 the Rev. George Soley acted as curate-in-charge here. But then on 29th January 1907 the aforementioned Dr. Robertson, Bishop of Exeter, came down to the gymnasium and, in the presence of a large congregation including Thomas Lockyer the Mayor of Plymouth and his Deputy, he publicly licensed the Rev. J. L. Nightingale, MA, as curate-in-charge of the new district to be known as St. Gabriels.

The name, St. Gabriel, was chosen because of that Saint's close association with the Emmanuel, mirroring the new church's links with the parish church of Emmanuel, which had itself been begun in 1869. In the event, the actual construction of St. Gabriel's (as chronicled by George Manuell in a booklet on the church), began exactly 50 years after Emmanuel—its foundation stone being laid on 22nd May, 1909. The site for this new church was at the junction of Hyde Park Road and Peverell Terrace and the land was the gift of the Rev. Dr. Trelawney-Ross and his son the Rev. W. Trelawney-Ross; the gift having been made to the Vicar of Pennycross (St. Pancras), the Rev. W. E. Waddington, in memory of a beloved daughter and sister. The site for the church was actually in the parish of Pennycross, although it was obvious that part of the parish of Emmanuel would be carved out to make up the new parish of St. Gabriels—a parish which was formally created on the day the church was consecrated, 26th July 1910. In those days the boundaries were marked by Ford Park Road and the cemetery, Hyde Park Road, Barn Park and Ganna Park roads, stretching up through the Mutley House grounds to the playing fields of Mount House School (now Plymouth College Preparatory School) and including Glenhurst Road. In 1962 these boundaries were pushed further out to include Burleigh Park Road, Burleigh Lane, Tor Lane, Mannamead Road, Mutley Plain, Ford Park Road and right back across the eastern line of Central Park to Burleigh.

By this time the church had almost been completed. The Lady Chapel, which stands on the nearest corner here, had been shelved on completion of the Church and

Chancel back in 1924 and was only begun, 30 years later, in December 1954. Work was swift, however, and on 11th June, 1955 the new Chapel was opened. Designed by W. D. Caroe, the original architect of St. Gabriel's, the Chapel was constructed in the same Doulting Stone as the rest of the building—the stone for it coming from the Church of St. George, in Durnford Street, Stonehouse, which was bombed during the last war.

St. Gabriel's Church hall on the other side of the church is, meanwhile, a remnant of the First World War. Described as being temporary in 1924, the hall originally stood in the playground of Hyde Park School, where it had been erected at the suggestion of Colonel Mildmay. During the First War the school was used as a military hospital and the Mildmay hut served for recreation and refreshment. St. Gabriel's Vicar, the Rev. C. W. H. Sewell, acted as the Hospital Chaplain here and after the war Colonel Mildmay—now Lord Mildmay—and Lady Mildmay gifted the hut to St. Gabriel's. By May 1915 the hut had been re-erected on its present site and the following month it was officially opened by the Headmaster of Plymouth College, the Rev. H. J. Chaytor. The hall was extensively refurbished in 1969.

In 1960 the church celebrated its jubilee year by installing a figure of St. Gabriel in the external niche in the eastern end of the church, thereby fulfilling another part of the original plan. Incidentally there is no traditional east window in St. Gabriel's because the Building Committee and the architect thought it inadvisable given 'the closeness of the road and the proximity of the tramways'.

Today St. Gabriel's continues to draw on a strong local congregation. The present incumbent, the Rev. J. J. Stark, arrived here in 1979, following the Rev. C. H. J. Treneer and the church fosters a healthy and friendly relationship with its Catholic and Methodist neighbours.

25th July, 1987.

Plymouth College Preparatory School

For the first fifty years or so of its existence, Plymouth College Preparatory School was based at the main school in Ford Park. It was started, in a 'very small way' in 1890, by the then head of Plymouth College, Mr. F. H. Colson. Colson had been appointed the previous year and was the fourth head at the school since it had opened in 1877.

By all accounts the 'Prep' grew very rapidly. Initially it was conducted in a room in the headmaster's house but a move soon became inevitable and operations were transferred to a house near the south gate which had been specially rented for the purpose. In 1921 another move saw the Prep take over No. 1 Shaftesbury Villas, one of the ring of grand Victorian residences that surrounded the headmaster's house, No. 1 Valletort Villas. Then in 1929 No. 2 Valletort Villas, backing on to the headmaster's house, was taken over by this expanding section of the school. (Not that attendance at the Prep automatically led to a place at the main school—there was still an examination to pass).

Up to this point the Prep appears to have been run entirely by female staff, and it is thought that the appointment of Charles Firman in 1935 as head of the Prep was the first break with this 'tradition'. Whether it was or not, one thing is certain, under E. C. A. Firman the Prep was built up and established as a major institution in its own right.

Firman's first staff appointment followed in 1936 and it was another male, 25 year old James Westhead, who, apart from a five year spell in the army during the Second World War, taught at the school right through to 1977. However, there has been a

Westhead at the school every year since, as Jimmy's son and grandsons all went through the school, the last one leaving this year. Certainly such continuity is a common feature of the Prep, and another young man who arrived just after the war was to spend an unbroken 33 year spell teaching at the school. This young teacher was Len Coombe, and he had only been with the school for a year or so when it moved from Ford Park to the site here, at the end of Hartley Road. This move came about largely as a result of the post-war Butler Act under the terms of which Plymouth College became a Direct Grant School. Among the conditions pertaining to this new status was the setting up of the Prep as a separate school physically as well as administratively. The Act also required the Main School to admit 25 'free place' pupils a year, and effectively this meant the school would soon need all its extra classrooms anyway.

The search for a new home fortunately did not prove to be a difficult one as Mount House School, which had been based in this grand edifice at the end of this small approach road off Tavistock Road, had evacuated to Tavistock (via Helston!) during the war and there they have stayed ever since. Dr. David Owen was one of its first post war pupils. Mount House School was established here in 1900 by a Miss Foulger Tubbs who had been born in Mount House. It was the third home for this school since its founding in 1881 in Alton Terrace. In 1890 it had moved to North Hill House, moving from there when it was condemned after a diphtheria epidemic in 1899.

Following the wartime evacuation of the building, Mount House was requisitioned by the Wrens and it was during their stay here that the swimming pool was constructed. Once the Wrens had gone Mount House became available—and very soon overgrown—and in 1947 Plymouth College Preparatory School began preparing it for their use. Chairman of the Governors at the time, and a leading figure in the move, was Sir William Munday and it is in his honour that the Mount House building was renamed Munday House.

Meanwhile Westfield House, from which this view was taken, was occupied in 1947 by the Busy Bees girls' school. Miss Smith was then head of Busy Bees and under her it moved to Thorn Park in 1948, from where it has only recently moved. Westfield, or the Red House as it was later known, then became the residence of the Prep school headmaster and here Charles Firman and his wife Molly lived until 1964. Molly Firman, a well loved figure about the school, is, like Jimmy Westhead and Len Coombe, still around today although she now lives in Tavistock. Jimmy Westhead's wife, incidentally, took over from Miss Smith as Headmistress of Busy Bees.

J. D. Hope Simpson followed Charles Firman at the Prep and in 1978 he was succeeded by the current headmaster, Tony Hudson. Apart from the war years, when Mr. Richards, a retired headmaster of Salisbury Road School, was at the helm, Plymouth College Preparatory School has had but three heads in the last 53 years. Certainly change is not a major feature of the school although new buildings and extensions have appeared at regular intervals—the School Hall, 1954, and the Library or classroom buildings, 1970, being the two that stand out in this particular view.

16th July, 1988.

Fives courts, Plymouth College

'Sir . . . I am surprised that so little attention has been paid to Fives this term. It cannot be the expense attached to the game that prevents those who like the game from playing; for it is the least expensive amusement we have. It is a pity when we have such splendid courts, pronounced by some to be among the finest in England—that so little interest should be taken in the game . . . Hoping that this letter will not be unheeded, I remain, Yours truly QUADRANGLE.'

Quadrangle, whoever he may have been, was addressing his comments to the editor of the first ever edition of the *Plymothian*. The *Plymothian* was, and indeed still is, the school magazine of Plymouth College and Vol. 1 No. 1 was published on 1st December 1883. The Fives Courts, like the rest of the school, were relatively new in 1883, being part of the original development at Ford Park and, therefore, dating from the late 1870s. Fives itself, or at least the variety played here—Rugby Fives— was also relatively new in 1883, having grown out of a game developed at Rugby School around 1850. Like most ball games it is essentially quite simple; the ball is served onto the front wall above a line about $2\frac{1}{2}$ feet above the ground and has to strike a side wall and bounce to the liking of an opponent, who has in turn to make the ball strike the front wall again above the line, either directly or indirectly, off one of the other walls. In Eton Fives, a slightly earlier version of the game, there is no back wall. Irish handball is another similar sport played in a much longer court or 'alley'.

No one is quite sure where the name 'Fives' came from; it seems unlikely that it was ever played by teams of five; singles are usual, but doubles are often played. A suggestion that scoring up to 15 was originally divided into three fives also seems unlikely as other variations score to 11, 20 or 25 points and the popular notion that a hand is a bunch of fives (five fingers—an expression common in Scotland) also seems unlikely as the first recording of that expression appears long after the first written reference to the game Fives. Earliest references to the sport, incidentally, are all around the Somerset area, Banwell 1634, Babcary 1765 with the first court noted at Lord Weymouth's school, now Warminster School in Wiltshire, in 1773.

Quadrangle's remarks did not, apparently, go unheeded and in *Plymothian* No. 3

(March 1884) it was noted that 'One of the best events this term has undoubtedly been the Fives competition.' Two of the five Whiteford brothers (of the family whose name is remembered in Whiteford Road) entered; the older brother lost the Senior Cup he had won the previous year, but the younger brother won the junior tournament. The youngest of the Whiteford boys was later responsible for setting up Hill Lane Tennis Club and, just as tennis had originally grown out of hand-tennis, it would appear that the origins of squash are to be found in fives. The courts are similar, as is the play and the size of the balls, except that rackets are used rather than gloved hands to strike the ball (although 'Tom Brown' mentions his Five's bat in 'his schooldays' at Rugby published in 1857). Fives was played as a school team game at Plymouth College for a good many years after Quadrangle's outburst. However, a combination of poor weather and poor playing surfaces (the floors became pitted and uneven), led to a weakened school side and in 1948 the School Captain of Fives, P. W. J. Luddington, reported that the team had been 'soundly defeated' by Kelly College and reiterated the 'time worn plea' that something be done about the courts. It wasn't and Fives was reduced to a break-time sport, more often than not played with bare hands and a tennis ball. However, by 1958 the school was at the forefront of the newer sport of Squash Rackets, as it was then known, as they were among the first in the area to have a squash court.

Now, nearly 30 years later, the completion of their new Sports Hall sees the College pioneering another game in the city—Tchouk ball. Popular on the Continent, it is a non-contact hand/ball game played with a ball about the size of a small football. A game that the very young of either sex can play alongside much older men or women, it is being hailed as a game of the future.

But Fives too could well have a healthy future. Kelly College at Tavistock have recently reactivated their Fives Courts. After many years of lying dormant, they were reopened by the Secretary of the national Rugby Fives Association. Blundell's at Tiverton play very enthusiastically and Warminster's oldest court in the country is still in use. An easy and exciting game to play using both hands and no rackets, with simple courts, it may yet reach a wider audience.

29th November, 1986.

The Barton Building

In 1870 James Starley, foreman of the Coventry Machinists Company, invented the Ariel bicycle—the first penny farthing. Fifteen years later his nephew, John Kemp Starley, produced the first 'modern' style bicycle with a sloping front fork and chain to drive the rear wheel. He called it the Rover Safety Bicycle. By 1903 the first Rover motor cycle had appeared, followed, a year later, by the first Rover motor car.

Meanwhile, back in the 1890s London born Frank George Barton, just in his twenties and then living in Oxford, had also entered the bicycle business. But his interest was by no means limited to working hours, he raced both penny farthings and the new safety bicycle. Indeed on the latter, he became Oxfordshire County cycling champion. Around the same time, 1893, sixteen year old William Richard Morris began business as a cycle repairer in a shed at Cowley, near Oxford. Morris also took up amateur cycle racing as his sport and later made his own cycles and motor cycles. Then in 1911 he made his first motor car, the Morris Cowley. That same year F. G. Barton joined Morris Garages. He stayed until 1918, by which time he had become general manager. Morris had made great inroads into the motor industry, at last offering the British public a dependable motor car which, selling at £165, no longer made motoring the monopoly of the very rich.

At the 1921 Motor Show Morris cut £100 off the latest price of all his cars and precipitated a huge demand; 65,000 cars were produced in a twelve month period soon after. Figures which all augured well for F. G. Barton who, having already

opened his first garage in Torquay, was about to move to Plymouth. Here in 1922, he opened a business on Ford Park Corner, Mutley, the present Gateway corner site of the old Mutley Cinedrome (only ever a silent movie house, it was also known as the Argyle Cinema). In 1924 Barton's also opened in Fore Street, Exeter. Later, advertising as 'The Morris People', business continued to thrive. In 1923 the first MG had been assembled, on a Morris 'Oxford' chassis and in 1927 Morris took over Wolseley Motors Limited.

Then in 1930 this fine piece of period architecture was constructed to house the expanding Barton Motor Company. It was opened by William Morris himself—by then Sir William and soon to become Lord Nuffield. As Lord Nuffield, Morris's name came to be linked with far more than motor cars, founding Nuffield College, Oxford and the Nuffield Foundation, a charitable trust devoted to medical research; the development of medical and health services; trade and industrial research; social studies and the care and comfort of the aged. His total benefactions had exceeded £25 million pounds over 30 years ago.

In 1951 Morris—by then the Nuffield Organisation—merged with the Austin Company to form the British Motor Corporation and it was BMC Cars that Barton's sold until their closure at the end of the sixties. F. G. Barton himself had died some years earlier, at the grand old age of 88, and a great many Westcountry motor-trade people had attended his funeral at Emmanuel Church, including W. Roy Mumford. Mumfords had had a nineteenth century base on Mutley Plain and one of their principal showrooms, Abbey Garage (now demolished) in St. Andrews Street, was built in 1933 and shared certain architectural features with the Barton building.

Prior to the building of Barton's here on Hyde Park Corner, a residence known as Cleeve Villa had occupied much of this site. In private hands until the beginning of this century, it was for a time used as a local Salvation Army Rescue Home and later, the premises of C. A. Edmonds, dentist. W. H. Thorn, cab proprietor, had operated from another building previously on this site. Originally of course, the Hyde Park Hotel was not on an 'island' and at the rear of the Hotel, on the Hyde Park Road side, were stables. The short lane on the north side of the Barton building ran right along the back and was an extension of Ford Park Lane.

Closed now for over 15 years, the Barton building is just about to receive a new lease of life and is now in the process of being tastefully refurbished and redecorated by its new owners, Sims Brothers, Builders. Always an impressive edifice, the grand entrance sports a fine wrought iron Barton's insignia and two coats of arms. One, a common sight locally, the Plymouth Crest, the other more of a rarity, bearing the motto *Semper Fidelis* (always faithful), is the crest of the City of Exeter, Barton's other erstwhile base. Strangely enough, however, the signature tune of Plymouth Argyle is also called *Semper Fidelis*!

11th October 1986.

150

Mutley Plain

There was a time when the road leading out of Plymouth via North Hill and along what we now call Mutley Plain, was the only way out of the town that did not involve crossing water. Those were the days when Stonehouse Creek was tidal as far as Pennycomequick and three small rivers flowed down from below Torr/Venn, Oxford Avenue and Houndiscombe valley to meet it. At the same time, to the west, the tidal waters reached Lipson beyond Trefussis Park and two streams ran down to it; one roughly along the line of Alexandra Road, the other running almost due south, a little below Compton.

Much the same situation existed north of Mutley and as the road to Tavistock made its way out to Roborough, its path was determined by the succession of small river and stream sources it had to avoid. The same was true of the east-west road, which ran from Plympton to Saltash Passage. This road crossed the Tavistock Road at Torr just between Hartley Reservoir and Sungates. The ancient granite cross, now set in a roadside wall between two very old local boundary stones, marks the approximate site. From the Iron Age through to the seventeenth century at least, these were the two principal thoroughfares for travellers in the area. Here many a man or woman, on foot, would have crossed paths and it comes as no surprise, therefore, to learn that the two small manors which ran south of Torr from the Venn estate and west of Tavistock Road as far down as Houndiscombe Road, appear to owe their name to a corruption of two words; Gemot-leah, meaning the place of meeting. Over the years this became Motte leigh, then Mutley. At the time of Domesday, the name was recorded as Modlei and around 1500 we find mention of Motley Park Lane (the present Weston Park Road). Part of the original Mutley, primarily the northern manor, was later destined to become split three ways; part in Peverell, part in Mannamead and part in Hartley. The modern Mutley comprises all of the southern manor of Modlei plus lands, originally part of Lipson and Compton, that lay to the east of Mutley Plain. The name 'Mutley Plain' itself quite probably dates from the time of George III when, as a consequence of the various Turnpike Acts, many local roads were improved and the Mutley section of Tavistock Road was raised and levelled, thereby giving more the appearance of a plain. As R. N. Worth noted at the end of last century, 'the original ups and downs were far more considerable than is now apparent'.

All this took place at the beginning of last century. A turnpike or toll gate, later known as the Lewis Jones Gate, was established near another ancient stone set in a wall at the south end of Mutley Plain (it bears the legend '1 mile to the King's Arms'; this Inn no longer stands, but it was about 50 yards from the 'King's Head' at Breton Side). The Lewis Jones gate, just below the end of North Hill, more or less occupied the most obvious point of attack for the Royalist forces during the Civil War, bearing in mind the small local rivers that were still flowing back then. And again, to quote Worth—'The sea formed a natural moat, except towards Mutley and there lay the main strength of the defence'. The base for this defence was Maudlyn Fort, which was constructed on the site of the local Maudlyn or Leper House, where the old Blind Institute, now part of Plymouth High School for Girls, stands. There were various

other forts along a northern line principally at the heads of the creeks at Lipson and Pennycomequick.

At this time, there was little or no development along the length of Mutley Plain, save for the section of Drake's Leat which ran straight along its western side, turning into what is now Houndiscombe Road (which is curved along the path of the leat). Today, that leat runs below street level, many sections of it being covered in the 1860s and 1870s. It was around this time that the development of Mutley Plain began in earnest. In 1850 there were but a few houses set back from the road in Ford (formerly Foard's) Park, examples of which survive behind the shops that front the street, adjacent to the Swarthmore Adult Education Centre. Six or seven detached and impressive villas were built soon after this, just off Ford Park. These are now almost all owned by Plymouth College, itself established in the adjacent field in 1880.

The main housing development took place soon after 1868 when Miss Cordelia Yonge sold two large fields west of the Plain to the builders Benjamin Call and John Pethick. In no time at all Seaton Terrace, Ermington Terrace, Seaton Avenue, Coryton Terrace, Trematon Place and Pentillie Road had risen out of the ground.

The rest of modern Mutley soon followed and most of Mutley Plain itself, excepting modern shop fronts, is substantially Victorian and most of it is still standing. Gone, however, are the tram lines, a few of the trees, Mutley Station (1849–1939) and Mutley Methodist Church 1881 (closed 1977, demolished 1979).

Gone too are some of the long established businesses, although C. J. Park's the Chemist, one of the more famous, was reconstructed in the Merchant's House soon after it closed a couple of years ago, while another Mutley veteran, Charles Harding's furniture business, established here in 1894, has only recently closed its doors. Meanwhile, the Plain continues to thrive, although increasingly, fast-food shops, travel agents, estate agents and building societies have been taking the place of one or two of the more traditional businesses.

17th October 1987.

Plymouth High School

In 1848 two young ladies, Dorothea Beale (17) and Frances Mary Buss (21) were among the first ever pupils at the newly opened Queen's College in London's Harley Street. In 1849 Bedford College, part of the University of London, became the first such college to admit women, although it was almost another 30 years before women were allowed to study for degrees. Miss Beale and Miss Buss, after going on to Bedford College, both then went on to become great pioneers in the cause of female education.

At a time when education as a whole left much to be desired, secondary girls' schooling was particularly wanting. In 1857 Dorothea Beale was appointed head of the newly established Cheltenham Ladies' College (1854). Here she enjoyed much success, both inside the school and outside; in 1869 she published the report of the 'Commission on the Education of Girls'. The following year, Miss Buss handed her North London Collegiate School over to a trust so that it might serve as a model for others. This school, reorganized in 1850, had been established by her mother and her handing it over in this way, marked the beginning of the Girls' Public Day School Trust. Two years later the Devonport Branch of the National Union for the Education of Women held a meeting at which their treasurer, Mrs. Metcalfe, suggested that a school should be established in Plymouth by a Public Trust, on exactly those lines. In February 1874 the Devon and Cornwall Girls' School Company was formed under the presidency of Frederick Temple, the Bishop of Exeter, who became the first chairman of the new school council. (He also later became Archbishop of Canterbury.)

The new school began on the 14th September that year; Miss Kendall was its head and Sherwell House was its home. In the meantime a fund had been set up for the building of a new school and the purchase of its site. In the event, the current main school building was opened in 1877. Erected by Messrs Blatchford of Tavistock, the architect was Mr. Paull. It cost £10,000 for the structure and an additional £3,000 for the site. A Jacobean dwelling known as 'North Hill' with its adjacent land made up the site and the original house itself stood until 1939 when it was demolished to make way for the new wing. It had served, incidentally, until 1931 as the Headmistress's residence. When the school opened there were but a few major buildings on Tavistock Road, above Sherwell Church; Sherwell House itself (where Queen Anne Terrace now stands), Mount Drake House, North Hill Cottage, North Hill House (where now stands the masonic building next to Charles with St.

Matthias), a few shops, 'North Hill' and of course the Blind Institute, completed a year before the school, in 1876. Messrs. Palk and Partridge were the contractors for this building and Mr. H. J. Snell was the architect. Today all of the old part of this building has been annexed by the school, a process begun in the early 1960s and completed around the time the building celebrated its centenary in 1976. While this building has seen some fairly major changes internally, over the years the old school building, seen here from St. Matthias tower, is today much as it was 110 years ago, although the uses to which many of the rooms are now put is quite different from their original conception. So, indeed, is the standard of education received and the curriculum that goes with it, much of the recent developments following on from the creation of new universities in the 1960s and the greater number of places available to women. However, the basic tenet, voiced by Bishop Temple at the school's opening, still holds good today. 'School', he said, 'must be the anticipation of practical life', and in this he echoed Cicero's saying, later adopted as the school motto, and also used by Queen's College, Taunton, *Non Scolae sed vitae discimus*—'we learn not from school but from life'.

In the early part of Plymouth High's history, school was not somewhere that all children had access to, boys or girls, and indeed there were those who felt that it should stay that way. Until 1917, Plymouth High was strictly a fee-paying school and, although Plymouth Education Authority bought the school that year for £9,000 and scholarships were introduced, fees weren't phased out until 1925–30. In 1933 fees were reintroduced on a limited and means test basis but after the war, when many pupils had been evacuated, first to Fowey then Newquay, fees were abolished again—but who is to say they won't ever come back?

Something else that was introduced in 1933 was compulsory school uniform. Miss Violet Turner was the lady responsible for this change, although a hat band and tie had been worn since the turn of the century. Present Head, Muriel Newman, who arrived here in 1973 has since decided that the hat has had its day, while her immediate predecessor Margaret Farrar waived the wearing of uniform for 6th Form girls. It's interesting to note that Miss Farrar and her two predecessors Miss Miller 1954–62 and Miss Brogden 1962–67 are still alive today and, furthermore, that Plymouth High is perhaps unique among its peers in having a succession of unmarried headmistresses since the day it opened.   »Postscript

7th November, 1987.

152

Charles with St. Matthias

On 25th October 1887, Dr. Bickersteth, Bishop of Exeter, came to Plymouth to consecrate the city's newest church which had just been built on land which had formerly been part of the gardens of North Hill House. Prior to the building of the church, these gardens were surprisingly extensive, despite all the development around them. Within a few years, however, the church and then Wentworth and Bedford Park Villas occupied at least three quarters of the gardens. So it was that North Hill House, which only 40 or 50 years earlier had stood in fields well outside the city boundary, was now all but swallowed up by it. Clearly this expansion was partly the reason for the creation of the Church of St. Matthias in the first place and although originally planned as a Chapel of Ease to the Parish Church of Charles, such was the rate of the development of this neighbourhood that within two years of its consecration, St. Matthias had its own parish assigned to it.

That the church is as impressive and substantial as it is, is undoubtedly thanks to Mrs. Anne Watts, who founded a trust fund for 'The erection of the church intended to be built at, or near, North Hill' back in August 1855. To this trust fund she left £8,000. Under its terms the church was to be built in memory of her late husband and this, perhaps, gives us a clue to the naming of the church for it appears that her husband's name was Matthias. Certainly Matthias is an unusual dedication; the name is actually a shortened form of Mattathias. Matthias was the one chosen of two appointed to take the place left by the traitor Judas Iscariot; 'And they gave forth their lots; and the lot fell upon Matthias; and he was numbered with the eleven apostles' Acts 1, 26. In Christian art Matthias is generally portrayed with an axe in his right hand, the symbol of his martyrdom, a stone carving in the church shows him thus. Sometimes, he is depicted bearing a stone 'in allusion to the tradition of his having been stoned before he was beheaded'. Substantial though the church is, in its early days it was also a little on the empty side, not in terms of its congregation, but in terms of its furnishings, as the money in the fund, while going a long way towards the completion of the building, left nothing for fittings. These came with time, however, and curiously enough by 1924, St. Matthias had become one of the first parish churches in Plymouth to abolish pew rents. Some twelve years before this, the church hall was erected on 'The Bowling Green Field of North Hill'. This new hall was designed, among other things, to accommodate 400 'Sunday scholars'. Through its association with Charles Church, St. Matthias can lay claim to a link with, undoubtedly, the most famous and probably the first purpose built Sunday School in Devon—'The Household of Faith'. This was founded in 1787 by Charles Church's most celebrated and longest serving incumbent, Robert Hawker (1784–1827). The Sunday School movement was then in its infancy, having begun in earnest in 1780 in Gloucester, under the guidance of Robert Raikes. Raikes was horrified by the condition and behaviour of children in the streets of Gloucester and by the rioting, gambling and swearing which disgraced the Sabbath. He quickly organized his own schools and soon his example was being followed across the country. By 1831, 103 parishes in Devon claimed to have such schools, 41 of which appeared to have no other provision for educating the poor. It is no surprise, therefore, to find that at least one authority felt that these institutions were 'the root from which sprang the system of day schools'.

In 1837 Charles National School, which later became Charles Secondary Modern, grew out of this and although that school closed in 1985 the Sunday School, with its 200 year tradition, still thrives.

Arguably of course, while St. Matthias is about to celebrate its first centenary, its tradition dates back nearly 350 years to the founding of Charles Church. Following the bombing of Charles Church in 1941 its congregation moved here, or to its earlier daughter church St. Lukes and then after the closure of St. Lukes in 1962 they all came here. In 1964 the parish was retitled Charles with St. Matthias.

Designed by James Hine, the church with its 120 foot tower, the top of which some say is the highest point in the city, was perhaps itself lucky to survive the Blitz. Legend has it the Germans felt that it was too important a landmark to target, and they used it as a ready means of getting their bearings on their way in and out of bombing raids. Prominent it certainly is, and those interested in a fuller picture of its place in local history may like to know of a centenary 'Past, Present and Future' exhibition to be held in the church on the 23rd, 24th and 25th of this month, and an updated history of St. Matthias that Vicar, David Littlefair, has had written by one of his congregation, Desmond Joyce.

10th October, 1987.

Prison Hill

'The new Borough Prisons, erected without the precincts of the town, in a field situated in a healthy and commanding position near what was once Lewis Jones' Turnpike-gate, on the northern entrance to the town, are now completed . . .' So ran the opening paragraph of a news story in an April edition of the Plymouth, Devonport and Stonehouse Herald in 1849.

An impressive pile of buildings in a rural setting it must have been too, being constructed well before the neighbouring workhouse and hospital and even most of the adjacent housing.

Standing on about three acres of land, the prisons, surrounded by a lofty wall, were in the centre of the ground and were: 'disposed in three large wings, comprising the governor's offices, apartments for the matron, a chapel and surgery, visiting cells, convalescent rooms, a bath room and cells for 60 prisoners, including six for male and three for female debtors for whom there are comfortable day rooms and airing-grounds. There are four solitary cells, so constructed as to admit air, but no light; and there are 24 airing-grounds radiating from a common centre, and each to be occupied by only one prisoner at a time, whilst an officer is so placed as to be able to see into all the yards.'

There was also plenty of space available so that, if necessary, the prison could be extended.

Completed around the same time as most closed prisons in Britain today, and two months before a similar institution at Pennycomequick (Devonport Prison, which was demolished, all but its warders' accommodation, in 1881–2), Plymouth Borough Prison never did need to expand. From the census returns of 1861, cited by W. N. Bryant in the journal Devon and Cornwall Notes and Queries, we learn that there were then only 30 prisoners here, all male, although a somewhat higher figure was recorded, on census day 1871, when 25 adult men, 16 females and two teenage girls were shown as being held here. Governor of the Prison at the time of both surveys was John Simon and it was he who likely succeeded T. Plimsaul, the first governor here. A Northumberland man who lived here with his wife and children, John Simon had a regular staff of about seven—mainly prison officers, living on site, in some cases with their wives and children. Indeed in 1871, there was a prison child

156

recorded as living here, less than a year old and presumably a daughter of one of the female inmates. Interestingly enough, 80–90% per cent of the inmates were born well outside Plymouth, there were more Cornish and Irish-born prisoners than there were Plymothians. By 1878, in the wake of the previous year's Prison Act, this Gaol and that at Pennycomequick came under central control along with 113 others nationally, of which 38, including Devonport, were closed. Here on Greenbank Road, the gaol continued to operate but with 'considerable changes in the arrangements'. 'The principal employment of prisoners at this time, 'was in mat-making, oakum picking, and shoemaking'. Oakum being the loose fibre obtained by untwisting and picking old rope; oakum literally means 'off-combings' and this material was commonly used for caulking or stopping up the seams of ships to prevent leaking.

Some 50 years or so after the changes were rung internally at HM Prison Greenbank Road, as it became known, changes took place in the structure of the place. Originally built, like Devonport, to the almost Italian style designs of Messrs Fuller and Gingell and erected by local builder William Clift in limestone with Caen stone dressings, most of the iron work was soon to be ripped out as the original buildings were, for the most part, converted in 1935 to accommodate the Plymouth Police Force HQ, which moved up from Catherine Street that year. There had long been complaints that the Catherine Street police station (occupied until recently by the City Treasury and soon to be taken over by the Plymouth studio centre of BBC Radio Devon), was too cramped and, although it had been extended in 1925, the space was still too small.

The local Fire Brigade—then administered by the Police—had also outgrown their base at the back of Catherine Street and they too moved to new premises on the Prison site in 1936.

For more than 40 years the Plymouth Police HQ, then, was based here at Greenbank; the old prison entrance was refashioned and the archway came down. Cars were introduced into the force soon after the police moved here, and over the years these buildings grew to accommodate the latest innovations. Come the mid seventies, however, even Greenbank was becoming too small and in 1976 the local HQ moved out to new buildings in Crownhill while the following year, the major City sub-divisional station was established at Charles Cross and Greenbank was left empty.

Today the Health Authority occupy these buildings which, remarkably enough, have no official DofE listed status. So who knows what may happen here when they move out, as seems likely in the next few years? Having survived the Blitz and a direct hit from a 1,000 lb bomb which came to rest on the Court landing but failed to explode, it would be a shame to see these historic buildings now disappear; a sentiment that members of the District Health Authority Staff Club are keen to endorse, having recently refurbished the old police social club at a cost of £32,000, which is more than $2\frac{1}{2}$ times what the prison cost to build in the first place, but of course, that allows nothing for inflation! »Postscript

5th September, 1987.

Greenbank Fire Station

Stern war's alarms, they have their charms,
And with powder shot and guns,
Foes of great might are put to fight
By England's gallant sons.
But our fire brigades, our fire brigades,
Are merciful and brave;
Our mission is *not* to destroy,
But rescue, help and save.

The first verse and chorus from a piece written over 100 years ago by 'West of England' Fireman, John Good. The 'West of England' was an Insurance Company and from the records it would appear that it was they who established the first effective fire-fighting service in Plymouth back in 1838. It consisted of a Chief Officer, one Foreman, 14 Firemen and 2 Torch Boys. Capable of covering up to a radius of 20 miles around Plymouth, they worked with a 30 man, manual fire engine. An account of Fire Fighting history in Plymouth, published in 1959, paints a vivid picture of these Brigades '. . . as they dashed along darkened roads with torch bearers standing on the front of the engine holding flaming torches to light the way, their appliances swaying along behind four galloping horses with postillion riders, and frequently with the fire-dog in close attendance, such dog mascots being a feature of early Fire Brigades.' Indeed, just such an image as the pictorial design employed by the 'West of England' and used above the many published poems of Fireman Good. Another of these works, written towards the end of his long service with the Brigade (he joined in 1838 and was with them 50 years), was entitled 'An Old Fireman's Advice' and provides us with a further insight into Victorian fire fighting and prevention.

Be sure to keep your chimney clean,
'Twill cost but a few pence,
From them I scores of FIRES have seen
Through want of common sense.

Don't read in bed by candlelight
Which many do no doubt
Or smoke a pipe in bed by night
Turn gaslight safely out.

Insurance companies were, undoubtedly, the prime movers in the establishment of Fire Brigades in this country, indeed the first recorded brigade was set up by Nicholas Barbon in 1684 to protect houses that were insured by the Phenix (sic) Fire Office. A company formed just four years earlier in the wake of the Great Fire of London. However, fire fighting by insurance company brigades, was not without its problems and there is at least one instance on record in Plymouth, of rival company firemen fighting each other in the street at the scene of a conflagration. But there were also, in certain areas, modest Municipal Fire Brigades and, although Plymouth did not establish a Corporation Brigade until 1863, there is a record of a fire engine being brought into the town in 1673 along with a supply of buckets.

Before the Fire of London, there was little in the way of fire fighting regulations in this country although in some areas it was a requirement that 'a barrel full of water for quenching fires should be placed before the doors of buildings' and it was common for bell men to ring their bells at night and call out 'Take care of your bell and candle. Be charitable to the poor and pray for the dead'!

The earliest reference to a fire brigade anywhere is in China, around 4,000 BC. The Egyptians also appeared to have some sort of fire fighting organization around 2,000 BC and, as you might expect, the Romans, by 40 BC, had a highly trained and efficient Brigade. But when they 'disappeared' so did a good many of their innovations.

In 1890 Plymouth Police, who had no doubt evolved from the officers and watchmen who were also the beginnings of the Fire Brigade, took over responsibility for the Brigade and they remained in charge until July 1941, when Plymouth City Fire Brigade was formed. That year, as with the Great Fire of London, the Blitz forced a reappraisal of our fire fighting measures and in August 1941 the National Fire Service was inaugurated. This ran for a few years into peace time when control was again passed back to local authorities, on 1st April 1948.

Just a few years later, Greenbank Fire Station, built in 1936 on the site of Plymouth Prison, was expanded. Previously two storeys with officers' flats above, another floor was added in 1952 and the building made to look as it does today. All but the Christmas message that is, a feature that has been attended to by the Firemen here for many years now. Although, they did miss one year, when they were on strike, and they had a number of complaints from the Hospital and surrounding areas that the place didn't look the same without this seasonal touch.

Today the work of the Fire Brigade has changed greatly from its Victorian counterpart. They do much more fire prevention and special service calls these days—chiefly attending to road traffic accidents. Known as the Devon Fire Brigade since 1973 and one of the best equipped in the country, the changes in their workload are about to be recognized in a change in name. From 1 January 1987, they will become the Devon Fire and Rescue Service.

20th December, 1986.

Greenbank Hospital

Plymouth's first proper general public hospital had been opened on the corner of Sussex Street and Notte Street in 1840 and by the time of its closure, it had 8 wards with an average of 55 patients at any one time, and a total of 75 beds. At times however, this proved to be all too few and in emergencies a tent would be erected in some spare ground behind the hospital to squeeze in a few more beds, but there wasn't room for many. In contrast, the new South Devon and East Cornwall Hospital had room for 130 beds, it also had much-improved sanitary arrangements.

The move from the one institution to the other was reckoned to take no more than a day—'by nightfall the whole work of transference will be completed'; most of the patients being transported in 'military ambulance wagons lent for the purpose'. There was of course no motorized road transport then, indeed other modern conveniences were also in their infancy. Thus although there were no telephones, it was proudly announced that 'speaking tubes have been fixed from the centre of the administrative block to each of the wards; and electric bells are fixed all through the establishment.'

The new hospital was altogether an improvement on its predecessor and it was estimated that more than 7,000 people turned up on the Saturday before the hospital was put into service to inspect the wonderful new premises. Furthermore it was noted that 'a good proportion of the visitors were more or less from the working classes'. A fact that was deemed to be very encouraging, 'seeing that the hospital is an institution directly for their benefit'.

The somewhat patronizing tone of this sentiment appeared largely because hospitals were not then funded out of the public purse; the health service, such as it was, was paid for by voluntary subscription, and while there were regular public collections (in 1883 £891 was raised on Hospital Sunday and £538 on Hospital Saturday), most of the early hospital foundations locally and in the country as a whole, were the product either of the compassion of various religious orders or the generosity of certain private individuals.

In the case of Greenbank the whole project was made possible thanks largely to two of the great local families, the Edgcumbes and the Lopes. Born at Maristow House in 1818, Sir Massey Lopes like his father before him, had been connected with the earlier Sussex Place hospital and became President of the New Hospital in Greenbank Road. The Lopes and Maristow Wards were constructed, mainly through contributions by him, in 1884. The Chapel was built by him in 1895 and endowed with £2,000—indeed between '1891 and 1899 the Hospital was endowed by him from time to time with sums amounting in the aggregate to £14,000'. Some scale to the total of 'these munificent benefactions' can be gleaned when it is shown that the entire cost of the original development was only £32,000 plus a further

£6,259. 11s. for the purchase of the site. Incidentally the foundation stone was laid on this site back in 1881 by the fourth Earl of Mount Edgcumbe—William; after him is named the Mount Edgcumbe Ward, while the Countess Caroline Ward was named after the Dowager Countess of Mount Edgcumbe who died in 1881. The Lady Alberta Ward is named after the fourth Earl's second daughter who married Henry Yarde-Buller Lopes, the elder son of Sir Massey. There were of course many who contributed generously to the fund in accordance with their means. One of the great names in the history of the South Devon and East Cornwall Hospitals has been Prance and the Prance Ward is named in memory of William, son of the first treasurer of the first hospital.

Prance and Mount Edgcumbe were at least two of the ward names to be perpetuated in the new building; Radford was another, while Bewes, Gill and Dawson were all named after other generous benefactors. For the most part, the honour of naming a ward fell upon those donating in excess of £1,000, and in this way, Mrs. Rooker named the Rooker Ward in memory of her late husband, and former Mayor of Plymouth, Alfred Rooker. There was however another massive contribution and this came from Mrs. Elizabeth Hains of Alton House who gave in total, just under £20,000 to the hospital and sadly died just before the completion of the John Hay Wing, named in memory of her brother, in 1899. The Hains and Elizabeth Wards are both named in her honour.

As well as financial gifts, though, many gave in other ways and six of the original wards were painted 'in a soft green colour with a salmon colour dado' free of cost, by 'some of the principal painters of Plymouth'.

All in all the original hospital was an impressive collaboration of effort and resources. A great asset to the city, it was not long before the original designs of Coe and Robinson were being added to here and there and the hospital as it stands today has been much extended and updated. Princess Mary laid the foundation stone to the main extensions in 1928. A private patients ward was added by 1936. It was later named the Sister Francis Ward in memory of the much thought of Matron, Muriel Francis (1937–59).

A full account of the main points of interest of Greenbank's history is provided in the absorbing book produced by Hilda Goodman, in 1977, which can be found in the local history library. Since that date there have been few changes here; the future of Greenbank however promises a somewhat different picture. Once Phase 2 of Derriford Hospital is under way and completed Greenbank will quite simply close down and it is quite likely that some time in 1993–4 the building and the site will be sold off in their entirety.

5th March 1988

Freedom Fields

In August and September 1849 Plymouth was ravaged by cholera. The city's Workhouse, founded in 1630 and otherwise known as the 'Hospital of the Poor's Portion' in Catherine Street, was already heavily over-burdened. It was over-crowded, badly ventilated and dysentery was widespread. There was only one bath and seldom any hot water. One contemporary report noted that the hospital 'sometimes is so full that the sick have to be laid on the floor'. Meanwhile Gibbons, the local Superintendent of Police, said that at night his station was besieged with destitute people who could not find accommodation at the Workhouse. Even then such lodgings were no guarantee of creature comfort. Indeed, earlier in the year, the Guardians of the Workhouse decided not to press libel charges against the *Herald* after the paper had made the following comment on one woman's fate at their establishment: that she had been 'permitted to go down to the grave with no greater degree of attention to her wants than she would be likely to have received in a land of barbarians, and certainly not one half the care which an English gentleman would have felt it his duty to bestow upon one of his dogs!' The case was not brought because too many of the Guardians felt that it was probably all too true. The woman, Mrs. Henrietta Beer (whose husband, a marine, had been drowned at sea five years earlier), died leaving two young children, but not a single possession as they had all been pawned.

So it was against this backdrop that the Guardians decided to go ahead with a scheme that many had been advocating for some time; namely the building of a new workhouse on a four-acre site they owned on the 'outskirts of town'. The site was part of Speccott's Fields, near Freedom Park. It was just behind a small group of houses known as Green Bank and just up from the 'Borough Prisons' which were completed in 1849.

The foundation stone for the new workhouse was laid on Tuesday 16th March 1852. Henry Greaves the vicar of Charles Church, was present at the ceremony as was the Mayor, Alfred Rooker. At a celebratory dinner later that day at the Globe Hotel, the Mayor said, 'One cannot help looking back to the time when the present workhouse (in Catherine Street), now clearly in the centre of the town, was in the suburbs and, in the present rapidly increasing state of the town, I have little doubt that that which we are now building will, in 200 years, be included in its limits'.

In the event of course, Freedom Fields Hospital, which now occupies the old workhouse, is not only well inside the city limits, but is about to be superseded by the new, much larger, hospital at Derriford, itself bordering on the city limits. In another 100 years, however, who knows how it will stand in relation to this continually expanding city.

Plymouth Workhouse was completed by 1858. Built to the designs of Messrs. Arthur and Dwelley, it cost around £12,500 and could accommodate 600–700 inmates. Because of all its free labour, this workhouse was kept impeccably clean and the inmates worked and prayed hard for their 'dinner of the day'. It had extensive gardens in which the fitter inmates were kept busy cultivating '20,000 leeks and 11,000 cabbages', or however many thousands of potatoes, depending on the cycle. It was an unenviable existence and the only ones likely to escape were the children of unmarried mothers who were cared for there and, ultimately, the mothers themselves, who might later be released as domestic servants.

These imposing old buildings continued to be known as Plymouth Workhouse until the Local Government Act of 1929, which enabled authorities to run Poor Law institutions as hospitals. Bert Medland, one of the newly elected Labour councillors and leader of the local party (and later MP for Drake), was then chairman of the Public Health Committee and he saw to it that Plymouth Workhouse became the City Hospital.

Within a few years, however, the name changed again as Royal approval of the amalgamation of the city's hospitals led to them being grouped under the general title of 'Prince of Wales's Hospital'. This included the South Devon and East Cornwall Hospital (Greenbank, built 1881–84), the Royal Albert Devonport (recently closed) and the Central Hospital in Lockyer Street (finally closed in 1977).

In 1951, soon after the passing of the National Health Act under which everyone became entitled to free hospital treatment in this country, the hospital was renamed again and, from that day to this, has been known as Freedom Fields, although it is part of 'Plymouth General Hospital'.

And what of the old workhouse buildings? For the most part they stand little changed from the outside, although inside they now house departments and wards the like of which few Victorians would ever have dreamed.

Visible here is the Neuro and Diabetic Clinic, while other original buildings behind and to the right of it, variously house Casualty, the Intensive Therapy Unit, Wards 5, 7, 8, 12–17, Haematology, the Geriatric Day Centre, Ante Natal, the Special Treatment Clinic, Neuro X-Ray, Colposcopy (laser treatment) and Endoscopy (Fibre Optics). The Maternity block, nurses' home and other buildings to the left are more recent and stand on the vegetable gardens of the old workhouse. However, with some departments due to move out to Derriford next year, who can say what Freedom Fields will be like in ten years time, let alone 100?

St. Simon's Church

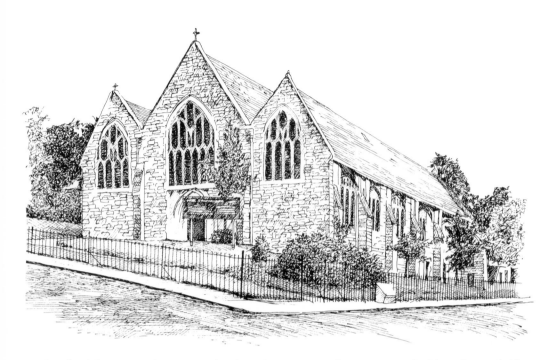

On the 8th November 1905 the foundation stone for St. Simon's Church was laid here in Farringdon Road at the eastern end of Salisbury Road. It was an occasion marked with great pomp and ceremony; 170 clergy and lay readers from the Three Towns and further afield were present. The Bishops of Exeter and Crediton were there, so too were the Archdeacons of Exeter, Totnes and Barnstaple, and the foundation stone itself was laid by no lesser dignitary than the Archbishop of Canterbury, Randall Thomas Davidson. Davidson of Lambeth, as he was known, had only become Archbishop two years earlier and for some time served as Queen Victoria's domestic chaplain. He was in Plymouth to speak to the Diocesan Conference on the subject of Church Extension in the Three Towns, so in some respects the timing of this ceremony was particularly symbolic and we are told the site was 'covered by an awning and was gay with flags and bunting'. However in the event, building did not begin on the site until well into the next year.

Already fully five years had passed since the site had been purchased and eight since the idea had first been mooted. Indeed back in 1898, a site not quite so far down Salisbury Road had been acquired for the Church but this was, by 1900, deemed to be too small and was sold off. Salisbury Road Baptist Church now stands on that ground.

The fact that the actual fabric of the church did not begin to appear until 1906 however, did not hamper the establishment of the congregation of St. Simon's. The first ever service was held in an 'Upper Room' in 49 Durham Avenue on the 4th March 1900 and on 1st June the Reverend W. F. Wiltshire was appointed Curate in Charge of the Mission District of St. Simon's. Twelve months later, on 12th June 1901, the foundation stone of the Parish Hall was laid and by November the building was opened and complete with a font, organ, choir chancel, altar and seating for 400. This was used as a church until the church itself was completed.

As it turned out the church was not completed for another 57 years. It was however, consecrated in September 1907 and opened then with a temporary, galvanised-iron west wall. Funds, a problem from the outset, were not available in sufficient quantity to complete the architect's original vision—a vision which had the church almost two bays longer, with a bell tower, two porches and a cloister. Even then, plans for a simplified completion of the church, in the form of a stone built west wall, were twice foiled—in 1914 and 1938/9—by the onset of war. In 1954 the first major step was taken towards this work with the purchase of a quantity of stone made available by the demolition of Granby Barracks, Devonport, that year. Three years later in July 1957 work on the wall began and the following July it was completed, the Bishop of Plymouth formally opening the new west door at the special Dedication Festival that summer.

This now left only one other major piece of work to be done on St. Simon's land; the building of the vicarage. The site was already available and had been part of the original plans and in 1962, after two years of deliberation, work began. Then in April 1963 the Reverend John Llewelyn moved out of the old vicarage, 5 Lipson Terrace, which had served in that capacity since the beginning, and into the new quarters which front on to Edith Avenue. Reverend Llewelyn went on to become one of St. Simon's longest-serving vicars, his stay here being only marginally surpassed by the Reverend Charles Maldram, who spent nearly 23 years here from 1930. During that time Reverend Maldram reckoned to have officiated at somewhere between 700 and 800 weddings and he would have baptized about twice as many children.

Reading Gordon Brayley's absorbing account of St. Simon's, it is clear that the total number of such ceremonies performed here over the last 90 years must of course be several times greater, and hopefully the church has long-since fulfilled many of the dreams of James Yonge Woollcombe and John Shelley who, with the help of others, purchased the first site for the proposed church back in 1898.

Certainly the present incumbent, the Reverend David White, whose stay here ends soon, has been as keen as anyone to promote the role of the church in the parish of St. Simon's, a parish principally bounded by Ladysmith Road to the north, Pentyre Terrace to the west and Lanhydrock Road and the Embankment to the south and east.

28th May, 1988.

Astor Institute, Mount Gould

Standing right at the eastern end of Mount Gould Road is this simple yet not unimpressive building best known as the Astor Institute. Commanding fine views of Dartmoor, Saltram, the Plym estuary and across Plymouth, it is hardly surprising that this site was occupied by a small fortification during the Civil War. Small but very strategic, it was an 'entrenched outpost with three cannon, in itself of little strength'. However here on Sunday 3rd December, 1643 began the Sabbath Day Fight described by historian R. N. Worth as 'one of the most memorable days in the history of Plymouth'. It all began in the small hours of Sunday morning when, at low tide, 400 musketeers, under cover of darkness, crossed the almost dry Lipson Creek (which ran up to Trefusis Valley) and then, hidden by the steep ridge, came around and surprised the guard at the Point here. Dawn was still 3 hours away. The alarm was raised and at daybreak '150 horse and 300 musketeers fell in above Tothill to repel the attack'. A lot of fighting followed around this area before Prince Maurice's Royalist support forces arrived and the Roundheads, 'outnumbered ten to one', were 'driven back in absolute rout for the space of three fields'. The next round of serious fighting then took place at the top of Freedom Fields. The King's men were kept at bay and eventually driven back after sixty garrison musketeers had come up behind Prince Maurice's men and Colonel Gould, at a given drum signal, pushed forward in a general assault and the enemy were repelled in a chaotic dash to get back across the Creek. It was a victory celebrated for many years thereafter, every 3rd of December, when the bells of St. Andrew's would be rung in memory of this great deliverance. Many men and many horses were killed or drowned on both sides that day. William Gould, who was then in charge of the Plymouth Garrison, had one horse shot and another wounded under him that day. Wounded himself in the fighting in October 1643 over by Mount Batten, Colonel Gould died in Plymouth the following year. His memory however was perpetuated by the naming of this area—Mount Gould—after him. Although due to a small error somewhere along the line it was, for a good many years, incorrectly referred to as Mount Gold; the name reverted back to its proper form in the late 1960s.

Meanwhile, in the 1920s the memory of another great figure in Plymouth's history, Waldorf Astor, was recorded 'in perpetuity' here in his gift of the Astor Institute to the people of Mount Gould. Opened by his wife, Lady Nancy Astor, in April 1929 and built at a cost of £10,000, Lord Astor's idea was for the Institute to serve the tenants of the Astor Trust Housing Estate, which they had earlier been responsible for having built in the area. Aware that his development, together with that of Plymouth Corporation, would create a large new population in this area away from the public halls and recreation areas of town, he felt that this well-equipped Institute would provide the foundation upon which to build a fine focal point for the community. 'Here are the bones' he said at the opening 'it is for the

people to see that a soul is put into them'. This gift, he added, was not for the moment, but for the future. But its future has to date been one of mixed success. Well equipped with a fine gymnasium, added by Lord Astor in 1936, meeting rooms, a hall and a kitchen, the Astor Institute in the early days had a fine sporting reputation and several of its 'old boys' went on to play for Argyle, including Pat Jones, Paddy Blatchford and Dave Hatherley. Running the Institute, however, has never been an entirely easy task and even at the 21st party celebrations for the Institute there was mention of a 'none too sound' financial position. Nevertheless, it carried on providing an excellent facility for the neighbourhood. In 1944 Lady Astor bought the present scout hut from the RAF. In the 1970s, however, interest appeared to dwindle and those groups that were active experienced difficulty with booking the building. Such was the consequent lack of use that the building was quietly sold in 1977 to the Hospital, the Charity Commissioners approving the sale on the basis that there was insufficient use being made of the building. Subsequent attempts by Mount Gould Community Association to regain the building or the proceeds of the sale, have failed. However their endeavours have been 'rewarded' with the Social Club newly established across the road. With financial assistance from many quarters, including the brewery—keen to gain a foothold in this dry area—the Astors were temperate and Mount Gould has no pubs at all—the social club entertains many locals. David Astor, grandson and prospective MP, has visited here. But despite its success it fails to cater for the young and old and larger groups, all of whom lament the transition of the Astor Institute to the Astor Clinic.

26th July, 1986.

Old Road Inn

'When we started, beer was basically 5d [2p] a pint, whisky 12s 6d [62½p] a bottle and a drop or tot of whisky 7d [3p].' So said 75-year-old Ted Dyer a week before he retired as publican of the 'Old Road Inn', Laira, back in April 1965.

Ted Dyer had started out in the trade when he took over the ertswhile 'Albert Oak' from his aunt Emma Morris in 1919, since when he had witnessed 'colossal changes'. 'The hours have become too stretched' he said 'although some of the younger ones don't think so. We used to open from 12 p.m. to 2.30 p.m. and 6 p.m. to 10 p.m. This seemed to be very reasonable.' Ted and his wife Laura had moved to the 'Old Road Inn' just before the outbreak of the Second World War and had taken over from Fred Pine, who himself had been there almost 10 years. A long serving and very active member of Plymouth's Licensed Victuallers Association, Ted Dyer counted amongst his regulars in 1965 Alderman T. H. Watkins, then Lord Mayor of Plymouth. Ald. Watkins said the 'Old Road Inn' had for years been his 'local' and described Mr. Dyer as a friend and 'a wonderful example of the fidelity of the licensed trade'. Certainly such fidelity is one quality all 'Old Road Inn' licensees would appear to possess. Since 1909 it seems just five licensees have shared the task of running this Inn.

Before the above mentioned Messrs Pine and Dyer came John Alway, who was here some 20 years and after them Wally Fenwick arrived at the Old Road, having almost completed 20 years himself, at the Patna in North Road. Wally then turned in another 16 years here before handing over to Graham and Rose Lavers, fresh from the Breakwater in Coxside, exactly five years ago.

Much changed internally at least, over the years the 'Old Road Inn' has a large lounge that was formerly living accommodation and a large public bar that was once the stables. Built at a time when horsedrawn vehicles were the main means of road transport, the present pub sign of the 'Old Road' shows the Inn as it appeared when new. The Northern side of the road was undeveloped, a draycart has been painted in where a contemporary photograph shows a horsedrawn coal wagon, and the new bit of the Old Laira Road itself had not yet been constructed. This was done by the City Corporation in 1912, by way of an improvement to the road from Mutley to the Embankment. Alexandra Road, from Mutley to Lipson, had been made around 1863.

Plymouth had expanded its boundaries in 1896 less than 10 years after having been made a county borough and this expansion included the incorporation of the Compton, Weston, Peverell and Eggbuckland parishes. Laira was part of the latter and among the many consequences of this change was an almost immediate doubling of the rates and a great deal of building and development along both sides of the Old Laira Road. The change in the path of the road, in front of the pub, is commemorated in the granite steps that lead from one to the other with a large carving of the civic crest flanked by the date '19–12'.

Still a busy road today, long gone are the days when the Old Laira Road was known as the Old London Road, or even doubtless the London Road, when traffic used to have the awesome task of going up or down Lipson Hill before winding its way round to here. The laying down of the Embankment, then the 'New London Road', in the first half of last century, altered all that; it also paved the way for the setting up of Plymouth's first railway terminus at Laira Green, by the heart of the old Village of Laira, all of which can be panoramically viewed from on high from the small, but pleasant, beer garden at the rear of the 'Old Road Inn'. From here can be seen the expansive and expensive High-Speed Train complex in British Rail's Laira Yard, parts of the Plym Estuary, the woods of Saltram and some of the older houses of Laira around The Avenue, just off Old Laira Road. Houses that in the 1930s flooded when the brook coming down Pike Road was blocked. Situated more or less below sea level, they took a long time to clear and GWR, who were held responsible for the 'disaster', agreed to pay compensation. Rumour has it that nearly everyone claimed for a new three-piece suite, but all they got was about £12 per household!

19th July, 1986.

St. Mary The Virgin Laira

Laira has been a parish in its own right for little more than 50 years, the name 'Laira' however has been around in one form or another for centuries. 'Leurie Point', between Lipson and Tothill creeks, appears on a seventeenth-century map; we also find part of the Plym estuary being referred to as Leeri or Lary and the English Place Name Society suggests that this derives from the Celtic 'Llaeru'—'to ebb or grow shallow'—a notion supported by neighbouring Efford or Ebb Ford. Whatever its early history however (like many other parts of modern Plymouth this was the scene of much activity during the Civil War), Laira owes its more recent prominence to the gradual improvement of communication between Plymouth and all parts east of the Plym.

Prior to the Turnpike roads of the mid 1700s the fords here were unreliable and Plymbridge (which once had a Chapel dedicated to St. Mary the Virgin standing on it) was the surest route. However with the Turnpiking and the construction across the marshes of the raised road known as Longbridge, together with a new bridge over the river, the situation was much improved as it was also by development of the Laira embankment road, sanctioned in 1802 and completed by 1811. Although the new roads were in many ways a great asset to the area it was the arrival, on 5th May, 1848, of the first South Devon Railway engine at Laira Green that really put the place on the map (it was almost another year before the line ran through to Millbay).

Today, the Church of St. Mary the Virgin Laira enjoys wonderful views of the Plym estuary together with the adjacent Laira goods yard. However although all this to-ing and fro-ing helped establish Laira, the initial impetus for a religious building came from the War Department's concern to provide for the needs of the garrison and their families based at the Victorian Laira fort. In 1874 therefore a school-chapel was erected at Crabtree and at last the 200-odd residents of the area had a local place of worship—thereby saving a 2-mile walk to their parish Church of Egg Buckland. This Mission, which went on to serve the community for another 40 years and more, stood until the busy Embankment road was widened and improved in 1971. In the meantime, however, the building of the Church of St. Mary the Virgin had begun—work, which although in some respects complete, may never fulfil the architect's original intentions. In 1906 Mrs. Lucy Clark, of Efford Manor, conveyed 4,840 square yards of land here to the Church (the Clarks had been Lords of the Manor of Efford since 1784). The following year a decision was taken to proceed with the building of a church and a Mr. T. R. Kitsell, a member of the Egg Buckland congregation, was chosen as its architect. Once drawn up it became apparent that the cost of the church would easily exceed available funds and although Lady Clark laid the foundation stone on 16th September, 1911, and the Diocesan Committee for Church Extension in the Three Towns eventually contributed over £5,000, there

was still a great shortfall. On top of this the Church Building Committee—in the face of difficulties with the contractors—eventually took the work into their own hands, a move that later cost them hundreds of pounds in a court settlement.

Nevertheless by 1914 phase one of the church had been completed and now, like Emmanuel, it awaits completion of its tower. It also awaits more major work as the 'temporary' slate-hung western wall testifies. Designed to accommodate 750 people the church, without a major part of its nave and its baptistry, does well to seat 250. However notwithstanding these problems it was announced in the London Gazette of Tuesday, December 18th, 1931, that St. Mary the Virgin, Laira had been separated as a parish and Father Leonard Strong, Priest in Charge since 1922, was appointed first vicar here; a post he held until 1947.

At that time the church was a prominent landmark, virtually at the north-eastern tip of the Plymouth boundary. Well inside such boundaries today of course, this pleasantly situated, pseudo-Gothic structure is now surrounded by urban development—including, since 1961, the Vicarage which today houses the Reverend A. G. Cookman.

23rd November, 1985.

Plym Estuary

Over the last forty years or so there can be few who travel along the Embankment, particularly rail travellers, who have not noted the gradual deterioration of this beached trawler. A favourite perch for curious cormorants, the boat was brought up here just after the war by the late Harry Blagdon. Harry was one of the last old barge builders in the area and one of the many Blagdons who, since the 1920s at least, have been associated with boat letting and building along the Embankment and around at Richmond Walk. He brought the *Antelope*, as she was called, up here in the wake of the post war wood shortage and sold her mast and a few other of her useful timbers and then left her stranded, a relic of times past, to become a landmark since known to thousands.

Built around 1906, the *Antelope* was a sailing trawler and, towards the end of her days, was one of the last working examples of the erstwhile large fleet of these big Brixham craft. Last working in the late 1930s, just before the second world war, the *Antelope* was used in the first world war as a fishing protection vessel. Today, however, she little reflects her size and former glories and indeed, in the last couple of years the deterioration process seems to have accelerated.

Stuck fast in the sand and silt of the Plym, it is hard these days to imagine that large craft used regularly to come up the Plym—not just to this point, but well beyond. The passage of time and silt and waste matter from local medieval tin streaming operations meant that much of this area became negotiable only at high tide, if at all. Plympton once had a thriving maritime trade; a cargo of slates is recorded as leaving Plympton for Southampton as long ago as 1178. However, as Crispin Gill tells us in his first volume of Plymouth History, the Plym, the Meavy and the Tory Brook which all feed the estuary—the latter coming down through Plympton itself—were all from tin streaming valleys and prompted protests about the silt which date from earliest records through to Elizabethan times. So it was that centuries ago Plympton lost its sea trade to its younger neighbour Sutton and the increasing use of this alternative would appear to have been instrumental in this town becoming known as the town at Plym Mouth. In the Pipe Rolls of 1211 the name Plymouth first occurs together with its first cargoes.

Just two hundred years ago, however, large craft were recorded opposite here as 'a flotilla of sloops and boats' with ship following ship, marking the progress of George III and his entourage to Saltram where he was based during his 1789 visit to the City. A visit, incidentally, that saw him attend the City's pre-Foulston theatre in George Street, thereby occasioning its owners to dub it the 'Theatre Royal', a name which subsequently stuck, despite its unofficial status. At the time of George's visit, the Amphitheatre at Saltram would have been but a decade or so old and it is believed that the area behind these three pseudo-Roman arches was then roofed, covering the large chamber hewn out of the shale bank. Last century, the Amphitheatre fell into disuse and any roof has long since gone. However, the National Trust, who now administer the Saltram estate, are currently working with Manpower Services to tidy up the area around the Amphitheatre. To this end the sea wall is being repaired, some forestry work carried out and the impressive figureheads, that had fallen from the folly over the years, will soon be re-erected, ensuring that this landmark at least will see out a good many more years yet.

12th October 1985.

Crabtree Town Hall

In 1974 the 'Crabtree Inn', which had hitherto occupied one of the oldest inn sites in Plymouth, was pulled down to make way for the new stretch of dual carriageway from Laira to Marsh Mills. Situated on what is believed to be the second oldest thoroughfare in the city, the 'Crabtree Inn' overlooked the Ebb Ford which, at low tide, provides the lowest crossing of the Plym. Two causeways across the sands have been identified as being from Arnold's Point to Saltram Point and from Crabtree to Blackstone Quay.

As to the origin of the name Crabtree, Crispin Gill remembers 'the channels in these muddy rivers being marked by branches of trees stuck upright and irreverently called "winkle-trees"' and goes on to beg the question 'were there even earlier such branches to mark the line of the ford and were these the "crab-trees"?'

Crabtree was a busy little place in the eighteenth century. Much traffic was generated by the five lime kilns known to have existed in the area. Indeed the remains of one stood until the road was widened in the early 1970s. The demand for lime for manuring was at that time high with neighbouring Plymouth and Plymouth Dock (Devonport) expanding rapidly. Then, not long after the building of Dartmoor Prison, Sir Thomas Tyrwhitt persuaded Plymouth Chamber of Commerce to support plans for a horse drawn railway from Crabtree to Princetown. Designed to bring granite down from the moor for building purposes and take lime up to the moor for fertilization, the line opened in 1823 but sadly never paid its way. By the middle of last century imported and chemical manures had replaced lime and the Crabtree works had fallen into disuse.

However, around 1834 another, albeit frivolous and comparatively short lived, chapter began in the history of Crabtree. Around this time a number of patrons of an ancient and long since demolished hostelry in Treville Street, called the 'Pack Horse', decided that it might be a merry jape to hold an annual outing on the first holiday in Spring and that Crabtree would make a good place to hold this 'high revel'. Politics and politicians were made even more fun of in an active way then than they are today and so these gentlemen decided that they would form 'a mock Corporation with a mock Mayor, a mock Recorder' and enact 'a general travesty of municipal proceedings'. So popular did this annual event become that on the given day children would line the streets as the 'Mayor' and his immediate confederates made their way by coach along 'Britonside, Exeter Street and Jubilee Street'. Many would follow on foot and a large band orchestrated the proceedings. Passing the Embankment turnpike was frequently a riotous affair and it was not unknown for the toll house to be taken by storm so that the revellers could pass without paying their halfpennies. On reaching Lower Crabtree 'the ancient Dame known as Granny Tupper duly made her appearance' and presented them with a bountiful bowl of cockles. At Higher Crabtree they were met, amid much rejoicing, by a 'mass of many sorts and conditions of men, women and children'. Slowly the mayoral party would make its way into Crabtree Town Hall preceded by the bearer of the Great Cockle, which was set on a crimson velvet cushion embroidered with gold lace and adorned with tassels. Crabtree Town Hall was but a large room in the Rising Sun and here the new mayor was elected. On receipt of the robes and chain of office he would then be sworn in. 'I, Anthony Tutton (twice elected and many times Recorder), being this day fully and freely elected by the burgesses of the ancient cockle borough of Crabtree, do promise and vow to do all that in me lies for the benefit of the said Borough and the preservation of all its time honoured rights and privileges touching the catching and selling of cockles, so help me Bob.'

After this three men would appear with monster bowls of cockles and a good time would be had by all. In 1845 the date changed to Good Friday after the 'Astronomer Royal of Crabtree' announced that the almanacs were wrong that year in their calculation of Easter. Each year on the Whit Sunday following this revelry a more sober expedition would arrive at Eggbuckland Church for the service and this second trip saw them leave their regalia in the Rising Sun for another year.

Sadly by 1854 'none cared to carry on the burlesque' and, writing over 100 years ago, John Webb noted that 'the drowsy prosy life of a roadside inn, deprived of all the bustle that thronged around it when coaches were and railways were not, has fallen to it . . .', it being the Rising Sun.

Renamed the 'Roundabout' in 1973 when developments at Marsh Mills guaranteed a new level of neighbourhood bustle, this roadside Inn is soon to be no more. However, its licence will be adopted by nearby Marsh House.

18th October, 1986.

Triumphal Arch

In the golden age of the Roman Empire a 'triumphus' was the solemn and magnificent entrance of a general into Rome after he had won some great victory and such was the fervour and significance accorded these returns that Lucius Stertinius erected two magnificent commemorative arches, one in Rome's Circus Maximus and the other in the Forum Boarium. In the centuries that followed successive emperors built between them some 40 Triumphal Arches in Rome, of which only 3 now survive. The newest of these dates from around AD 317 and was built by the Emperor Constantine. A few other examples survived in other parts of the Roman Empire including one at Orange in France.

Many centuries later another Empire builder, this time a Frenchman, Napoleon, resolved to decorate Paris in the same way. In 1806 he was responsible for the building of the Arc de Triomphe du Carrousel, which stands between the Louvre and the Tuileries (built in the pattern of one of Rome's two other surviving Arches, that of Septimius Severus, AD 203), and the beginning of another Arch, just beyond the Champs-Elysees, the Arc de Triomphe de l'Etoile, a structure that was not completed for some 30 years. However, it remains the largest and most famous Triumphal Arch in the World.

Standing 162 feet high 147 feet wide and 72 feet deep it saw the addition, this century, of the tomb of an unknown French soldier from the First World War. At the head of this tomb there is a flame kept perpetually alight.

Whilst this celebrated Arc de Triomphe was being constructed, however, Marble Arch, modelled on Constantine's Roman Arch, was constructed in 1825 as the front entrance to Buckingham Palace, itself begun in that year but not completed till the mid 1830s. Also the Arch which, since 1888, has stood at the top of Constitution Hill was, in 1828, built as the original North Entrance to Buckingham Palace (Marble Arch itself was moved to its present site in 1851).

Meanwhile, back here in Devon we find by this time, that Plympton had been blessed with its own Triumphal Arch. However, exactly who built it and when, appears to be a matter of conjecture as indeed, does the reason for building it. The City Librarian, when replying to an inquiry about the Arch in 1971 from a lady, Mrs. Mannell, who was then living in the Triumphal Arch Cottage which forms part of the structure, dated it around 1720 and described it as 'purely a piece of landscape architecture'. George Parker of Boringdon who, a little earlier, bought Saltram House was the man accredited with its construction. A City of Plymouth guide to 'Buildings of Architectural and Historical Interest', however, dates the Arch from 1783 and suggests that John Parker, by then of Saltram, was responsible for this 'eye-catcher' built 'to be seen from Saltram' and that it was based on a design by the Scottish architect Robert Adam (1728–1792).

Commanding superb views of Plymouth and the Plym Estuary, the Arch would appear to have marked the entrance to Saltram from Plymbridge Road which itself sported two entrances on its north side to Boringdon Hall. After their move to Saltram, the Parkers soon left Boringdon altogether and by 1836 at least, Boringdon, while 'it still retains indication of its ancient importance', was occupied as a farm. The only building other than Saltram itself with Grade 1 listed status in Plymouth, Boringdon Hall (parts of which are fourteenth century) was almost beyond repair earlier this year. However, now in the careful hands of restorer Peter Malkin, the building is, happily, well on the way to being completely returned to its former glory by the end of next summer. The future of Triumphal Arch cottage, condemned by the City who also class it a Grade II listed structure of particular importance, is not presently so rosy however. Empty for more than over a year now, the cottage, like its immediate neighbours, has no gas, electricity or water supply. Alf Dell, in 'Hilltops' next door, who must have one of Plymouth's few surviving households without these not so mod-cons, however, says there is talk of a friendly ghost in the Arch cottage and there is talk of an underground passage from here to Boringdon Hall. Whether the one amounts to anything or the other leads to anywhere may never be known. The mystery of the Arch itself, however, may perhaps be uncovered yet, along with its true age.

16th November, 1985.

Boringdon Hall

Some parts of Boringdon Hall are believed to date back to the fourteenth century, a substantial section of the western end of the building (to the left as we see it) is regarded as being fifteenth century, while the bulk of the building is thought to be Elizabethan. The completed sixteenth century rebuilding would have been largely symmetrical about the central tower and of the many alterations and additions that have taken place over the years since it is the disappearance of this East Wing, for whatever reason—fire, decay or demolition—that has undoubtedly made the biggest impact on the appearance of the place.

Impressive it still is, however, and today it stands as the oldest substantial building in the area that is both open to the public and offers accommodation, entertainment and refreshment for the visitor. And yet just a few years ago this historic building was virtually written off. In a deplorable state, it had been looked at by a number of potential restorers and/or developers, all of whom had either got cold feet soon after starting or had been forced out by the costs involved.

A newspaper report of ten years ago painted the scene graphically, 'It won't be long now before Boringdon Hall finally crumbles into ruin. The roof has great gaps, the floors, sodden with rain, have finally subsided. Even the staircase has slipped and collapsed.' The City's Assistant Planning Officer was quoted, at the time, as saying 'I think Boringdon Hall is probably too far gone now. I wouldn't dream of guessing how much it would cost to restore.' By 1984 the building had deteriorated further; fortunately for the City, however, that was the year Peter Malkin saw Boringdon Hall, and fell in love with it. This week his dream of restoration becomes a reality, as two years of investment and rebuilding, involving a tremendous personal, physical and financial commitment from Mr. Malkin come to an end. Although it is by no means *the* end as a number of adjacent buildings remain to be further developed.

Of the early history of Boringdon Hall comparatively little is known. In 1121 the manor lands of Boringdon (sometimes known as Colebrook Manor) were granted to the newly founded Priory of Plympton. A substantial Grange was then erected on this land which remained in the hands of the Priory until Henry VIII's 'dissolution of the Monasteries'. Boringdon was thereby appropriated by the Crown and in 1547, the year Henry VIII died, his 'Garter King of Arms' (a title given to one of the King's most trusted servants) Sir Thomas Wriothesley, Earl of Southampton, was granted Boringdon, Wembury and Broadhembury. The following year Sir Thomas was granted permission to transfer the ownership of Boringdon to Richard Mayhow (Mayhew?) of Tavistock. In 1558 Richard died; his wife remained at Boringdon, but with no children to pass his property on to, it soon after came into the possession of his nephew Jerome (Jeronemy) Mayhew.

By this time John Parker had appeared in the records as a tenant of Boringdon and in 1583 John Parker married Frances Mayhew, only child and heiress of Jerome. Jerome Mayhew died four years later, 400 years ago, and from that year on down to the 1920s Boringdon remained in the hands of the Parker family. John's father, Edmund Parker of North Molton, had ensured that Boringdon would pass into his family by paying Jerome Mayhew £3,000 as part of the marriage settlement and it is believed that it was probably Edmund Parker who was responsible for rebuilding Boringdon. Although, as stated, Boringdon stayed in Parker hands until this century, the families represented locally, moved to Saltram at the beginning of the eighteenth century. Boringdon was then let out to tenant farmers, but it was always too big and not designed as a farm building and that was when the rot first set in. It is indeed thought that the demise of the east wing may, in part, have been due to a desire of the tenants to use the stonework to provide more suitable farm buildings adjacent to this part of the house.

Certainly Peter Malkin feels that this is so, although he says that part of his extension to the main hall building, while built with available stone he found around the grounds, also incorporates part of the rear wall of the original east wing which he unearthed soon after beginning to work on the site.

Today, Boringdon Hall stands as proud as, doubtless, it has ever done; internally and externally walls, windows and rooms have been rebuilt and replaced as close to their originals as it is possible to imagine. The Great Hall, the Minstrels' Gallery and the impressive coat of arms, above the main fireplace have, one way or another, been reinstated. Plymouth has every reason to be grateful to Peter Malkin, for in making his dream come true he has provided the means for many to come and visit this 'Elizabethan' hotel, perchance to dream of times gone by themselves.

9th May, 1987.

The Colebrook Inn

'The Colebrook Inn . . . Once was the site of four small cottages. Small boats brought pilchards and other wares past its door on the "Brook" or little river that ran under the bridge thro' the village.' So proclaims the signboard to the left of the front entrance of this large, comfortable and inviting village inn. The little river, Tory Brook, tidal at least as far as here, has long since been filled in. Recent excavations, however, across the road from the pub, revealed sea, sand and shells about ten feet below street level.

The sign on the side of the inn, a colourful representation of an older design to be seen on a window at the back of the lounge bar, is a fanciful interpretation of how the inn may once have been set. Certainly, the deeds of neighbouring cottage 'Sunkist', home of Roy Blackler, indicate that the 'dwelling house called the "Colebrook Inn" had a large garden and an orchard opposite and suggest that the pub may date from the 1750s. Meanwhile a chart in J.Brooking-Rowe's *History of Plympton Erle*, shows us three local roads over the '*Torrey Brook*', one of which could be almost as near the Inn as the picture suggests.

Various theories have been put forward for the derivation of the name Colebrook; one suggests that the Saxon 'coln' meaning 'pebble' has given us the pebbly brook—Colebrook; another possibility is that 'col' is the celtic ridge which appears in Coleland. Then again Bill Best-Harris, in his *Place Names of Plymouth, Dartmoor, etc.*, suggests that it is either Cola's Brook or Cool Brook. Certainly, until recently, the naturally arising water opposite the pub was used to keep milk churns of the local dairy cool. Whatever the explanation, however, it is likely that it will apply equally to the two other Colebrooks to be found in Devon, the largest of the three being near Crediton, the other just a hamlet of Cullompton. Whatever its derivation, in the middle of last century it would appear that Colebrook was owned, in its entirety, by the Earl of Morley—the family having acquired it by marriage with an heiress of the Mayhews. The 'Colebrook Inn' and surrounding acreage was purchased from the Earl in 1861 by John Stephens, for five hundred and seventy pounds.

Stephens had already been landlord here for more than a decade and the Inn subsequently stayed in his family until 1911 when it was purchased by the Octagon Brewery. Today a Courage house, the pub has seen three long-staying landlords since the last war; Harold Luscombe, Cliff Dyer and the present licensee Derek Barrett, who took over from Dennis Perry eight years ago. Cliff Dyer was an ex-dockyard electrician whose father, for some time, kept the Old Road Inn at Laira. Tragically, however, Cliff literally dropped dead one night behind the bar, having just 'commented' on Plymouth Argyle's prospects against Brian Clough's Brighton the following day. 'The Colebrook' was thus Cliff's one and only pub. For Derek Barrett, however, it is currently the sixth. Having now spent twenty years in the trade, Derek began at the 'West Hoe' (now the 'Swallow'), then went to the 'Royal Oak' (Bigbury), 'King's Arms' (Salcombe), 'Penguin' (Mutley) and the 'Navy' on the Barbican, before arriving here. Happy to be in such a local 'local', Derek, a few years back, instigated a photograph hunt which produced the various old pictures that have been copied and now hang around the bar. One of these is a copy of Plympton artist Sir Charles Eastlake's painting of the Bellerophon, anchored in the Sound, with Napoleon on board. One bar of the Colebrook has now been renamed the Eastlake lounge after the great man and a descendant of his still lives in Plympton. Meanwhile, the other bar is named the 'Pryer of Plympton', after local journalist and editor of the *Star* Bill Anderson, who searched out the copy of the painting, along with various other scoops and stories on the area.

18th January, 1986.

Elize Hele School

Chapter VIII of J. Brooking Rowe's great, 400-page 'History of Plympton Erle', published in 1906, is titled 'Elize Hele's School'. However, this was not the official name of the school as the first sentence of the chapter tells us it is generally called—'Plympton Grammar School' and 'was founded by John Maynard and Elize Stert, the surviving donees under a deed dated 9 January 1632–3, whereby Elize Hele of Cornwood and Bovey Tracey granted, enfeoffed, and confirmed sundry manors and lands to and for godly and charitable uses'.

The nature of these godly and charitable uses was left to the three trustees, Maynard, Stert and John Hele, who died sometime before 1658 when, as Brooking Rowe puts it, 'The intention with regard to the foundation of a grammar school at Plympton was carried into effect by Indenture of Lease and Release date 6 and 7 September' of that year. Elize Hele (sometimes written as Ellis or Ellys Heale) owned much land and the revenue from it was substantial and in 1658 it was 'declared and directed that one thousand eight hundred pounds' should be 'employed for the building of a schoolhouse and purchasing lands of inheritance for the maintenance of a Schoolmaster and a dwelling place for the said Master'.

As it turned out, the school was built just off Old Street, 'beginning March 1663 and ending October 1671', at a total cost of 1,099 pounds 17 shillings and sixpence; and it still stands today. The Master, however, had no new building then and for two centuries at least, the Schoolmaster lived in already existing, adjacent premises.

Although still carrying two rusty, old crests bearing the wording Plympton Grammar School, the large wrought iron gates of the old school, off what is now the bottom end of George Lane, St. Maurice have, since 1980, been part of the independent Sir Joshua Reynolds School.

Named after the most illustrious pupil ever to be taught here (his father was schoolmaster at the time), the school, on many occasions through the years, had less than 10 pupils, and well before its recent revival as a private school had seen days as a

174

fee paying school. In 1882 boys under ten were charged 2 guineas a term; boys over ten, 3 guineas.

The headmaster then received £120 per annum. There were around 50 pupils and 8 staff throughout the 1880s but towards the end of the century the number dwindled and, after the forming of the School Board and the new initiatives in education, the school closed.

In 1921 it was revived as a secondary school. However, the old building was deemed unsuitable as a school and the new school was housed in Castle Barbican, strangely enough, as this was the former private residence of the school's aforementioned chronicler, J. Brooking Rowe. Recounting episodes from its later history, Brian Mosely, writing in 1967, notes that by 1928 Castle Barbican itself had become 'grossly overcrowded' and, after early hopes to secure a new school were dashed by the 1931 financial crash, the old seventeenth-century building was brought into use again.

On Friday 11th June 1937 however, this building was opened a mile or more away in Stone Barton as the new home for the co-educational Plympton Grammar School. Fees were now £3 10s 0d per term and the school had considerable playing fields. Establishing itself a fine reputation as a Grammar School over the next 40 odd years, in 1983 yet another development in local education saw this and Plympton Secondary 'go comprehensive'. A change that was accompanied by the name Elize Hele at last being officially adopted as the school's title. And what better time to change, as when looking at the original clauses of the schedule relating to the original school being set up by Elize Hele's trustees over 300 years ago, we read that it was always intended to be 'a free School for all poor person's children whatsoever of Plympton, Brixton, or elsewhere who are not able or shall profess themselves not well able to pay for their children's schooling'.

2nd November, 1985.

Post Office Inn

On 31 July, a little over two weeks ago, the Post Office celebrated its 350th birthday with a colourful issue of postage stamps.

Back on the auspicious day in 1635 Charles I had issued a proclamation extending the use of the Royal Mail to the great British public. As with most older countries the Post Office here grew out of an organisation of King's messengers.

Henry III (1216–72) employed such figures and by the time of Edward III (1312–77), there were already various private posts.

The first 'Master of the Post' seems to have been appointed in the time of Henry VIII around 1512, the first Postmaster General two hundred years after that, in 1711.

Between the two dates, 1635 marks the time when the King first allowed private letters to be carried alongside State mail, with, for the first time, regular rates being fixed for such public correspondence.

Traditionally, inns were used as staging posts, usually 12 to 15 miles apart. They would have provided both refreshment and a change of horses.

From Tudor times onwards the London–Plymouth post road, thanks to the importance of the town as a naval base, had been one of the four main post routes in Britain. However, prior to the construction in 1758 of the new Great West Road, the principal route to London from Plymouth had been via Tavistock and Okehampton and not through Plympton.

Indeed, even some time after the new road had opened the post went through Plympton St Maurice and it was not until the institution of the mail coach, 1784 onwards, that the post ran past here.

Consequently, by 1798 we read in the Universal British Directory of that year that the post goes through Ridgeway and the postmaster waits at the 'George Inn' to take the bag. The era of the mailcoach however was a comparatively short one and by 1847, just seven years after the national adoption of the penny post and the world's first postage stamp, the penny black, the railway arrived in Plympton.

Another directory, this time from 1850, tells us that the Post Office is once again located in Plympton-Earl (St Maurice) however by 1857 John Cook is listed as Postmaster followed soon after by Ralph Cook 'sub-master' at the 'Post Office, Ridgeway'. Quite how this relates to the building we see here known since 1870 at least as the 'Post Office Inn', is unclear.

We do know however that William Head was here throughout the 1870s as a victualler or beer retailer somewhere in the Ridgeway.

At that time there were three other inns on the Ridgeway, the 'Devonshire Arms', the 'Plymouth Inn' and the 'George'. The 'Devonshire Arms', a few doors along from the Post Office, has not been an inn since the late 1930s when it was first converted as Plympton Library. The 'Plymouth Inn' is now the 'Sir Joshua Reynolds' while the 'George' remains unchanged.

Philip Head, presumably a son, followed William at the Post Office in the 1880s to be succeeded in turn by Philip Foster. More recently the ex-naval John Hawkins and his wife Pat took over this Starkey, Knight and Ford house from Beatrice Brimacombe who left soon after the death of her husband in 1965.

Prior to the Brimacombes (whose son, Tony, played for Argyle), was Fred Jolley, who left to go to the erstwhile 'Barleysheaf', now 'Trader Jack's', in the City Centre.

Ten years ago Whitbreads took over the 'Post Office Inn' and a tasteful refit reinstated a period flavour into this fine local tavern of uncertain age that stands, as we are told by local historian Henry Wheeler, upon the site of Crossman's Tenements.

17th August, 1985.

Mayoralty House, Plympton

Like the Guildhall it stands next to, the 'Forester's Arms' in Fore Street, Plympton St. Maurice, is thought to date substantially from the late seventeenth century. Together, the two buildings are historically and architecturally listed as a group and indeed, their individual histories are very much interwoven.

In 1602 Plympton St. Maurice, feeling its position of local eminence being eroded by its rapidly growing and younger neighbour Plymouth, petitioned the Queen for a Charter of Incorporation which it was hoped might herald better times for the ancient and depressed borough. The charter was granted and from that year, 1602, Plympton St. Maurice was entitled, amongst other things, to appoint its own Mayor. Later that century, presumably to accommodate this new body and provide it with a better 'Council house . . . that they may there assemble, meet, councell etc . . .', the present Guildhall was built, by all indications on the site of its 13th century predecessor. Around the same time it would seem that the building we now know as the 'Foresters', was built as the Mayoral House and evidence suggests that there were internal interconnecting doorways, between the two, on both the ground and the first-floor level.

For some 250 years the authorities appointed their chief magistrate and dispensed local matters and justice. However, in 1859 the passing of the Victorian Acts establishing a county police led the Court of Aldermen and Common Council to feel that they no longer had any 'franchises or immunities granted by the borough charters of any value to the inhabitants of Plympton' and that 'the interests of the inhabitants would best be consulted by suspending the operations of the charter, by refraining from the election of a chief magistrate in the year 1860'. Consequently Walter Hele Molesworth, elected in 1859, became the last ever Mayor of Plympton. Regarded by many as a great loss to the community, local historian J. Brooking Rowe, in his history of Plympton Erle, went so far as to say, 'There can be no doubt that a mistake was made in taking the course the mayor and aldermen did'. Writing in 1906 he went on to add a long, familiar and almost universal lament '. . . had younger men been consulted and confided in, steps could have been taken which would have resulted in benefit to Plympton and the neighbourhood . . .'

Nevertheless, the immediate practical consequences of the elders' actions in 1859 were that the Guildhall and other property of the 'dying corporation' were conveyed to trustees. The corporation had been in a state of decline since the passing of the Reform Act in 1832, when the financial support of this rotten borough was no longer forthcoming from one of its two principal owners, the Earl of Mount Edgcumbe. The others, the Treby family of Plympton House, remained loyal. However, to raise money a certain amount of property was sold, as was the portrait of Sir Joshua Reynolds (Mayor in 1733). Meanwhile other important paintings appear to have been divided among members at the same time. Funds were still wanting though and by 1860 the Guildhall was 'miserably decayed and dilapidated', so the trustees oversaw the formation of a company which by 1862 had restored and redesigned the interior of the building. In 1859 Mayoralty House had been passed by the trustees of Paul Treby Treby to Richard Redpath, a local carpenter. Then in 1862 the house was divided and part of it was passed to Henry Ford, the Clerk of Peace, and subsequently used as a Police Station. The building to the west of the 'Foresters' served as Plympton's Police Station for the next 76 years and once again there appear to be interconnecting doorways between these two properties. In 1938 the Police Station moved up to the Ridgeway.

Meanwhile, back at the 'Foresters', it would appear to be some time late in the 1860s that it assumed its new name and became a licensed premises. Prior to that Thomas Stanbury had conducted his grocery business from here for a number of years. It's not at all clear when it properly ceased to be the Mayoralty House in all but name. The property, known now as Mayoralty House, on the south side of Fore Street, does not appear, according to Brooking Rowe, 'ever to have been connected with the Corporation in any way'.

Bought by Plymouth Breweries in 1937, the last private owner of the 'Foresters', Sidney Cutliffe, bought the pub 50 years ago for £3,300. It has seen several minor changes externally since 1860; the large window on the left was originally two, similar to those directly above, while the window and doorway to the right was at one time all together. Inside has recently been restructured quite extensively, but Jack Lycett, the current licensee, is keen to recapture as much of the original flavour of the place as possible.

13th September, 1986.

Pomphlett

'Woolly mammoth, woolly rhinoceros, reindeer, bear and other animals found shelter in the caves at Stonehouse, Oreston, Mount Wise and Pomphlet as bones during the late eighteenth and early nineteenth centuries testify.' So writes John Gerrard in his 1982 *Book of Plymouth*. For the most part these bones were unearthed in Pomphlett and Oreston as a direct result of the quarrying undertaken in the course of the construction of the Breakwater. This work began in 1812. Finds at Stonehouse had occurred earlier. In 1776, while waiting with Captain James Cook to set sail for the South Seas, Sir Joseph Banks was in Plymouth when, among the many limestone caves in Stonehouse, one was found to contain prehistoric bones. When work, therefore, began on other parts of this limestone ridge which runs through Stonehouse, the Hoe, Cattedown, Mount Batten, Turnchapel, Oreston and Pomphlett, Banks wrote to the Superintendent of the Oreston Quarry asking him to keep a special look out for caves and bones. By now Sir Joseph Banks was 69; he had been made President of the Royal Society back in 1778.

Caves and bones were found as early as 1816 but it was not until 1887 that any of the sites yielded human remains and they were found just off the mound visible here across the Plym Estuary at Cattedown. Of course the Plym Estuary presented quite a different picture when these bones were laid to rest. As Crispin Gill reminds us 'with the unquarried white cliffs of Oreston and Cattedown just 300 yards apart, the river flowed through a minor Cheddar Gorge from Pomphlett to the Sound'.

All Ice Age images of the area, however, are necessarily products of speculation and the imagination and it is not until 1330 that we find our first written reference to Pomphlett or Ponnaflute. The early spelling of the name suggesting that it may derive from an old English personal name Puna, or Punna, coupled with ' fleot', again an old English word meaning 'a place where water flows; a creek, inlet, run of water'. Thus we have Pomfleet as it's called in Bellamy's handwritten History of Plymstock (1843?). Bellamy, however, prefers to interpret the Pom as coming from Pilim, that is the 'rolling river adjacent'. Making Pomphlett the 'creek of the Plym', an attractive enough idea, but unlikely. Certainly it is easy enough to see how a double 'e'–'t' when handwritten can so easily become 'e'–double 't'.

Incidentally 'The Fleet' originally described the run of water that flows into the Thames between Ludgate Hill and Fleet Street; today it is a covered sewer. Pomphlett Creek, meanwhile, at low tide when the sun shines, smells like an uncovered sewer and it's no surprise to find that the old Pomphlett Mill, at the end of the creek, was replaced by a sewage installation after the Mill had been demolished in January 1969. Although this development apparently improved the creek water and allowed seaweed to grow there once more, the old Mill did not go without attempts to save it. Known locally for centuries as Abbot's Mill, it had a pedigree dating back to the fourteenth century. It was in 1392 that Tavistock Abbey was first seen to be running two grist mills at Pomphlett, and it is known that the reigning Abbot of the Abbey had been Lord of the Manor at Plymstock for at least 200 years before that. The manor had been bequeathed to the Abbey by the Saxon Prince Eadwig who should have succeeded his brother Edmund (Ironside) to the throne in 1016 but was thwarted by Swegn Forkbeard's younger son, Cnut.

In addition to running the mills, the reigning Abbot also had Pomphlett as his demesne farm. A few years before Henry VIII dissolved Tavistock Abbey the mills were let out to a father and his two sons and for the next 360 years the mill was leased to a succession of local people. In 1892 William Mitchell bought it and worked it with his family until he, in turn, sold it to the Plymouth Co-operative Society in 1922. Today that 'Freehold, Tide Water Grist Mill with Dwelling-house, Coal stores and Stabling attached' has gone for good, as have the neighbouring cottages and railway bridge at Stamps Corner, and now most of the traffic that bustles along Billacombe road is unaware of what lies here behind the hoardings and the advertisements that line the south side of that road. While on the creek itself the traffic is but a fraction of what it once was and one can barely imagine big ships 'nearly the width of the Mill' carrying coal and grain along here. But it does still have a charm of its own and however narrow and silted up it may be (and here it is shown at very low tide) it would be sad to see another of the city's creeks infilled. Although such plans, already mooted in the past, can never be far away in the present climate.

4th July, 1987.

The Old Smithy, Elburton

Pedestrianisation, a long word and one not even found in most dictionaries. The notion that we would one day be creating areas just for people to walk in would have struck a lot of our forebears as absurd. Walking on two legs is, after all, what sets us apart from other species. However, there are those who would have us believe now, that it is the ability to drive a motor car, amongst other things, that sets us high above lesser mortal creatures. Perhaps they're right, for by association, pedestrian has come to mean 'uninspired, flat or commonplace' simply by virtue of the walker not being 'mounted on Pegasus'. And long before the motor car became an extension of the human arms and legs there weren't many who could afford their own horse, let alone a winged one, so most people did have to make do with their legs, handed out to them by mother nature.

There was a time, though, when horses were a lot more commonplace than they are today. A time when we relied on them for our speediest form of transport and for most of the hard work around the farm. In the middle of last century there were 37 blacksmiths and farriers operating in Plymouth alone and you could more than double that number if you included all those smaller towns and villages that now find themselves inside the City boundary—Devonport, Stonehouse, St. Budeaux, Tamerton Foliot, Eggbuckland, Plympton St. Maurice, Plympton St. Mary and Plymstock. And there were even further divisions within those titles. The older inhabitants of Turnchapel, Hooe, Oreston, Pomphlett and Elburton did not, and do not, readily regard themselves as coming from Plymstock. Elburton itself still maintains a village atmosphere, but the arrival of the motor vehicle, the property developer and the age of the nuclear family has done much to blur its identity.

Here in the heart of Elburton, however, we find a touch of the past in the present. It was around 1840 that the local blacksmith moved his tools and forge from around the corner in Springfield Road to this building in Haye Road South and for the next hundred years it operated as the village blacksmith's. It passed through various hands until 1866 when William Coleman took it on and it stayed in his family until Whitsun 1919 when Harold Coleman sold it to Philip Truscott. A little over thirty years later Philip's son, Trevor, became the last to shoe a horse in 'The Forge' as it was then known. By then change had already dictated a different workload for the village smithy. The demand for working on old ploughs, harrows, children's hoops, the 'drills' to propel them and making the old heater pieces for ironing boxes had long since fallen off and Trevor Truscott started selling anything and everything, ultimately using the smithy as a store for the general shop the family had, just across the way. In 1960 he sold the lot, however, and, although still used as a store, the smithy began to deteriorate and was in danger of being pulled down to make extra space for the village car park.

However, two sisters, both local girls whose family had a market garden in Elburton, had other ideas and with the help of their husbands they soon transformed the building and gave it a new life. Sadly, it had been gutted by its previous owner and the forge, with many other traces of its former existence, removed, but the basic layout remained the same.

The windows have been given fresh lintels from the loft and the former little lean-to with its corrugated-iron roof has been built up using old stone and given a new tiled top. Inside the walls remain uneven but now have a coat of white paint where they were black from the fire. The old steps up to the forge are further worn away today, but it is not the pungent smell of burning hoof that greets the nose but the rather different aroma of flowers, herbs and pot pourri.

Diane and Patrick Trerise, with Lorna and Stuart Brace, have certainly changed the smithy and everyone is happy about it, especially Trevor Truscott, who is delighted that the building not only still stands but is a busy workshop. For it is not only flowers and craft items that now fill the old smithy. There is a new 'smith' in the place, for Patrick, a full-time fireman, is also a qualified silversmith and he has the Freedom of the City of London to prove it!

Meanwhile, brother-in-law Stuart once enjoyed the freedom of Home Park, in the 1960s before he swopped his shirt for a succession of other league clubs, eventually hanging up his football boots about five years ago, preferring now to play cricket for Plymstock.

This view of the old smithy, incidentally, will be familiar to all the erstwhile patrons of Nellie Martin's shop (Wrigley's) which now houses the Elburton veterinary surgery, having been drawn from just outside the door.

7th February, 1987.

Elburton Cross

'Elburton—Ael—celtic a brow or commanding spot. Bur (Saxon) dwelling, also storehouse (as in farming ...) ton or tan (Saxon) primarily an enclosed space (as for agricultural purposes) a village ... According to this the above name will imply a dwelling, farm or barn having the quality of being located on the brow of a hill and so the present village grown up probably from a single habitation or a barn really is.'

So says Bellamy in his manuscript—*History of Plymstock* written in the 1840s.

More recently, however, in the *Place Names of Devon* we find Elburton explained as probably being 'Aeþelbeorht's' farm or 'tun'. Aeþelbeorht or Aeþelberht presumably being the name of an early, if not the first, owner of this farmland. The first known spelling of the name we have is Aliberton and that appears in 1254. Later variations are Ailberton (1423) Aylberton (1480) and in 1485 Elberton.

Whatever the true derivation of the modern name one thing about Elburton does seem certain, that since 1485, if not before, the two large stones in the foreground of this picture have stood somewhere in the heart of the village. These stones are part of Elburton Cross and as such have occupied various locations this century and doubtless stood much higher above the ground well into the beginning of last century, during which it would appear that a local farmer removed the shaft in order to get a roller he could use for breaking up the ground. Fifty years ago, E. N. Masson-Phillips, in a paper entitled 'The Ancient Stone Crosses of Devon', expressed his outrage at such 'wilful desecration for utilitarian purposes' which he said 'is without excuse, and to our shame has to be guarded against even at the present time'.

However, although now moved to an apparently safe haven here at the junction of Springfield Road and Wembury Road, no one yet appears to have located the original shaft which would have stood the head impressively high above the ground. Perhaps it has been broken up. Arthur Clamp, in his second booklet on Elburton, noted that parts of the cross were said to be buried on Candishes farm, land now occupied by Willets and Hawkins (Plant Services); and he speculates on their rediscovery should that site ever be disturbed.

Some 250 or so 'Mediaeval and later' crosses have been noted in Devon, generally falling into five basic categories. Churchyard crosses, village crosses, market crosses, boundary crosses and wayside crosses. Elburton cross, we know, was used as a market cross. With its earliest known location being in the middle of the junction of four roads at the top of what is now Doreena Road, just up from Revell's Cottages, here sermons would have been read, preaching conducted, proclamations made and manorial dues collected. Serving, as Masson-Phillips puts it, as 'a reminder of Christianity in the midst of business', markets and fairs would have been held around the cross.

Again quoting Bellamy in the 1840s we read: 'At the central cross at Elburton was held a sort of market within living memory.' Nowadays the notion of Elburton as an isolated farming community is just within living memory but the train, the motor car and the attendant development of the area for private housing makes it difficult now to fully appreciate the once rural atmosphere of this 'village on a brow'. If you look around though many traces are still there; seven of the ten major local farmhouses still stand, the old smithy has recently been restored, although not as a smithy, and many old cottages and barns still stand. And of course there is still the ancient village cross, moved a couple of times for road widening in modern times, it stood for many years on a brick base which had a tap inside from which local people 'drew water for washing etc.'

More recently it stood outside the Co-op next to the old telephone kiosk there, until it finally found its way here on what might—almost—pass for a small village green and, in the absence of any inscription, might almost lead the casual observer to assume that it always had been here ... After all, the village chapel is just across the road.

8th August, 1987.

Radford, St. Kevin's

In 1772 Messrs. Baring, Lee, Sellons and Tingcombe established Plymouth's first bank and indeed it later became known as the Plymouth Bank. The following year Messrs. Harris, Harris, Turner and Herbert established Plymouth's second bank, which later became known as the Naval Bank. In 1825 the Plymouth Bank, with a deficiency of £70,000, crashed along with a number of other banks around the country. The panic was said to be precipitated by the failure of a bank in York, which in turn could be traced back to a period of reckless speculation by the Bank of England. Worth notes, in his history of Plymouth (1890) that there was 'widespread suffering'. The Naval Bank, however, continued to thrive and, by the end of the nineteenth century, there were nine banks in Plymouth. In 1914, however, the Naval Bank itself failed and, for at least one of the families involved with the Bank, this led in 1917 to the sale, in bankruptcy proceedings, of their entire estate: an estate which covered over 600 acres and included many 'Capital Farms with Residences and Homesteads'. It was a sad day for the Bulteels and a sad day for Radford House.

The Bulteels had become linked, by marriage, with the Harris family in the middle of the nineteenth century and, as well as establishing the Naval Bank, the Harris family had owned the Radford estate for well over 400 years. Before them it had been passed down through the heads of the Radfords or Redfords—the name generally assumed to have been adopted by Walter le Abbe, grandson of William le Abbe, in whose hands the estate is first recorded in the days of Henry II (1216–1272).

So it was then that an estate, which had been handed down through the generations of two families for some 700 years, came to be sold in 1917. William Alfred Mitchell, the owner of Pomphlett Mills, bought Radford House and Park, but he never lived in the house himself, opting rather to let it. In 1930 Councillor Billy Mitchell died suddenly and tragically, while addressing a sub-committee of the General Purposes Committee of Devon County Council. The house and park passed to his son. Within seven years the Radford House, a large and impressive mansion house, had fallen into a bad state of repair and it was agreed by the trustees of the estate to demolish it.

Built or rather re-built on the site of its early-Tudor predecessor, Radford House dated substantially from the late seventeenth and early eighteenth centuries. In the process of this re-building it is believed that certain parts of the earlier construction were re-erected on the edge of Radford Pond—adjacent to the Boat House. The layout of these little dwellings appears to have been fairly whimsical and they are often described as being part of a 'folly'. However, it is only in recent years that these buildings have become 'ruins' and, for at least one Plymstock family, this was home for a number of years this century. Mr. Southern was a gardener at Hooe Manor when he lived here with his wife.

Bomb damage and a fire just after the War in the Boat House, however, put an end to those days and there is little left but a shell of this building today, which has romantic connections back to Elizabethan times. Indeed, it is often referred to locally as 'Drake's Boathouse' and as we're told, 'at Radford, Christopher Harris entertained Drake, Raleigh, Howard and Hawkins and the other captains who fought the Armada' (Whitfeld, 1899). It is likely that all these men would have been familiar with this particular area (after all there was no pedestrian crossing from the Plymouth side, south of Plymbridge, at this time and so a small boat was easily one of the best ways of getting about). Radford Lake was not dammed then and was tidal beyond this point and the built-up southern bank suggests this was probably the scene of much coming and going from Radford House, which stood behind this vantage point, slightly around the side of the rise towards Hooe.

Of the buildings adjacent to the boathouse, the nearest here was described grandly, in the 1917 sale brochure, as 'The Chapel', '. . . an antique structure in which is a Massive Granite Fireplace and Mantlepiece dated 1640.' Now, while there seems to be no evidence that this was ever used as a chapel, the impressive fireplace can still be seen and the eastern door in the little building is said to be the original front entrance to the old Radford House. Other odd and ancient relics can be found in the adjoining structures; including part of a large circular stone animal-powered cider press, which is set in the grass beside the Boathouse. Also just up behind the Boathouse, in the trees, is a large lime-kiln which has had, rather incongruously, five granite pig troughs built into its wall while above its south door half of an eighteenth-century cheesepress can be found serving as a lintel. A true folly indeed, but it does not explain why this little group of buildings, or sometimes just the Boathouse, is often found referred to as St. Keverne's or St. Kevin's. Perhaps there was some distant link with one of the largest parishes in Cornwall—St. Keverne, or could it be an allusion to the story of St Kevin, an Irish saint of the sixth century? The legend is that St. Kevin retired to a cave, on the steep shore of a lake, where he vowed no woman would ever land. However, a girl called Kathleen followed him. There are two versions of what happened next; one story states that the saint flogged the girl with a bunch of nettles, the other suggests that he hurled her from a rock into the lake, but her ghost rose smiling from the tide and never left the place where St Kevin lived. Now, not far from the Boathouse in Ashery Wood, is the entrance to a network of caves and there are several recorded sightings of the 'White Lady of Radford', a female ghost 'seen' both in Radford Dip and the great old 50-roomed mansion itself!

27th February 1988

Burrow Hill

'On a high hill commanding a delightful prospect over the pleasant village of Plymstock and its neighbourhood, a half buried piece of ordnance remains as a monument of the civil commotions which so horribly disorted the reign of Charles I.'

This quote, apparently dating from 1825, appeared in a newspaper article written in 1963. The title of the piece was 'Ancient Gun Found In Ditch', and it went on to describe the cannon here as dating from the Civil War and having lately been 'tumbled down the hill into the ditch where it lies upside-down and half buried by weeds'. Restored to its mounting a few months later, the cannon, now described as dating back 'hundreds of years and evidently first used on a ship', was, and at present still is, upside down. This description though vague is likely to be the more accurate of the two. Civil War cannon are few and far between and at least one leading expert on guns and cannon is extremely doubtful that it would date from that time. Furthermore, although Burrow Hill undoubtedly commands an excellent, albeit a little distant, view of several of the known skirmish locations (Mount Batten, Stamford, Pomphlett and even one or two on the other side of the Plym) and we know Colonel Digby had formed his headquarters at Plymstock with '600 horse and 300 foot', there would appear to be no record of and indeed no reason for the defending Plymouth Roundheads attacking this position. But again its very prominence makes it an excellent choice to commemorate the bloodshed that would have been witnessed from here and it is only sad that the four cannon balls, which formerly accompanied the cannon, have long since disappeared.

Also lost are the railings that once surrounded the most recent arrival here . . . this simple yet impressive cross. Erected on this site (given to the area by William Cooke, the market gardener in 1919), it was designed as a memorial to those local servicemen who lost their lives in the First World War. A generation later names were added of servicemen who died in the Second World War plus those civilians whose deaths were due 'to the war operations.'

Here then on this one site we have at least three reminders of lost lives of local people all of which have, at one time or another or in one way or another, been vandalised. Ironically, however, beneath them all is a larger and altogether more ancient monument which to some extent has itself been desecrated by the arrival of these later additions. Marked on maps as a tumulus, this is the Bronze Age barrow that gives its name to Burrow Hill. While there are between 30,000 and 40,000 barrows in England alone and well over 500 in Devon, this is thought to be the only one within the modern Plymouth boundaries (although it is understood that two adjacent barrows were in recent years bulldozed in the levelling out of the field here).

In this context the latin word *tumulus* means burial mound, barrow. The most common type, the bowl barrow, round with a ditch skirting its edge, was introduced to this country by the Beaker people, settlers from the Rhineland around 1800 BC, at the dawn of the Bronze Age. Certainly the bronze hoard found at Oreston in 1869 indicates a presence here around that time and finds at Mount Batten go back further still. Copper and tin, the essential components of the Bronze Age, were both obtainable in Cornwall and having been brought down the Tamar would be traded near here. Indeed, it is believed that the Mount Batten peninsula operated like a mini Hong Kong of its day with traders arriving here from all parts of Europe and the Mediterranean.

Not all deaths in these ancient communities were marked with earth or stone mounds (cairns or carns) but chieftains, particularly important ones, would have been so honoured. 'The site chosen was usually a summit from which the mound is conspicuous over a wide tract of country . . . the dead were thus set apart from the likely settlement zone . . . but interred in places where they were brought to mind, as men and women moved about the hills with the herds [Aileen Fox].' This point on Burrow Hill is then a perfect text book location, all the more so as the old lane that runs up and down the hill doubtless marks the ancient road from Mount Batten to Dartmoor.

There is, however, another name on record for this barrow--Winnowing Hill, noted by Ivy Langdon as appearing in a Plymstock Manor Survey of 1755. It was also noted by Dr. J. C. Bellamy in 1853 who recorded the ancient practice of winnowing on this site as 'a public, inalienable easement'. Winnowing is the method of separating the chaff from the grain by wind but, although it is undoubtedly as good a place as ever for this occupation, it's hard to see anyone attempting to assert that public right today.

8th November, 1986.

Mount Batten Tower

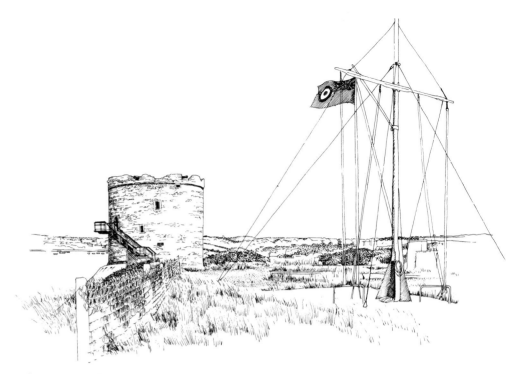

The name Mount Batten is almost contemporary with the building of the tower itself. Only the tower was commissioned by Charles II, some time in the 1660s, when the Citadel was being constructed; the purpose of both being to ensure that the people of Plymouth would not in future present a problem to the Royalist cause as they had during the Civil War ... while Mount Batten was named after Captain Batten who had fought so bravely to defend this headland for the Parliamentarians during the Civil War. A war where Englishmen fought and killed other Englishmen; where families often found themselves with divided loyalties and where even, within the two factions themselves, an act of cowardice might well result in Royalist killing Royalist, or Parliamentarian killing Parliamentarian, as indeed happened here in October 1643 when one ensign—in the face of a Royalist advance—quit his position. However for the most part the Mount here was defended valiantly and this particular piece of high ground, deemed crucial to both sides, saw intense fighting in late October and early November 1643, until eventually the surviving Parliamentarians were forced to surrender and leave the headland. Although the King's men subsequently held this position until their cause was lost and took pot shots at Plymouth from it, it would appear that little damage was done, no-one was killed although a few buildings were hit and one vane on the windmill on the Hoe was knocked off.

Apart from this windmill and the Henry VIII artillery tower at Fisher's Nose there was little or no development of the Hoe at this time. Outside the young town that grew up around Sutton Pool, the Hoe derives its name from Hawe, meaning high place, and this high ridge originally ran right down to West Hoe until quarrying at that end hacked much of it away. Across the water here at Batten this Mount was similarly far more extensive than it is today. It was only the quarrying of the limestone in the eighteenth century for agricultural use and then in the nineteenth-century for the building of the present Fort Stamford that led to the precarious situation whereby this tower now stands on the edge of a cliff. However, if one imagines the extent and overall height of this area one can see why it was known, prior to the Civil War, as Hoe Stert (Husteart, Hawe Stert); that is a high place with a headland. Today Hooe is the only area south of the Cattewatter to preserve a derivation of that name.

Meanwhile Captain Batten later became governor of this headland and was promoted to the rank of Admiral. It would appear that the original fortification at Batten was replaced by this present tower a little later. Originally furnished with a cellar and with two floors of living accommodation above, the tower has a minimum of windows and a doorway well above ground level for the sake of security. In recent years, three seventeenth-century cast-iron cannons have been hoisted up to the top of the tower. These guns are placed on reconstructed wooden truck-type carriages of the kind used on ships of that period. It is thought that in arming positions such as this weapons would have been lifted wholesale from existing ships rather than brought new from a foundry. The tower's top was built with a small magazine and a toilet for the sentry, while the thick walls contain the stairways which run from deck to deck, and originally the furnace which heated the roundshot so lethal against wooden ships.

For many years this tower was known as the Castle and the popularity of this headland, on which it stands, with nineteenth-century day-trippers from Plymouth plus the buzz of activity from local coastguards, fishermen and mariners of other descriptions, prompted the construction of the Castle Inn just below it which, for over 100 years, looked across the Cattewater. However, soon after the first flying-base was established here in 1913, the old inn became the home of Mount Batten's first Station Commander and was renamed 'Greenleaf House'. Then in 1962 it was pulled down to make way for the present Sergeants' Mess. 1962 almost saw the demolition of Batten Tower as well, when the Air Ministry claimed that the expense of saving it—primarily the bolstering up of the rocks on which it stands, which they said had become unsafe—was prohibitive, and they had no alternative but to take down this ancient edifice that during the last war was used as a water tank. However, thanks to the vigorous campaigning of local MPs, notably Sir Henry Studholme, the Old Plymouth Society and some angry Plymothians, the tower was eventually saved and, thankfully, today is in the care of the ancient monument branch of the Department of the Environment.

5th July, 1986.

Boringdon Arms—Turnchapel

There was quite a sizeable Ancient British Camp at Boringdon at one time and this, along with Wembury, was evidently granted to St. Peter of Plimton by King Edgar (957–975). Some time later the Manor of Boringdon was bought by Richard Mayhew (Mayhow) and for some 500 years it remained within the Mayhew family. Then in the 1580s Boringdon passed into the hands of the Parker family by the marriage of Frances Mayhew to John Parker. Two hundred years later the great great grandson of Edmund Parker, brother of this John Parker and also called John Parker, was created 1st Baron Boringdon. He, in turn, was succeeded in 1788 by his son John. Born in 1772, this John Parker appears to enjoy the possibly unique distinction, almost two centuries on, of having two public houses, each established in his day, bearing his Coat of Arms, but each having a different title. For in 1797, as the second Baron Boringdon, he enclosed part of Turnchapel as a dry dock and, doubtless, then gave rise to the naming of Turnchapel's main concourse, Boringdon Road, which included this inn, the 'Boringdon Arms'. Then in 1827, the year the iron bridge he

commissioned from Laira to Pomphlett was completed, we find an early reference to the newly built Morley Arms. An inn so named after the Baron's elevation to the title the 1st Earl of Morley (and Viscount Boringdon of North Molton) in 1815.

By this time the Parkers had long since moved to Saltram and the brother of the 6th Earl, great great grandson of the 1st and also named John, still has a residence there, although the Earl himself now lives in Yelverton.

Not long after the first Earl had set up the dry dock at Turnchapel, two large warships were built here by Isaac Blackburn. The *Clarence* and the *Armada*, laid down in 1809, each had 74 guns and were then the largest ships to have been built outside the dockyard at Devonport. Strangely enough, had the Admiralty been able to find someone prepared to undertake the task of building the first English stone dock in the Cattewater at Turnchapel in 1689, then the history of this area and of Devonport and Plymouth might have been quite different. However, they didn't and when, in December 1690, Robert Waters of Portsmouth was given this contract, the site was settled at Point Forward on the western side of our modern city.

Turnchapel, however, had had a long tradition of shipbuilding and it is likely that, together with the other early yards at Teat's Hill, boats that fought in the Armada were refitted here. Until recently, such traditions were still reflected, within these communities, in the naming of two local pubs, both called the 'Shipwright's'. Today only the Coxside inn remains; the Turnchapel 'Shipwright's' having recently closed. Not that that is unusual, a good many of the commercial concerns in this 'village within a town' have closed their doors in the last few decades, reflecting changes in the village's fortunes. Changes which, in part, one local, Cyril Thomas (born in No. 8 Boringdon Road 75 years ago and still living there today), puts down to the arrival of the bus service at the top of the hill. This, he says, effectively killed off the ferries which had travelled back and forth from here to the Barbican for over 80 years and which only outlasted Turnchapel's passenger railway link (1897–1951) by some 10 years.

The severing of these links, however, makes this now 'one-shop—two-pub village' quite a restful haven today, but one which may yet see a new life depending on the outcome of the various developments planned for neighbouring Hooe Lake and Mountbatten. But whatever happens Nigel Smith, his wife and in-laws, who arrived at the 'Boringdon Arms' last year with a good deal of catering experience previously gained in Leamington and Norfolk, are determined that this pub, far from closing, is going to grow. The building, they believe, once housed the Quarrymaster and was built around 1760. No longer worked today, and fondly remembered, by the writer J. C. Trewin, for their scaly spleenwort fern, part of these quarries form the backdrop to Boringdon Road and may yet afford the pub an attractive beer garden.

Meanwhile, Turnchapel itself may yet prove an attractive proposition to many Plymothians who perhaps do not even know at present how to get there.

8th March, 1986.

Staddon Heights

'In the month of May, Staddon Heights may be explored to much advantage; not by an undeviating march along the beaten footway, but by penetrating into the bosom of every bushy glen, and wandering quietly over the smooth carpets of sandy beach which interrupt the bold rocky margin.'

So began five pages of gushing prose describing the delights of Staddon Heights in an edition of the *South Devon Monthly Museum* from the summer of 1833. Today, it is not unknown for stray golf balls to penetrate into bushy glens . . . Back in those days though the idea of siting a golf course here would have been almost inconceivable. After all there were then no seaside courses outside Scotland, indeed apart from at Blackheath, which was an extension of the Royal Court, there was little golf at all played south of the border.

In Scotland itself reliable documentary evidence of the game goes back much further; in March 1457 'goff' was prohibited by an Act of Parliament, one of several such acts during the century. It was feared that the compulsory sport of archery might be neglected. However, James IV himself was known to play the game and Mary, daughter of James V and later Queen of Scots, is said to have founded St. Andrews, the first royal course. Mary is also credited with being the one who brought into general usage the term 'cadets' to describe pupil players: the word later evolved into 'caddie'.

However popular the game may have been with Scottish Royalty and other members of society in the sixteenth century, it was of course bowls that Francis Drake and his fellow naval officers played overlooking Plymouth Sound in 1588. Three hundred years later, however, golf was beginning to catch on in this country and by 1904 senior naval officers were regularly to be found playing golf here overlooking that same stretch of water. From here though they could see much further along the English Channel.

The exact origins of golf are quite obscure. China, Italy, Scandinavia and Holland are among those claiming the earliest known form of the game, dating as far back as the second century BC. The popular theory in Scotland though is that the game began with shepherds using their crooks to knock pebbles into rabbit holes. Early, formal golf balls tended to be made of boxwood, then came leather balls stuffed with feathers and in 1848 the famous 'guttie' or gutta-percha ball was introduced. The modern rubber-cored ball was not devised until 1899, the year tees were first used, but it wasn't until 1902 that rubber-cored balls went into general circulation.

By this time the Commander-in-Chief, Plymouth had already expressed concern at the lack of golf facilities in the immediate area and a nine-hole course was laid out on War Department land at Staddon Heights. Every officer's mess in the port was to share the expenses. So was born the United Services Golf Club, the President of which was always to be the Commander-in-Chief, Plymouth. The War Department had for years owned vast areas of land around Staddon and the area is littered with defence works that form the last south-eastern links in Palmerston's famous defensive chain around Plymouth, Stonehouse and Devonport.

For more than 60 years the club survived here as the United Services Golf Club. However, within the first ten years there were a few civilian members and by 1925

there were more civilian than service members. And yet it was not until 1968–9 that service personnel lost their preferential treatment, a move which followed the purchase of the club from the War Department by the now very large civilian membership. With this change came the new name, the Staddon Heights Golf Club. This move also led, indirectly, to the removal of cattle from the course, a feature which had previously been regarded as a natural hazard as a local farmer had grazing rights here.

The irony of all this being that the name Staddon itself is said to derive from 'stot-dun' meaning, literally, 'the bullock hill'.

Cattle weren't the only source of trouble here however. The changing demands of the RAF caused substantial course alterations in the past; then during the Second World War an estimated 150 craters were made on the course by enemy action. And there were always the stray picnic parties, particularly prevalent in the days when the Turnchapel ferry service offered the quickest escape from Plymouth for thousands of day trippers. It was also, incidentally, the route many golfers took to get to the course.

Sporting some of the finest views of almost any course in the world, Staddon has, in recent years, considerably improved upon its 19th hole, the Clubhouse. The view here is taken from the balcony of the new building which was opened three years ago by George Smale. Son of a pre-First World War steward of the Club, George, who celebrated his 90th birthday recently, was club professional here for over 50 years.

As with most other sporting clubs in Plymouth, however, Staddon has yet to produce a champion of national acclaim. Perhaps one day the establishment of a municipal course at Saltram, something which has been on the cards for years, will go some way to rectifying this situation.

18th June, 1988.

Plymouth Breakwater

'It was noon; the military were assembled, in gorgeous display on the grand parade at Mount Wise, to do honour to the natal day of their Prince; the ships and vessels at anchor, in the Sound were decorated with colours, over which waved, in lustre and dignity, the Royal Standard . . . a vast assemblage of spectators, in their gayest attire filled the grand parade, and crowded every eminence, far and near, that could command a view of the beautiful scene. It was a delightful day too: the glorious sun poured forth his beams in all their splendour . . .' So ran a contemporary account of 12th August 1812, and the occasion for which all this pomp and ceremony had been arranged was the laying of the first of the hundreds and hundreds of thousands of stones that eventually made up the 3½- to 4-million-ton deposit that is known as PIymouth Breakwater. It was also the fiftieth birthday of the Prince Regent, George Augustus Frederick, who became George IV eight years later.

The order for the construction of the Breakwater had actually been given by the Prince Regent's Council in June of the previous year and the Admiralty had immediately given John Rennie (Snr) the go ahead to produce detailed plans. Rennie, together with Joseph Whidbey, the other chief engineer of the scheme, had been working together on the project since 1806. After consulting with a number of civil, military and naval authorities they had four main plans to consider. All of them, however, involved the construction of piers; from Penlee Point 1,040 yards out and sheltering Cawsand; from Staddon Point out a massive 2,640 yards to Panther Rock; from Audurn Point to Shovel Rock, approximately the middle of the present Breakwater and representing a distance of some 1,700 yards and finally the longest of the lot, 2,920 yards from Audurn Point to Panther Rock.

A problem with all of these schemes would have been the inevitable problem of silting and so ultimately the plan that was put forward was for a free-standing, solid breakwater along the line of Panther, Shovel and St. Carlos Rocks with a complementary pier of around 400 yards from either Staddon or Audurn Point. In the event this secondary pier was never constructed and indeed the main Breakwater was not finally approved until a number of other schemes had been considered, including the mooring to the rocks of 117 huge wooden frames and the dropping of 140 hollow stone towers fifty feet high to be laid in two rows and later filled with stones to weigh them down. A similar scheme to this last one however had already, unsuccessfully, been tried at Cherbourg 30 years or so earlier. Not that the idea of dropping a stone rubble breakwater was anything new as John Rennie junior, a noted engineer in his own right (he helped complete the Breakwater with Whidbey after

his father's death in 1821 and was also responsible for the Victualling Yard) observed: 'The foundations of the moles of Tyre and Carthage are said to have been made in this manner.' The Greeks and Romans used similar methods of constructing and Kingstown (Ireland) and Holyhead (Wales) both antedate the Plymouth Breakwater.

Throughout the early stages of the Breakwater construction, Whidbey always favoured a 1-in-3 stone gradient at the front of the surface line and 1-in-2 behind it. In practice, however, the sea repeatedly wore the front gradient to Rennie senior's preferred 1-in-5 slope and that is how it is today beneath the waves. In addition to this work incidentally Rennie senior's credits include many other harbour and dock works, including the London and East India Docks, Southwark Bridge, the old Waterloo Bridge and the Bell Rock Lighthouse.

Although not officially completed until 1841 and although work has continued to be done on the Breakwater over the years its benefits were very early felt. A mile long and 120 yards wide above the sea, its promenade 16 yards wide, the Breakwater is mainly straight with its two wings inclining to the middle at angles of about 120 degrees. Substantially constructed with 30 acres of stone from Oreston and around the Cattewater, which was for the most part transported by the world's first rail ferries, the Breakwater was a phenomenal undertaking.

Originally it was to have two lighthouses then in 1820 Rennie snr. produced designs for a lighthouse and beacon, but these weren't erected until 1843–5 by which time Whidbey was also dead. Whidbey had overseen most of the work, up until his death in 1835, from Bovisand House. Bovisand Pier, below Staddon Point here, had been completed in 1824 for the shelter of the working men and boats. In the 1860s it was built on to with the construction of Bovisand Fort, one of Palmerston's defensive ring of establishments which included the Breakwater Fort (an idea first mooted back in 1820 by the Duke of Wellington).

Abandoned by the military in 1956, since the early 1970s Bovisand Fort has been developed by two men, Alan Bax and Jim Gill, into a Diving Centre of world renown. The largest underwater centre in Europe, here both recreational and commercial diving is taught, many people coming purely for a diving holiday. With accommodation for up to 120 visitors and enjoying superb views above and below the water, the centre has prospered, thanks to the increasing demand for diving workmen on the world's oil rigs and thanks also to the large number of shipwrecks dotted around this famous harbour.

22nd August, 1987.

Postscript

Rather than attempt to ensure that all the information on the foregoing pages is correct up to one particular point in time I have, as before, decided to let the pieces stand as they were originally published. There follow however a few notes concerning one or two major changes, original inaccuracies, obvious omissions and points of interest.

Latimer Trend   Among the productions not mentioned in the article are, of course, the two volumes of *Plymouth – As Time Draws On.*

Southside Street   Parade Printing Works was sold not long after this article appeared and, after major refurbishment, two new shops appeared on the ground floor and the rest of the building was converted into flats. Meanwhile the neighbouring 'Maritime' public house has since doubled in size, taking over premises at the rear, fronting on to the Parade, and Archie Roberts and his mother, Mabel, have since moved to the 'United Services Inn'.

Jacka's Bakery   The oldest commercially working bakery in Great Britain has indeed now changed hands and is run by one of the youngest and biggest commercially working bakers in Britain – Roger Compton.

Looe Street   I am informed by Stanley Goodman of the Old Plymouth Society that Drake lived at the bottom of Looe Street and not the top as stated and as commemorated by the presence of a plaque. He attributes this mistake to someone, at some stage, reading an old map on the street upside down.

Ebrington Street Nissen Huts   These are not, as thought, the sole surviving Nissen huts in the city. There are others; there are two by the School of Navigation.

Central Library   Wyn George's mural is no longer visible.

Phoenix Way   Following the appearance of this article in the Herald, G. Bowyer from James Street, Devonport, wrote in to Postbag and threw welcome light on the story of the 'Phoenix'. It transpires that the figure was the work of Plymouth sculptor Samuel Trevenan (to whom the correspondent's father was apprenticed between 1893–1898) and that it is in fact an eagle. 'This bird originally surmounted the conical tower at the eastern end of the old municipal buildings on the north side of the Guildhall Square and can clearly be seen on contemporary photographs'. The writer then goes on to lament the vandalism that has blighted the bird over the years and suggests that 'the vacant plinth on the gable apex of the (erstwhile) City Treasury at the east end of the Guildhall' would be a suitable place for it – putting it virtually 'back home' again!

The letter also noted that a statue of Sir Francis Drake once stood on this plinth but was removed after it was found to be unsafe, and the question was mooted 'where is this statue now?'

Civic Centre   The Lord High Steward is not in fact an agent of the Crown, rather it is an office that carries 'great dignity and some influence, but ... practically no duties or emoluments.'

I received a letter rightly pointing out that Viscount Astor was Lord Mayor on more than one occasion—but his terms of office ran consecutively. George Creber's did not. However although listed as having been Mayor twice, George Creber's second term of office was really a quirk of administration. It arose out of local government reorganization when certain powers were transferred from Plymouth City to Devon County Council. As this changeover was effected George Creber, then leader of Plymouth City Council, held the office of Lord Mayor for a few hours on the morning of 1st April, 1974.

Armada Way   As the City celebrated the 400th Anniversary of the Armada, the pedestrianisation of Armada Way was almost complete. However it is open to debate whether its present form is quite as glorious as Paton-Watson might have hoped.

The Odeon   The answer to the question posed here for the time being at least is ... a disco/nightclub called 'Monroes'.

Edgcumbe Street Stonehouse   The buildings in this scene have now all been demolished.

Victualling Office Tavern   It turns out that the picture of Victoria referred to is a comparatively recent addition.

Tamar High School   John R. Goodall wrote to Postbag from Seasalter in Kent after this article appeared and said '. . . as one who joined Tamar School as a new boy in September 1939, my memory is quite clear that at that time the school had been transferred to Johnston Terrace and I never attended the military hospital building. At this time the Johnston Terrace building was jointly used by Tamar and another school, which, if memory serves me right, was Camel's Head . . . ,

'. . . When the Johnston Terrace building was destroyed by bombing, Tamar was accommodated at North Prospect and it was from this site . . . that the school was evacuated . . .'

The correspondent also thought that the two temporary members of staff were probably not temporary at all – Mr. Johns and Mr. Stribley.

The sad news now for all old boys and girls of the school is that it rather looks as though it will close in the very near future.

Devonport High School   More wartime recollections were stimulated by this piece and V. G. Saundercock wrote in from Colebrook to expand on the experiences of Stoke Senior Boy's School . . . 'I was one of the many boys who moved from York Street Junior School after the summer holidays of 1939 to Stoke Senior Boys' School.

Within a short time we were moved out and into King Street School, Devonport.

Unfortunately with the girls in situ, there were far too many of us to be accommodated there at the same time so a shift system was arranged, boys from 9 a.m., to 1 p.m., girls 1 p.m., to 5 p.m., changing around each week. This worked fairly well until the blitz then we had no school at all. It was several months before a master came around telling parents that Cornwall Street School had been opened. Once again this proved to be too small and a few rooms that survived the bombing at York Street School were used to accommodate us. This was short lived and once again we moved, this time to the Devonport High School for Boys – they had been evacuated – at the top of Albert Road Devonport.

I left in 1942 . . . Mr. Kitt was the headmaster.'

New Pier Inn A letter from Albert E. Grose who was born in what was No. 54 James Street, directly opposite the pub, followed this article. Full of reminiscences of James Street and surrounding area, one shop was recalled which 'sold hot Udder and Tripe' and which 'was greatly patronized at lunch times by the very poor who would perforce make a meal from a pennyworth of either one of the foods, and which again was busy in the evenings'.

St. Levan Road Viaduct Other articles, St. Aubyn Church, St. Levan Gate, etc., clear up this so called 'mystery' caused by a momentary lapse of reason on the part of the author as noted by more than one correspondent.

Ham House B. Wilkinson, formerly LAC Clarke of the WAAFS, from West Park, wrote to say that I did not mention that during the last war Ham House was used as '934 Squadron Balloon Barrage Headquarters'.

Burrington The school was officially opened in 1961. However, as J. L. Williams (deputy head 1958–83) pointed out in Postbag, the school effectively opened three years earlier with Bill Button as its head. Meanwhile another former Burrington master, Gerald Durston, dropped me a line to say the school motto did not come from the arms of the Were family but rather was 'imported' from South Africa from a school in which Gerald had previously taught. In the last few months it has been my pleasure to design a badge, tie and school colours and to suggest a new motto for the new comprehensive school, the John Kitto School, to be based on this site. I am only sad that Mike Bender, a very popular teacher at the school, will not see any of the changes he had hoped for. From the first meeting I attended at Burrington as a school governor he always insisted that I should cover Burrington in 'As Time Draws On'. Tragically he died in the same week that I wrote the article.

Lord Seaton Soon after this article appeared, the swords referred to were stolen along with many other valuable items and although much of the haul was subsequently retrieved, much wanton vandalism and unnecessary upset occurred. Fortunately the police felt there was no possible link between the publicity generated via the *Herald* and the theft.

Fursdon Barn Tony Tucker subsequently informed me that the two lines of square holes weren't there for ventilation at all, rather they were there for the birds— pigeons mainly.

Far Post Club Currently no less than 75 player cartoons appear above the bar, almost all of which escaped damage when the Club's flat roof caved in after collecting a huge amount of rainwater.

Peverell Park Methodist Church While William may have been the last of the male Chapell-Hodges, Joyce Knight wrote to say that 'A Miss Chapple-Hodge, probably his daughter, lived at Crapstone and rode a motorbike during the last war . . . She told me she used to live at Pounds House'.

Plymouth High School for Girls At one time there was a mixed infants' school here in which the Right Hon. Michael Foot was a pupil.

Prison Hill Stanley Pearce was on duty in the building when the bomb fell – amazed that he survived, he says there was a story that the bomb later did explode when it was being disposed of on the moor, killing members of the disposal squad that were with it.

Bibliography

Abbreviations: *WEH—Western Evening Herald*; *WMN—Western Morning News*; *Trans PI*—Transactions of the Plymouth Institution; *Trans DA*—Transactions of the Devonshire Association; ALC—Arthur L. Clamp, Publisher; PLHL—copy in Plymouth Local History Library.

Dates when known are those of editions referred to.

The Admiral MP . . ., A. J. Collins, *South Devon Times* (28.6.1974)

Anchor Development, H. L. Dove, Naval Architect (July 1972)

Anchored For Good, Bill Anderson, *Devonport News* (April 1980)

Anchors, Bronze Age, Stone Age, Honor Frost, *Marriners Mirror* (Nov 1970)

Ancient Stone Crosses of Devon Pt. 1, E. Masson-Phillips, Tavistock (June 1937)

Armada Memorial Proposals, Henry J. Waring, Mayor, Plymouth (April 1888)

Barbican, The, and its People Remembered, Arthur L. Clamp, ALC (1985)

The Bear's Head and Queen Anne's Battery, *The Perambulator*, South Devon Monthly Museum (1.12.1835)

Biographia Navalis, John Charnock, London (1798)

Boniface of Devon, John Cyril Sladden, Jarrold (1975)

Borough of Crabtree, A History of the Mayor & Corporation, John Webb, *Doidge's Almanac* (1882)

Brunel's Royal Albert Bridge, Thomas Bowden & Bernard Mills, Peter Watts (1983)

Brymon and the History of Plymouth Airport, Malcolm Ginsberg (1.10.1984)

Budshead, St Budeaux, G. W. Copeland, Plymouth (undated, 19—)

Burrow Hill, Ivy Langdon, *Plymstock Chronicle* (April 1972)

Business Houses of Plymouth Vols 1 & 2, W. J. Power, typescript PLHL (1982)

Captain Robert Falcon Scott, RN, L. M. Forbes, Plymouth (1965)

Chamber of Commerce First Report, Henry Woollcombe (1814)

Chiropodist, Department of Health and Social Security (revised ed. Feb 1982)

Church of St Nicholas, A Short History, BCJR, Plymouth, C-i-C (19—)

Citadel—A History of the Royal Citadel, F. W. Woodward. Devon Books (1987)

City of Plymouth, European Architectural Heritage Year, City Planning Officer (1975)

Cookworthy, A Man of No Common Clay, Douglas Selleck, Baron Jay, Plymouth (1978)

Corinthian, Jeremy Greenaway (1977)

Crabtree Limeworks, J. W. Perkins, *Devon & Cornwall Notes & Queries* (1968–70)

Crownhill Fort, the Significance of, Dr. David Evans (1986)

Crownhill, Reflections, Arthur L. Clamp, ALC (198–)

Crownhill, Story of a Crossroads, Crispin Gill

Days in Devonport, Parts I–VII, Gerald W. Barker, ALC (1982–5)

Day's Diving Disaster, Frank Beer, ALC Plymouth (1982)

Devon and Cornwall, Early Tours in, ed R. Pearse Chope 1918, David & Charles (1968)

Devonport Dockyard Story, K. V. Burns, *Maritime* (1984)

Devonport, Hail and Farewell to, F. S. Blight, *Trans PI*, xii (1951)

Devonport, History of, R. N. Worth, W. Brendon (1870)

Devonport, Inns and Beer Houses of, 2 vols, Henry Horwill, manuscript PLHL (1975)

Devonport, Official Guide to, Burrows (190–)

Devonport Services R.F.C., A History 1912–81, T. Fraser-Dunbar (1981)

Devonport, Stoke and Morice Town, Stonehouse & Plymouth, John Sanford (1830)

Documents Relating to Manadon, West Devon Record Office, Plymouth

The Drainage of Town, A. Hamilton Bampton, Plymouth & Devonport (1849)

Drake's Island, Mayflower Centre Trust (198–)

Drake's Island, a Brief History of, P. J. Mowan, Old Plymouth Soc (1951)

Efford, J. Hopkinson, Efford (July 1977)

Elburton, Ten Farms of, Arthur L, Clamp, ALC (1981)

Elburton, The Making of a Village, Arthur L. Clamp, ALC (198–)

Elize Hele, Winslow Jones, *Trans DA* (August 1889)

Emmanuel, The Parish of, Compton Gifford, Roy Harris, Church (1970)

English Terraced House, Stefan Muthesius, Yale University Press (1982)

Fighters of the Old Cosmo, A History of Plymouth Boxing, 1907–24, Clive Mumford (1975)

Fire-Fighting in Plymouth, the Early Days 1673–1959

Floating Bridge at Saltash, I. M. Rendel, Plan (1831)

The Four Ark Royals, Michael Apps, William Kimbel (1976)

Gardens of Saltram House, Mary Crosse, *Devon Life* (May 1983)

Gateway to Cornwall, Joan Rendall, Bossiney Books (1981)

Gaumont Palace, Grand Opening Programme (16.11.1931)

George Rundle Prynne, A. Clifton Kelway, Longmans, Green & Co (1905)

Greenbank Hospital, Hilda Mary Goodman, Plymouth (1977)

Ham, An Account of, G. W. Copeland, Plymouth (1947)

Ham, Field Meeting Report, *Trans DA*, Vol. 72 (1940)

Hamoaze The Meaning of, Phoenicians in the West, Rev Worthington-Jukes, typescript, PLHL

Higher Stoke & Milehouse, a Short History of, David Ayres, Plymouth (1965)

HM Naval Base Devonport, Historic Architecture of, Jonathan Coad, National Maritime Museum (1983)

HMS Drake, Wardroom Mess (Dec 1973)

HMS Thunderer, Geoffrey Penn, K. Mason (1984)

The Hoe, Chatty Joe, *Doidge's Almanac*, Plymouth (1882)

Honicknowle Remembered, Arthur L. Clamp ALC (198–)

Hooe, The Story of, R. H. C. Fice, *South Devon Times* (26.2.1960)

Hooe and Turnchapel Remembered, Arthur L. Clamp ALC (1981)

Inn Signs, Introduction to, Eric R. Delderfield, Pan (1971)

It Came to Our Door, H. P. Twyford, Underhill (1946)

John Colborne, The Life of, G. C. Moore-Smith, John Murray (1903)

John Macbride Esq., *Naval Chronicle*, Vol 19 (1808)

Kelly's Devonshire, Directory also published by White & Billings (1856–1928)

Kings Ships Vol. 3, Halton Stirling, Horace Lecky, Muirhead (1914)

The Law Courts, Plymouth, Geoff Clarke, Latimer Trend & Co (1963)

The Libraries, Public and Private, of Plymouth, W. H. K. Wright, Library Assoc (190–)

London and South Devon Railway Vol 2, R. A. Williams, David & Charles (1973)

The Lonely Sea and the Sky, Francis Chichester, Hodder & Stoughton (1964)

Lord Morley's Flying Bridge, Keith S. Perkins, *Rendel's News* (1982)

Making of a Cornish Town, Gladys & F. L. Harris, Torpoint Town Council (1976)

Manadon, Desmond Wettern, Navy (Dec 1970)

Manadon, G. W. Copeland, Plymouth (undated 19—)

Mannamead School, Story of, C. R. Serpell (1945)

Mount Batten, Archaeology of, Cynthia Gaskell-Brown (March 1985)

Mount Batten, the Story of, Arthur L. Clamp ALC (198–)

Mount Edgcumbe, a Walk Around, W. Byers (1836)

Mount Edgcumbe, Duprez's Visitors Guide to, W. H. K. Wright, Duprez (1871)

Mount Edgcumbe Park, William Crossing, Hoyten & Cole (18—)

Mount Edgcumbe, Survey, Colin Griffin, Cornwall (1983–84)

Mr Jacka the Baker, Mark Brayshay, *Devon Life* (April 1984)

Old Devon Bridges, Charles Henderson & E. Jervoise (1938)

Old Plymouth, Sybil Jerram, *WMN* Book (1913)

Old Plymouth, Ecclestiastical History of, J. Brooking Rowe (1876)

Old Plymouth, Nooks and Corners of, John McDonald (1883)

Old Plymouth, New Light on, James Barber, Plymouth Atheneum, Vol. lV (19—)

Old Plymouth, Streets of, C. Eldred & W. H. K. Wright (1901)

Old Plymouth, Views of, Sarah Foot, Bossiney Books (1983)

Oreston and Its People Remembered, Arthur L. Clamp ALC (198–)

Palmerston's Follies, John Babbs, manuscript PLHL (1980)

Parish of Charles with St Mathias, John G. Byrnell (March 1964)

Pennycross, Story of, Robert Groves (1964)

Peverell Park Methodist Church 1896–1986, Leslie Jenkins Plymouth (1987)

Pictorial Plymouth, Robert K. Dent. J. J. Allday (1900)

Plan for Plymouth, A. J. Paton-Watson & Patrick Abercrombie, City Council (1943)

Playbill, A History of Theatre in the Westcountry, Harvey Crane, McDonald Evans (1980)

Plymouth, History of, Llewellyn Jewitt, W. H. Luke (1873)

Plymouth, History of, John Harris, typescript PLHL (1808)

Plymouth, A History of, C. W. Bracken, SR (reprint) (1931/70)

Plymouth Albion R.F.C., Centenary Handbook, History Roy Watson (1976)

Plymouth, Ancient Heraldry of, some notes, R. N. Worth, Journal PI (1877)

Plymouth and Devonport Guide with Sketches, H. E. Carrington, Byers & Son (1838)

Plymouth and Devonport in Times of War and Peace, H. Whitfeld, Plymouth (1900)

Plymouth and Its Polytechnic, Report for PPSU, David Brunskill & Barbara Courtney-Wildman (1978)

Plymouth and Plymothians Photographs & Memories, Andrew Cluer, Lantern Books (1974)

Plymouth and Plymothians more Photographs & Memories, Andrew Cluer, Lantern Books (1975)

Plymouth and the West, Early Newspapers in, James L. Palmer, *Trans PI* Vol XIX (1944)

Plymouth and District Illustrated Commercial Guide, W. H. K. Wright

Plymouth, the Ancient Buildings of, G. W. Copeland & E. N. Masson-Phillips, Old Plymouth Soc (1958)

Plymouth, A New History of, Vols I & II, Crispin Gill, David & Charles (1979)

Plymouth, Arms of, Chris J. Smith, *Standard Triumph Review* (1961)

Plymouth's Bicentenary (Synagogue), Edgar R. Samuel, *The Jewish Chronicle* (9.6.1961)

Plymouth Blitz, The Story of the Raids, F. Crisp & H. P. Twyford *WMN* (194–)

Plymouth Blitz, S. M. Green & R. F. O. Cock, *Western Independent* (194–)

Plymouth Blitz, the Story of, Frank Wintle, Bossiney (1981)

Plymouth, Book of Reference, F. E. Sach, F. E. Sach & Co (1916)

Plymouth Buildings of Architectural & Historical Interest, City of Plymouth/DOE

Plymouth Cathedral, souvenir booklet, (undated 19—)

Plymouth Churches, Layman's View of Same, 2 vols, W. J. Power, typescript PLHL (1977)

Plymouth College, Ten Decades of Growth, John Spear, Plymouth College (1977)

Plymouth Daily Newspapers and Their Founders, James L. Palmer, *Trans PI* (1946)

Plymouth Dartmoor Etc, Place Names of, W. Best Harris, W. Best Harris (1983)

Plymouth, Devonport & Stonehouse, The Strangers Handbook to (1842)

Plymouth, Devonport, Stonehouse etc. Handbook of, Henry Besley (186–)

Plymouth, Devonport & Stonehouse (Post Office) Directories of (between 1812–1955) various publishers

Plymouth, Devonport, Stonehouse & South West Devon, various editions, Ward Lock (18—)

Plymouth, Devonport, Stonehouse, Wood's Handbook to, various editions, W. Wood (18—)

Plymouth Division Royal Marines, Col. R. D. Ormsby, Globe Laurel (1930)

Plymouth Dock Guide Etc, The, Hoxland, Dock/Devonport (1792)

Plymouth Friaries, New Light on the, Jennifer Barber, *Trans DA*, Vol 105 (1973)

Plymouth's golden Age of Trams, Arthur L. Clamp, ALC (1985)

Plymouth Health Authority, *Evening Herald 'Citizen's Guide'* (1984)

Plymouth, Heard its first telephone conversation, A. G. K. Leonard, *WEH* (1952)

Plymouth High School, History of, J. Turner (July 1954)

Plymouth's Historic Barbican, Arthur L. Clamp, ALC (1985)

Plymouth's Historic Hoe, Arthur L. Clamp, ALC (1985)

Plymouth's Historic Synagogue, M. E. G. (undated 196–)

Plymouth, History of, R. N. Worth, William Brendon & Son (1890)

Plymouth in old picture postcards, Mary M. Devonport, European Library (1985)

Plymouth in Pictures, Crispin Gill, David & Charles (1968)

Plymouth, Industrial Architecture of, ed Cynthia Gaskell-Brown, Plymouth City Museum (1980)

Plymouth Institutions in the 1861 Census, W. N. Bryant, *Devon & Cornwall Notes & Queries*, Vol XXXV (1982–86)

Plymouth Libraries, Arthur Maddison, The Municipal Review (June 1965)

Plymouth Library, Architectural Notes, H. J. W. Stirling (1956)

Plymouth Memoirs, Dr James Yonge (1647–1721), ed John J. Beckerlegge (1951)

Plymouth Methodist Central Hall (1940–65), Silver Jubilee brochure, various authors (1965)

Plymouth Municipal Records, ed R. N. Worth, Plymouth (1893)

Plymouth Naval War Memorial 1939–45, Imperial War Graves Commission, London (1924)

Plymouth's New Central Library, W. Best Harris, *Library Association Record* Vol 88 no 11 (Nov 1956)

Plymouth Old and New, Owen A. Baker, EP Publishing (1976)

Plymouth – 100 Years of Street Travel, R. C. Sambourne, Glasney Press (198–)

Plymouth's Past Through Postcards, Guy Fleming, ALC (1985)

Plymouth Polytechnic, thesis, Avril Hodge (March 1978)

Plymouth, A Portrait, J. C. Trewin, Robert Hale (1973)

Plymouth Public School, CWB, *WMN and Mercury* (10.9.25)

Plymouth's Ships of War, Lt. Com K. V. Burns, Greenwich (1972)

Plymouth Steam 1954–63, Ian H. Lane, Ian Allen (1984)

Plymouth, Stonehouse & Devonport Illustrated, Handbook to, W. H. K. Wright, W. H. Luke (1879)

Plymouth, Stonehouse & Devonport, Nettleton's Guide to, George Wightwick, E. Nettleton (1838)

Plymouth, Story of, R. A. J. Walling, Westaway (1950)

Plymouth, Story of, for young and old, W. H. K. Wright, A. Wheaton & Co (18—)

Plymouth's Synagogue, History of, Rabbi Dr B. Susser (1962)

Plymouth Theatres & Cinemas, P. F. Ghillyer & W. J. Power, typescript PLHL (1983)

Plymouth, The Book of, John Gerrard, Barracuda (1982)

Plymouth Through the Lens, Vols. 1–3, Brian Moseley, Plymouth (1985–87)

Plympton Erle, A History of, J. Brooking-Rowe, James G. Commin (1906)

Plympton Grammar School, A Short History, Brian Moseley (Oct 1967)

Plympton, History Beginnings of, R. N. Worth, Plymouth (1887)

Plympton St Mary, J. Mercer-Cox, Plympton (19—)

Plympton St Maurice Guide, Audrey F. Mills, Civic Association (1981)

Plymstock Area, Recollections of, Dorothy Warley Pitt, Plymouth (1985)

Plymstock in Perspective, Arthur L. Clamp, ALC (1982)

Post School Education in the Three Towns 1825–1975 , ed Alston Kennerley, Learning Resources Centre (1976)

Private Papers of Hore-Belisha, Leslie Hore-Belisha, Collins (1960)

Proposed Civic Centre for Plymouth, H. J. W. Stirling, *Municipal Journal* (12.11.1954)

Public School, A History of, Muriel Graham, *WEH* (5.3.1983)

Radford House, Vanished Glories of, G. W. Copeland, *WEH* (1954)

Raglan Barracks, *Navy and Army Illustrated* (1.5.1896)

Rattles to Radio, Ernest Dickaty, typescript PLHL (1977)

Reconstruction Committee Minutes, Plymouth (15.12.1947)

Register of the Names Inscribed on the Naval War Memorial Erected at Port of Plymouth, by Imperial War Graves Commission, London (1924)

Royal Chapel of St Katherine Upon Upon the Hoe, booklet (1965)

Royal Citadel, Arthur L. Clamp, ALC (198–)

Royal Naval Hospital Plymouth, History of, Surg Capt P. D. Gordon Pugh (1972)

The Royal Navy, Wm Laird Clowes, London (1899)

St Budeaux, H. Montagu Evans, *Trans PI* (1913)

St Budeaux, Growth of Through Peace & War, Rev T. A. Hancock, *WEH* (23.1.34)

St Budeaux, Historic Treasures, Rev T. A. Hancock, *WEH* (16.2.1934)

St Budeaux, the Ancient Parish of, Marshall Ware, ALC (1983)

St Budeaux, Yesterday's Village, Marshall Ward (1982)

St Dunstan's Abbey, prospectus (1987)

St Dunstan's Abbey School, The History of, Margaret Teresa, Plymouth (1928)

St Edward, King & Martyr, Christopher Wood, G. Cumming (1959)

St Gabriel's, Story of, George Manuell, Plymouth (Nov 1978)

St Judes Church, A Story of, Clifford Tretheway, Parish Church (1976)

St Mary's Church, Tamerton Foliot, P. S. Bebbington (1981)

St Peter's, Plymouth 1850–1950, B. M. Vere, Church (1950)

St Simon, Mount Gould, The First Sixty Years, Gordon Brayley, Plymouth (1967)

Saints of Cornwall Part 2, Gilbert H. Doble, Cornwall (1962)

Selevan, the Fisherman Saint, Richard Angove, *Cornish Life* (Feb 1985)

Sherwell Story, Stanley Griffin, Plymouth (1964)

Ship's Figureheads, Peter Norton, David & Charles (1976)

Sir Francis Drake and the 'Golden Hinde', Alex A. Cummin, Jarrold (1975)

Sir William Morice, C. W. Bracken, *Devon & Cornwall, Notes & Queries*, Vol 21 (1940–41)

Smeaton's Tower and the Breakwater, L. H. Merrett, Graphritre (19—)

Some Medieval Devon Coroners, RBM, *Devon & Cornwall Notes & Queries* (1935)

South Devon & East Cornwall Hospital, George Wightwick, *Architectural Magazine* Vol VII (1836)

Southway, One Hundred Years of, ed Peter M. Bindschedler, Plymouth (1981)

Staddon Heights in May, JB, *South Devon Monthly Museum* (1833)

Stoke & Morice Town, F. S. Blight, *Trans PI*, vol XXII (1951)

Stonehouse, Archaeological Survey, Cynthia Gaskell-Brown, Plymouth (1975)

Stonehouse, Early History, R. N. Worth, *Journal of the Plymouth Institution* (Nov 1886)

Stories from Plymouth's History, W. Best Harris, W. Best Harris (1985)

Stuart Road Higher Grade School, an 'Old Boy' 1893–98, typescript (1960)

Sutton Harbour, Crispin Gill, Sutton Harbour Improvement Co (1976)

Tamar Secondary School, A History 1930–1958, H. W. A. Warren (1958)

Tamerton Foliot, Arthur L. Clamp, ALC (198–)

Tamerton Foliot Village, II, Portrait of, Betty Bryant and Arthur L. Clamp, ALC (198–)

Technical Colleges in the Three Towns, Terry J. Bickford and Digby Hole, Learning Resources (1976)

Theatre Royal, Plymouth, Building Study, Peter Moro Partnership (1982)

The English Inn, Thomas Burke, Herbert Jenkins (1948)

The Inn, Explorer's Guide, Frank Bottomley, Kaye & Ward (1984)

The Obsolete Plymouth Manors of Sutton Pyll, C. W. Bracken, *Trans DA* Vol 74 (1942)

A Torch in Flame, Henry Whitfeld, *Devon Books* (1987)

Toucher & Rubs (Bowles), Humphrey J. Dingley, Glasgow (1893)

Transport Bygones in the Plymouth Area, Sydney V. C. Goodmann, ALC (1984)

Turnchapel, Gordon Hines, *South Devon Times* (21.1.1965)

Twelve Men of Plymouth, Gerald Hamilton Edwards, Plymouth (1951)

Tything of Compton Gifford, R. N. Worth, *Trans DA*, Vol. 28 (1896)

Unitarianism in Plymouth, Minister & Trustees, *South Western Press* (1958)

United Services – Staddon Heights Golf Club, Jack Urrell, typescript (1972)

Universal British Directory of Trade, Commerce and Manufacture, Champante & Whitrow (1798)

Vanishing Plymouth, Brian Moseley, B. S. Moseley (1982)

Vanishing Street Furniture, Geoffrey Warren, David & Charles (1978)

Water from the Moor, David J. Hawkings, *Devon Books* (1987)

Western Morning News, History of, supplement *WMN* (4.1.1960)

White's 1850 Devon, William White, David & Charles (reprint) (1850/1968)

Widey Court, G. W. Copeland, *Trans DA* (1955)

William Cookworthy, John Penderill-Church, Bradford Barton (1972)

William Cookworthy, Theodore Compton, London (1895)

Unlisted but rich in information are: the many street and survey maps of Plymouth—Several of which are available as prints from Plymouth Local History Library or Museum; various editions of, *Doidges Almanac* which were produced between 1868–1955 and the 'Christmas Cheer' booklets that followed it for some years; countless newspapers and magazine articles; souvenir programmes; advertising brochures; a variety of general reference volumes, books of facts and encyclopedias; census returns, old telephone directories and electoral registers. Copies of which can generally be found in the local history or reference rooms of Plymouth City Library.

There follows a list of just some of the articles used, credited where possible.

Army That Refused to Run, Guy Fleming, *WEH* (7.5.1986)

Baker Pledges Royal William Yard Aid, Nick Oldham, *WEH* (28.2.1986)

Back Track, Plymouth Railway Series, Bernard Mills, *WEH* (1981–84)

Blue Monkey Puzzle and the Missing Camel, Marshall Ware, *WEH* (24.2.1982)

Blue Print for Success – Plymouth Poly, Pamela Leeds, *WEH* (9.5.1977)

Boringdon Hall the Sad Saga, Carol Howland, *Sun. Ind.* (5.6.1977)

Bumps in the Night, Douglas Selleck, *WEH* (4.7.1987)

Chance to Capitalise on the Past, Roger Malone, *WMN* (1.4.1987)

Church Born 300 years Ago, Anthony J. Cross, *WMN* (25.10.1962)

Church That Says We Agree to Differ, Bernard Harris, *Sun. Exp.* (14.12.1958)

Curtain Calls, Harvey Crane, *WEH* (8.3.1984)

Death of Lord Astor, Great Western Benefactor, *WEH* (30.9.1952)

Death of Mr C. Norrington, *Western Daily Mercury* (21.6.1900)

Devil's Point, R. V. Walling, *Sun. Ind.* (13.6.1965)

East Stonehouse, Pat Twyford, *WEH* (23.1.1953)

8 Acre District Centre, Geoffrey Hanks, *WEH* (17.12.70)

Estover, a Pattern That Shouldn't be Repeated, Jean Campbell, *WEH* (17.1.1980)

Faith & Renewal, Fraser Massey, *WEH* (26.5.1984)

50 Years of Plain Dealing at Mutley, John Melvin, *WEH* (23.5.1977)

Fire Brigade, Judy Cannon, *WMN* (29.7.1967)

Fire! Fire!! Fire!!!, R. V. Walling, *Independent* (19.7.1964)

Grand House on the Hoe That Few People Use, Veronica Horwell, *WMN* (26.11.65)

Ham, the Oldest Inhabited House in Plymouth, Audrey Hawkins, *WEH* (30.4.1939)

John Kitto, Gerald K. S. Edwards, *WEH* (22.9.34)

Judges' E90 a Head Lodgings . . ., Michael Miller, *WEH* (23.2.1972)

King Billy's History, Ken Burns, letter to *WEH* (17.7.1984)

King's Ransom to Save Tudor Hall, Sheree Dodd, *Sun. Ind.* (22.10.1978)

Leslie Hore-Belisha, Will Stewart, *WMN* (6.10.1983)

Manadon to Greet Queen, Michelle Sammons, *WEH* (7.1.1983)

Memorial Key to Plymouth Plan, feature *WEH* (21.5.1952)

Memories of Southside Street, R. D., *Western Independent* (30.5.52)

Mr E. A. Pearns' Munificent Gift, *Western Daily Mercury* (25.2.1892)

Mr Rawlinson's Report on the Sewerage, Drainage. . . of Plymouth, *P.D.&S. Herald* (12.3.1853)

My Priorities by City's New Bishop, Kevin Maguire, *WMN* (21.11.1985)

New Prisons, *P.D.&.S.* (28.4.1849)

New Start for City Athletes, Julie Fleet, *WEH* (20.7.1986)

Oil Bonanza Gave New Life to Old Fort, Peggy Archer, *WMN* (12.11.1984)

Old Barn Blooms at Estover Leisure Complex, Dick Benson-Gyles, *WEH* (10.12.1982)

Opening the Way for a New Brickfield Pavilion, Alan Endean, *WEH* (25.9.1963)

Ordnance Land at Devonport, *Western Daily Mercury,* (May 1857)

Palmerston Folly for Sale, Ralph Dunn, *WMN* (19.3.1986)

Paradise for Purdah? Michael Miller, *WEH* (15.5.1966)

Pearn Home, *South Devon & East Cornwall Hospital Report* (23.2.1892)

Pioneers in the Air, Walter Taylor, *WMN* (22.6.1965)

Plan for a New Theatre, Angela Rippon, *South Devon Times* (25.11.1965)

Plymouth High in 1936, an Echo of, Marcia Treece, Plymouth Times (12.2.1981)

Plymouth Man's Empire of Cinemas, Bob Ainsworth, *WEH* (23.12.1969)

Plymouth Market, feature *WEH* (7.9.1959)

Poly All Set to Take Status of a University, Mark Duff, *WEH* (5.11.1986)

Presentation of Hoe Fountain, *Western Daily Mercury* (30.6.1881)

Raglan Barracks, Godfrey Wycisk, *WMN* (13.4.1970)

Raglan Barracks, feature *WEH* (1.8.1936)

Regiments of Foot, Godfrey Wycisk, *WMN* (15.11.1971)

Restored Regency Grandeur, Ronald R. Gatiss, *WMN* (27.7.1973)

Retiring from Dealing with Death, Philipa Foster, *WMN* (24.4.1979)

Rich Young Man's Amazing Flight, *Daily Mail* (21.12.1929)

St Joseph Gets Church Back Among the People, Linda Jackson, *WEH* (21.10.1985)

Slice of Plymouth History, Guy Fleming, *WEH* (16.9.1983)

Southside Street Memories, Stephen Barrett, *Barbican Voice* (Nov 1983)

Southway's 'Pioneers' Settling Down, *WEH* (6.9.1957)

South Devon & East Cornwall Hospital, *Western Daily Mercury* (July 1884)

Stoke Damerel, Ann Chiswell, *WEH* (20.11.1980)

Stonehouse Set to Regain its Former Style, Dick Benson-Gyles, *WEH* (25.9.1963)

Street of History, Douglas Selleck, *WEH* (11.1.1985)

Tales of Old Pomphlett, Dorothy Warley Pitt, *Plymouth Times* (1982–83)

This Was Blitz, the Mascot, Gossip of Plymouth, *Western Independent* (7.9.1958)

Tourism Bid May Save Fort, Mark Duff, *WEH* (20.3.1986)

Tower of Mount Batten to Go, L. K. Way, *WMN* (17.5.1962)

Village Inside a City, Nigel Howard, *Plymouth Times* (20.1.1978)

When Saltash Ferry Vanished in Night, A. G. K. Leonard, *WEH* (10.8.1956)

Where the First Telephone Was Installed, Patricia O'Neill, *WEH* (25.5.1937)

White Elephant Mausoleum, Rosemary Burnett, *WEH* (18.9.1980)

Index

200